THE REDEMPTORISTS IN IRELAND, 1851–2011

In memory of
Frs Paddy O'Donnell, Michael Baily, Fred Jones and Seán O'Riordan

In aeternum vivant!

Brendan McConvery CSsR

The Redemptorists in Ireland, 1851–2011

the columba press

First published in 2012 by
the columba press
55a Spruce Avenue,
Stillorgan Industrial Park,
Blackrock, County Dublin

Cover by David Mc Namara CSsR
Origination by The Columba Press
Printed by MPG Books Limited.

ISBN 9781 85607 759 0

Contents

List of Tables

Foreword

For many Irish people, the word 'Redemptorist' is synonymous with 'parish mission' or solemn novena. There are few parishes in Ireland that have not experienced at least one Redemptorist parish mission in the last 160 years. Parish missions traditionally have been the flagship apostolate of the Redemptorists since the first mission was preached in Limerick more than a century-and-a-half ago.

The Synod of Thurles in 1850 sought to bring discipline and renewal to the Irish Church after the desolation of the Great Famine. One of the main agents of its renewal programme was the parish mission. Missions and their preachers offered comfort, won back the lost and built up parish communities. They also provided colour and entertainment in times when there was little of either, especially in the countryside. As the account of the 'poitín missions' of the 1920s and 1930s in this history will show, the missioners offered more than 'hellfire and brimstone'; they were socially engaged, according to the understanding of their times. Their impact has left its mark on the Irish Church, on Irish literature and on the Irish Catholic psyche.

But, of course, parish mission work isn't the only ministry in which Irish Redemptorists have been engaged since 1851. According to their Constitutions, 'Redemptorists have as their special mission in the Church the explicit proclamation of the Word of God to bring about fundamental conversion' (Constitution 10).

This 'explicit proclamation of the Word' has taken many forms. Annual solemn novenas have had extraordinary success in recent decades and continue to attract young and old in their thousands. Ministry to young people has developed very significantly over the years. Redemptorist retreat house, church and parish ministry continue to serve the needs of the Irish Church. Individual Redemptorists have ministered to the Traveller community, to people from other lands who have made their home in Ireland, as well as serving as chaplains in universities and hospitals and in many other pastoral settings.

From the beginning, 'overseas mission' has been an integral component of the Irish Redemptorist story. The first Redemptorist missioner in Ireland was a man who was born near Kiev in modern-day Ukraine, Vladimir Petcherine. Other early missioners included Austrians, Dutchmen, Flemish-speaking Belgians as well as English and Scots converts from the Church of England.

The newly-established Irish Province of the Redemptorists of 1898 included an overseas mission in Australia.

The setbacks and the successes of the later missions to the Philippines, India and Brazil are well recorded in these pages; that each of the missions is flourishing today is a tribute to the efforts of these pioneers and their successors. That our communities in Ireland contain so many returned missionaries has added a richness and an appetite for fresh thinking that has been of tremendous benefit to the Province at home and to the Irish Church.

Not least among the works of Redemptorists in recent years has been the peace ministry, which helped in no small way to bring about a resolution to the Northern 'Troubles'. It goes hand in hand with the ministry of ecumenism that has helped build bridges and forge links with members of the other Christian churches in Ireland. The apostolate of the pen, so important to St Alphonsus, the founder, has also been a significant ministry of the Irish Province, especially with the establishment of Redemptorist Publications in 1936.

This book provides more than an account of the work and ministry of Irish Redemptorists. It tells the story of the Irish Redemptorists from the inside, as it were, offering an insight into the difficulties and challenges, the triumphs and failures, the setbacks and successes of a small band of different characters over a century-and-a-half as they have sought to be faithful to St Alphonsus's mission to preach the Gospel to the poor and the most abandoned. It tells the story of a group trying, with various levels of success, to put structure on its missionary efforts.

Ireland is experiencing a time of great changes, of great storms. At times of storms, it is important to recognise some fixed points from which we may take our bearings. Such times are a challenge to clarify again the basics: who we are and what are we about. Fr Brendan McConvery's book will help us as Redemptorists as well as our friends and those who are interested in the story of the Irish Church to remember that Jesus Christ, the Redeemer, is our Light, the Sun by which we plot our course. We are disciples of Jesus Christ in the tradition of St Alphonsus Liguori. We are called to be distinguished by missionary dynamism, to keep our eyes fixed on Jesus and our feet rooted in local communities. In this context, one interesting aspect of our Irish Redemptorist story over the years is the serious commitment to co-working with lay people in missionary efforts, through, for example, confraternities and credit unions.

To chronicle the history of the Irish Redemptorist Province has been a major undertaking, requiring work over many years. I thank Brendan for the time and effort he has put into this task; he is a worthy successor to John Sharp whose study, *Reapers of the Harvest: the Redemptorists in Great Britain and Ireland 1843–1898* (1989) chronicled the beginnings of that story. It has clearly been a labour of love for Brendan, who is not only interested in his subject, but has a passion for the tradition in which he was reared. His conviction that what Irish Redemptorists have contributed over the past 160 years is valuable gives clear hope for the future.

This book is a tribute not only to Brendan's diligence but also to those who kept documents and records over the years. Brendan dedicates the book to the late Paddy O'Donnell and celebrates the memory of Michael Baily, Fred Jones and Seán O'Riordan. I join him in recognising and paying tribute to these men and to all those who have gone before us. Brendan's work is a living history and a clear invitation to others to continue his good work in the future.

In chapter one, Brendan tells how, according to the memoirs of Fr Joseph Prost, one of the first Redemptorist missioners in Ireland, the people of Limerick honoured those strange preachers with the title 'holy fathers'. I was born in Limerick, literally in the shadow of Mount St Alphonsus, which has always been known locally as 'The Fathers'. I'm not sure when or why the 'holy' was dropped, but in many ways I'm relieved it's gone. In these challenging times, it's good for us to remember that God alone is holy and that we live by God's grace. I thank God for the abundant blessings bestowed upon Irish Redemptorists over the last 160 years and I offer thanks for all that God has done through Redemptorists, the Redemptoristine Sisters and their co-workers during that time. May this book remind us of the great heritage we possess, of the gratitude that we owe to so many, and inspire us to do our best to preach the Gospel ever anew in our time and place. I hope too that it may open some windows to those who are curious about the Redemptorists and the part they have played in shaping Irish Catholicism for more than a century-and-a-half and that it will enable them to discern a history, that like the history of the Irish Church and society, is complex and still unfinished.

Fr Michael Kelleher CSsR
Provincial

Introduction

'These are the researches of Herodotus of Halicarnassus, which he publishes, in the hope of thereby preserving from decay the remembrance of what has been done, and of preventing the great and wonderful actions of the Greeks and the barbarians from losing their due meed of glory; and withal to put on record what were the grounds of their feuds' (*Histories*, 1.1). So begins the work of 'the father of history.' It sums up rather elegantly my purpose in putting together this outline of the Redemptorist story in Ireland. It is a provisional work that awaits someone with better history-writing skills than mine. Yet, it is worth putting together even a faltering remembrance of what the great men and women of our past have done, giving them their due meed of glory, and (occasionally) putting on record the grounds of their feuds.

John Sharp's masterly study, *Reapers of the Harvest*, has covered the story of the Redemptorists in these islands from their arrival in England in 1843 up to the separation of the English and Irish Provinces in 1898 in great detail. His painstaking care has freed me from the burden of having to rework that formidable body of material in any detail but my debt to him will be apparent throughout. I had initially intended to pick up the narrative where he had left off, or at most to lightly sketch in the story of the first period in the broadest strokes possible. In the end, I decided to begin at the beginning, if for no other reason than to make the Irish part of the story accessible in one place. If there are differences of interpretation or an occasional filling out of detail here or there, there is little of moment that Sharp has not already taken into account. As he noted, the Archives of the Dublin Province of the Redemptorists are thin. I was able to visit the General Archives in Rome on several occasions and to its archivists, I record my debt.

Several shorter studies, in the form of commemorative brochures published to celebrate the anniversaries of houses like Limerick, Dundalk, Clonard and Esker have preserved many details of earlier times. In many of the later ones, the hand of the late Fr Paddy O'Donnell CSsR can be detected. Telling the story of the Province from independence in 1898 to recent times has proved daunting, as little of this material has been published. It is rich in detail, particularly the story of the foundation of the three Vice-Provinces of the Philippines, India and Brazil. The former two are now provinces in their own right. The late Fr Michael Baily CSsR has written an accomplished study of the early years of the Philippine Mission, *Small Net in a Big Sea*, which I have drawn on fully. The late Fr Joseph Morgan CSsR has also sketched the beginnings of the Indian mission, of which he was a participant, in his memoir, *A Time to Remember*. Fr Philip Hearty CSsR has gathered much of the material of the early years of the Brazilian mission in a useful but unpublished memoir. Fr Brian Holmes CSsR, as Vice-Provincial, commissioned a history in Portuguese to mark the golden jubilee of the Vice-Province in 2010, *A Vice-Provincia Redentorista de Fortaleza* (2011), by Gilberto Paiva, but it has appeared only after the completion of this work. A proper study of the Irish Redemptorists as foreign missionaries might provide several students with ample material for doctoral study. That kind of attention to detail will not be found here: the strokes are broad, some may judge unjustly so.

The aim of this sketch is modest: it is to spin a thread of narrative for Redemptorists, their co-workers and friends, to recall the names of people and places that shaped the Irish Redemptorist Province in more than a century-and-a-half of its life. I have contented myself with a rapid and impressionistic survey of the period from about 1970 to the present, in the spirit of the wise tradition in archival practice of keeping material under embargo for a period of years.

The place of the Redemptorists in the history of Irish church and society is not an undistinguished one. Some of our younger members may find much here that is new to them. They may also find some of the internal debates that drew such passion from older generations bewildering.

I make bold to dedicate this work to four Irish Redemptorists. Fr Paddy O'Donnell, as my novice master, introduced us to the quirky history of the Irish Province in Esker many years ago. He faithfully stayed with the work of telling the story in his own unostentatious style. His succinct but meaty articles in *Search*, an internal journal of the Province that flourished for some years, have been of immense value in building up this work. Sadly, Fr Paddy died the day the page proofs arrived. Fr Michael Baily was both a biblical scholar and a historian from whom I have learned much. Fr Frederick M. Jones was an accomplished historian and biographer of St Alphonsus. Many hoped he would eventually turn his hand to writing a history of the Province, but death came too soon. Fr Seán O'Riordan was both a historian and a theologian by training. Seán's apparently limitless memory passed on much oral tradition and kept the memory of great men of the past green with much humour and always kind observation. I am grateful for Paddy O'Donnell's guidance through several early incarnations of this work. The others would have saved me from many errors of fact or interpretation, so I must accept full responsibility for the weaknesses that remain.

To those who helped, critiqued and encouraged along the way, I offer my thanks. Máire Ní Chearbhaill was a meticulous editor who reviewed several drafts and brought her historical and archival training to bear in correcting my short-cuts and lapses of style. Seán O Boyle of Columba Press encouraged the proposal from the beginning, but has had to wait many years for delivery. Fr Michael Kelleher is the last of a series of provincials that includes Raphael Gallagher, Brendan Callanan and Con Casey who have supported this undertaking both financially and humanly. I thank Fr Kelleher especially for his Foreword. Fr George Wadding took the risk of publishing early drafts of several sections in his *News from Home.* The late Fr Leonard Martin of the Vice-Province of Fortaleza challenged me to begin writing and enquired about progress, usually as we trudged through the forests of Luxembourg each summer. Fr Raphael Gallagher gave several chapters an informed and much-needed critique. Fr Anthony Mulvey generously checked some sources in the General Archives in Rome. He and Brother Patrick McCrave also checked dates in the mission chronicles of Dundalk and Limerick respectively. Successive rectors of Marianella and the members of that community provided me with a home and did not ask too many questions when I pleaded historical research as an excuse to be released from community responsibilities, especially during the busy summer months. The communities of Esker and St Alphonse in Luxembourg ('*die Paaterskierch*' or 'the Fathers' Church', as it is known to the locals) frequently provided the space and the kind of fraternity that is congenial for writing. To all of them, much thanks.

Brendan McConvery CSsR
Feast of St Clement Hofbauer,
15 March 2012

Note on Archival Sources

The research for this book was done in the Redemptorist General, Provincial and Domestic Archives of the various Redemptorist communities in Ireland.

The Redemptorist General Archives in Rome (RGAR) are extensive but the material relating to Ireland is catalogued in a number of different ways. Before 1898, Irish material is catalogued as part of the English province to which the Irish houses then belonged. After that date, early material is catalogued as XIII-Hib, while later material is catalogued as 13-D, reflecting the change in the naming of provinces after the place of residence of the provincial superior. More recently still, an electronic cataloguing system has been introduced that uses a multi-digit system. All these cataloguing systems will be encountered here.

The next major source used is the Redemptorist Provincial Archives of the Dublin Province (RPAD). Each community retains its own domestic archive and these are signalled by the name of the community, for example, Limerick, Dundalk, Clonard, Esker.

Abbreviations

EDACALF	*Editiones Academiae Alphonsianae*
IER	*Irish Ecclesiastical Record*
ITQ	*Irish Theological Quarterly*
RGAR	Redemptorist General Archives, Rome
RPAD	Redemptorist Provincial Archives, Dublin
SHCSSR	*Spicilegium Historicum Congregationis Sanctissimi Redemptoris*

CHAPTER ONE

Foreign Missioners in Ireland

In a monastery room in Liverpool in October 1851, five priests met to make the final arrangements for the journey to Ireland they were to begin later that day. None of them knew Ireland well. One of them, a Russian called Vladimir Petcherine, had given a few days' retreat to a community of sisters in Omagh, County Tyrone the month before.[1] The superior of the group, an Austrian called Joseph Prost, had met many poor Irish emigrants in both England and the United States where he had previously worked. Unlike Petcherine, who had rather romantic views about the downtrodden Irish peasantry, Prost harboured few allusions about the Irish Catholic laity or their clergy. He had met enough displaced emigrants fleeing from the ravages of the Great Famine to know what poverty and hunger had done to them. A priest in Liverpool had pointed out to him a street where many poor Irish lived, ready to fight for the faith when drunk, but with little enthusiasm for its regular practice when sober. Two of the five were Flemish-speaking Belgians, John van Antwerpen and Leo Van der Stichele. The fifth, and the only native English speaker, was Edward Douglas, a convert from the Church of England and heir of a wealthy Scottish aristocratic family. When the final travel arrangements had been made, Prost took what he was later to regard as a sensible precaution. He asked his companions to join him in a pledge not to drink whiskey while they were in Ireland. As he recorded later in his memoirs:

> Before we departed, I called the Fathers together and told them how much the Irish like 'whiskey punch'. I told them the Irish are accustomed to it and therefore can take a good deal of it. We on the other hand are not used to it and it could easily happen that a missioner could get drunk at a social gathering. We therefore all promised ... not to drink whiskey. They all agreed and this promise was kept at all times as long as the mission was under my supervision.[2]

---

[1] There are several variant renderings of the Slavonic spelling of Petcherine's name (e.g. Petcherin, Pecherine). In the text, the most common form in English is used here, while preserving in the sources quoted the form used by the authors.

[2] *Redemptorist Missionary in Ireland: 1851–1854: Memoirs by Joseph Prost, CSsR*, ed. Emmet Larkin and Hermann Freudenberger, in Irish Narratives Series, ed. David Fitzpatrick (Cork:

The five priests were members of a missionary congregation known as the Redemptorists. They were the heirs of a tradition that had been given its distinctive shape by three men. The first of these was the founder, a Neapolitan priest called Alphonsus de Liguori, born in 1696, who had abandoned a promising career at the bar in his mid-twenties for the priesthood. As a member of the minor nobility of the kingdom of Naples, Alphonsus's family had ambitions for his future ecclesiastical career. Instead, he chose to devote himself to preaching parish missions among the urban poor and the shepherds of the mountainous regions along the rugged Amalfi coast.[3]

In the village of Scala high above the town of Amalfi, Alphonsus and a small group of priests and laymen had formed a community in November 1732 that would be devoted to the work of missions in remote country districts. The enthusiasm of the group lasted only a few weeks. Alphonsus was soon left alone, except for one of the laymen, Vito Curzio, who became the first brother of the congregation. Undaunted, Alphonsus and Vito bound themselves by a vow to persevere in the work unless God showed them otherwise. In time, a few more generous spirits joined them, and by 1749, the congregation had three communities and had gained official Roman approval as the Congregation of the Most Holy Redeemer.[4]

The Redemptorist Congregation was born in difficult times. While the Bourbon rulers of Naples and their ministers, like Bernardo Tanucci (1698–1783), were often devoutly Catholic in their private lives, they were driven by an obsessive desire to control virtually every element of Church life in the kingdom. Alphonsus spent many years fighting off their attempts to bring his congregation under royal control. By 1780, he was eighty-four years old and chronic illness had made him increasingly reliant on his advisors. They set aside his forty years' resistance to royal control and acquiesced to a royal decree reducing the religious vows to simple promises and forbidding any appeal to the Pope regarding the government of the congregation. They had hoped that, by outwardly conforming to the royal regulations, they might survive as a missionary community, living their rule in the privacy of their religious houses as though nothing had changed. The handful of Redemptorist communities in the Papal States beyond the rule of Naples

Cork University Press, 1998, 35. See also Edward Hosp, 'First Redemptorist Missions in Ireland according to Fr Joseph Prost's Diaries' in *Spicilegium Historicum CSsR* (hereafter *SHCSSR*), vol. VIII, no. 2 (1960), 454–85; *idem*, 'Leben des Paters Josef Prost, 1804–1885, nach seinen eigenen Aufzeichnungen' in *SHCSSR*, vol. XI, no. 2 (1963), 375–432.

[3] For a biography of Alphonsus, see Frederick M. Jones CSsR, *Alphonsus Liguori: The Saint of Bourbon Naples* (Dublin: Gill and Macmillan, 1992).

[4] For an early history of the Redemptorists see Francesco Chiovaro (ed.), *The History of the Congregation of the Most Holy Redeemer. Vol. 1: The Origins, 1732–1793*, ed. J. Robert Finelli (Liguori, MO: Liguori Publications, 1986).

were appalled by what they regarded as the treachery of their Neapolitan brethren. They appealed to the Holy See, with the result that they were declared the legitimate heirs of the congregation approved in 1749, to which their Neapolitan brethren, including the founder himself, were deemed no longer to belong. Alphonsus lived for a further seven years after these events, feeble and virtually blind but sufficiently in touch with the affairs of his disciples in the Papal States to hear of the entrance into the Redemptorist congregation of the next major figure in the foundation story.

John Dvořák (1751–1820) was a Czech, better known to history as Clement Mary Hofbauer, from the German form of his surname and the two religious names he had adopted while living as a hermit for a period during his youth.[5] Clement had dreamed of becoming a priest from his earliest years, but his family's poverty made it an impossible dream. Like the Bourbons of Naples, the Hapsburg Emperors of Austria regarded the Church as their loyal servant and resented the control of Rome. Clement Hofbauer had little desire to spend his life as a functionary of the state, administering the sacraments and preaching the Gospel according to state-approved forms. His sense of the Church's universalism drew him towards Rome. He walked there several times on pilgrimage, and spent a period as a hermit near Tivoli in the hills above Rome. In 1784 he made his last pilgrimage with a companion named Thaddeus Hübl. One morning, the pilgrims wandered by chance into the small Redemptorist church of San Juliano close to the basilica of St Mary Major. Hofbauer already knew something of the founder of the Redemptorists, since translations of the spiritual writings of Alphonsus Liguori had already been circulating in German-speaking areas for some years.[6] Within a matter of hours, the two pilgrims asked to be admitted into the congregation. After a brief novitiate, and a cursory study of theology, both completed within a year, they were professed, ordained and sent back across the Alps with instructions to plant the congregation wherever they could.

Late eighteenth-century Austria was every bit as hostile to new religious groups as the government of Naples, so the two new Redemptorists soon sought refuge in the more benign city of Warsaw in 1787. They were given charge of a church belonging to the German confraternity of St Benno. The

---

[5] For a biography of Clement Hofbauer, see Kornelius Fleischmann, *Klemens Maria Hofbauer: Seine Leben und seine Zeit* (Graz: Verlag Styria, 1988). At the time of writing, there is no up-to-date critical biography available in English but Josef Heinzmann CSsR, *Preaching the Gospel Anew: Saint Clement Maria Hofbauer* (Liguori, MO: Liguori Publications, 1998) is a good introduction.

[6] For German translations of the works of Alphonsus, see Maurice de Meulemeester, *Bibliographie Générale des Écrivains Rédemptoristes I* (Louvain: Imprimerie St Alphonse, 1933), 202–21.

small church was soon throbbing with energy. The two young priests kept up a continuous round of services from opening time at 4.00 a.m. until 9.00 p.m. In addition to a full schedule of church services, they ran a school for boys and an orphanage. Within a few years, young men came knocking on the door to be admitted to the novitiate. The arrival of Napoleon Bonaparte in 1807 on his way to the Russian front spelled the end of community life at St Benno's. Hofbauer returned to Vienna where he remained virtually alone for the next twelve years. His companions in the meantime wandered through Austria, Switzerland and Alsace in search of a permanent home. Hofbauer found work in Vienna as chaplain to a community of nuns. Devoid of any intellectual pretensions, his style of preaching and his lively interest in people and in the events of the larger world drew around him a circle of intellectuals, artists and university students. The little chapel of the convent and Hofbauer's small apartment became like another St Benno's until his death in 1820. The imperial decree recognising the Redemptorists was signed in time to be laid on his coffin.

The pent-up energy of the proceeding years of struggle finally found release as the Redemptorists spread throughout Europe with extraordinary rapidity. At the time of Hofbauer's death, there was but a single community of twenty-seven members north of the Alps living in a dilapidated former Carthusian monastery at Valsainte in Switzerland. There was one professed Redemptorist in Vienna who had been Hofbauer's companion in his latter years. A handful of others lived in twos and threes in the principality of Walachia and in Poland. Thirty years later there were forty-five houses north of the Alps. By 1850 there were nearly 500 priests and brothers and over 120 students and novices

The expansion of the Redemptorists after Hofbauer's death was overseen by the third major figure in early Redemptorist history. Joseph Passerat (1772–1858) was born in Joinville in eastern France.[7] His studies for the priesthood were cut short by the outbreak of the French Revolution and his conscription into the army of the Republic. Passerat deserted after a few months and made his way through Belgium and Germany in search of a seminary where he could continue his studies. His wandering took him, with four companions he had met along the way, to Warsaw where he entered the Redemptorists under Clement Hofbauer in 1796. When the community of St Benno's was dissolved, Hofbauer placed Passerat at the head of the group of students and novices that wandered through Switzerland and Alsace in

---

7 Despite the introduction of his cause and the great respect in which he was held for over a century in the Congregation, Passerat has been much neglected in recent Redemptorist historical research. The only comprehensive, but uncritical, life in English is Henri Gerouille, *Father Joseph Passerat: A Great Pioneer Redemptorist*, translated by John Carr (London: Sands and Company, 1928).

search of a home. On Hofbauer's death in 1820, he succeeded him as vicar general of the transalpine communities, that is, those outside Italy. The years of wandering had taught Passerat the importance of a solid formation in the spiritual life for holding men together in hard times. He was not a theologian like Alphonsus Liguori or an innovator who could make the best of difficult circumstances like Hofbauer. He was a man of prayer and was able to inspire others to pray. Yet he was also clearly a man of some organisational ability who managed to hold the group together and to keep their minds fixed on the essential nature of the Redemptorist vocation as an apostolic community, responding creatively to pastoral need. When the first Redemptorists came to Ireland in 1851, Passerat was still alive and revered as the 'Patriarch of the North' whose wise stewardship of the legacy of Hofbauer was bearing rich fruit.

Alphonsus Liguori, Clement Hofbauer and Joseph Passerat had shaped the Redemptorist tradition that made its first appearance in Ireland in 1851. From Alphonsus, it had received in its rule a strong commitment to the 'salvation of the most abandoned, especially those who live in remote country districts', a tradition of moral theology that respected the conscience of even the most unlettered believer and a spirituality that stressed sanctity as the response to the love God has shown his people in the story of Redemption.[8] Hofbauer had seen that, when prevented by circumstances from adopting the itinerant preaching apostolate of parish missions, a Redemptorist community could find ways of expressing its zeal in liturgy, catechesis, education and personal contact in an urban setting that would have all the marks of a 'perpetual mission'. From Passerat, it learned that a commitment to prayer and regular observance of the rule were the principles that guaranteed stability in hard times.

Before their arrival in Ireland, the Redemptorists had eventually found a congenial home in Belgium in 1831. From there, they spread to England in 1843. Some of its first English members, who had belonged to the Oxford Movement and followed John Henry Newman into the Roman Catholic Church, joined the Redemptorist Congregation. If the Redemptorists were known at all in Ireland, it was due to the popularity of the writings of their founder, Alphonsus de Liguori. Daniel O'Connell considered his book of meditations, *Preparation for Death*, as his essential spiritual reading. Many of his shorter works had been translated and published in cheap editions by Fr

---

8 Alphonsus's moral theology went through nine editions in his lifetime. His canonisation in 1839 and subsequent proclamation as a Doctor of the Church in 1870 gave his work a particular authority. His devotional writings were addressed to priests, religious and lay people. For a useful and representative selection of his writings see *Alphonsus de Liguori: Selected Writings*, ed. Frederick M. Jones CSsR, Classics of Western Spirituality Series (New York and Mahwah, NJ: Paulist Press, 1999).

Nicholas Callan, professor of natural philosophy at St Patrick's College, Maynooth. Callan is today best known as a scientist who pioneered early development in the use of electricity. He was also a man with a deep pastoral sense. He had first read the writings of Alphonsus while a student in Rome, and had translated many of them in cheap 'penny editions' under the pseudonym of 'A Catholic Clergyman' for the Dublin publisher, James Duffy, so that they could circulate as cheaply as possible among the poor.[9] Liguori's reputation as a moderating influence in moral theology was also becoming more widely known among Irish clergy due to the work of another Maynooth professor, Edmund O'Reilly.[10]

Work of the Missions
The systematic preaching of the Word of God and administration of the sacraments by visiting priests with a view to reaching the spiritually-neglected had been a feature of life in the Catholic countries of the European mainland since the seventeenth century. The pioneer of the parish mission movement in France was St Vincent de Paul (*c.*1576–1660), founder of the Congregation of the Mission. In Italy, notable promoters of the mission movement included the Franciscan, St Leonard of Port Maurice (1676–1751), the Passionist founder, St Paul of the Cross (1694–1775), and Alphonsus Liguori. Due to the operation of the Penal Laws in Ireland, missions were virtually unknown. The first mission in Ireland was given in Athy, County Kildare in 1842 by a group of young Maynooth priests who had formed themselves into a society modelled on that of Vincent de Paul and which would eventually be incorporated into the Congregation of the Mission in 1847.[11] The years immediately following the Great Famine proved to be particularly favourable to the parish mission movement. By the time the Redemptorists arrived in Ireland in 1851, the Jesuits and a number of newly-arrived religious congregations, including the Rosminians (1848) and the Passionists (1849), were already engaged in mission-giving.

---

[9] For a biography of Nicholas Callan, including his interest in Alphonsus, see Patrick McLaughlin, *Nicholas Callan: Priest-Scientist 1799–1964* (Dublin: Clonmore and Reynolds, 1965).

[10] According to Patrick Corish, Edmund O'Reilly (1811–78) introduced Alphonsus's moral theology into the Maynooth curriculum: see Patrick Corish, *Maynooth College 1795–1995* (Dublin: Gill and Macmillan, 1995), 122. O'Reilly later entered the Jesuits and became rector of Milltown Park, Dublin. See also his obituary, 'In Memoriam: R. P. Edmundi J. O'Reilly, SJ', in *The Irish Monthly*, vol. 6 (1878), 695–700.

[11] For an account of early Vincentian missions, see James Murphy, 'The role of Vincentian Parish Missions in the "Irish Counter-Reformation" of the mid-nineteenth century' in *Irish Historical Studies*, vol. xxiv, no. 94, 1984, 152–71.

The five Redemptorists who left Liverpool for Ireland in 1851 were bound for Limerick, where they had been invited to give a mission in the old St John's church by Bishop John Ryan. Earlier that year, William Monsell, MP for County Limerick, had invited Fr Frederick de Held, superior of the Redemptorist house in Clapham, London, to stay at his estate at Tervoe near Patrickswell with a view to exploring the possibility of a Redemptorist foundation in Ireland. Monsell had been received into the Catholic Church the year before and with the zeal of a recent convert, was determined to do something for the Church of his adoption.[12] Shortly after de Held's visit, Monsell's brother-in-law, Edwin Richard Wyndham-Quin, third Earl of Dunraven, had intimated to the bishop that he would welcome a foundation of the Redemptorists on his estate in Adare.[13] Lord Dunraven was still an Anglican but was on the threshold of entering the Catholic Church. While no decision about a foundation had been reached, it was clear that the Limerick mission was a step towards gaining a foothold in Ireland.

The missioners had their first brush with the punch that Prost feared so much on the night of their arrival. Unknown to them, Bishop Ryan had travelled from Dublin on the same train. When bishop and missioners met on the platform at Limerick, he invited them to join him for dinner at his residence. The fare offered was plain enough, and the only drink on the table was water. When they adjourned to the sitting room after dinner, the whiskey bottle and the kettle made their appearance. To the bishop's surprise, the missioners declined his offer of hot punch, so a bottle of sherry was hastily produced for them.

Next morning, the mission was launched. Prost had a poor view of the liturgical expertise of the Irish clergy, but he was determined to cut a dash with the opening ceremony of the mission. He insisted on a solemn liturgical reception before the 11.00 a.m. High Mass. With the bishop seated on an improvised throne in the sanctuary, the four missioners entered in procession, carrying the tall mission-cross through the nave of the church. The evening service began at 6.30 p.m. Recitation of the rosary was followed by

---

[12] Matthew Potter, *The life and times of William Monsell, first Baron Emly of Tervoe, 1812–1894: A Catholic Unionist* (Limerick: Treaty Press, 1994).

[13] A copy of a note from Bishop John Ryan dated 5 July 1851, reads: 'The Earl of Dunraven has called on me this day for the purpose of obtaining my consent to the establishment of a foundation of the Order of the Redemptorists on his property in the town of Adare in this diocese. With this request, I most cheerfully concur, while I am most thankful to his Lordship for his charity and generosity in affording us the prospect of having the aid of such valuable assistance in the work of religion in the present various difficulties of this distressed country.' Copy in 'Domestic and Apostolic Labours, vol. 1, 1851–1868' in Redemptorist Provincial Archives, Dublin (henceforth RPAD).

a short catechetical instruction, preparing the way for the 'great sermon' of an hour's duration. Within a few days, the fruits of the mission were becoming apparent. Knowing that the confessionals would soon be thronged, Prost asked the sexton to open the church at 4.00 a.m. To his amazement he found on entering the church at that early hour people already crowding around the confessionals: someone in the crowd had managed to cut a hole in a windowpane and the people streamed in through the open window. Prost commented on the results with some satisfaction:

> We took people as they came, without distinction. We made no difference between the well off and the commoners, between the rich and the beggar, the well dressed and the ragged, the well educated and the ill educated. The people soon learned that we drank no whiskey and accepted no invitations, that we sacrificed ourselves to the poor and to the sinners with love. Consequently, they honoured us with the name 'holy fathers'.[14]

Urban poverty in the decade following the Famine had horrific consequences. As Prost would admit later, long hours in the confessional did not come easy. The confessor's day lasted from before dawn to almost midnight, broken by a three-hour interval for lunch, recreation and a nap to compensate for the short night's rest. At the end of the day, the missioners had to search their clothes for vermin and 'the lice were unusually large, so that they brought us to the point of wanting to vomit'.

When the mission ended on 2 November 1851, it was hailed on all sides as a magnificent success. Monsell invited the Fathers to take a few days' holidays at his estate at Tervoe. Like many wealthy converts of the Oxford Movement, Monsell had initiated a rigorous spiritual regime in his house. There was Mass each morning in his private chapel, with a further hour's devotions for the household and staff before dinner. It did not prove an altogether relaxing time for the missioners. Despite her husband's best efforts, Mrs Monsell remained a convinced Evangelical and played the part of the missionary with every bit as much zeal as the Redemptorists. Each of them found by his bedside a Protestant bible and a small bundle of tracts, a gift from the lady of the house. The silence of the monastic refectory had not equipped them for dining in polite society. As they gathered in the drawing room before dinner on the first evening, Monsell told Prost that it was his privilege as guest of honour to escort the lady of the house to table. When it was explained that he should offer her his arm, he refused, saying he would simply walk alongside her. Looking back on the incident years later, he

---

[14] Prost, *Redemptorist Missionary in Ireland*, 39.

reflected ruefully on the deficiencies of Redemptorist training in the social graces:

> On this occasion and on several others, I felt a deficiency in our training. We had not been instructed in the ceremonies of the country. This appears to me to be essential for a missioner of our day. One looks very inept and it is as if one lacks good upbringing, like a peasant. The judgement of the people about the training of a missioner has important repercussions in regard to his usefulness. The Jesuits excel in this respect. They know how to behave in company, whereas we often demonstrate a lack of understanding of the rules of good behaviour and are therefore often censured and consequently, we are not as useful as we should be.[15]

At the end of the week, the missioners moved on to begin their next mission in Omagh, County Tyrone. The weeks in Limerick had left Prost convinced there was still much work to be done there, and that large sections of the population had not been able to avail of the mission. They returned the following May to preach a second mission in Limerick, this time in the church of St Michael, lodging in a house that Monsell had rented for them in Bank Place. Invitations to preach missions in Ireland were rapidly increasing, so they retained the house for the rest of the year. In November 1853, Limerick was formally established as the first Redemptorist community in Ireland.

Over the following months, missions were preached in Westland Row in the city of Dublin, Enniskillen, County Fermanagh, the Waterside in Derry, and in Letterkenny, County Donegal. The missioners were growing more accustomed to the etiquette of polite society. After the Derry mission, they stayed for a few days with another family of benefactors. They still withdrew, however, when the punch appeared at the end of dinner.

> We usually went to the living room and sooner or later the ladies joined us there and tea would be served. There was a wonderful *fortepiano*. Fr Coffin [who joined the mission team after the first Limerick mission] is a master on it. We chanced to talk about the *Marsaillaise* and I said I had never heard it. Fr Petcherine and Fr van Antwerpen volunteered to sing it and Fr Coffin accompanied them on the *fortepiano* …[16]

The dreaded punch played something of a providential role in the Letterkenny mission. The first meeting between Bishop Patrick McGettigan of Raphoe and the missioners was not an auspicious one. To Prost's eye, the

---

15 Ibid., 43.
16 Ibid., 59.

bishop was 'like in every way a rough Austrian village priest ... but able to behave himself, if a little crudely, in polite company'. Like Bishop Ryan of Limerick, Dr McGettigan was taken aback by their refusal of his punch. Within a few days, relations between bishop and missioners had deteriorated. To the missioners' consternation, the bishop appeared to have gone back on the agreement that there would be no admission charge to the evening mission service. He announced a charge, with the stipulation that those unable to pay would be given a free ticket. Few came forward to claim the free tickets, but the collection went on. Believing he had found a diplomatic way to end the collection, Prost launched a sharp attack on the wealthy Catholics of the town. Their refusal to support their bishop, he thundered, meant he was forced to set a price on poor people's access to the Word of God. The point was not lost on the bishop who sat in the sanctuary in stony silence. He stalked out of the church as soon as benediction was over. Realising his tactical blunder, Prost hurried after him. When they met at McGettigan's front door, Prost broke the embarrassed silence. 'My Lord, I am so exhausted I could stand a glass of whiskey.' The bishop was magnanimous. He fetched up a bottle of his oldest whiskey from the cellar and mixed his guest a stiff glass of punch. They sat by the fire chatting amiably, with neither saying a word about the evening's events. Although the collectors disappeared the following day, the bishop was to have his revenge. When the mission was over, Prost recounts, he bade his farewell to his guests without bothering to ask if he owed them anything for their travelling expenses.

Parish Missions in Post-Famine Ireland

The success of parish missions in mid-nineteenth century Ireland was due to the convergence of a number of factors. The social and personal upheaval caused by the Great Famine and its aftermath had created a sense of desperation, which led to an increasing dependence on the consolations of religion. Missions were a call to spiritual renewal, especially in rural areas where people had every reason to feel abandoned by the earthly powers. With its dual emphasis on the precariousness of mortal life and the certainty of ultimate salvation, mission preaching provided a map in which the stark 'great truths' of Christianity became a horizon of meaning that enabled people to leave the suffering of the famine years behind. The emphasis on the day-to-day living of the gospel – keeping the commandments, daily prayer, practical neighbourliness, as well as virtues like sobriety and family values – was intended to enable them to begin to construct a better life for themselves, where older traditions had broken down. The missions, too, were seen as a plank in the policy of church reform implemented by Paul Cullen on his arrival in Ireland as archbishop of Armagh in 1850. He launched his reform programme at the Synod of Thurles in 1850. One of its decrees, 'On Avoiding Dangers to the Faith', specifically instructed bishops to organise missions as a means of instructing the people in the faith and of driving away the danger of error.[17] Following his translation to Dublin in 1852, Cullen was to play a major part in the life of the Irish Church in the second half of the nineteenth century. He was convinced that the Irish Church needed to conform more whole-heartedly to the Roman model. In addition to their role in local Church reform, Cullen also hoped that the missions would serve to counter the proselytising efforts of Protestant missionary societies on the one hand and the growing political influence of secret societies on the other. Writing to Monsell in the same month as the second Redemptorist mission began in Limerick, he assured him that 'the clergy have done everything in their power to banish secret societies. A mission given lately in Dundalk by the priests of St Vincent has done more good than ten special commissions could ever effect.'[18]

Especially along the western seaboard, the years before the Famine had been marked by an upsurge of activity by Evangelical missionary societies. These societies were confident that the time was ripe for a 'Second Reformation' which would succeed where the first had failed.[19] Some leaders of the missionary societies even believed that the Famine was a sign that God was prospering their work and drawing the Irish away from Romish idolatry. In places such as Achill, County Mayo, Clifden, County Galway, Doon, County Limerick and Dingle, County Kerry, the missionary societies founded colonies or settlements where education, training in domestic skills and food was provided to converts. Such was their success that many Catholic church-men feared them as a genuine threat to the faith in impoverished country districts in the west of Ireland. The effects of the campaign were long-lasting. As late as 1904, Redemptorists giving a mission in the Erismore district of Clifden observed that

---

[17] *Decreta Synodi Plenariae Episcoporum Hiberniae apud Thurles habita Anno MDCCCL* (Dublin: James Duffy, 1851). See also Ciarán O'Carroll, *Paul Cardinal Cullen: Portrait of a practical Nationalist* (Dublin: Veritas Publications, 2009).

[18] Paul Cullen to Edward Monsell, 3 May, 1852, Monsell Papers, Ms 8317(3), National Library of Ireland (NLI).

[19] See Desmond Bowen's two studies, *The Protestant Crusade in Ireland, 1800–70: a study of Protestant–Catholic Relations between the Act of Union and Disestablishment* (Dublin: Gill and Macmillan, 1978), and *Souperism: Myth or Reality?* (Cork: Mercier Press, 1970). Miriam Moffitt has produced a detailed study of the evangelical crusade in Connemara, *Soupers and Jumpers: The Protestant Mission in Connemara 1848–1937* (Dublin: Nonsuch Publishing, 2008). See also Irene Whelan 'The stigma of souperism' in Cathal Póirtéir (ed.), *The Great Irish Famine* (Cork: Mercier Press, 1995), 135–54.

between fifty and sixty years ago Erismore was in the hands of the Jumpers [mission society converts], the people having renounced the faith for food in famine times. There are now only four or five Jumper families in the place but the evil effects of the lamentable occurrences of half a century ago are still only too visible in the religious indifference of the people with regard to Mass and the manner in which they bring up many of their children without sacraments or Mass or school. We discovered children of 16, 17 and 18 years of age who had never received any sacrament but baptism and some of them had never entered a church.[20]

Some bishops saw parish missions as a sort of pre-emptive strike in areas targeted by the mission societies. Archbishop John MacHale of Tuam, who was in the forefront of the battle with the Evangelical societies, invited the Rosminians to conduct a series of missions throughout his extensive diocese where many of the more remote areas were exclusively Irish-speaking. Preaching in English posed problems enough to the Dutchmen, Austrians and Russian among the Redemptorists or for the Italian Rosminians and Passionists, so that sermons in Irish-speaking areas were often delivered through an interpreter: the Vincentians, for example, used Irish Christian Brothers in this capacity.[21]

Following the success of the Redemptorist missions in the first season of 1851–2, demand steadily increased. Six were preached the following year and following the opening of the Limerick house in 1853, nine were given in 1854. According to the index at the end of the first volume of the mission chronicle of the Limerick community, 125 missions (excluding parish and other retreats) were given in the seventeen years between 1851 and 1868.[22] Depending on the population and physical size of the parish, the mission normally lasted between two weeks and one month. A distinctive feature of Alphonsus's system of mission preaching was the 'renewal'. This was a return visit after an interval of several months for a shorter period of preaching and confessions. Its objective was to promote a deeper 'renewal of spirit' and to consolidate whatever good work had been done during the mission proper. Not every mission had a 'renewal', but it was a feature of a sizeable number of the early missions. In those times of the year when no missions were preached, retreats were undertaken to clergy, religious communities and groups of lay-people, such as confraternities or to the inmates of workhouses or other institutions. The Fathers were also in demand as preachers of special sermons, often as fund-raising appeals for church buildings or other charitable

20 Mission in Erismore (part of Clifden parish), 26 June to 3 July 1904. Esker Mission Chronicle, vol. 1, 170, Esker Domestic Archives.
21 Murphy, 'Vincentian Parish Missions', 158.
22 'Domestic and Apostolic Labours', vol. 1: 1851–1868', RPAD.

causes. The number of Redemptorists was also increasing. The continental pioneers were augmented by new entrants from Ireland and England and their training finished, they promptly took their places in the mission work. The cramped temporary residence in Limerick city centre was replaced, first by two cottages on the outskirts of the town, and eventually by a more spacious purpose-built monastery on the same site.

The mission generally followed the plan outlined by Alphonsus and developed in subsequent 'mission directories' or instructions on how to give a mission. Departures from the plan were few. A notable exception was the work of Fr John Furniss, a pioneer of missions for children, whose work will be considered in somewhat greater detail in a later chapter. While a short 'children's mission' was often the curtain-raiser to a parish mission, Furniss was regularly invited to give special missions to children in the more indus-trialised parts of the country where children were sent out to work from the age of twelve or even earlier.

The flavour of some of the early missions and the missioners' daily life can be gleaned from the lively accounts in Prost's memoirs and the first volume of the Limerick mission chronicle mentioned above. Accustomed to the flourishing Catholic life of Austria and Belgium, the early Redemptorists were often aghast at the poverty they met in Ireland. In the parish church of Enniskillen, County Fermanagh, for example, a trunk near the high altar did duty as a sacristy. The church itself was

> low and the altar small, with a torn picture above the altar. The church was dirty, and one could see here and there cobwebs. Our first task was to clean out the cobwebs and sweep the church, which every one of us did … We covered the torn picture and replaced it with a picture of the Mother of God we had brought with us for the devotions and put the crucifix we had brought on the altar. The Catholic people looked extremely miserable, even pitiable.[23]

Since there was no pulpit, the parish priest, wearing his everyday clothes, gave the missioners a somewhat perfunctory welcome from the altar steps, 'barely different from the way in which gentlemen are introduced at a social gathering'. He made it plain to the congregation however that he expected handsome offerings during the time of the mission, citing the example of a mission in Derry where two hundred pounds had been taken in.

The standard of cooking in the average parish house was considered monotonous and unattractive by men accustomed to the variety of simple country food of the continent. During the mission in Fermoy, County Cork (May–June 1855), for example, the missioners lodging with the 'saintly bishop

---

23 Prost, *Redemptorist Missionary in Ireland*, 54.

of Cloyne' observed that his table was 'simple and frugal, the usual fare of the Irish clergy, a portion of meat and potatoes without any pudding or other delicacy'.[24] A striking feature of this mission was the large number of soldiers from the garrison who approached the sacraments prior to their departure for the Crimea. More than eighty were confirmed during the mission. Several Protestants were received into the Church, including an eighteen-year-old English soldier who followed their carriage sobbing as they left the town. A mission in Doe, near Creeslough, County Donegal, revealed the still more naked poverty of a country church. The chronicle entry describes it as a rough country chapel perched between the Atlantic and high steep mountains.[25] The people covered long distances on foot to come to the mission. The church possessed no tabernacle, not to speak of pyx or monstrance, so a blessing with the great mission cross took the place of Benediction. The mission was so successful that the sermons of the final days had to be held out of doors for the benefit of the crowd estimated at about 10,000 people. On their way to their next engagement in Killybegs, they made what amounted to a triumphant three-day progress through Donegal. At Dungloe, where they had planned to stay for the night, the whole parish came out to meet them, and escorted them to the parish church where they led the rosary and gave a short sermon and a further sermon after Mass the following morning.

Elsewhere, movement towards reform with an accompanying programme of church-building was already well under way in the 1850s. There are several references in the chronicles to handsome new churches built to the plans of Pugin and his disciples. The mission in Kilkenny during Advent, 1858 ran into difficulties before it had even begun. Bishop Edmond Walsh, who had recently expended a great deal of money on completing and decorating St Mary's cathedral, did not relish the prospect of poor people bringing in mud on their boots, night after night. One of the more dramatic highlights of the mission was a solemn act of reparation to Jesus in the Blessed Sacrament for sins of irreverence, especially neglect of holy communion. The Blessed Sacrament was exposed on an altar ablaze with candles and the missioner invited the people to respond to his invitation to repentance by crying out for mercy as he chanted the *Miserere* psalm. They did so with an enthusiasm that the bishop clearly thought inappropriate. 'Stop the singing!', he ordered. Turning to the people, he said: 'You have disgraced yourselves! Leave the church immediately.' In their rush to comply, the people stampeded, overturning and damaging several of the benches in the process. The bishop

---

[24] The bishop in question was William Keane. Appointed bishop of Ross in 1851, he was translated to Cloyne in 1857, where he remained until his death in 1875. 'Domestic and Apostolic Labours, 1', 19, RPAD.
[25] Ibid., 25–6.

ordered the cathedral to be closed and the mission abandoned. The day was only saved by the intervention of his nephew, the dean of the diocese. Bishop Walsh was diplomatically 'out' when the missioners called to bid farewell, but the members of the corporation arrived to present them with an address of thanks, printed on silk.[26]

The mission chronicle affords interesting glimpses into the social life of the time. For some women, the only escape from the trap of poverty seems to have been through prostitution. Prostitution was not confined to larger towns or cities. During the mission given in Queenstown (Cobh) in 1855 'fifteen girls of ill-fame' converted. The missioners found them a place of safety and rehabilitation, noting how generous the people of the town showed themselves in their regard.[27] The previous year, eight women in Mallow converted from prostitution and 'the ladies of the town subscribed some money to support them for some time in Mallow and then at the earliest opportunity, they will send them to Australia.'[28] In Glyn, County Limerick, the wretched state of the morals of the young was blamed on the influence of a local landlord – or, as the chronicler put it in elegant Latin, '*ob praevaritatem cujusdam viri nobilis ibidem commorantis*' ['on account of the depravity of a certain nobleman who lived there'].[29] Places were found with the Good Shepherd Sisters in Limerick for three girls from the village, while a further three were sent to the workhouse.

The difficulty of Irish-speaking missions mentioned above seems to have first presented itself to the Redemptorists during the mission in Athenry, County Galway in 1854. To their surprise, 'the sermons could not produce all their effect on account of the people not understanding well the English language.' Fr Bernard Hafkenscheid, the Dutch preacher at the solemn service of reparation to the Blessed Sacrament, 'was forced to have recourse to violent means to make them cry out "Mercy! Mercy!"' In Mitchelstown, County Cork, the Irish-speaking population of the hinterland was sufficiently large for the missioners to draft in a team of local priests to help with the confessions. Neglect of the sacraments, especially confirmation, but some-times also first communion, was a feature of Catholic life in Ireland in the mid-nineteenth century. Archbishop John MacHale of Tuam attended the close of the Athenry mission and confirmed 600 people in the parish church and a further 550 in the out-church at Newcastle. The same year (1854) in

---

[26] Ibid., 50–7. The address is pasted into the volume.
[27] Ibid., 20–1.
[28] Ibid., 9.
[29] Ibid., 32. The nobleman in question was probably John Fraunceis FitzGerald, twenty-fourth Knight of Glin, commonly known as Ridire na mBan ('the Knight of the Women') who reput-edly sired fifteen children out of wedlock: see obituary of Desmond FitzGerald, twenty-ninth Knight of Glin, *Daily Telegraph*, 16 Sept. 2011.

Mallow 'a remarkable number of young men and young girls between 15 and 22 or 25 years of age had not made their first communion.' They were prepared during the mission and approached the altar rails with a lighted candle in their hands. In other places, the mission provided an opportunity to rectify illicit marriages. In Kingstown (Dún Laoghaire) in 1855, fifty couples 'who were supposed to be married' received the sacrament.

Public religious controversy was a feature of some missions in the period, especially where the influence of the Evangelical societies was strong. The Redemptorists did their best to avoid confrontation, regarding it as counter-productive. In Mitchelstown, County Cork, an Evangelical minister offered to debate the errors of Rome publicly with them, but the challenge was ignored. Public controversy during the Kingstown mission in October–November 1855 led to a legal trial.[30] Given its influential Protestant population, public displays of Catholicism were rare there. Crosses marking missions were normally of impressive dimensions, but that made for Kingstown was unobtrusive. The chronicler observed that this was deliberate 'owing to the fear of the parish priest from the Protestants who were exceedingly alarmed and embittered on seeing great crowds of men and women lying down before the cross'. One Protestant resident complained in a letter to a Liverpool newspaper pasted into the chronicle that 'the Redemptorist Fathers were doing all the mischief they could and now idolatry is no more hiding itself, but it showed itself as barefaced as in any popish town on the continent and that under the fostering care of the government.'

Fr Vladimir Petcherine, the Russian Redemptorist, had arranged a public burning of immoral books as the climax of the Kingstown mission. Due either to his carelessness or to a deliberate attempt to embarrass him, several Protestant bibles were included among the books destined for the pyre. The charred remains of the bibles were retrieved from the ashes and brought to the local police barracks as evidence that Petcherine had burned them. According to his biographer, unpublished documents among the state paper archives suggest that the police were slow to act on the evidence, and only took action when political pressure was applied by some extremist Protestant organisations.[31] Petcherine was charged with the crime of blasphemy. His trial in Green Street court house in Dublin lasted from 27 November to 8 December 1855. He was defended by the leading Catholic barrister of the day, Thomas O'Hagan, later the first Catholic lord chancellor of Ireland. The

---

[30] Ibid. An account of the Kingstown mission along with press cuttings has been inserted into this volume between pages 22 and 23.
[31] Eóin MacWhite, 'Towards a Biography of Vladimir Petcherine' in *Proceedings of the Royal Irish Academy*, 1981, 109–58, here 138. Dr MacWhite was a distinguished Irish scholar and diplomat who appreciated Petcherine's significance in both Irish history and Russian literature.

trial attracted enormous publicity; the account of it in the Irish daily papers was given extensive coverage. Petcherine was acquitted and given a hero's welcome on his return to Kingstown.

Crisis for the Missions

Petcherine's bravura performance in Kingstown disquieted some of his confreres. Louis de Buggenoms (1816–82), his Belgian superior, gave him only very lukewarm support. The bible-burning charge, he feared, was symptomatic of an attitude that was threatening to undermine much of the good that had been done in Ireland over the previous four years. The small band of Redemptorists was doing a prodigious amount of work, travelling long distances to put themselves at the disposal of parishes that wanted missions. In a sober reflection on shortcomings of the Kingstown mission, the chronicler may have caught something of the mood of his colleagues. The mission, culminating with Petcherine's new status as an Irish Catholic hero, should have been a success, but 'there appeared always the want of one strong, able and experienced head of the mission, owing to which there were sometimes as many systems as there were Fathers.' Joseph Prost, the first superior of the missions in Ireland, had tried to follow Alphonsus's methods of mission-giving with almost literal exactness, despite the fact that many of them had already been abandoned as impractical by his confreres in Austria and Belgium. One of the more intractable problems proved to be the financing of missions. With the building of new churches and other religious institutions in the nineteenth century, missions were sometimes seen as a welcome source of revenue for such projects. The unpleasant consequences of this have already been seen in the case of the Letterkenny mission, but collections proved a headache elsewhere. The Redemptorists in Britain and Ireland had very little by way of regular income. The first Irish missions had been funded thanks to gifts from the inherited income (patrimony) of members like John Furniss who had given Joseph Prost two hundred pounds to finance the missions. Such a system could not continue forever and Prost was enough of a realist to recognise that he had to find ways of making the missions pay for themselves, yet he remained implacably opposed to fixed admission charges or collections at church doors. He was prepared to countenance a collection plate being passed around before the evening sermon or a token levy of one penny for a seat in the gallery on better-off folk who wanted a clearer view of the proceedings. The Sunday collection went to the parish, while the night collections were for the missioners. From the proceeds, all the expenses of the mission were defrayed and no further stipend was asked from the parish. Vegetables, bread and chickens were sometimes sent in as gifts for the missioners' table, especially in country districts.

Prost was replaced as superior of the missions by the Dutchman, Fr Bernard Hafkenscheid, in 1854. Like Prost, Hafkenscheid had spent some years on the American mission. He was less attached than Prost to the literal following of Alphonsus's mission methods and was determined to put the Irish missions on a businesslike footing. The two were clearly set on collision course, and Prost was recalled to Austria shortly afterwards. For all its idealism, there was much in Prost's mission system that was impractical. The renting of a separate house as a dwelling for the missioners where they could continue to live a modified form of their religious life proved to be unworkable. His missions were also open-ended: he did not declare the mission closed until he felt sure that all the confessions had been heard. Hafkenscheid's personality was also more capable of attracting the loyalty of his fellow missioners, and of gaining the support of the parish clergy and bishops.

The compiler of the report of the Dundalk mission of 1859 may have been drawing on the collective experience of his brethren who had served on the Irish missions for the previous eight years. As it lists the most distinctive characteristics of Irish missions, it is worth quoting at length.

1. Many of the poor people remain for several nights in the church if they can; if not, somewhere near to it.
2. Many remain for one, two or even part of a third day without food [while waiting for confession]; often they ask for Holy Communion after sunset.[32]
3. In seeking to be admitted to confession, they often tell *publicly* [emphasis in the original] the great number of years they are absent from the sacraments and the great sinners they have been.
4. They have such faith in the Fathers that they present themselves and their children to be cured of every disease and to this there would be no end if the Fathers did not do all in their power to prevent it. They often try to touch the hem or some part of the religious habit.
5. They manifest their strong feelings during the sermons with sobs, sighs and tears and at the closing sermon, their wailing is loud, long and heart-rending.
6. Many of the poor people have no shoes. In the depths of winter amid rain, hail and snow, they come before the *aurora* [dawn] and remain the whole day barefooted on the cold damp floors of the village churches. The

---

[32] Even at the turn of the nineteenth century, lengthy vigils for confession were still occasionally encountered. The report of the mission in Virginia, County Cavan (10 June to 1 July, 1899), for example, recorded that 'the people remained up the whole night in order to secure confession the next day, taking their place at the confessionals before the rosary began [at the evening service] and staying until 2 or 3 p.m. next day.' Esker Mission Chronicle, 1, 29, Domestic Archives, Esker.

floors are sometimes of stone flags, but more generally of earth or clay. At the departure of the missioners, they cannot be prevented (although the Fathers always try to stop them) from accompanying them, often for several miles.

7. The crowds are so great, they are often packed together and the heat of the church is so intense that not only do women but sometimes men sink into a faint and are carried out almost dead.

8. The people generally are very poor, yet they purchase on every mission from the hawkers who follow the missioners everywhere, one, two, or sometimes even three hundred pounds worth of pious books, scapulars, rosaries, crosses, medals etc.

9. On *every* mission people are met with of 50, 60, 70 years of age who have never received a sacrament except baptism, and perhaps marriage, and who are in excellent dispositions, shedding abundant tears when they hear they are deemed worthy to receive our dear Lord in the holy sacrament of the Eucharist.

10. Rarely are any sinners found in any of the parishes who do not attend the mission and receive the sacraments. The exceptions are principally in the larger towns and are made up of drunkards who cannot or will not give up their habits and a few of the better classes who if they do not avail themselves of the graces do nothing to retard the progress of the mission.

11. In all our missions (except a few at the beginning), we announce often and adhere to our word that we shall receive the confessions only of the people of the parish. In this we differ from all the other missionary bodies and this is the one great cause of the success of our missions. No doubt the mission loses a part of its exterior *éclat* or glories, but the sinners of the parish are all heard, which would not otherwise be possible.[33]

Difficulties in Limerick

The incessant activity of the new Limerick foundation gave superiors some cause for concern about the quality of the religious life being lived in the community. The communities of England and Ireland continued to be composed for the most part of Dutch, Austrians and Belgians, with a small scattering of English and Irish. They may not always have been, humanly speaking, easy places to live. A larger set of questions was also beginning to emerge. Old rivalries, which had split the Redemptorist congregation in the last years of the life of the founder had left their legacy. The wars and revolutions of the nineteenth century had done nothing to improve communications

---

33 'Domestic and Apostolic Labours, 1', 95–6, RPAD. Although the English is grammatically accurate, an occasional stiltedness of style betrays the pen of a non-native speaker of English.

between the houses north of the Alps and what was nominally the Italian superior general. In the thirty years since the death of Clement Hofbauer, the transalpine communities had increased phenomenally and were under the strong leadership of a vicar general who enjoyed almost all the powers of a superior general. Although the Neapolitan houses that were separated from the main stem shortly before the death of Alphonsus had been reunited with the houses of the Papal States, a great deal of distrust still remained. Pope Pius IX had ordered the Redemptorists to put an end to their divisions and to prepare for a general chapter to be held in 1855 in Rome with the objective of uniting the entire congregation under a single superior general who would live in Rome rather than in the mother house of Nocera dei Pagani near Naples.

The superiors of the transalpine branch were determined that their stricter interpretation of the rule of Alphonsus, particularly in the interpretation of the vow of poverty, would prevail. This was an issue so complex and acrimonious that many, like Prost, confessed that they did not quite understand some of the points at issue.[34] For the partisans of strict observance of a monastic kind, the ideal of community life was summed up by a saying, ascribed to Alphonsus, which defined the true Redemptorist as 'a Carthusian at home and an apostle abroad'. Although the phrase has become consecrated by generations of Redemptorist usage, it cannot be found in precisely this form in the writings of Alphonsus. In one of his short works on vocation, for example, he writes that the members of his congregation could call themselves apostolic workers (*operai*) when out of the house and hermits (*romiti*) when at home. Santino Raponi, an authority on early Redemptorist history, suggests that the Carthusian/apostle contrast, which gained currency in the nineteenth century, was borrowed from the Vincentians, as it is ascribed in this form to St Vincent de Paul by Louis Abelly, his first biographer.[35]

The partisans of 'strict observance' proved victorious at the general chapter. One of their number, Nicholas Mauron (1818–93), a Swiss-born disciple of Fr Passerat, was elected superior general. He would rule the congregation for the next thirty-eight years. As political conditions made the holding of another general chapter impossible until the one for the election of his successor in 1898, Mauron's firm interpretation of strict observance would shape Redemptorist identity for the rest of the nineteenth century.

Some of these tensions were already making themselves felt in Limerick in the early 1850s. Writing to the Scottish-born Redemptorist, Edward Douglas, then resident in Rome, Louis de Buggenoms confided his fear that

---

[34] Prost, *Redemptorist Missionary in Ireland*, 86.
[35] Santino Raponi, *The Charism of Redemptorists in the Church: a commentary on the Constitutions* (Rome: Centre for Redemptorist Spirituality, 2003), 93–101.

'the chief misery of this house arises from the fact that several Fathers are not at all fond of the interior life.'[36] He attributed this to the baneful influence of Bernard Hafkenscheid. While acknowledging his undoubted gifts as a missioner, de Buggenoms believed some of Hafkenscheid's less spiritual side had also to be reckoned with: Hafkenscheid, he complained, had taught them to be *gaillards* (a French word that might be translated roughly as 'one of the lads'), 'full of merely human life, rejoicing when nature is flattered and attaching more importance to external show and success than to more hidden good'. Nor was de Buggenoms without his critics. Some of his confreres considered that he shirked the burdens of mission work and was only too happy to use the excuse of the growing popularity of the temporary chapel of the Limerick house to stay at home cultivating the spiritual lives of a coterie of female penitents he was grooming for the convent. Others were critical of his tale-bearing and gossipy nature. In his favour, it should be allowed that de Buggenoms had borne the burden of most of the foundations in England and Ireland. He had calculated that for more than fourteen years he had either been the founder or at least a member of the first community in every community in which he lived. Now in his mid-forties, he was beginning to find the constant upheavals and uncertainty rather wearisome.

Hafkenscheid was of more optimistic cast of mind. He reported to the 1855 general chapter that Limerick had the potential to become one of the most important houses of the congregation, but it needed more men.[37] John Baptist Swinkels, the provincial of the Anglo–Dutch province to which Limerick now belonged, took a gloomier view than Hafkenscheid.[38] While admitting that the Limerick Fathers were 'virtually worshipped by the people', he feared that the incessant demands of preaching and providing confessional service in their own church, in addition to the regular mission work, were becoming an intolerable burden on the community. As far as regular religious observance went, he considered Limerick to be the worst house in the province. Like Louis de Buggenoms, Swinkels ascribed this to the baleful influence of Bernard Hafkenscheid. Many regular acts of community life had been virtually abandoned. The weekly study meetings prescribed by the rule, for example, were held only by way of exception. Nor did some of the English Fathers pass muster: while Coffin had not enough of a religious spirit and was too English in manner, the only thing Redemptorist about John Furniss was his habit!

---

[36] Louis de Buggenoms to Edward Douglas, Limerick, 24 Sept. 1853, Redemptorist General Archives, Rome, hereafter RGAR.

[37] Mémoire du P. Bernard au P. Mauron, 1855, Prov. Anglica, RGAR.

[38] John Baptist Swinkels to Nicholas Mauron, Oct. 1855, Prov. Anglica, RGAR. It seems like an account given at the end of a provincial visitation.

Casualty of the Missions

The intense round of mission work, complicated by tensions within the community, took its toll on the health and wellbeing of some of the missioners. Several died while still relatively young. Others, like Joseph Prost, headed back to the quieter pastures of their homelands. The story of Vladimir Petcherine is particularly tragic.

Petcherine was born near Kiev in the Ukraine in 1807. His intellectual abilities led him to the universities of St Petersburg and Moscow where on completion of a doctorate in 1835, he was appointed extraordinary professor of Greek philology. He was a writer of at least minor talent, whose place in the history of Russian literature has been belatedly recognised. Tiring of the controlled world of Tsarist Russia, Petcherine decided to travel in western Europe. While in Belgium in 1838, he came under the influence of a Redemptorist and converted to Roman Catholicism. He entered the Redemptorist novitiate in 1840 and after a short course of theology, was ordained priest. He was sent first to the new Redemptorist community in Falmouth in Cornwall and after a spell in London, came to Ireland as a member of the Limerick mission team.

Petcherine's Russian experience and passionate nature led him to see the lives of the oppressed peasants on the large estates he had known in his youth reflected in the struggles of post-Famine Ireland, and he was an outspoken champion for social change. He seems to have been the only member of the mission team to recognise that the most urgent Irish mission field was in the west of Ireland. He believed it to be the closest equivalent to the experience of spiritual abandonment that had led Alphonsus Liguori to found the Congregation of the Most Holy Redeemer in the mountain villages to the south of Naples. He wrote:

> The Irish in the West, and especially in County Galway, are apostasising *en masse* because of the extreme ignorance and poverty of the people. That is where the most abandoned souls are. Missioners should be flying there. It is our misfortune to be going to places where we are least needed. We are being invited to places where there are zealous priests and a population that never wavered in the faith … No one is inviting us to Galway where souls are perishing in thousands. But again, no one invited Alphonsus to evangelise the goatherds of Scala.[39]

Petcherine's relationship with his Dutch and English superiors was not easy. By 1861, he was in the depths of an emotional and spiritual crisis.

---

[39] This passage is quoted in a letter of Louis de Buggenoms to Rudolph von Smetna, the vicar general of the transalpine provinces, 27 Oct. 1854, RGAR. De Buggenoms claims to be quoting from a letter of Petcherine.

Swinkels, the provincial, felt compelled to confront him with some of the accusations that had been made against him in the course of the canonical visitation earlier that year.[40] There were three specific areas of complaint. First, he was accused by confreres and parish priests alike of being too expeditious in hearing confessions: it was alleged he heard 180 confessions in an eight-hour period, and that he did not encourage people to make general confessions, which was a regular feature of mission-practice. Second, he did not support the temporal power of the papacy, had even spoken against it and had voiced criticisms of the Roman superiors of his own congregation among his confreres. Finally, he was regarded as being 'exclusively Irish' in his sympathies.

Even before he received Swinkel's letter, Petcherine had already written one of his own asking to be dispensed from his vows on the grounds that he was weary of the missionary life. As a Russian, he claimed, he was familiar with only one kind of monastic life, that of strict contemplatives who buried themselves in silence and austerity. He raised some questions about the lifestyle of his brethren. The thought of growing old in a Redemptorist community with little to do but follow the regular spiritual exercises and hear the confessions of a few devout penitents terrified him. He was especially critical of what he felt was a growing preoccupation with money in the communities:

> I have never been able to bear having to handle money or to hear it discussed. Imagine then what I feel every day when I come out of the confessional with my pockets laden down with money.[41]

Now in his fifty-fourth year, he claimed that his energy was fast running out and that he needed to prepare for death in a contemplative monastery, preferably among the Carthusians. He had refrained from posting the letter at the time, but Swinkel's rebuke opened old wounds and triggered a few more months of soul-searching before he dispatched the letter to Nicholas Mauron, the superior general in Rome, the following August.[42]

Mauron's official response was dry. He summarised Petcherine's points and assured him that, if he were still in the same frame of mind and were to apply for his dispensation from vows, it would be granted without further

---

[40] The main source for this period of his life is the valuable collection of letters edited with commentary by Andreas Sampers, 'Wladimir Sergejewitsch Pecherine (1807–1885). Sein Austritt aus der Kongregation der Allerheiligsten Erlöseres (Redemptoristen), 1861' in *SHCSSR*, vol. XXI, no. 1 (1973), 165–97. Jean Beco CSsR has collected many of his letters and a memoir in *Vladimir Petcherin (1807–1885): Mémoires et Correspondance* (Rome: Redemptorist Historical Institute, 2006).

[41] Letter from Petcherine to Nicholas Mauron, in Sampers, 'Wladimir Sergejewitsch Pecherine,' 176–80.

[42] The Redemptorist major superior's official title at this time was rector major. The terms 'rector major', 'superior general' and 'general' are used interchangeably.

ado. The curt official note was accompanied, however, by a longer personal letter, whose tone was scarcely calculated to mollify Petcherine. Mauron accused him of lacking the spirit of the congregation. Particularly insulting from the young superior general must have been the suggestion that Petcherine re-read the novice's rule in order to regain a proper perspective on his vocation. Mauron concluded: 'I do not think you can remain long in our congregation. It only remains for you to ask for a dispensation from your vows.' The next exchange of letters brought the dispensation. Not a man to do things by halves, Petcherine left for France within a few days of receiving it with the intention of entering the Carthusians. A retreat in the remote monastery of the Grande Chartreuse in the French Alps with winter fast approaching convinced him that he was in the wrong place. He decided he would be better off returning to Ireland and applying for admission to the Cistercians of Mount Melleray in County Waterford.

Petcherine arrived at Mount Melleray on 29 October 1861. He was formally received into the community and given the habit on Christmas Day. Despite his protests that he needed solitude, his nature was too passionate for silence. Within a month, he had left and taken rooms in Dublin. A contrite letter to Mauron followed at the end of January 1862. It was supported by an appeal from the Irish Redemptorist, Fr William Plunkett, written the following day. Plunkett urged Mauron to show Petcherine some sympathy and to take him back, 'if not for our sake, then for his'. Petcherine had worked unselfishly for the congregation, Plunkett argued, and whatever faults he had sprang more from faulty judgement than from ill-will. Mauron was inflexible: under no circumstances would he take Petcherine back.[43] He rejected the claim that Petcherine could appeal to the canonical privilege that permitted an active religious to try his vocation in a contemplative community and guaranteed his return to his original community without prejudice, arguing that the Russian had sought and been granted his dispensation on the grounds that he was disillusioned with the Redemptorists, not that he wanted to try a more perfect way of life.

---

[43] Petcherine's case bears some similarities to that of the American Redemptorist, Isaac Hecker (1819–88). Wishing to encourage a more indigenous spirit among his brethren in North America, Hecker had gone to Rome in 1857 against the will of his local superiors to plead this cause directly with the superior general. Mauron regarded this as an act of insubordination, and despite Hecker's protest that the Rule permitted such recourse in urgent cases, he expelled him from the Congregation: see Maurice de Meulemeester, *Histoire Sommaire de la Congrégation du Très Saint Rédempteur* (Louvain: Imprimerie St Alphonse, 1950), 158. Hecker founded the Missionary Society of St Paul the Apostle (Paulists). On Hecker's significance in the development of nineteenth-century American Catholicism, see John Farina, *Hecker Studies: Essays on the thought of Isaac Hecker* (New York: Paulist Press, 1983).

Vladimir Petcherine found work in the diocese of Dublin as chaplain to the Mater Hospital. He spent the next twenty-four years living in rented rooms in Capel Street, working quietly at his hospital duties to the edification of the Sisters of Mercy. There is some evidence that he resumed literary contact with the Russian men of letters he had known in his youth. Many of his confreres believed that a grave injustice had been done to Petcherine. Joseph Prost, who could be scathing on the defects of his confreres, glosses over his shortcomings as a missioner with the comment that 'he was very lovable.'[44] Henry Harbison, who had entered the Redemptorists as a result of seeing Petcherine in action as a missioner in the parish where he was curate, visited him a few days before his death. His name was held in honour and affection by later Irish Redemptorists who regarded Vladimir Petcherine as one of the founding fathers of what was eventually to become the Irish province. Justice was finally done to his troubled spirit. On 1 May 1999 his remains were exhumed from their neglected grave in Glasnevin cemetery, and re-interred among his brethren in the Redemptorist plot at Deansgrange cemetery in County Dublin.

[44] Prost, *Redemptorist Missionary in Ireland*, 34.

CHAPTER TWO

A Church and a Confraternity

The house at Bank Place, Limerick, rented as a temporary residence during the mission in St Michael's parish, continued to serve as a home between missions for the rest of the summer of 1853. In November of that year, it was granted the status of a canonically-constituted community with Fr Louis de Buggenoms as superior. In addition to the superior, the first community consisted of two priests, John Schneider and John Furniss, and one brother, Peter Franken. Over the following weeks, they were joined by Frs Bernard Hafkenscheid, Vladimir Petcherine and Francis Theunis. Redemptorist houses had the canonical right to open a public church with a daily and seasonal round of liturgical and devotional services. Especially important was the availability of confession, so that people who had benefited from the mission preaching could continue to receive spiritual guidance from the fathers. The largest room on the ground floor of the Bank Place residence was set up as a chapel, and confessionals were erected wherever space permitted. On the eve of major feast days, there was a constant stream of penitents from 4.30 a.m. until the door closed at 9.30 p.m. Limerick was a busy port, and many emigrants on their way to Australia or the New World made their last confession on Irish soil in the little chapel.

Writing to his superior, Louis de Buggenoms recorded that on the first Christmas Eve, the chapel was thronged all day with people waiting for confession and asking the Fathers to give them a midnight Mass. When the chapel was finally cleared late in the evening, 'I believe they spent the night outside in spite of the cold, waiting with a patience worthy of the shepherds of Bethlehem.' Bank Place, situated on one of the city's main business streets, with no room for expansion, could only be a temporary expedient so it was imperative to have a site for a proper monastery and church. Three sites were considered, before they eventually settled on a property called Courtbrack at the suburban end of Henry Street.

The Redemptorists took possession of Courtbrack in the late spring of 1854. Two reconditioned cottages on the land were fitted up as a home for the community and with the help of James Walsh, an Irish Christian Brother, as clerk of works, a temporary chapel was completed within six weeks at the cost of about £800. A newspaper report described the church on the opening day:

The church, though temporary, is commodious. It is 120 feet long by 40 feet broad ... At the eastern end are three altars: the middle and the largest is dedicated to St Alphonsus, whose sculpted effigy dressed in episcopal robes, with outstretched hand over a beautiful child who looks up to him for protection, is a conspicuous object in a niche immediately over the tabernacle ... The other altars are dedicated to the Blessed Virgin and St Joseph and with the wax lights that burned on them and about them all, and the simple but elegant decorations with which they were ornamented the effect was exceedingly impressive throughout.[1]

Conditions in the new church were more spartan than this account implies. De Buggenoms remarked in a letter to Edward Douglas that many regarded it as fine enough for the poor, but better-off people who had a horror of vermin were already demanding a permanent church.

When the Redemptorists came to Limerick, Bishop John Ryan was already planning to build the new cathedral of St John (built 1856–61). They assured him that they would provide the funds for the new monastery out of their own resources. This was to prove an over-optimistic promise. The truth was that the Redemptorists had very limited financial resources, and these had been stretched by the expansion of the previous thirty years. They had arrived in England at a time when a stream of conversions in the wake of the Oxford Movement presaged a Catholic revival on a grand scale. The reality proved very different. Several temporary foundations made before they settled on two permanent houses at Clapham and Liverpool had stretched their already meagre financial resources to the limit.

Several of the first English and Irishmen to join the Redemptorists were men of property in their own right. The Scots convert, Edward Douglas, had considerable personal wealth and it was anticipated that he might provide something for the new foundation. Before work could get under way, however, he was called to Rome in 1853 in preparation for the forthcoming general chapter to be held in 1855. Pius IX had instructed Redemptorists to move the seat of their general government to Rome. With their central resources every bit as limited as those of the Limerick house, Douglas's money was the only way a rising congregation might buy itself the kind of prestigious site needed to make its mark on Rome. With Douglas's funds, the former Villa Caserta on the Via Merulana was bought and construction of the church of San Alfonso began.[2]

---

[1] *Limerick Reporter*, 30 May 1854.
[2] For an early history of the house, see A. Walter, *Villa Caserta, 1855–1905: Ad aureum domus generalitae jubilarum* (Rome: CSsR, 1905).

William Plunkett (1824–1900), younger son of the Catholic earl of Fingall, who had entered the Redemptorists in 1850, put his patrimony of £2,500 into the building fund. Given the straitened circumstances, John Baptist Swinkels, the Dutch provincial superior, was inclined to allow events in Limerick to take their natural course. The Limerick community, thought otherwise. Louis de Buggenoms argued strongly that a start should be made immediately on building a permanent church and monastery. Many sacrifices had been made for England, he pleaded, but little had been done for Ireland and the Limerick foundation had not only proved to be financially viable, but it was subsidising the English houses with Mass-offerings. Nor were prospective candidates likely to be impressed by the makeshift living conditions at Courtbrack: the few who had recently visited with the intention of applying for admission had gone off to the Vincentians when they saw the primitive living conditions. Swinkels reluctantly gave permission to begin building, but the Redemptorists now had to go back, cap in hand, to ask Bishop Ryan's permission to begin a public fund-raising campaign.

Church and Monastery of Mount St Alphonsus
The architect for the new building, Philip Charles Hardwick, came with the recommendation of Lord Dunraven. Apart from St John's cathedral in Limerick, his Irish work included the design of the manor house and the restoration of the medieval friaries at Adare for Dunraven and St Columba's College, Rathfarnham. The foundation stone of the monastery was laid on the feast of St Alphonsus, 2 August 1856.[3] The community took possession of the completed building on 24 June 1858. A newspaper report of the dedication of the church some years later described the building:

> The convent, spacious enough to accommodate forty guests together with a community equally numerous, contains a cloister, library, refectory, and all the apartments suitable for its sacred destination. This convent was completed in 1857 at a cost of £7,000 and this large outlay of £9,000 was defrayed wholly, or nearly so, out of the personal fortunes of the Redemptorist Fathers.[4]

Some weeks before they took possession of the completed monastery, the foundation stone of the new church was laid in what was to become one of the massive pillars on the Gospel side of the sanctuary. Although all trace of

---

[3] St Alphonsus's feast day was observed on 2 August until it was transferred to the previous day in the reform of the Roman liturgical calendar in 1969.
[4] *Freeman's Journal,* 8 Dec. 1862. The dimensions of the building are somewhat exaggerated as the circular appealing for funds sent out in 1860 says that it contains 'some twenty apartments fitted up for priests and laymen desirous of performing the spiritual exercises'.

it has disappeared, the chronicle reveals that it bore a Latin inscription which is translated as follows:

> Pius IX Pont[ifex] Max[imus], Victoria Queen of Great Britain /in the one hundred and twenty-sixth year of the Congregation/Nicholas Mauron rector major/John Baptist Swinkels, superior of the Anglo-Dutch Province/John Baptist Roes rector of this house of Limerick/this foundation stone of the Church of St. Alphonsus was laid by D. John Ryan, Bishop of Limerick/on the 30th day of May, in the year of Our Lord MDCCCLVIII/William Corbett, Contractor: P.A. Hardwick Architect.[5]

Progress on the building of the church was slow. The chronicler noted wryly that there were sometimes so few workers on the site that it might be safely said of this church, as was said of Solomon's Temple, that 'neither hammer nor axe nor any tool of iron was heard in the temple while it was being built' (1 Kings 6:7). It was finally dedicated by Bishop George Butler, coadjutor bishop of Limerick, on 7 December 1862, with the special preacher for the occasion being Bishop David Moriarty of Kerry. It had taken almost seven years to complete the shell of the building, and substantial additions would continue to be made to it for the next half-century. The architectural taste of the age, especially among the Oxford converts, was in favour of the gothic revival. R. A. Coffin, a future provincial superior of the Redemptorists, who made his novitiate in Rome as one of the first members of Newman's oratory, for instance, thought that Michelangelo's *Last Judgment* in the Sistine Chapel should be painted over and 'something Christian and edifying' painted in its place.[6]

Hardwick took his inspiration from the early gothic period. The result was an impressive structure, whose interior measured 173 feet from the crown of the apse to the front door, and was 36 feet in maximum breadth. *The Freeman's Journal* report quoted above observed that 'the great breadth of the nave and the height of the arches give the church a remarkable air of lightness, while the solidity of the piers and the great size of the limestone blocks employed give also the idea of prodigious strength.' The interior of the church was still incomplete when it was opened for worship. The high altar had been simply taken over from the temporary church. The attendance at the opening ceremony was large and fashionable, including Lord Dunraven and several members of the Plunkett family. The price of admission tickets (five shillings for the front seats, two shillings and sixpence for the rear seats

---

[5] 'Domestic and Apostolic Labours, 1', 44, RPAD.
[6] Samuel J. Boland: 'R.A. Coffin and the English Oratory' in *SHCSSR*, vol. XXVIII, no. 1 (1980), 147–74.

and one shilling for the aisles) meant that few working people could afford to attend, while in the evening 'silver will be expected for the reserved seats and a collection will be made at the door'. As Solomon celebrated the dedication of his temple with seven days of festivity, the Redemptorists celebrated the opening of their new church with a two-week mission ending on Christmas Day 1862.

Furnishing the church
The liturgy of the new church was marked by a degree of external solemnity unusual in Ireland at the time. Many of the founding fathers of Limerick were continentals, used to the colourful displays on feast days common in Belgium or Austria, while the English converts had all been shaped by the ritualist and sacramental theology of the Oxford Movement. Before the new church was opened, a young Belgian had been engaged as an organist. On arrival in Limerick, he organised a 'vocal institute' to give instruction in music to boys and young men in return for their service in the choir. By the time of the dedication, his choir of seventy-four male voices had built up a rich repertoire, including 'harmonised Gregorian chant', for the proper of the Mass.

Thomas Bridgett, who had a more than passing interest in the details of liturgical observance and church art, initiated a programme of furnishing the church during his period as rector that made it a significant witness to the liturgical arts of the nineteenth century in Ireland. The first step was the provision of a dignified high altar. It, together with the matching communion rail in Caen stone, were designed by George Goldie and were the gift of the wealthy Limerick merchant, John Quin. It was restored to its former glory in 2008. The high altar was complemented by a fine matching pulpit, also in Caen stone, gift of a Mr Sheehan, a tallow chandler in the city. It was used for the first time on Christmas Day 1866.

The fourteenth-century icon of Our Lady of Perpetual Help came into the possession of the Redemptorist Congregation in Rome in 1866. In handing it over to the superior general, Fr Nicholas Mauron, Pius IX charged the Redemptorists to 'make her known to the world'. Copies of the icon quickly made their way to every Redemptorist community. Limerick received its copy towards the end of the following year and it was solemnly unveiled in the church in December 1867. A chapel worthy to receive the new icon was planned on the site of a porch on the right hand side of the church. The foundation stone of the new Lady chapel was laid in October 1868 and opened for worship on the feast of the Assumption, 15 August, the following year. The members of the recently-founded men's confraternity defrayed most of the cost. Further embellishments were added to the chapel at the end of the nineteenth century, most notably a series of mosaics on a Marian theme executed under the direction of George Ashlin in 1893.

An organ was installed in 1869, replacing the harmonium that had done duty until then. The cost of fitting up the two side chapels in honour of Our Lady of Grace and St Joseph was defrayed by two more benefactors, Edward Murphy and Dr Enright, the community's physician.

John Quin was the most generous of the early benefactors of the church. Apart from the high altar and donations of sacred vessels and vestments, he later defrayed the cost of building the tower and peal of bells, though Redemptorist superiors needed some persuasion about the wisdom of building the tower. Other generous benefactions followed in the course of the late nineteenth and early twentieth centuries. Two ladies who lived near the monastery, the Misses Margaret and Mary Anne Kelly, commissioned no less than three side chapels for the church, in honour of the Sacred Heart and Our Lady of Dolours.[7] To mark the solemn consecration of the church, planned to coincide with the golden jubilee of the foundation of the house in 1903, they crowned their benefaction by erecting a new side chapel in honour of the recently-canonised St Gerard Majella.

Uneasy Relations

Governance of the diocese of Limerick passed in all but name to George Butler, who had been named coadjutor bishop with the right of succession to John Ryan in 1861. Bishop Ryan had encouraged the Redemptorists during the decade since their first mission in the city but, according to John Sharp, Bishop Butler was determined to exert his authority as soon as he was consecrated.[8] The first trial of strength came over the attendance of the fathers at the diocesan theological conferences that Butler had instituted in June 1861.[9] In vain did they plead that their rule and pontifical privileges exempted them from attendance. Butler took advantage of a visit to Rome to exert pressure on Nicholas Mauron, the superior general, to compel the Redemptorists to attend. Edward Douglas wrote from Rome that Mauron had had two firm interviews with the bishop and, although unwilling to concede fully to his demands, he thought a compromise might 'contribute to the peace of the

---

[7] The generosity of the Kelly sisters was acknowledged when they were made Oblates of the Congregation on 12 May 1888: see Andreas Sampers 'Institutum Oblatorum in Congregatione Ss Redemptorist, Rectore Maiore N. Mauron 1855–1893' in *SHCSSR*, vol. XXVI, no. 1 (1978), 75–142. They continued to be generous donors to new Redemptorist houses in Esker and Belfast.

[8] John Sharp, *Reapers of the Harvest, the Redemptorists in Great Britain and Ireland 1843–1898* (Dublin: Veritas Publications, 1989), 67.

[9] 'Domestic and Apostolic Labours, 1', 121, RPAD contains a lengthy note in Latin on the question of attendance at the theological conferences.

Fathers at Limerick. Two fathers can go, says the R[ector] M[ajor], to the four or five conferences, which the bishop holds every year, without accepting dinner or other annoyance.'[10]

Butler was determined to win this battle of wits and he limited the faculties of the confessors for absolving from reserved sins and commented adversely on the presence of English fathers in the community. Most of the bishop's restrictions seem to have been directed at curtailing the influence of all the religious clergy of the city. He forbade the celebration of Mass in private houses for the sick or recently-deceased, a long-standing custom in Limerick but one of which the Redemptorists rarely availed. More of an irritant to them was the bishop's prohibition on blessing and imposing the brown scapular on the sick. Rightly or wrongly, they saw this as aimed in a particular way at themselves, since people, concerned about the spiritual state of a sick relative, often asked them to call and impose the scapular as a way of disposing the sick person to receive the sacraments.

Worse was to come as the date for the consecration of the church drew near. Butler wanted to manage all the arrangements for the occasion, including the choice of preacher. Coffin, the vice-provincial, was prepared for a show-down and instructed Plunkett to defer the opening, informing Butler of the decision, but without giving any particular reason. Coffin's patience was clearly at breaking point, as he confided to Edward Douglas in Rome:

> I fear we are gradually and yet more surely slipping into the hands of Dr Butler, forfeiting our independence as a religious order and creating difficulties for ourselves and for our successors from which years and years may not release us ... I will never consent, for the honour of the Congregation, for the peace of our successors and for my own conscience's sake, to be his train-bearer ... our position as Redemptorists is at stake, and our religious liberty endangered.[11]

Sharp considers this episode as representing 'the most sustained attack made upon the Redemptorists ... by a bishop in the whole of the nineteenth century'.[12] If Bishop Butler eventually lost the battle for control, it may have been due as much to the patience and equanimity of Mauron and Plunkett as it was to the steel of Coffin's resistance.

Clergy Retreats in the Monastery

By a tradition going back to the earliest days of the congregation in Naples, Redemptorist houses were usually built larger than the immediate needs of

---

[10] Ibid.

[11] Robert A. Coffin to Edward Douglas, 9 May 1862, RGAR, cited in Sharp, *Reapers of the Harvest*, 69.

[12] Sharp, *Reapers of the Harvest*, 69.

the community required. Alphonsus Liguori had envisaged them as centres of spiritual renewal for clergy and laity, with sufficient rooms available to allow them to come on retreat either as a group or individually. Less than a year after the community moved in to their new home, the first retreat for the clergy of the Limerick diocese was announced.

In pre-famine Ireland, the annual clergy retreat had been rather informal in structure, with the priests of several deaneries gathering in a convenient place for several days of clerical fellowship. Each priest made his own arrangements for lodgings, either with friends or in a local hotel or inn. There was common prayer in the parish church and instead of lectures by a visiting retreat director, they took turns to read aloud from a spiritual book for a period in the morning and afternoon. They made their confessions to one another, and the clerical host inevitably entertained his colleagues to a good dinner or two. As part of its reform of priestly life, the Synod of Thurles in 1850 insisted that annual retreats be made in the more disciplined setting, either of a religious house or the diocesan college.

Two five-day retreats were arranged for the new monastery during June 1859, with accommodation for twenty-five priests on each. The Limerick chronicle for this period describes the event in some detail. The clergy had made it clear that they were not going to adopt the new form of retreat without at least a token show of resistance. They objected, for instance, that the arrangements for confession did not respect their freedom of conscience, since they would be compelled, like it or not, to confess to a Redemptorist. Fr Coffin, who was responsible for the arrangements of the retreat, was willing to concede the point and arrange for a few non-Redemptorist confessors to be available. The bishop was adamant that there would be no change until a delegation of two of his senior priests made him change his mind. Strict silence and a rigid order of the day were surely trying for men used to more easy-going ways. As a concession to Irish clerical custom, dinner was served at 3.00 p.m. and a glass of punch was offered at the conclusion of the meal. 'This was the first time,' notes the chronicler, 'that whiskey was used in any form in one of our convents.'[13]

The Limerick diocesan retreat continued to be held at Mount St Alphonsus annually until a purpose-built Redemptorist retreat house was established in the city almost a hundred years later, in 1954. Retreats for laity were slower to develop. The first was held from 11 to 17 December 1866 with 'forty lay gentlemen in attendance', eighteen of whom lodged in the house. Retreats for laymen continued for some years, but were discontinued when numbers began to decline. Individual priests and laymen came for

---

13 'Domestic and Apostolic Labours', 1, 64–7, RPAD.

retreats at other times in the year. Until the arrival of the specially-dedicated 'retreat house' in the 1940s, all Redemptorist houses were designed with provision for prospective retreatants in mind.

Confraternity of the Holy Family

The arrival of the picture of the Mother of Perpetual Help at the end of 1867 was celebrated, in customary Redemptorist style, with a mission for the men of the city. It began at the end of December and continued for three weeks. Some sense of its impact might be gauged from the fact that 1,333 men and boys were prepared to receive the sacrament of Confirmation on the final Sunday. The chronicler records that 'many who had not kneeled to a priest in their lives' came to confession. The crowd was so large that some benches had to be removed from the church to create more space. Rumours of an impending Fenian rising had been circulating for much of the previous year, so crowds of men moving around the city before dawn and again in the evening gave some people the impression that trouble was brewing. The chronicler notes:

> Much alarm was felt at the beginning of the mission by the Protestant residents in Limerick at seeing such crowds of men passing through the streets, many of them with measured step. Thoughts of the Fenians, of insurrection, of fire and slaughter presented themselves to their minds, and many a door was bolted and barred. But when they learned the peaceful nature of the work which was being accomplished, their fears were dissipated and they joined heartily in promoting the work of the mission, sending those in their employment and giving them the time and opportunity to avail themselves of the mission.[14]

A large crucifix with a bronze figure still stands near the entrance to the church as a commemoration of this mission. It was the gift of the drapers' apprentices in three of the main business houses of the city who raised the sum of £27 from collections among their workmates. The night following the mission, men thronged the church once more. This time, it was to hear an explanation of the Holy Family confraternity from Fr Thomas Bridgett. Over the following days, about 1,300 men gave their names as prospective members.

The Archconfraternity of the Holy Family had been founded in Liège in Belgium in 1844 by a devout military engineer called Henri Belletable (1813–55) as a support for the christian life among working men. The Belgian Redemptorists took Belletable's project under their wing and quickly

---

14 Ibid., 292–300.

promoted it throughout Belgium, Luxembourg and Germany. Several branches had already been established in Ireland during Redemptorist missions, notably at Ennistymon, County Clare and in Wexford. Bridgett promoted the confraternity enthusiastically in Limerick, especially as it seemed to provide an answer to the growing threat of Fenianism. So successful was the confraternity that within a few weeks, a second division had to be formed to cater for the men who could not gain entrance to the church.

The format of the confraternity was simple. The weekly meeting, consisting of prayers, a sermon and a short benediction service, lasted about an hour. The members were arranged into sections under a prefect and sub-prefect who kept attendance records and hunted up backsliders, before passing on their names to the director should more persuasive action be deemed necessary. Members were expected to receive communion as a body on one Sunday each month, preparing by confession on the previous day. Confraternity work had a special attraction for Redemptorists. As a young priest in Naples, Alphonsus Liguori had worked with small groups of working-class men in the 'evening chapels' (*cappelle serotine*). These groups met in any convenient place available, such as a barber's shop or the corner of a piazza. If no priest were available, the members led the prayer and discussion themselves. Belletable's original idea for the Holy Family confraternity was similar, and he tried in vain to resist its transformation by the Redemptorists into a mass-movement meeting in a church.[15] The confraternity was destined to play a controversial role in the Catholic and social life of the city of Limerick.[16]

Some Confraternity Members

An important source of information about the early days of the Limerick confraternity is the 'Obituary of the Holy Family Confraternity', held in the confraternity archives in Limerick. It covers the period from the foundation to the end of 1951. Bound in two large manuscript volumes, it records the death-notices of some 7,955 members and quotations in this section are taken from it. The majority of the entries are one-liners, recording little more than the man's name, section and circumstances of death. Many of the early entries are more detailed and put a human face on the confraternity and the social world of working-class Limerick in the mid-nineteenth century. The lot of working men was hard, and it comes as little surprise to find that many

[15] Maurice Becqué, *Le Cardinal Deschamps* (Louvain: Biblioteca Alphonsiana, 1956), vol. 1, 74–6.
[16] On the origins and early years of the confraternity, see Brendan McConvery, 'Confraternity spirituality: the case of the Limerick men's Holy Family Confraternity', *Spirituality*, 5(26): (Sept.–Oct. 1999), 291–4, and 'Male spirituality in nineteenth-century Ireland: the case of the Limerick Holy Family Confraternity', *Spirituality*, 5(27): (Nov.–Dec. 1999), 360–3.

of the members died as a result of industrial injuries. A fifteen-year-old boy was killed in a fall from scaffolding on the site where he was employed as a builder's labourer. Another young man was scalded to death when the hot-water system on which he was working exploded. Firemen and railwaymen were killed in the course of their duty. Fishermen and crewmen of dredging craft on the Shannon drowned in stormy conditions. Many were carried off by the diseases endemic among the urban poor, such as alcoholism, lung and chest complaints, consumption or the vague expression 'decline', or delicate health.

Of the first twenty entries, eleven are described as 'young men', often in their teens or early twenties. William Cusack died at the age of seventeen on 30 September 1868, about nine months after the foundation of the confraternity and had attended the meeting just some days prior to his death.[17] Michael Kenny is described as 'a young man, who, with his brother, worked hard in the midst of poverty to support his little brothers and sisters when death deprived them of their mother and insanity of their father's assistance.'[18] James Noonan died at the age of twenty-one in 1869: he had been a regular monthly communicant, but a short time before his death, 'his fervour and piety increased in a wonderful way as though God wished to make him, without his knowing it, prepare for what was to come.'[19] The death of Michael McInerny, a young fisherman, was 'caused, or at least hastened, by his zeal in attending the retreat in spite of poor clothing and terrible weather morning and evening'.[20] Lawrence White, a former soldier, 'without pension, without regular work, without strength, without food and drink, often cold, hungry, wet, miserable, yet never failing without cause to attend his section which was the singing section, has gone home to his Father's house where there is no want or poverty'.[21] Thomas Ryan, who died of consumption, was 'an orphan of nineteen, of no settled condition'.[22] John Griffin had been a gardener at the Good Shepherd convent but 'was in great poverty for the last ten years of his life. He was buried at the expense of the present prefect and the section attended his funeral and had the Holy Sacrifice twice offered for his soul.'[23] James Burke came to live in the city after being unjustly deprived of his smallholding near Hospital, County Limerick. Left a widower

---

[17] 'Obituary of the Holy Family Confraternity', vol. 1, no. 1, Limerick Confratenity Archives. Since page numbers are lacking in the latter part of the book, entry numbers are standard reference.
[18] Ibid., no. 12.
[19] Ibid., no. 25.
[20] Ibid., no. 44.
[21] Ibid., no. 1447.
[22] Ibid., no. 1545.
[23] Ibid., no. 2097.

at a relatively young age, he devoted himself as best he could to the upbring-
ing of his young family. His life was not easy on account of his poverty,
ill-health and failing sight, yet he was regarded as a devout and good man,
and one of his sons entered the Christian Brothers community.[24]

Other members are recorded as having rendered charitable service
towards the poor through their membership of the Society of St Vincent de
Paul. Lawrence Ryan was not alone a member of the confraternity and the
Society of St Vincent de Paul, he was also 'an active and zealous defender of
Catholic interests in the Town Council and other places'.[25] Bernard Kirby is
credited with having recruited several hundred members for the confraternity.
In search of a more solid life of prayer, he 'had formed a little society of the
Blessed Sacrament whose members met on Sundays and Thursdays in a room
hired out for the purpose.'[26] This informal association, about which we know
little beyond this note, seems closer to Belletable's ideal of what the confraternity should be and it anticipates the basic Christian communities of a
more recent age.

Alcoholism was one of the major dangers in Irish male social life, and
membership of the confraternity was no guarantee of protection against its
ravages. While never a temperance movement in the strict sense, the confraternity did promote the virtues of moderation and sobriety by frequent
admonitions about temperance from the pulpit. These were common around
St Patrick's Day or at the time of the Limerick races. Many men found the
discipline of frequent reception of the sacraments and the camaraderie of
other men a help in the battle against drink. One man, whose testimony is
recorded in the obituary, reckoned that 'he owed his salvation to the confraternity, for it was by means of it that after many years of drunkenness and
neglect of the sacraments, he was brought back to God some months before
his illness seized on him.'

The great men's mission and the foundation of the confraternity appears
to have had a striking effect on the morale of working-class men in Limerick.
According to a newspaper clipping inserted in the domestic chronicles
for July 1867, the judge at the summer assizes said that he had nothing to
address to the grand jury and that the city of Limerick was in the happy
position of having only one case to be heard, that of a nine-year-old boy
accused of perjury! Subsequent developments of the confraternity will be
considered in later chapters.

---

[24] Ibid., no. 1504.
[25] Ibid., no. 1879.
[26] Ibid., no. 1366.

CHAPTER THREE

Four Englishmen and an Irishman

Although the majority of the first Redemptorists who came to work in Ireland were from the old Catholic lands of continental Europe, several Englishmen and one Irishman have been mentioned in this narrative so far. Three were converts from the Anglican Church at the time of the 'second spring' associated with John Henry Newman and the Oxford Movement. One was a priest from an old Catholic recusant family, and the other was the younger son of an Anglo-Irish noble family that included in its family tree the martyred archbishop of Armagh, St Oliver Plunkett. Newman himself briefly considered the Redemptorists before making his final decision to found an English branch of the Oratorian community. Of those who joined the comparatively unknown Redemptorist community in the late 1840s and early 1850s, several were university men, a number were converts, and the majority were approaching middle age. None of them has yet received a full-scale critical biography, so in re-constructing their lives, the only sources available, for the most part, are extended 'necrologies' or death notices circulated within Redemptorist communities for the edification of the brethren and drawing attention to the virtues of the deceased while drawing a discreet veil over whatever vices or weaknesses may have been apparent. An exception is the work of Fr Samuel S. Boland CSsR, whose biographical studies of two of them, based on the original sources, will be referred to here.[1]

The Scottish Millionaire

Edward Douglas (1819–98) was born into a wealthy and aristocratic Scottish family in 1819. His father had been secretary to one of his kinsmen, the fourth Duke of Queensberry, and on the duke's death, he inherited a very

---

[1] Samuel J. Boland, 'The Conversion of Fr Robert Coffin CSsR' in *SHCSSR*, vol. XXVI, no. 2 (1979), 355–74; 'R.A. Coffin and the English Oratory' in *SHCSSR*, vol. XXVII, no. 1 (1980), 147–74, 'R.A. Coffin's departure from the Oratorians' in *SHCSSR*, vol. XXVII, no. 2 (1980), 431–56 and 'The conversion of Edward Douglas CSsR' in *SHCSSR*, vol. XXIX, no. 2 (1981), 291–322.

considerable fortune.[2] Edward's father died when he was eleven years of age. As an only child, he inherited the sizeable fortune that had come to his father from his Queensberry relatives. Edward was raised by his mother, a devout Anglican. He was educated at Eton, from where he went to Christ Church, Oxford, in 1837. When Douglas arrived in Oxford, John Henry Newman, a don of Oriel College, was the most controversial figure in the university. His *Tracts for the Times* had begun to appear in 1833, advocating a *via media*, or middle way, for the Anglican Church between Protestantism and Rome. By the time of the publication in 1841 of the best known of the series, *Tract 90*, 'Remarks on Certain Passages in the Thirty Nine Articles', which argued that the Anglican articles of religion could be interpreted in a sense consonant with Catholic doctrine, Edward Douglas had already left the university, having failed his final degree examinations.

At Oxford, Douglas had been devout and earnest about religion, but had 'kept aloof from the busy debates aroused by the Tractarians'.[3] The publication of *Tract 90* ignited a furious debate within the Anglican Church, with those who identified with Newman's search for the *via media* on the one side and those who vehemently opposed it as a sell-out of the Protestant birthright of the Church of England on the other. A visitor to Douglas recalled the excitement with which he and an Oxford friend pored over 'multitudes of pamphlets, newspaper articles and private letters, all tending to the momentous question of whether we could remain in the Anglican Church or not'.[4]

By the end of the debate, Douglas was convinced that his future lay in the Church of Rome, and towards the end of 1841, he travelled there with his friend, Charles Scott Murray. His first contact with the person who would make the taking of that step easier was by way of what might be called a happy accident.[5] While assisting at a papal ceremony for the feast of St Peter's chair in the Vatican basilica, Scott Murray had stowed his umbrella for safe-keeping in one of the confessionals. When they returned to retrieve it

---

[2] Despite the important role he played in Redemptorist administration in the latter half of the nineteenth century, no complete study of Douglas exists in English. Two short and largely edifying sketches of his life were produced for circulation among his confreres and friends, the first in Latin, by Frederick Kuntz, *De Vita Eduardi Douglas, Presbyteri Congregationis Ssi Redemptoris* (Rome: 1907, privately published) and the second in English by Fr George Stebbing CSsR, *Father Edward Douglas* (London, also privately published, 1917). For a more detailed study of his early life, see Boland, 'Conversion of Edward Douglas', 291–322.

[3] Boland, 'Conversion of Edward Douglas', 296.

[4] Lady Herbert of Lea's recollections of Fr Douglas, written for Thomas Livius who was collecting material for Douglas's necrology, and reproduced in Boland, 'Conversion of Edward Douglas', 319–21.

[5] The story of how Douglas met his spiritual guide was recounted in a letter from Scott Murray's widow to Fr Edward Livius. See Boland, 'Conversion of Edward Douglas', 318.

after the ceremony, they found the confessional locked. Since Scott Murray was a member of parliament and had to leave Rome to be in time for the opening of the next sitting of the house, Douglas undertook to recover the lost umbrella. His search led him to a Carmelite friary near St Peter's. The confessor, Fr Simone Spilatros, asked one of his students, a young priest called Angelo Savini, to accompany Douglas to St Peter's to recover the umbrella. Douglas and the young Carmelite priest formed a warm friendship. With his encouragement, Douglas applied to be received into the Catholic Church. He was baptised conditionally on 22 February 1842, some three years ahead of Newman, and within a few days had received the sacraments of the eucharist and confirmation.

His mother, to whom Edward, an only child, was deeply attached, was horrified by the news of his reception and dispatched an Anglican clergyman to Rome in an attempt to reconvert him. Douglas returned to England after a few more months in Italy. In 1845, he left for a lengthy pilgrimage to the Holy Land with a group of Catholic friends, one of whom, John Furniss, a diocesan priest, is the subject of the following portrait.

Douglas had entertained the possibility of becoming a priest at the time of his conversion but it was a step he was reluctant to take for fear of the additional pain it might cause his mother. Relations between the two seem to have been restored relatively smoothly, for by June 1848, Douglas was arranging to be ordained under the tutelage of his Carmelite friend, Padre Savini. Boland observes that his theological training for priesthood, like that of many other convert Anglicans of the time, must have been limited in the extreme. R. A. Coffin, himself a convert clergyman, complained that 'all young converts brought up at school and college in the same way and with very little more than book knowledge, are made priests without any training and confessors with as little.'[6] Douglas was ordained in Italy in June 1848 'on the title of his patrimony' (i.e. not for the service of any particular diocese or religious order). Shortly after his ordination, he made a pilgrimage to the tomb of St Alphonsus at Pagani to pray for guidance in making the right decision about his future as a priest. He had considered the Franciscans for a short time, but by the end of 1848, he was in the Redemptorist novitiate at St Trond in Belgium, where made his vows on the feast of the Immaculate Conception, 8 December 1849. He was the first Briton to be professed in the congregation.[7]

---

6 Boland, 'Conversion of Edward Douglas', 305.
7 He had another Englishman as a fellow novice, Francis Weld, a member of an old recusant family, who was professed but left the congregation after a few years.

After profession, he was sent to the house of studies at Wittem in Holland to complete his studies, especially in moral theology, but by the end of February 1850, he returned to England as a member of the newly-founded Clapham community. After spending time in Ireland between 1851 and 1853, he returned to Rome, where he spent most of the rest of his life until his death in 1898. A man of Douglas's background, as Samuel Boland remarks, was bound to attract attention in Rome.[8] His opinion in matters relating to Britain, and especially Scotland, was sought by the Holy See. He also became a point of reference for English converts coming to Rome to work out the final stages of their decision about joining the Catholic Church and is reputed to have prepared about fifty converts for their entrance into the Church. He served the congregation as a general consultor, as provincial of the Roman province and as rector of the House of S. Alfonso on the Via Merulana, which had been purchased with the fruits of his patrimony. When the forces of Italian reunification invaded Rome in 1870, Douglas saved the house by running up the Union Jack and claiming that it was British property. Edward Douglas died in Rome in 1898.

The Old English Catholic

The year after Douglas was professed, John Furniss (1809–65), one of the companions of his Holy Land pilgrimage, entered the Redemptorist novitiate. Furniss was born near Sheffield into a Derbyshire Catholic family.[9] His father was a wealthy master cutler. After studies in Ushaw College, he was ordained priest in 1834 for the Northern District, one of four administrative areas of the Catholic Church in England before the restoration of the hierarchy in 1850. Furniss spent the first years of his ministry in Bradford and Doncaster. From 1840 until 1847, he travelled in Europe for the sake of his health. He spent the winters for the most part in Rome, where he availed of the opportunity to undertake studies at the Roman College. It was here that he first encountered the moral theology of Alphonsus Liguori. The summers were spent visiting the major and lesser shrines of Europe. Somewhat fastidious about his health, he had been recommended to use goat's milk and he brought a goat around with him as part of his baggage.

The pilgrimage to the Holy Land with Edward Douglas in 1845 was an eventful journey. It lasted from April until July, and the pilgrims travelled by boat, horseback and camel. When Furniss returned to England in 1847, he was able to resume limited pastoral ministry, first as chaplain to a convent

---

8 Boland, 'Conversion of Edward Douglas', 311.
9 From Thomas Livius CSsR, *Father Furniss and his work for Children* (London: Art and Book Co., 1898). See also account of children's missions in Sharp, *Reapers of the Harvest*, 135–7, 194–5.

and then as an assistant priest in the parish of Islington in London. Irish immigrants, in flight from famine, were beginning to arrive in droves in London. Furniss was especially struck by the plight of the children, who had no schools and were more or less abandoned. He began to devote the greater part of his time to the pastoral care of children, a work to which he was to return as a Redemptorist.

Furniss's fellow-pilgrim in the Holy Land, Edward Douglas, had returned to Clapham as a professed Redemptorist. Furniss's work with emigrant children brought him to identify with Alphonsus Liguori's charism for the most abandoned and he applied to join the congregation. Despite the poor state of his health, he was accepted, entered the novitiate at St Trond in 1850 and was professed the following year. After the course in moral theology at the house of studies in Wittem, Holland, obligatory for former diocesan priests who entered the Redemptorists, Furniss returned to England. Given his talent for engaging with children, Furniss soon developed a special mission for children as an element within the parish mission. His travels had furnished him with a wealth of stories, sermon illustrations and even visual aids. Years of ill-health had given him a gaunt and sickly look but he also had the trick of making a virtue out of his eccentricities. Sharp remarks:

> His ascetic appearance, for example – thin, worn, emaciated – caused people to ask whether he did not live on bread and water. His clothes were old and shabby, sometimes dirty and ill-fitting, while his manner was such that he gave the impression of great antiquity; although only 53 when he finished his labours, he was believed to be 107.[10]

Furniss preached several children's missions in Ireland, the first of which was in St Michael's parish in Limerick in 1852. His style had its limitations. Many of the stories he told had an element of the fantastic, or even lurid. Nevertheless, he anticipated some of the movements in modern catechesis, especially in the way in which he led children through the stages of the Mass while it was being celebrated by another missioner, as well as in his use of simple hymns and music as a technique in communicating the message. His biographer, Thomas Livius, points out that, while the proper manner of religious instruction might have included a systematic presentation of the faith, Furniss's audience was for the most part made up of illiterate children who, for reasons of grinding poverty, were either early drop-outs from education or who never had sat in a schoolroom.

> Father Furniss set before these children ... as in one moving panorama, the whole cycle of Christian doctrine: their last end, the value of the

---

[10] Sharp, *Reapers of the Harvest*, 104.

soul, sin and its consequences, redemption, the sacraments, the dangers to salvation, prayer, the Blessed Virgin Mary and the saints, heaven and the means of attaining it … in this way, Fr Furniss revealed to the children, so to say, another world, about which they had hardly thought before. He brought them into this spiritual world; the land of faith which through his graphic instructions and discourses, he made a reality to them, and peopled for them with Jesus Christ the redeemer, his Blessed Mother and the saints.[11]

Following a career as a parish missioner that had lasted eleven years and included more than one hundred and fifteen missions and events for children, Furniss's health collapsed. After a three-year illness, he died in 1865.

The Oxford Vicar
Despite his significance in the history of the English and Irish Redemptorists, and indeed of the English Church in the nineteenth century, it is regrettable that there has been no full-length study of Robert Aston Coffin (1819–85).[12] He was born into a prosperous merchant family in Brighton and was the eldest of five children. He received his early education in Harrow, the great public school rival of Douglas's Eton. As a child, he had wondered whether he should become an opera singer or a bishop, but decided the matter by going on to read theology. After ordination in 1843 in the Church of England, he was appointed vicar of St Mary Magdalene's, one of the more fashionable churches in Oxford. It was inevitable, given his influential role in the Oxford of the time that Coffin should become embroiled in the theological debates of Oxford. It was in this way that he became a member of Newman's circle. The debate that followed the publication of *Tract 90* in the Anglican establishment was an unsettling time for him.

Coffin's personal moment of crisis came when he was summoned to the bedside of a dying parishioner. He ministered to her according to the rites of the *Book of Common Prayer* but, as he began the words of absolution, the woman interrupted him: 'I believe you don't know whether you are a priest or not.' Samuel Boland's account of the incident continues:

---

11 Livius, *Father Furniss*, 90.
12 See B. Guldner, 'Coffin, Robert Aston' in *The Catholic Encyclopaedia*, ed. Charles Herbermann (New York: Robert Appleton, 1907–1912), vol. 4, 93–4. There is also a short entry on him by Michael Clifton, 'Coffin, Robert Aston (1819–1885)' in the *Oxford Dictionary of National Biography*, Oxford University Press, 2004 (http://www.oxforddnb.com/view/article/5810). Coffin receives mention in many of the studies and biographies of Newman. For the story of his conversion and sometimes stormy relationship with Newman, see Boland, 'Conversion of Fr Robert Coffin CSsR', 'Coffin and the English Oratory', 'Coffin's departure from the Oratorians.' See also Sharp, *Reapers of the Harvest*, 35–46.

In some consternation, Coffin asked her what she meant, and discovering that she believed that the Christian priesthood existed only in the Catholic Church, he very generously went to fetch the priest from the Catholic Church. Rev Mr Newsham received the woman into the Church and heard her confession before she died.[13]

The gossip circulating in Oxford after this incident, 'that the vicar was with the woman at eleven o'clock and the priest at noon', did little either to enhance Coffin's standing or to set his doubts about the nature of the Church of England to rest.[14] Newman had withdrawn to his residence in the village of Littlemore to escape the storm following the publication of *Tract 90*. It was there he preached the famous 'Parting of Friends' sermon in September 1843, signalling his break with the Church of England but it would be two more years before he entered the Roman Catholic Church, in October 1845. Coffin continued to hesitate. When they met at the end of that month, Newman took the initiative by asking him why he was not yet a Catholic and offering to bring him that very afternoon to Prior Park near Bath, the seminary established by Bishop Baines of the Western District, to be received into the Church. Coffin was received on 3 December 1845. He spent the next years as tutor to the family of another convert, the rich but eccentric Ambrose Philipps de Lisle.

After much hesitation about which religious community he should join, Newman finally took the decision to establish a branch of the Oratory of St Philip Neri especially for converts. The Oratory had the advantage that each community, although inspired by the spirit of Philip Neri, was independent and self-governing. Newman assembled a group of six prospective novices at Santa Croce in Gerusalemme in Rome in early 1847. All were convert clergymen who had either been, or who hoped to be, ordained as priests. They made a novitiate under the direction of an Italian Oratorian and Coffin was ordained priest on 31 October of the same year. The newly-professed Oratorians returned to England in 1848 and established their community at Maryvale near Birmingham. It soon became clear that Coffin's heart was not in the Oratory and tensions were beginning to show between himself and Newman.[15] By 1851, Coffin had left the Oratory for the Redemptorist novitiate in St Trond. There he was professed in February 1852.

Coffin's undoubted talents and social contacts with both recusant families and many of the new Oxford converts marked him for leadership in the English Church. He was part of the early Irish Redemptorist mission in Ireland. When the original Anglo–Dutch province divided in 1865, he was

---

[13] Boland, 'Conversion of Robert Coffin', 360.
[14] Ibid., 361.
[15] Boland, 'Coffin's departure from the Oratorians', 431–56.

appointed provincial of the London province, which included the houses in Limerick, and later Dundalk. He held that office until he was nominated bishop of Southwark in 1882. As will be seen as the later history of the Irish province unfolds, Coffin's lengthy period as provincial did not endear him to all his Irish brethren. On his appointment to Southwark, he entertained the brief hope that he might be permitted to combine his offices as bishop and provincial, or at least to reside in the community at Clapham. His episcopate lasted a mere three years, and he died on 6 April 1885 in the Redemptorist house of studies at Teignmouth in Devon that he had founded.

The Cambridge Convert

Thomas Edward Bridgett (1829–99) was the youngest of the first group of Englishmen to enter the Redemptorists. He was born in Derby, the child of a successful silk-manufacturer.[16] His religious background was mixed. His father was a Baptist and his mother a Unitarian, so Thomas was not baptised until he requested it himself as a pupil in his minor public school. In 1847, Bridgett entered St John's College, Cambridge.

Bridgett was not as exposed at Cambridge to the feverish religious disputes that wracked Oxford. Nevertheless, the questions raised by Newman's *Tracts* were influencing Anglican opinion far beyond his own university and exposing wide diversities in churchmanship. Bridgett had read theology with a view to entering the ministry of the Church of England. Apart from a few holidays abroad, his contacts with Catholicism were slight. Later in life, preaching to the men's confraternity in Limerick, he told a story of his first brush with Irish Catholicism while a student at Cambridge. He and a fellow-student wished to visit the local Catholic chapel. It was a small building in an obscure street and as they returned the key to the Irish labourer who looked after it, Bridgett's friend joked: 'Why Paddy, do you think you have the truth all to yourselves down this little back street and our learned doctors and divines in the university are in error?' The Irishman answered: 'Well, sir, I suppose they are all very learned, but they can't agree together, while we are all one.'[17] It was an answer that remained with the young student, as its very simplicity seemed to reduce complex debates to their essence.

As he departed for the long vacation at the end of the academic year of 1850, he remarked to his friends: 'It is not likely that I shall return to Cambridge, but if I do, I shall be a thorough Protestant, and not a High

---

16 See Cyril Ryder, *Life of Thomas Edward Bridgett* (London: Burns and Oates, 1906). For a sketch of Bridgett's life, see 'Bridgett, Thomas Edward' by H. Castle in *Catholic Encyclopaedia*, vol. 2, 782–3.
17 Ryder, *Life of Thomas Bridgett*, 12.

Church Anglican.'[18] In the early summer, he attended some of Newman's 'Lectures on the difficulties of Anglicans' in London. The lectures began in May and by 14 June, Bridgett was taking steps to be received into the Roman Catholic Church at the London Oratory. He says that he stumbled into the Oratorian residence and 'stammered out that I wanted to be a Catholic. I was alarmed when the words were spoken.'[19] The priest gave him no instructions, simply told him to return the following day to make his confession. Bridgett was twenty-one years of age. As he had foreseen, he did not return to Cambridge. As a Catholic, the 'test acts' of the penal laws prevented his taking his degree without acknowledging the Anglican articles of religion and royal supremacy, which as a Catholic he could not do. These religious tests were only abolished in 1871.

Soon after this, he made a retreat with the Redemptorists at their house in Hanley Castle, Worcestershire. He had entered Cambridge intending to be ordained. The vocation to priesthood remained, but it could now only be fulfilled in the Catholic Church. He felt little attraction to Newman's Oratory as he believed its members were straining to be ultra-Catholic and 'I wished to be thoroughly Catholic, but among those to whom it came easily and harmoniously.'[20] An uncle had prophesied, even before he became a Catholic, that he would end up a Jesuit one day but Bridgett was determined to disappoint him. His reading of the life of Alphonsus Liguori and a meeting with Louis de Buggenoms guided him towards the Redemptorists and by the end of September 1850 after a mere three months as a Catholic, he was on his way to the novitiate in Belgium along with a young Irishman, William Plunkett.

Bridgett received the fullest Catholic theological education of all the converts. Having made his profession in 1851, he was sent to Wittem in Holland for five years of ecclesiastical studies. He returned to England as a member of the Clapham community in 1856. The years 1862 to 1871 were spent in Ireland as a missioner and giver of retreats, especially to clergy. As rector of Mount St Alphonsus in Limerick (1865–71), he introduced the Archconfraternity of the Holy Family, founded a Catholic lending library and was responsible for the building of the chapel in honour of the Mother of Perpetual Help. After Limerick, Bridgett was rector of Clapham from 1871 to 1874. He returned to Limerick for a further term as rector from 1881 to 1884, and was briefly rector of the house of studies at Teignmouth from 1893 to 1894.

---

18 From his own account in his *curriculum vitae* written as a Redemptorist novice, cited in Ryder, *Life of Thomas Bridgett*, 16.
19 Ibid., 19.
20 Ibid., 29.

On account of ill-health, Bridgett dedicated much of his later life to writing on subjects of theological and historical interest. His style of writing has been described as a kind of scholarly apologetic. Abbot Aidan Gasquet described him as 'a collector of facts from old books which would serve to illustrate Catholic teachings and practice in the age of faith'.[21] He spent many hours reading in the British Museum but was not ashamed to use helpers to cull a vast amount of literature. His writings display an encyclopaedic knowledge of English Catholic history, for example *Our Lady's Dowry: Devotion to the Blessed Virgin Mary in England* (1875), *The History of the Holy Eucharist in Great Britain* (1881), *The Life of Blessed John Fisher* (1888). They introduced him to a growing circle of intellectual Catholics in Britain, including Frederic Baron von Hügel, the lay apologist and theologian, who became a regular correspondent. Bridgett's legacy to the Irish Redemptorist province is an enormous one. As has been shown in the previous chapter, his aesthetic sense contributed to the adornment of the church at Mount St Alphonsus. The confraternity he founded in Limerick would continue to grow and to be a force in the city and it was he who initiated devotion to the Mother of Perpetual Help which would flower pastorally in the modern age in annual celebration of the solemn novena.

The Irish Aristocrat

William Plunkett (1824–1900) was born in Killeen Castle, Corbalton, County Meath. He was the third son of the Earl of Fingall, a member of the Irish aristocracy with a seat in the House of Lords.[22] Although long regarded in the folk-tradition of the Irish province as the first Irish Redemptorist, he was not the first Irishman to make profession in the congregation. Two young emigrants, John Baptist Duffy and Peter McGrane, had entered the Redemptorists in the United States and both were professed in 1848. John Duffy was born in Kill in 1826, ordained 1849 and died in 1874 in Chatawa, Mississippi. Peter McGrane was born in Dublin in 1815 and was dispensed from vows in 1861.[23]

The Plunketts had a distinguished family tree, stretching back to Norman times. The family managed to keep control of much of its estates as one

---

[21] 'Introduction' to Ryder's *Life of Thomas Bridgett*, xiv.

[22] The information on William Plunkett is the most scant of all and depends on slender archival sources in the Dublin provincial archives, especially his *curriculum vitae* and the necrology composed at the time of his death. On the Fingall family, see Mary Rose Carty, *History of Killeen Castle* (Dunsany: Carty/Lynch, 1991).

[23] See *Annales Congregationis SS. Redemptoris Provinciae Americanae*, cura Josephi Wuest (Ilchestriae: Typis Congregationis Sanctissimi Redemptoris, 1899), vol. 1, 457 and the alphabetical entries in *Catalogus CSsR* (1884). I am grateful to Fr Raphael Gallagher CSsR for drawing my attention to these sources.

branch, the Dunsanys, conformed to the Established Church. William Plunkett was educated in England at the Prior Park, near Bath, which had been established by Bishop Barnes as a Catholic school in 1830. At the age of sixteen, he was given the choice, common for younger sons of aristocratic families who did not stand in the direct line of inheritance, to serve in the army or navy. He chose the army and was given a commission in the Welsh Fusiliers, with whom he spent some years in service in the West Indies and Canada.

The demands of military life were difficult for a young man of Plunkett's piety as he felt drawn towards religious life. While on leave in London in 1850, he wavered between applying to the Passionists or to the Redemptorists. It is said that he solved his dilemma by deciding that, if the next omnibus took him to Clapham, he would join the Redemptorists; if Highgate, it was to be the Passionists. The Clapham omnibus arrived first, so a visit to the Redemptorist house concluded with his acceptance for the novitiate. He left for Belgium in September 1850 with Thomas Bridgett. A three-year course in theology followed his profession. He was ordained in 1854 and assigned to the Clapham community for a short time before coming to Limerick in 1857, at the time when the community was still living in the temporary accommodation at Courtbrack. Plunkett placed his fortune of some £2,500 at the disposal of the superior for the building of the new house and monastery.

Plunkett remained in Limerick until 1865, serving as rector of the community from 1862. During his term as rector, the church of Mount St Alphonsus was solemnly dedicated. Apart from two spells, the first from 1880 to 1882 and the second from 1884 to 1887 in Limerick, William Plunkett spent the greater part of his life as a Redemptorist attached to houses in England and Scotland.

In 1888, at the request of the Australian bishops, the London province agreed to send a team of Redemptorists to begin parish mission work in Australia.[24] Despite being at the relatively advanced age of sixty-four for a new undertaking in difficult terrain, William Plunkett offered himself as one of the pioneers. His offer was accepted and he was destined to spend the rest of his life in Australia. He was appointed as assistant to Fr Thomas O'Farrell, the first superior of the Australian mission, which nominally covered the entire continent and succeeded him as 'visitor' or regional superior from 1894 to 1898. William Plunkett died in Sydney in 1900, having gone there to represent the congregation at the dedication of the cathedral and the opening

---

[24] For a history of the Redemptorists in Australia, see Samuel J. Boland, *Faith of Our Fathers: The Redemptorists in Australia 1882–1982* (Armadale, Victoria: H. H. Stephenson, 1982).

of the Australian Catholic congress, planned as the first major public gathering of all the agencies of the Catholic Church on the continent.

Despite his aristocratic origins, Plunkett remained a modest man of delicate conscience, with a tendency to scrupulosity. If he is no longer considered as the first Irish-born Redemptorist, he might be considered as one of the pioneers in that province's tradition of service to struggling churches in new lands.

CHAPTER FOUR

Redemptorist Women in Dublin

The second foundation of the Redemptorist family in Ireland was not another missionary community of men but a convent of contemplative sisters of the Order of the Most Holy Redeemer at Drumcondra in Dublin in 1859. The expansion of the Redemptoristines in the nineteenth century was of a piece with the growth and expansion of the male branch with whom they shared a common narrative of origins. Some of the people who have already appeared in this narrative played a part in the expansion of the women's order.[1] Before entering into details about the foundation at Drumcondra, it will be necessary to trace in outline something of the history of the Order.

The Order of the Most Holy Redeemer: Beginnings

The Redemptoristines, the Sisters of the Order of the Most Holy Redeemer, are, in fact, the 'older sisters' of the Redemptorist men. Their community was born on Pentecost Sunday 1731, more than a year before that of their brethren. Redemptorists and Redemptoristines are bound by a common story of origins and spirituality. When Alphonsus Maria de Liguori went to the hill town of Scala overlooking Amalfi in 1730 to recover his shattered health, he found a community of sisters living in an old monastery according to the Visitation rule but with no canonical links to that order.[2] It is likely that

---

[1] Besides the contemplative sisters of the Order of the Most Holy Redeemer, several active congregations of women were founded with the encouragement of Redemptorists who passed on to them the spiritual patrimony of the Redemptorists. They include Sisters of the Immaculate Heart of Mary, founded in the United States in 1845, the Oblatas del Santisimo Redentor (Madrid, 1870) and the Missionary Sisters of the Most Holy Redeemer (Gars, near Munich, 1957). *The Dictionary of Redemptorists*, ed. S. J. Boland (Rome: Redemptorist Historical Institute, 1987) contains entries for ten women's congregations associated with the Redemptorists.

[2] In addition to the biographies of Alphonsus already mentioned, the fullest sources for the history of Redemptoristine origins are: D. Capone and S. Majorano, *I Redentoristi e le Redentoriste: Le Radici* (Materdomini: Valsele, 1985) and S. Majorano, *L'Imitazione per la Memoria del Salvatore. Il Messaggio Spirituale di Suor Maria Celeste Crostarosa 1696–1755*. Bibliotheca Historica CSsR, VII (Rome: EDACALF, 1978). For the later history, see Clement Heinze, *Die Redemptoristinnen* (Bonn: Hofbauer Verlag, 1931).

Alphonsus's choice of a holiday location was due to his spiritual director, Thomas Falcoia, bishop of Castellamare di Stabia near Naples, who was also director of the community. The community was at that time in something of a ferment and Falcoia may have been hoping to draw on Alphonsus's advice. One of members of the community, Sr Maria Celeste Crostarosa, like Alphonsus a native of Naples and born in the same year, 1696, had been having mystical experiences for some years. God, she claimed, was calling her to reform the convent at Scala and was providing it with a new rule that was being revealed to her. The distinctive feature of this rule was its stress on a contemplative spirituality that the community, and each sister in it, was called to become a 'living memorial' of God the Father's love, as revealed in the mystery of the incarnation, passion and resurrection of Jesus Christ.

Both Maria Celeste Crostarosa and Alphonsus Liguori were at turning points in their lives at this time. Alphonsus had considered abandoning his priestly career in Naples in order to dedicate himself full-time to preaching missions in country districts. The encounter with the spiritual poverty of the shepherds on the hills around Scala during his holiday convinced him that it was there rather than in Naples that God wanted him. At Falcoia's insistence, he investigated Maria Celeste's visionary experiences, decided she was a reliable witness and encouraged both bishop and sisters to act on them. On Pentecost Sunday 1731, the sisters adopted a distinctive red and blue habit and undertook to live according to the vision of the still incomplete 'Rule of the Most Holy Saviour'. Maria Celeste's visions included a congregation of missionaries, imitating the active life of Christ the saviour, who would be the male counterpart of the women's contemplative community. On 9 November 1732, Alphonsus assembled a group of priests and layman who were prepared to share his vision. They made their first home in the guesthouse of the convent, following the same rhythm of prayer and contemplation as the sisters. Alphonsus did not accept all of Celeste's recommendations. He had more experience of active ministry than she had and drew a very firm line under her urging that they adopt the same red and blue habit as the sisters.

Within a few months, the two communities were experiencing difficulties. Bishop Falcoia proved a controlling director who wanted all matters relating to the two new religious groups to pass through his hands. Although Alphonsus was inclined to defer to the bishop's judgement, Maria Celeste put up a more spirited resistance. Matters were not helped when some members of the men's community began to interfere in the affairs of the convent by undertaking the spiritual direction of individual sisters. Marie Celeste grew increasingly isolated within the community that she had founded. When she refused to submit without question to Falcoia's direction, she was expelled from the convent at Scala. Given shelter by a number of different communities, she lived an itinerant life until she succeeded in founding another house according to her rule at Foggia in 1738, where she died in 1755.

Given the stormy history of the Scala community and the departure of the men's community in 1737, relations between the two branches of the Redemptorist family were not especially close. Perhaps in the light of his dealings with the nuns of Scala, Alphonsus included in his rule a prohibition regarding the taking on of the direction of convents of women, but some early Redemptorists, including St Gerard Majella, continued to be close friends of Maria Celeste Crostarosa. Official contacts between the two communities were few. When Alphonsus became bishop of the diocese of S. Agata dei Goti in the province of Benevento near Naples, however, he invited the sisters of Scala to make a foundation in his cathedral city in 1766. There were now three communities following Crostarosa's rule, but her last troubled days in Scala had driven a breach between them and her final home at Foggia remained isolated from the other two. By the end of the eighteenth century, the Redemptoristine communities seemed destined to meet the same fate as other small communities that had risen in the relative isolation of the small towns and villages of rural Italy, flourishing for a generation or two before passing quietly into oblivion.

A New Beginning in Vienna

Like the Redemptorists, the Redemptoristines were saved from such a fate by the energy of Clement Hofbauer, the vicar general for the northern European houses, and his successors. He had little knowledge of the sisters' communities beyond what he had read in the life of Alphonsus. It is all the more surprising then to find him informing Pietro Blassucci, the superior general, in 1808 that he had applied for the royal assent to found a community of Redemptoristines in Warsaw.[3] Clement's intention was that this community of sisters would undertake the education of girls as counterpart of his own educational work for boys. Nothing came of the plan, as Clement had to flee the city later the same year before the advance of Napoleon.

It was left to Joseph Passerat, Clement's successor as vicar of the transalpine houses, to bring his plan to fulfilment. In 1822, Passerat gathered a group of women to run a shelter for homeless women in Vienna.[4] In time they would become the nucleus of the first Redemptoristine community outside of Italy, but for the next ten years they carried on running the hostel, with their transformation into a contemplative Redemptoristine community seeming ever more remote. Passerat eventually acceded to their pleas to

[3] Heinze, *Die Redemptoristinnen*, 93.
[4] Girouille, *Father Joseph Passerat*, 353.

establish a community entirely devoted to the contemplative life. With the agreement of the superior general, two of the longest-serving members of the group, Eugenie Dijon and the Countess Antonia von Welsersheimb, set off in 1830 for the monastery of S. Agata dei Goti to gain first-hand experience of the Redemptoristine way of life.[5]

Eugénie Gauvenet Dijon was born in Brittany in 1793. Her family had been forced to flee revolutionary France on account of their royalist sympathies. Brought up in Vienna, Eugénie came under the influence of the Redemptorists and was one of the first members of the group running the women's refuge. Antonia Suaradi was born in Graz, Austria in 1772. After a brief marriage to Count Joseph Von Welsersheimb, she was widowed in 1811. The two women left Vienna for the monastery of S. Agata in September 1830. Their journey took six weeks. Passerat had carefully prepared it through his contacts with the Redemptorist general and the Holy See. The papal secretary of state wrote no less than five letters of introduction on their behalf, including one to the nuncio to Naples and another to the bishop of S. Agata.[6] While the sisters of S. Agata dei Goti were happy to receive them, the unsettled political condition of the Papal States made it unwise to receive them formally as novices. After a stay of less than six months, the two women departed for home, bearing with them the habit of the order and a copy of the rule. During a brief halt in Rome, the Roman procurator of the Redemptorists, who attended to the congregation's business with the Holy See, arranged for Cardinal Carlo Odescalchi, prefect of the Congregation for Bishops and Regulars, to clothe them with the habit on Easter Saturday 1831. He also arranged an audience with Pope Gregory XVI.[7]

Back in Vienna, the two newly-professed sisters began the task of initiating the women they had left behind into the first Redemptoristine community outside of Italy. This might be said to mark the 're-founding' of the Redemptoristines. Like all attempts at re-founding, the past was not the sole arbiter of how the future might be constructed. Eugénie Dijon, now Sr Mary Alphonsus of the Will of God, and Antonia von Welsersheimb, now Marianne Joseph of the Resurrection, had brought back a copy of the Redemptoristine rule which they set about translating into French and German. They interpreted it as best they could in the light of the daily routine they had lived during the months in S. Agata, but their brief stay had scarcely allowed them to assimilate the history and traditions of the order

---

[5] Andreas Sampers, 'L'ingresso di Eugénia Dijon e Antonia von Welserheimb nel monastero delle Redemptoristine di S. Agata dei Goti, 18 November 1830' in *SHCSSR*, XX (1972), 15–23.

[6] Heinze, *Dei Redemptoristinnen*, 101.

[7] Ibid., 104–5.

with any depth. For the rest, they depended on their own good sense and on the guidance of Passerat to give the essentials of the Redemptoristine rule a new expression in the situation of Northern Europe in the early years of the nineteenth century.

In the years that followed, the Redemptoristines spread almost as rapidly as the male branch. Encouraged by the Redemptorists, they had established themselves in Bruges by 1841. Other convents followed in quick succession: at Reid, Austria in 1852; Gars, Germany in 1854; Marienthal, Holland in 1851, and at Malines, Belgium in 1855. Although Redemptorists and Redemptoristines share a historical and spiritual tradition, they were never a single religious family. There are important canonical distinctions between the two. The sisters are the *Order* of the Most Holy Redeemer, with solemn vows and strict enclosure, as opposed to the men's *Congregation* of simple vows. Each monastery of the order is independent, under the jurisdiction of the diocesan bishop. During their brief stay in Rome, Sisters Antonia and Eugénie had obtained permission for the future monastery to be placed directly under the authority of the Redemptorists. Given his attraction towards the interior life, it was inevitable that Joseph Passerat as vicar general would recognise the complementary vocation of the male and female branches of the Redemptorist family. He undertook the direction of the first community of women in Vienna, just as he was later to encourage his disciples in Belgium to take an active role in nurturing the community of Bruges. Rudolph von Smetana, Passerat's successor as vicar general, looked less favourably on this growing relationship between the two branches of the Redemptorist family, and strictly applied the letter of the rule which forbade Redemptorists to undertake the direction of women's communities.

By the end of the nineteenth century, there were about twenty Redemptoristine convents in a flourishing state. The three original Italian houses fared less well. They were seriously affected by the movement for Italian unification with its constraints on the property of religious communities. The independent status of each monastery left them to fend for themselves with poor results. By the early twentieth century, they were reduced to a handful of aging sisters living in crumbling monasteries. Their survival is due to the efforts of the Redemptorist, William van Rossum (1854–1932). While a member of the Redemptorist general council, he had saved the derelict monastery of Scala by negotiating its formal purchase from the state by the German Redemptorists. More importantly, he arranged for some Belgian sisters to come in an effort to revive the religious life in what was by then a community of a few sick and elderly sisters, living in poverty and near-squalor.[8] Cardinal van Rossum's experience in Scala convinced him

---

[8] Heinze, *Dei Redemptoristinnen*, 192–8.

that there was little future in individual communities maintaining independent status and that some form of federation was required. When he was made cardinal and prefect of the Congregation of Propaganda Fide in charge of foreign missions, he also arranged to have himself nominated as 'cardinal protector' of the Redemptoristine Order.[9] This was an ancient and largely ceremonial honour which he used to good effect to work for greater unity among the sisters. His proposal that the monasteries consider a form of federation was, however, not well received. Had it been, it might have had a different effect on the shape of the order in later years.

Foundation of the Monastery of St Alphonsus, Dublin

In August 1858, Reverend Mother Marie-Philomène, prioress of the Redemptoristine monastery in Bruges, Belgium, received a letter from Dublin. Her correspondent, a Miss Murphy, informed her that the Sisters of the Order of Charity, who had been conducting a Magdalene asylum in Drumcondra, had recently left their premises for a new home at High Park, Upper Drumcondra. According to the terms of the will of a Dublin priest, Fr James Smith, who had founded the house, if it were no longer required for the purposes of the asylum, it was to be offered to another community of sisters.

Mother Philomène wrote to Louis de Buggenoms, who had moved to the Redemptorist house at Bishop Eton, Liverpool, from Limerick the previous year. He travelled to Dublin to assess the property's potential as a home for a contemplative community. His first impressions must have been positive, for he returned a month later accompanied by Mother Philomène, and another sister from Bruges, the thirty-five-year-old Marie-Jeanne de la Croix. The sisters took a more critical look than de Buggenoms did and considered it to be in a poor state of repair. Nor was the question of the ownership of the property as simple as it had initially appeared. The final decision about the future use of the house rested with the archbishop of Dublin, Paul Cullen. Despite these obstacles, the sisters decided to make a foundation in Dublin if the ecclesiastical authorities were agreeable. Bishop Malou of Bruges made a formal request in their name to Cullen. Cullen signified his assent in a letter dated 4 February 1859.[10]

This account, from the chronicles of the Redemptoristine monasteries of Bruges and Dublin, gives the impression that the sisters founded their

---

[9] On van Rossum's career, see Joop Vernooy, 'Cardinal Willem van Rossum, CSsR: "The great cardinal of the small Netherlands", 1854–1932' in *SHCSSR*, vol. LV, no. 2 (2007), 347–400.
[10] A copy of the letter is in a preliminary account of the foundation in the monastery's Domestic Chronicle, vol. 1, Archives of Redemptoristine Monastery of St Alphonsus, Dublin.

Dublin home in a somewhat haphazard fashion. There are indications, however, that the idea of founding a community of Redemptoristines in Ireland had been maturing for some years. As will be clear from the historical outline in the previous section, Bruges, founded in 1841, was a relatively young foundation, but a vibrant one. In the first eighteen years of its life, it had founded several daughter houses. The entrance books for choir and lay sisters record the names of seven Irish women who entered the community between 1855 and 1859. The first of these was Alice Mary Devitt of Limerick, a grandniece of Daniel O'Connell, who entered in October 1855 at the age of twenty, receiving the religious name of Mary Seraphina of the Most Blessed Sacrament.[11] Alice Devitt had arrived in Bruges accompanied by her father and sister. Her sister was bound for the convent of Notre Dame in Namur in southern Belgium. This community had close associations with Louis de Buggenoms, so it was likely that he was instrumental in turning the thoughts of the two sisters towards convents in faraway Belgium.

In the late 1850s, a small but steady stream of Irish aspirants to the Redemptoristines made the journey to Belgium. Mary Malone of Limerick entered in January 1856 at the age of thirty-two, receiving the name of Mary Magdalene of Jesus.[12] Mary Louise Howley of Rich Hill, Lisnagry, near Limerick entered at the age of twenty-one to become known for the future as Sr Mary Gertrude of the Incarnation and was professed in July 1859. Two more candidates arrived in June 1858, one as a choir nun and the other as a lay sister. They were Henrietta Hart of Dublin and Brigid Kilmartin of Limerick. Miss Hart left before receiving the habit. Bridget Kilmartin may have received the habit and her new name of Sr Aloysia of Divine Providence with a degree of haste on 28 February 1859, for she left for Dublin with the founding group on the following day. Another lay postulant, Sophie Temple of Dundalk, entered in April 1859, receiving the name of Aloysius of Jesus and Mary. She was professed in 1863 and remained in Bruges until her death in 1868. She was followed shortly afterwards by Catherine Prositer of Tintern in County Kilkenny, who arrived as a choir postulant, but left the following January before receiving the habit.

Although the personal details on these women are scant, some general observations might be made. Four were from the Limerick area and the

---

[11] According to her mortuary card, Sr Seraphina of the Blessed Sacrament was 'the first Irish Redemptoristine'. She died in Drumcondra in 1905 at the age of seventy, 'in the forty-seventh year of her profession'.

[12] Redemptoristines were traditionally given a religious name on receiving the habit. Choir sisters added the name Mary as the first name, for example Sr Mary Seraphina, to distinguish them from lay-sisters. Each sister was allowed to chose her *predicat*, (e.g. 'of the Blessed Sacrament', 'of Divine Providence') in keeping with her special devotion.

remaining three from places where Redemptorists had preached missions. The driving force behind this recruiting campaign for the Redemptoristines appears to have been Louis de Buggenoms. Apart from the two lay sister candidates, the women belonged to the Catholic upper-middle or small landowner classes. Requirements for entry into a contemplative order were exacting. The applicant was required to have a fairly high standard of education, including sufficient knowledge of Latin to be able to recite the divine office. She also had to have a dowry sufficient to support her from its interest for the rest of her life. Given the expansion of the sisters in the preceding twenty years, it might appear that de Buggenoms guided young women who came to him for spiritual direction towards the Redemptoristines in the hope that they might form the nucleus of the first Irish foundation of the order.

Having obtained the consent of the archbishop of Dublin, Mother Philomène wasted no time in naming the seven sisters chosen for the foundation. They were Sisters Jeanne de la Croix as superior, Anne-Joseph of the Annunciation, Mechtilde of the Blessed Sacrament, Seraphina of the Blessed Sacrament, Magdalene of Jesus, Augustine of the Blessed Trinity and Aloysia of Divine Providence. Three were Irish – Seraphina, Magdalene and Aloysia – and Sr Gertrude Howley joined them after her profession. It is difficult to explain why Sophie Temple (Aloysia of Jesus and Mary) was left on in Bruges. Augustine of the Trinity was the only experienced lay sister among them and seems to have played the role of general home-maker of the community. Four sisters departed at once for Dublin, travelling in lay-dress from Ostend via London.

On their arrival in Dublin, they discovered that little by way of renovation had been done to the house. The builders seem to have taken literally the definition of 'an enclosed convent' for there was no door connecting the sisters' quarters with the outside. Although there had been Dominican, Carmelite, and Poor Clare communities in Dublin since the eighteenth century, none of them had been able to implement the strictly monastic style of life demanded by their rule. All these communities ran schools or orphanages and were virtually indistinguishable from the newer communities of Presentation and Mercy sisters. On 9 March 1859, the Redemptoristines moved into the still-incomplete convent. The only habitable room available served as refectory, kitchen, chapel and sleeping-quarters, while the sisters slept on the ground with mounds of straw instead of pillows. They attended Mass in the Jesuit church in Gardiner Street. Gifts for the future monastery began to arrive, and cheered the hearts of the sisters as they stepped around ladders and over piles of building rubble. Two weeks later, the remaining sisters arrived from Bruges accompanied by Fr Frederick de Held, an early disciple of Clement Hofbauer, and Mother Marie-Philomène, the prioress in

Bruges. Travelling with them was a Miss Augusta Lacy, who translated the community prayers and acted as organist in the new Dublin foundation until Sr Gertrude Howley had completed her novitiate.

The Beginnings of Community Life
The sisters resumed wearing their red and blue Redemptoristine habits for the first time in the new monastery on the feast of the Annunciation, 25 March 1859. That same afternoon, the ceremony of installation took place, at the end of which the visitors viewed the interior of the monastery. The external celebration was relatively simple, 'since it was Lent, wine and fruit only could be offered them.'[13]

Five days later, the monastery was solemnly enclosed, and the sisters took up the full observance of their rule with the solemn recitation of the divine office. Louis de Buggenoms preached the first community retreat, which began on the evening of the enclosure ceremony. Within a few weeks, the little community welcomed it first postulant, Anna O'Brien, who brought with her 'a handsome silver chalice and cruets that her grandmother, Mrs Seagrave, had given her on the occasion of her entrance'. Despite their poverty, the sisters had a good Easter: 'an abundance of lamb, chickens, ham, pastry, sweets, cakes, wine, fruit etc. sufficient not only for the Easter day, but for the Easter week' was provided by friends and well-wishers. Although their needs were simple, the books did not always balance, and caused the young superior some anxious moments. On Pentecost Monday, she asked the sisters to pray for a sign that the foundation was under the protection of God's will: the same evening, the chronicler recorded, the archbishop of Dublin, Paul Cullen, came on his first unannounced visit, leaving a gift of £50.

The sisters who came on the foundation were almost as mixed in nationality as were the founding fathers and brothers of Limerick. Apart from the handful of Irish, the remainder were French- and Flemish-speaking Belgians. Although Irish choir postulants presented themselves, there were few lay sister candidates. The mother-house at Bruges provided three additional lay sisters, including the German sister, Alphonsus of the Mercy of Jesus. As the Redemptorists were too far away to provide for the regular spiritual needs of the sisters, finding confessors for such a linguistically-diverse community as well as regular chaplains for daily Mass and benediction would prove a continuing headache.

---

[13] Unless otherwise stated, quotations in this section are taken from the Chronicle of the Monastery of St Alphonsus, Dublin.

Moving House

The sisters' first residence in Drumcondra could only be seen as a temporary solution. The enclosed part of the chapel set aside for the sisters' choir-chapel proved too small for the needs of the growing community. Since there was little money available for expansion or purchase of a new site, the sisters prayed earnestly that a postulant might enter with a dowry large enough to make the hope of building a reality. In any case, the cramped site on the Drumcondra Road gave scant hope for much by way of repairs or extension. In 1867, the superior, Sr Jeanne de la Croix, asked the community to make a novena to St Bridget to find a suitable place. As was her way, she joined a little spiritual bribery to her prayers by presenting a gold watch for the bazaar in aid of St Bridget's orphanage run by Margaret Aylward and her young congregation of the Holy Faith.[14] The contract was finally signed in 1871 for a new monastery to be built on a site originally destined for Newman's abortive Catholic university. George Ashlin, the distinguished church architect, was engaged to plan the new monastery.

In July 1872, the stone – blessed originally for the Catholic university by twenty-four bishops – was laid as the foundation of the new monastery. Owing to their rule of enclosure, the sisters did not attend the stone-laying ceremonies. According to the chronicler, 'we had also to stop the recital aloud of vespers, for at that very moment the procession of carriages, bands etc. playing national airs passing our windows to the ceremony, the noise was too great for us to hear each other.' After their prayers, they were allowed to go into the garden to listen to the music and 'we amused ourselves very much.'

Building work did not proceed smoothly. Jeanne de la Croix narrowly escaped serious injury when a plank gave way as she was inspecting progress on the building. Just as it neared completion, news came of the builder's bankruptcy. The delay was not helped by the bankrupt's claim that the sisters' failure to pay him on time was a contributory cause of his financial ruin. The first sister to enter the precincts of the new monastery was Sr Mechtilde of the Blessed Sacrament. She died on 29 May, 1874 at the age of thirty-five and was buried in the place destined as the future cemetery. The fine convent at the top of St Alphonsus Road remained the sisters' home until 2000. New needs and the difficulty of adapting an aging building required the construction of a new monastery on part of the original site.

---

[14] On Margaret Aylward and her Congregation, see Jacinta Prunty, *Margaret Aylward, Lady of Charity, Woman of Faith* (Dublin: Four Courts Press, 1999). Margaret Aylward had a strongly Alphonsian element in her spirituality.

Sisters and Friends

It may be useful here to sketch in broad strokes some details of the early members of the Redemptoristine community and their friends. The first superior or prioress was Julie Verhulst, known in religion as Sr Jeanne de la Croix. She was born in Courtrai, Belgium in 1826 and entered the monastery of Bruges at the age of nineteen. The evidence suggests that she was a woman of more than ordinary talent. She was made novice mistress at a young age and at a time when vocations were flourishing in the convent of Bruges. It had been able to supply fourteen sisters to make a foundation in Malines near Brussels in 1855. Three years later, Jeanne de la Croix helped in another foundation at Velp in Holland. The following year, she came to Dublin as foundress at the early age of thirty-three, and to her is due much of the early success of the venture. She proved a capable manager of the scant resources of the monastery, stretching them on occasion through the generosity of the members of her own family.

Jeanne de la Croix remained as prioress from the foundation until 1890, a period of more than thirty years. Such lengthy periods in office were not unknown in religious houses at this time but Jeanne de la Croix may have enjoyed the confidence of Paul Cullen and his successor as archbishop of Dublin, Edward McCabe, who allowed her to continue as superior for so long. She left Ireland in 1894 accompanied by her faithful friend, the lay sister Aloysia of Divine Providence, another of the founding sisters. Although sixty-eight years of age by then, her destination was the monastery of St Amand les Eaux, the most recent daughter house of Bruges and the first Redemptoristine monastery in France. When the French monasteries became victims of the 'Law of Associations' in 1901, which imposed severe restrictions on religious communities, the sisters were forced to find new homes in Belgium and Holland. Jeanne de la Croix found herself back in Velp where she had been a pioneer before coming to Dublin. There she died in 1902. Sr Aloysia, the former Bridget Kilmartin who had entered Bruges in 1858, survived her for almost two decades, dying in Velp in 1920.

The majority of the women who entered the Monastery of St Alphonsus in Drumcondra as choir-nuns belonged to the small Catholic gentry or professional classes. Women who did not enjoy such comparative privilege entered as lay sisters. The rule had ordained that there was to be a balance between choir-nuns and lay sisters, ideally, twelve of the former and six of the later. The principal occupation of the choir-nuns was the chanting of the divine office in choir while the lay sisters attended to the day-to-day running of the monastery, especially the chores of kitchen and housework.

Several of the original Irish members of the community have already been referred to here. The background of others is more obscure, as little has survived by way of personal records. The first new entrant to the Redemptoristine monastery in Drumcondra within a few weeks of its opening in 1859 was Anna O'Brien, who became Sr Mary Alphonsa in religion. She was distantly connected to William Smith O'Brien, the Young Ireland leader, and was a niece of J. L. O'Ferrall of Granite Hall, Kingstown, an early benefactor of the Redemptorists and commissioner of the Dublin Metropolitan Police.

Sister Gertrude Howley, who joined the community after completing her novitiate in Bruges, was from Limerick. Several of the early sisters came from Waterford. Josephine Power was daughter of James Power and Eleanor de Vere of New Ross. She took the name Teresa of St Alphonsus and was professed in 1862. She died 1891. When their first house was in need of repair the sisters turned in prayer to St Joseph to send them a postulant with enough money to see the project through. Their prayers looked as though they were being answered on the very first day of their novena, 23 September 1868, when an unlikely figure arrived on their doorstep. Maria Pereira was a Portuguese lady who had come from London to visit the convent with the intention of becoming a nun. The sisters were delighted 'for we feel sure we can have, if Miss Pereira perseveres, the long-wished for monastery, as she is very wealthy.' Unfortunately 'being of delicate health, she was unsuited even to the mildest of religious orders' and departed within the month. Despite the setback, Miss Pereira continued her friendship with the community until her death in 1902, and donated the money for the construction of the shrine of Our Lady of Perpetual Help in the new monastery chapel. She was made an Oblate of the Redemptorist congregation in 1874.[15]

Other women discovered that, despite their attraction to the contemplative life, they did not have the necessary health for it. Kate O'Brien of County Limerick served the sisters as *tourière*, or extern receptionist, for several years before entering as a lay sister. To her great disappointment, she was obliged to leave shortly afterwards for health reasons. On her death-bed, she asked the chaplain to ensure that her family would not try to reclaim the £100 she had brought to the community when she entered as she wished to make it a gift to God, even if it meant having a pauper's funeral. When she died on 1 June 1864 the monastery provided for her burial in Glasnevin and the chronicle speaks of her with evident affection. Another unfortunate sister had, what would be described today as a nervous breakdown. After several years in the convent, she became a little odd, entertaining, what the chronicle called 'strange ideas on the religious life'. On medical advice, she was forcibly dispensed from her vows, her dowry was returned and she was put into an asylum.

---

[15] She is listed in Andreas Sampers, 'Institutum Oblatorum in Congregatione Ss Redemptoris, Rectore Maiore N. Mauron 1855–1893' in *SHCSSR*, vol. XXVI, no. 1 (1978), 75–142.

One of the strangest stories of an Irish Redemptoristine took place, not in Drumcondra but in Italy. A little over a year after the foundation in Dublin, an Irishwoman turned up unexpectedly at the monastery of S. Agata dei Goti. The entry in the monastery profession-book deserves to be read in full.

> On the 15 August 1860, the noble lady Anna Maria Morphy [Murphy] a native of Ireland, educated in Bordo [Bordeaux] who had lived for many years in Tuscany and made twenty-two visits to Rome, at the age of 46 years of age, having received an inspiration from God, decided to become a nun of the Most Holy Redeemer in the Monastery founded by St Alphonsus. She set out from Rome, accompanied by a small retinue, and came to Naples, where she made her way to the Redemptorist Fathers. After a few hours' stay in Naples, the Fathers sent her to St Agata, accompanied by a trustworthy person. Not finding the bishop at home, she stayed for three days in our guesthouse. On his return, Monsignor Francis Paul Lettieri examined her about her reliability, and the letters concerning her dowry. He then summoned the chapter of the community to meet in his presence at the porter's lodge. As they decided to admit her, he had her enter at once. The said lady is educated in several languages, namely French, German and others. She knows music, drawing and miniature-painting.[16]

Anna Maria Murphy was born in the city of Cork and baptised in the church of SS Mary and Anne on 6 March 1814, the daughter of Stephen Murphy and Catherine Heffernon. The family appear to have left Cork as the profession-book records that she was confirmed in the convent of St Agatha in Florence in 1825. Florence was something of a Mecca in the nineteenth century for well-off foreigners, especially those searching for a milder climate for reasons of health. By the time of her entrance in 1860, she was already forty-six years of age. She took the religious name of Mary Addolorata of the Heart and Tears of Christ. By the time of her profession in October 1862, storm clouds were gathering. The monastery chronicle records that the ceremony was conducted behind closed doors, without the ringing of bells, fireworks or festive meal for the attending clergy and guests that were

---

[16] Translated by the author from photocopied extract of the manuscript, *Entrata, Vestitzione e Professione delle Revv Monache e Suore Converse del Venerable Monastero di S Maria di Constantinopile* ['Entry, Clothing and Profession of the Reverend Nuns and Lay Sisters of the Monastery of St Mary of Constantinople']. The author is grateful to Fr Emilio Lage of the Redemptorist Historical Institute in Rome who made available this extract, as well as several chronicle entries of the same monastery referring to Sr Maria Addolorata's stay there.

customary on such occasions. The kingdom of Naples had been brought to an end the previous year by the forces of Garibaldi. The movement for Italian unification was strongly anticlerical and leaned with particular severity on contemplative communities. Although the monastery of S. Agata managed to survive, with the sisters eventually receiving a small state pension,[17] Maria Addolorata was more vulnerable as a foreigner. She made her way to Rome with at least one companion. After several temporary residences, they found a home near the Irish College on its former site in the Via S. Agata dei Goti, which she regarded as a sign of heaven's providential care for her. Some short letters from her survive in the archives of the Irish College and in the Redemptorist general archives in Rome. The last is dated 1874. It has not been possible to discover the date or circumstances of her death. From the correspondence in the Irish College archives, it appears likely that Maria Addolorata and her companion continued to live their Redemptoristine life discreetly without habit or any other outward sign, but still signing her correspondence with her religious name.

One of the most unusual women to enter the Drumcondra monastery was Mrs Sophia Ainsworth, known in religion as Sr Mary Anne Liguori of Jesus Crucified. A sketch of her life together with a collection of her letters was published by her brother, who had preceded her into the Catholic Church under Newman's tutelage.[18] Sophia Hamner Ainsworth was the daughter of an Anglican clergyman. She had been received into the Catholic Church by John Henry Newman in 1851. Her husband had extensive property and business interests in Wales and the north of England. At the time of her conversion, the family was living close to the Redemptorist community of Hanley Castle, near Great Malvern in Worcestershire. On Newman's advice, she took the Redemptorist, Fr John Baptist Lans, as her spiritual director. Her husband was more interested in the traditional pursuits of the gentry than he was in religious matters, but their five children followed her into the church, one of whom became in time a sister of Notre Dame de Namur. She first met the Redemptoristines when she provided accommodation for the first sisters as they passed through London on their way from Bruges to Dublin, and for a time, considered offering a site for a monastery on her estate at Bron Erw in north Wales. Although the idea proved impractical, Sophia Ainsworth continued her friendship with the Dublin community.

After her husband's death in 1871, she asked to be received as a postulant although she was fifty-four years of age. Jeanne de la Croix accepted her and made arrangements to ensure her continued contact with her children despite

---

[17] Heinze, *Dei Redemptoristinnen*, 194.

[18] Anthony John Hanmer, *Mrs Sophia Ainsworth* (Privately published, 1889). I have consulted the copy in St Alphonsus Monastery library, Dublin.

the constraints of the enclosure. The monastery chronicle records occasionally that 'the two Misses Ainsworth have come over to see their mother'. Her business and family affairs were complex. She was obliged to interrupt her novitiate for more than eighteen months to attend to them and to care for one of her sons who had returned from the colonies in declining health. Jeanne de la Croix, who seemed to have had few scruples about leaving the cloister when business demanded it, went with her assistant to visit Mrs Ainsworth's Welsh estate for a week to assess its potential as a convent. The visit was enough to convince her that the community was not in a position to undertake a foundation there. Sophie Ainsworth died at the convent in Drumcondra in 1882.

Relationships between Redemptorists and Redemptoristines in the early years of the life of the Drumcondra community might be described as easy and informal. Since they had no house in Dublin, the Redemptorists stayed in the convent guesthouse on their visits to the capital. Although they could not enter the enclosure, the evening community recreation when they were visiting was held in the large parlour with the grill thrown open.

The professors of Clonliffe College would prove to be faithful chaplains for more than a century. The best known of them is Fr Joseph Marmion, chaplain from 1882 to 1886.[19] As a young priest, he was afflicted with troublesome scruples about the validity of his ordination. Early one morning in August 1884, he was summoned to receive the emergency profession of a dying novice, Sr Mary Claire. After the young sister's death, he asked her to obtain relief from his scruples, and the prayer was answered. Shortly afterwards, he decided to follow what he believed was a call to the contemplative life, entering the Benedictine abbey of Maredsous in Belgium in 1886. He eventually became its abbot, winning additional fame as a prolific spiritual writer. When the Germans invaded Belgium at the outbreak of the First World War, Marmion found a temporary home for the young members of his community at Edermine, County Wexford. In Ireland, the abbot resumed his friendly relations with the Redemptoristine sisters, visiting them frequently and, with typically Marmion good humour, leaving them the photograph of himself dressed as a cattle-dealer that had been used to procure his passport from Belgium. He was beatified by Pope John Paul II during the jubilee year in 2000 as Blessed Columba Marmion.

---

[19] See Mark Tierney, *Blessed Columba Marmion* (Dublin: Columba Press, 2000).

CHAPTER FIVE

On the Road to Independence

The three houses of Clapham, Bishop Eton in Liverpool, and Limerick became an independent province of the Redemptorist congregation in 1865, under the leadership of Fr Robert Aston Coffin. The new province shared the sense of optimism and expansion widespread in the congregation in the aftermath of the 1855 general chapter. Fr Edward Douglas, still in Rome, wished to build a house in Scotland from his large personal fortune. In 1868, work began on the first purpose-built religious house for men in Scotland since the Reformation on a hill overlooking the town of Perth where John Knox had launched his Reformation. The number of men entering the congregation justified the establishment of an independent novitiate for the new province at Bishop Eton, while students pursued their philosophical and theological studies either at Wittem in Holland or Teterchen in Alsace. Several years of living in a continental community did much to break down the insularity of men from Ireland and Great Britain, but there were inevitably difficulties with language, food and the clash of national temperaments. The health of several students suffered under such a regime, and it soon became clear that the best solution would be to establish a student house within the province's territory. Given the large number of Irish candidates, Ireland seemed like an ideal place. Instead, Coffin accepted the offer from Bishop William Vaughan of Plymouth of a foundation at Teignmouth in Devon for the future house of studies.

The decision was greeted in Ireland with a degree of exasperation. There were now four communities on the larger island while expansion in Ireland appeared to be proceeding at a snail's pace. The Roman superiors shared some of these misgivings and signalled to Coffin that his plans for a house of studies should not interfere with the foundation of a second house in Ireland.[1] Tentative offers of foundations in Kingstown and Belfast had been made since the foundation in Limerick, but the time had not been right to pursue them. Given the need to travel to missions, the ideal site for a Redemptorist foundation had to be close to a main railway junction. Limerick was ideal for missions in the southern part of the country, and even Dublin could be

---

[1] Sharp, *Reapers of the Harvest*, 42.

reached within hours. The northern part of the country was less accessible. The archbishop of Armagh, Daniel McGettigan, was well-disposed to a foundation in his diocese, and had even suggested his cathedral city as a location.[2] The pivotal position of Dundalk as a railway junction made it more desirable. It was also a thriving manufacturing and business town that promised opportunities for a lively local church apostolate. There had been a considerable degree of ecclesiastical expansion in the town in the preceding two decades. The parish church of St Patrick had been erected in 1848, followed by the chapel of ease of St Nicholas in 1860. The following year, the Marist Fathers arrived to open a college for boys while the Dominicans, long resident in the town, rebuilt their church near the railway station in 1866.[3]

Disputes between regulars and diocesan clergy in Ireland had a long history. There were two perennial sources of tension. The first was the ancient right of 'questing' for food and money claimed by the friars – Franciscans, Dominicans, Augustinians and Carmelites – for the support of the community within a certain radius of the monastery. The second was the right of 'exemption', or freedom from the control of the bishop in what concerned the interior government of the monasteries and, to a lesser extent, their churches, claimed by all clerical religious whose rule had been approved by Rome.[4] In times of scarce resources, the 'questing' of the friars within the boundaries of their parishes was resented by the diocesan clergy and the claim to 'exemption' was perceived as a way of avoiding control by the bishop. These ancient wars were to have unfortunate consequences when it became known that the Redemptorists intended setting up house in the town.

When Coffin made a formal request for a foundation in July 1876, McGettigan interpreted the general feeling in Dundalk towards the Redemptorists as positive:

> I came here [to Dundalk] chiefly for the purpose [of consulting the clergy] and I am glad to find that the clergy are not unfriendly. It would be distressing for the good Fathers and to me if all did not work out cordially in aiding the great and good work.[5]

---

2 Daniel McGettigan, bishop of Raphoe, had been appointed archbishop of Armagh in 1870.
3 *Centenary Souvenir: St Joseph's Dundalk, 1876–1976* (Dundalk: Redemptorist Community, 1976). The author of the historical note is Patrick O'Donnell CSsR.
4 *Codex iuris canonici Pii X Pontificis Maximi iussu digestus, Benedicti Papae XV auctoritate promulgatus* (Romae: Typis Polyglottis Vaticanis, 1917), Can. 500. The same privilege is maintained in the revised code, *Codex iuris canonici. Auctoritate Ioannis Pauli PP II promulgatus* (Città del Vaticano: Libreria editrice Vaticana, 1989). Can. 611.
5 Daniel McGettigan to R. A. Coffin, 7 July 1876, Dundalk Domestic Archives.

Coffin was aware that the arrival of the Marists several years before had stirred up some resentment among the parish clergy. They alleged that the Marists had broken some of the terms of their agreement with the archdiocese. It was not an opinion shared by Archbishop McGettigan. He continues in the same letter: 'I confess I could never discover the smallest departure from the original agreement on the part of the good Marists who are a most zealous and virtuous community.'

The following month, the archbishop drew up the formal agreement admitting the Redemptorists to his diocese, adding that 'it will be a great consolation to myself when I am dying that I offered no opposition to the great good being done in Ulster by those who have at heart the salvation of souls and the dearest interests of heaven.'[6] Coffin wasted little time. He had the superior general appoint Fr Henry Harbison superior of the new foundation on 2 August 1876 with instructions to find a temporary dwelling in the town, large enough for a mission community and with one room of adequate size for a small public chapel. Harbison took up his appointment six days later and began searching for a home for his community. The most suitable property available was owned by a Protestant clergyman. Fearing that the owner might be reluctant to sell if he knew the identity of the buyers, Harbison acquired it through an estate agent who gave the seller the impression that his client wanted to buy the property for use as a small hotel.[7] Harbison was joined a few days later by the first members of the community, Brs Patrick Hayes and Thomas Robinson. During the following weeks they were joined by Frs John Stokes, John Cleary and James Connolly. An early member of the community was John Urbany, a native of Luxembourg and a member of the German province who had taken up temporary residence in Ireland after his province had been dispersed by Bismark's *Kulturkampf* 'congregation law' of 1875 that prohibited religious communities.

Difficulties

The archbishop's assumption that there would be no opposition from the Dundalk clergy proved overly optimistic. The account of the early days of the foundation in the Dundalk domestic chronicle casts the Redemptorists in the role of victims of the prejudice of the clergy of Dundalk. Some of this may have been exaggerated, but there is no mistaking the fact that they felt decidedly unwelcome. The principal opponent was the administrator of St

---

6 Daniel McGettigan to R. A. Coffin, 8 Aug. 1876, Dundalk Domestic Archives.
7 Dundalk Domestic Chronicle, vol. 1, Dundalk Domestic Archives. The house was located in Park Street but no trace of it remains.

Patrick's church, Fr James McCann.[8] The Sunday before the Redemptorists arrived, Fr McCann had summoned a meeting of his parishioners after Mass to vote on a resolution of protest to the archbishop at the arrival of another religious order in the town. According to the account given at the beginning of the Dundalk domestic chronicle, and which is likely to have drawn on information obtained from some of the participants of the meeting, one of McCann's supporters put the motion, but it failed to find a seconder. The chairman of the town commissioners intervened to say that he thought it unlikely that the archbishop would welcome being dictated to by the laity and that in any case he gave little credence to the view that the Redemptorists would be draining money from the town.

Harbison was understandably concerned about entering Dundalk under such conditions. According to the same chronicle account, the archbishop advised him to take no notice. He suggested that Fr McCann was easily roused and when he was he could be 'as mad as a March hare' so the best way to deal with him was to ignore his public opposition and to invite him to the dinner for the opening of the house. Harbison duly dispatched the invitation.

McCann's reply was a blistering attack on religious orders in general and on the Redemptorists in particular. It began: 'Being perfectly satisfied that the establishment of your order in Dundalk will be of permanent injury to the cause of religion in the town, I cannot conscientiously aid it by my humble presence at your table.' It went on to say that despite its abundance of religious, Limerick was, 'with its teeming jails and internecine fights, the plague spot of Ireland'. His opposition hinged on the usual charges that religious took money and people away from the parish church.

> I am well aware that you do not quest from door to door. You find it more profitable to tap a few rich springs ... You do not say late Masses on Sunday, but those who have been invited to a feast of rhetoric in the morning will scarcely have stomach for our dull homilies at noon.[9]

There is no mistaking Fr McCann's hurt and anger, but there may have been some truth in the archbishop's assessment of the man.

The blessing of the temporary chapel went ahead on 8 September 1876. Archbishop McGettigan attended and formally welcomed the Redemptorists to his archdiocese, but no priest from Dundalk or the surrounding area attended the function.[10] The archbishop's words at the dedication probably

---

8 Since Dundalk was one of the archbishop's 'mensal parishes', providing him with a source of revenue, the priest in charge was an administrator, not a parish priest in the canonical sense.
9 James McCann to Henry Harbison (no date), cited in the Dundalk Domestic Chronicle account of the foundation.
10 Dundalk Domestic Chronicle, 80.

came as a crumb of comfort to the demoralised community. Given the mood of his clergy, it was a courageous statement of support. He reminded the congregation present that they were familiar with missions but that they were relatively new arrivals on the ecclesiastical scene, as the first mission he had attended had been in Omagh, some years after his ordination. It was during that same mission that Fr Harbison had decided to enter the Redemptorists. He concluded with the wise words of Gamaliel (Acts 5:39): 'This work is not of men but of God. If their work in this town is not of God, it will fail. But if it is the work of God, and I believe it is, and not mine or that of these Fathers, then it will succeed.'

Given the mood of the town, the religious exercises in the temporary chapel were discreet. No effort was made to form a confraternity. Despite the opposition, Harbison began hunting for a site for the permanent monastery and church. The site leased from Lord Roden proved to be swampy and needed to be drained before any building could begin. The architect was George Ashlin who had designed the Redemptoristine monastery in Drumcondra. The builder was James McAdorey, a Belfast man who had settled in Dundalk. After five years in the temporary house at Park Street, the community took possession of the new monastery in August 1881. The large room intended for the community refectory did duty as a temporary chapel until the church was completed. At the evening service on the opening day, Bishop Michael Logue of Raphoe, preached. He spoke of the blessings the new monastery would bring:

> Do you think this large house has been raised for the use of these holy men alone? Not at all. No doubt they will live in it during the intervals between missions, but one important reason for it is to give suitable accommodation to priests and laity to make in recollection the spiritual exercises of a retreat.[11]

The house cost £10,000 to build and the perennial problem of money postponed work on the church for a further decade. The foundation stone was laid in June 1890 and dedicated for worship in August 1892 by Archbishop Logue, who had succeeded McGettigan in Armagh in 1887. It is a graceful building of Mourne granite, in Ashlin's trademark 'Irish Romanesque' style. According to the domestic chronicle account of the opening, it was attended by a distinguished gathering of higher clergy and the preacher was Bishop John Healy of Clonfert.

Patrick O'Donnell has commented that the beginnings of the Dundalk foundation were the most difficult of any in Ireland and that the bitterness of the early days endured for decades. 'We were not wanted in Dundalk by

---

11 Dundalk Domestic Chronicle, 28 Aug. 1881.

the secular clergy and were often reminded of it during the years to come. During our five years in the temporary hospice the community tried to conciliate the clergy of the town but failed, seldom if ever being saluted by any of them.'[12] He observed that it was not until 1945 that an invitation came to preach in one of the local churches when Frs Michael Hickey and Jerry O'Shea gave the novena to St Brigid in St Nicholas's parish. The general mission of 1971 was the first given by Redemptorists in the town since 1867.

Robert Aston Coffin and the beginnings of 'Home Rule'
The seventeen-year reign of Robert Aston Coffin as provincial of the London province came to an end in 1882 with his nomination as bishop of Southwark. Coffin briefly entertained the prospect of combining the two offices, or at least continuing to reside at Clapham while bishop, but it was not to be. During his years as provincial, he had become an influential figure in the English Catholic Church and brought a measure of stability and esteem to the Redemptorists. Coffin was highly authoritarian by nature. As was seen in the sketch of his life in chapter three, he broke with Newman and his Oratory after little more than a year because his temperament needed the more disciplined form of religious rule he found among the Redemptorists.

The highly-centralised form of government put in place by the general chapter of 1855 and firm leadership of Nicholas Mauron, the general it had elected, was congenial to Coffin. He kept up a steady correspondence with Mauron throughout his time in office, with the result that each individual and every event was seen in Rome through Coffin's eyes. Sharp has observed that he displayed a dependence on, and a respect for, central authority that Mauron found gratifying, but which occasionally bordered on servility. 'The least desire of your Paternity',[13] he wrote, 'has always been to me like a formal order and long ago I made a firm resolution to place myself without question in obedience to your desires.'[14]

Despite his ability, many of his confreres felt that Coffin had a domineering manner and a disdain for foreigners including the Irish. Some Irish Redemptorists were determined that the superior general needed a more balanced view of affairs before he appointed the next provincial. One Irish priest, claiming to be writing on behalf of others, outlined what he perceived to be the dire straits of the congregation in Ireland as a result of Coffin's neglect.

---

[12] Patrick O'Donnell, 'History of St Joseph's, Dundalk' in *Search*, 4 (Dec. 1978).
[13] Formal title of address to the Redemptorist superior general.
[14] Sharp, *Reapers of the Harvest*, 38.

We are convinced that there has been a radical misunderstanding about Ireland for more than twenty years, and that this misapprehension has retarded the work of the congregation in that country and that great wrong has been done, not only to Ireland but to the whole province, and that it has prevented the growth of the congregation in England, Scotland, and in the colonies to the detriment of the souls of the faithful.[15]

Coffin's reluctance to increase the number of Irish foundations was regarded as symptomatic of his general disregard for Ireland. There had been an interval of more than twenty years between the foundations in Limerick and Dundalk. The formation of new members in the novitiate and house of studies was concentrated in England, despite the fact that the majority of candidates came from Ireland. Coffin's critics suspected he believed that the foundation in Dundalk had relieved him of further obligations to Ireland. Nor was Coffin sparing of his Irish critics in his voluminous correspondence with Rome. A painful thorn in his side was the English-born Fr Francis Hall. Hall had spent most of his life in Ireland, and it was believed of him that he had become 'more Irish than the Irish themselves'. The writer of his memorial notice may have been attempting to be charitable in recording that, as a student, he was subject to 'early attacks of the nerves and debility, which never completely left him'. Dismissing him as a case of 'nervous cerebral excitement', Coffin detailed to Douglas some of the difficulties Hall had caused him:

> … by his extravagant views and opinions on Ireland, the Irish, patriotism, the political and religious aspect of the papacy and temporal sovereignty, Zouaves and fighting to the use of blood … I ought to mention that Fr Hall does not consider the English government of Ireland legitimate as never having been accepted by the people. He also considers it his duty to keep alive the patriotic spirit so that in *tempore opportuno* [at the right time] the people would rise and throw off the yoke of the oppressor etc.[16]

Whatever antipathy there may have been among the Irish to the imperious style of government of an upper-class Englishman like Coffin, the campaign for an independent Irish Redemptorist province is a religious counterpart of

---

15 Memorandum 1882, LO I/2 539, RGAR. The original is written in French: at the end of the document is a note in another hand saying that the sender, Fr Morgan, was forwarding the translation on behalf of another priest.
16 Robert Coffin to Edward Douglas, 3 May 1875, XIII Hib., RGAR. The Zouaves referred to were regiments raised in Ireland and elsewhere to defend the Papal States against the movement for Italian unification.

the agitation for home rule which had been gaining momentum in Ireland throughout the 1870s.

Mission in Australia

One of Coffin's last acts as provincial had been to accept a mission in Australia. As early as 1848, Frederick de Held, superior of the Redemptorists in Belgium, had received a request from Archbishop John Bede Polding, archbishop of Sydney, then scouring Europe in search of priests, to send a group of Redemptorists to Australia.[17] Although de Held forwarded the request to Joseph Passerat, his immediate superior, scarcity of personnel made it impossible to comply. A direct appeal by James Murray, bishop of Maitland, to the superior general, Nicholas Mauron, in 1880 was more successful. Mauron passed the request to Coffin, and the first group of four priests and two brothers left for Australia in 1882, under the leadership of Fr Edmund Vaughan (1827–1909) and settled in Singleton, New South Wales. Staffing the Australian mission was to prove a further complication on the road to an independent Irish province.

Australia proved fertile ground for parish missions. The population had increased dramatically in the years following the discovery of the first gold fields in the 1850s from less than half a million to almost four million by the first decade of the twentieth century. Many of the newcomers were Irish, fleeing from hunger at home. With the earlier Irish settlers, many from the penal colonies, they made up about a quarter of the population. Much of Australia was undeveloped and distances between towns were enormous. The bulk of the Catholic clergy had been recruited in Ireland and they were pitifully few in number. Many Catholics living in the outback did not see a priest for Mass and the sacraments for years at a time. Leakage from the church, if not dramatic, was troubling. In such a setting, parish missions offered hope of a remedy and stories of the impact of the first missions seemed like a repeat of Irish missions of the 1850s and 1860s. According to Vaughan, many people came to the sacraments on the missions after years of neglect, often for the first time since leaving the 'old country'.[18]

The Irish brought with them to Australia a smouldering resentment of England and the English. Shortly after their arrival, Edmund Vaughan's name was mooted as a potential successor to his recently-deceased uncle, Bede Vaughan, as archbishop of Sydney. His credentials as a member of an old Catholic recusant family were impeccable. The Vaughans of Courtfield already formed an extensive episcopal network. In addition to his late nephew in the see of Sydney, his brother, William, was bishop of Plymouth

---

[17] Boland, *Faith of our Fathers*, 21.
[18] Ibid., 69.

and another nephew, Herbert, had been translated to Westminster in 1892 after twenty years as bishop of Salford. The clergy and laity of Sydney, however, were united in their opposition to another Englishman. Vaughan remained in Australia for ten more years, but by the time of his departure, the leadership of the Australian church was firmly in Irish hands. On his return to England in 1894, he was appointed provincial of the London province. He was wise enough to understand that the Australian mission should be staffed by Irishmen until there were sufficient native Australians to take over.

Many diocesan priests in Australia expressed an interest in joining the Redemptorists. Most of them had left Ireland as young men immediately after ordination in seminaries like All Hallows in Dublin that provided for English-speaking dioceses abroad. Years of isolation running vast parishes in the outback left many men yearning for the companionship and security of a religious community. As Boland has noted, only a small percentage of the priests who expressed an interest in joining the Redemptorists ever actually made a formal application or entered the novitiate. Sympathetic as their bishops were to the work of the Redemptorists, they were reluctant to part with any priest from their understaffed dioceses. Some bishops made it a condition that their priests could be released from diocesan service only when a replacement could be found to fill the vacancy his departure would leave, and this might entail a delay of ten years of more.[19]

After Coffin

Robert Coffin's immediate successor as provincial was a compromise candidate, the Scot, Hugh McDonald. He had a greater interest than Coffin in the ordinary round of parish missions, and he governed the province capably, if unspectacularly, for eight years until he was made bishop of Aberdeen in 1890. McDonald attempted to give some comfort to the Irish. Conditions in the French and Dutch provinces had made it desirable to set up small 'juvenates' or colleges for the secondary education of youthful aspirants to the congregation. When Mauron encouraged other provinces to follow suit, McDonald believed that Ireland would be a suitable place for such a college. In 1884, a small school with room for about twenty boys was established at Mount St Alphonsus in Limerick.

When John Bennett succeeded Hugh McDonald as provincial in 1890, it was clear that Nicholas Mauron's long reign as superior general was drawing to a close. The Mauron years had been a period of extraordinary growth and self-confidence for the Redemptorists. They had quadrupled their member-

---

[19] Ibid., 77.

ship worldwide in a little over twenty years. In 1867, the congregation had numbered 644 members: by 1890, there were 2,557 members in 132 houses.[20] It had also grown in prestige. The Redemptorists had campaigned for the proclamation of their founder, Alphonsus Liguori, as a Doctor of the Church and when this was granted in 1871, they basked in the reflected glory. The seal of approval on the moral teachings of Alphonsus led to an increase in interest in his writings. It also encouraged some Redemptorists to engage more seriously with moral theology. It saw the emergence of figures such as Anthony Konings (1821–94), Joseph Aertnys (1828–1915) and Leonard Gaudé (1860–1910), whose writings would shape much of the congregation's thinking on moral issues until the period of the Second Vatican Council.

Nicholas Mauron appointed Matthias Raus as his vicar general to assume responsibility in the case of his incapacity or death until a general chapter should meet. Mauron died in 1893 and the first general chapter since 1855 met the following year. The discontented among the Irish welcomed the chapter as a forum where they might air their grievances. By the provision of the constitutions then in force, the delegates to attend the general chapter along with the provincial were elected by a provincial chapter composed of delegates from each community. Although the delegates elected by the Irish houses did not arrive in London for the chapter with an agreed candidate to be elected as their spokesman, the voting from the outset showed that they were determined to flex their muscles and were in little mood for compromise.

Thomas Bridgett, living in Clapham and researching his books in the British Museum reading room, wrote a lengthy and gossipy account of the provincial chapter to Edward Douglas in Rome.

> The first scrutiny showed that there was to be a contest between Irish and English feeling – Father Hall, though an Englishman, represents the ultra-Irish sentiment. But it would seem that there had not been much concerted action beforehand, since the votes were divided between Geoghegan, Hall and Boylan on the Irish side … The second scrutiny showed that the single votes were dropped, and that minds were turning to Fr Boylan as acceptable to both Irish and English, though he had only become eligible [for election] about a month before. The third scrutiny [ballot] gave the required majority to Fr Boylan.[21]

---

20 De Meulemeester, *Histoire Sommaire*, 178.
21 Thomas Bridgett to Edward Douglas, 4 Jan. 1894, D00505, RGAR. Although Boylan was fifty-six years of age and more than thirty years ordained, he needed six years of profession before he was eligible for election as a delegate to a general chapter.

The second delegate elected was Fr George Stebbing, an Englishman. Substitute candidates had also to be elected. The first of these was Fr Edward O'Laverty, an Irishman acceptable to both Irish and English, 'but after a hard contest to get an English man elected', Fr Michael Geoghegan was chosen. John Bennett, the provincial, had not counted on the chapter taking such a political turn and was badly shaken by it. Bridgett continued his commentary to Douglas:

> My reply was that the result in no way surprised me: that this was the first opportunity the Irish Fathers had had of manifesting their discontent, and that I always thought there was discontent and jealousy towards England, from the provincial living in London, four houses in Great Britain as against two in Ireland. In fact, I heard some say in a moment of passion that Ireland supported the province and England took the honour and profit, that knowing there was smouldering feeling of this sort, I had always desired that his Paternity would visit us and give an opportunity to everyone to speak out. Let me add confidentially that more than once I have heard Irish Fathers say that they could not write their real feelings to Rome because they would be made known to the provincial.

As well as the Irish delegate and the two substitutes, another Irishman, Edward O'Farrell, represented the Australian houses at the general chapter. The first task facing the chapter when it met in Rome in March, 1894 was to endorse the mild-mannered Matthias Raus by electing him superior general. It then set in train a thoroughgoing reform of the Redemptorist general government, designed to take greater account of the increasingly international shape of the congregation. Consultors-general were given responsibility for groups of provinces, to be chosen in turn from the members of those groups of provinces. It was thus that the Irishman, John Magnier, was chosen as consultor for the region that included Ireland, England and Australia in place of the elderly and ailing Edward Douglas.

An Irishman in Rome

John Magnier had not been a delegate at the chapter which elected him to one of its highest international offices, that of a consultor-general, at the age of fifty-one. Born in Kildorrery, County Cork in 1842, he entered the Redemptorists in 1866. Following his novitiate in Bishop Eton, he studied philosophy and theology at Wittem in Holland, and was ordained in Liverpool in 1873. Three years later, he was appointed prefect of students at Teignmouth, a position he held for eleven years. In 1890, he was appointed rector of Limerick. At the end of his first term of office, he was appointed to Clapham as secretary and consultor to the provincial, John Bennett.

Prior to taking up his new position as a consultor general, Magnier was instructed to carry out a visitation of the houses of the province. His report on Limerick convinced him, if he needed convincing, that the separation of the houses on the two islands was imperative. Both local consultors were extremely critical of their English rector whom they accused of a litany of faults, including alleged favouritism to English members of his community. Magnier concluded his report:

> Most Reverend Father, there is now no doubt about the absolute necessity of forming a new Irish province. There are some people on both sides who are so stirred up that it is impossible to maintain peace in union. Religious and moderate men among the Irish who held out against the division even after the last provincial chapter, not indeed for any benefit it might bring to Ireland but simply because it was the best thing for England, now see that the good of the members, the growth of the congregation and the retention of its spirit dictate that we proceed to a separation.[22]

In his role as consultor general, John Magnier became increasingly the point of reference for many of the Irish Redemptorists, who by-passed the provincial in Clapham and referred directly to his judgement. The postal service between Rome and the continent at the end of the nineteenth century was more efficient than it was a hundred years later. Letters and replies could be received within a week and Magnier kept up a voluminous correspondence. The new superior general, Matthias Raus, took a cautious view of the proposed separation of the Irish houses, telling them that it was not the Lord's will to constitute the Irish houses as a separate province for the moment, and urged everyone to accept that decision in a joyful spirit.

Edmund Vaughan, who had succeeded John Bennett as provincial of the London province in 1895, was equally unwilling to contemplate separation. His years in Australia had put him at a remove from the new mood in Ireland. He believed that if separation had consequences for the future of missions in England, it would have even more serious ones for the fledgling Australian mission:

> Up until now, as the two nationalities formed a single province, these [Australian–Irish] prelates would tolerate an English superior, but once separation comes, they would be very hostile towards any arrangement which would detach them from the Irish province, and their displeasure could seriously, or even fatally, wound the work of the

---

[22] John Magnier to Matthias Raus, July 1894, LI/2 895, RGAR.

congregation here. You would need to be here in order to appreciate just how the majority of bishops bring nationality into religion.[23]

John Bennett, his predecessor, was more in touch with the current mood and knew that separation was inevitable. Writing to Edward Douglas, he confided: 'The new provincial is at present very much opposed to the division, as you know, but I believe he will be converted when he has to face the existing facts.'[24]

Irish classes and house-hunting

Magnier wasted little time in using his new authority to address some Irish concerns. The question of providing Irish language classes for the Redemptorist students in Teignmouth was a symbolic issue, but one on which he was determined to lay down a marker. Language revival and nationalism went hand in glove in the late nineteenth century. With the foundation of the Gaelic League in 1893, the language had became increasingly the badge of nationalism and separatism. The demand for Irish classes for the students was presented as the pastoral necessity of knowing the language for mission work in Irish-speaking areas in the west of Ireland. A proposal by Fr John McNamara, one of the Irish priests on the teaching staff at Teignmouth, for regular Irish classes met with stiff resistance from both the provincial and most of the English members of the staff who argued that Irish was in decline and that time given to it should not be taken away from that already devoted to French. Magnier took a hand in drafting the superior general's reply that from the beginning of the following academic year, 1896, all the Irish students would be required to take Irish classes.

A major grievance of the Irish had been Coffin's failure to establish a third house in Ireland during his term of office as provincial. In the ten years since his departure, both his successors had also failed to address the issue. Magnier turned his immediate attention to the matter, as a province could only be established when there was a minimum of three houses within its territory. The existence of the juvenate, or preparatory college, in a wing in the Limerick monastery presented one opportunity for dealing with the problem. The growing number of boys, with the full complement of missioners, brothers and sick members of the community, meant that the house was seriously overcrowded. Magnier asked the new rector of Limerick, Patrick Griffith (1844–1926), to explore the possibility of finding a new location for the college. Various locations were tried unsuccessfully including Sanderscourt, County Wexford and several locations in the Dublin area. Magnier then

23 Edmund Vaughan to Matthias Raus, 26 Aug. 1894, 11-LO 1.898, RGAR.
24 John Bennett to Edward Douglas, 14 June 1896, DO O544, RGAR.

embarked on a new tactic. He appointed Griffith and Fr Michael Somers (1848–1932) to 'prudently inquire, examine and report on the feasibility of a new foundation in Ireland'.[25] They embarked on an odyssey that lasted several years which Somers recorded in a notebook preserved in the provincial archives in Dublin.[26] As he was to remark in his notes, 'all the effort that was made in the foundation of the CSsR in the west of Ireland will never be known until the day of judgement.'

They were also to discover that their popularity as parish missioners gave them no guarantee of acceptance into a diocese. Their interview with the bishop of Derry, John Keyes O'Doherty, was brief but blunt. 'I like to call religious orders to work in my diocese from time to time, but not to live there', he told them. The former Jesuit college at Tullabeg, County Offaly which had closed in 1886, seemed a likely prospect for a foundation, but their request to buy it was met by a rebuff from the bishop of Meath, Thomas Nulty: 'All the vicars and priests of the King's County whom I have consulted are to a man opposed to the introduction of your congregation at Tullabeg in this diocese.' He attempted to soften the blow by adding that, while the services of the Redemptorists 'are most valuable where they are wanted, but they are not really needed here'. They were to find a friend at last when the newly-appointed bishop of Down and Connor, Dr Henry Henry, making his consecration retreat in Dundalk, spontaneously offered a house in Belfast. Belfast was then a rapidly-growing industrial city. It was expanding particularly in the western part of the city where Catholics had tended to gather along the axis of the Falls Road. While a Redemptorist church would certainly take the pressure off the already crowded churches of St Peter's and St Paul's, there was no compulsion to accept a parish but the parish mission work would be welcomed. At the end of a general mission in Belfast in October 1896, the first two Redemptorists took possession of Clonard Lodge, the former home of the mill-owning Kennedy family, when they celebrated Mass in it on 1 November. The last remaining obstacle to independence had been removed.[27]

Independent Irish Province

It remained increasingly difficult for Redemptorist superiors in both Britain and Ireland to maintain peace in the province. Edmund Vaughan was a man of sensitive temperament and ill-prepared for the storm of criticism that

---

[25] John Magnier to Patrick Griffith, 24 May 1895, XIII-D N 0882, RGAR.

[26] Michael Somers, 'Foundation at Carrick on Shannon, Rosses Point and Esker', Box D in RPAD. Quotations in text, unless otherwise noted, are from this source.

[27] For the history of Clonard Monastery, see James Grant, *One Hundred Years with the Clonard Redemptorists* (Dublin: Columba Press, 2005).

greeted him during his official visitation of the Irish communities on his appointment as provincial in 1895. He soon realised that his own preferred solution, a degree of limited independence for Ireland as a vice-province, would serve no useful purpose and that Irish sensibilities were too raw to entertain such a compromise.

Matters were not helped by what was seen as John Magnier's interference in the internal affairs of Irish houses or his tendency to act on the basis of gossip and petty criticism that flowed into him in Rome. Men like Edward O'Laverty, the rector of Dundalk, resented this kind of intrusion. Magnier, for instance, had demanded that O'Laverty take action against members of his community who were accused of 'carrying on unbecomingly'. The substance of the charge was that one young priest had ridden a bicycle on a public road during a mission and that another had sung a party piece at an entertainment in a convent parlour. O'Laverty writes with a finely controlled irritation: 'It almost makes me despair of the future when a boyish prank of that kind is thought to be material enough for a charge before the highest tribunal in the congregation.' As for the charge that singing in a convent parlour was unbecoming conduct in a priest:

> 'Carried on unbecomingly', now that is one of those nasty phrases which I am afraid shows the animus of the writer. I would beg your reverence to find me in what the 'unbecomingness' consisted, probably some little buffoonery, which when we consider the easy relationship between priest and religious in this country, had no evil except what an evil mind could read into it.[28]

O'Laverty himself had been accused of being over-generous in entertaining visiting missioners from England at the expense, it was alleged, of regular observance:

> The truth is that regular observance is not a matter of English or Irish ... man for man, I am satisfied that they are much as we are ... Regular observance is suffering far more with us now from a smouldering discontent and a readiness to criticise everybody and everything and to read into the most harmless actions deepest malice. Would to God that we had among us more of the charity that thinketh no evil ... Now with some of us there seems to be a determination to force things to a crisis and I am sore afraid nature and not grace has the upper hand. God help us in the days that are to come if this is so, and

---

28 Edward O'Laverty to John Magnier, July, 1896. Copy in Box LC, RPAD, original in RGAR.

if we get a province to ourselves in that way, we cannot expect God's blessing nor the favour of our Holy Father.[29]

One cannot help getting the impression that the deteriorating relationship between the Irish and English, and Magnier's role in it, was causing unease to fair-minded men like Edward O'Laverty in Ireland or John Bennett in Britain. Bennett confided in 1896 to Edward Douglas in Rome that the situation was getting so out of hand that 'we might have in this province what we have never thought possible before, a breaking out like that of the Paulists.'[30] Vaughan, he realised, was temperamentally incapable of breaking the logjam. He hoped O'Laverty might be appointed the next provincial but 'I am afraid he would not be acceptable to the Irish Fathers and I have heard and seen things lately which make me give up all hope of our remaining as we have been, and even those who have been most against division on both sides now admit that it must come.'

In the end, the final movement towards independence came swiftly and relatively painlessly. The superior general, Matthias Raus, ordered a consultation to be held in Clapham in September 1897 to consider the proposal for the separation of the Irish houses. His American consultor, Joseph Schwarz (1849–1927), presided over the meeting and the participants agreed unanimously that it was 'opportune and necessary' to divide the province and that this should be done as soon as possible. In January 1898, the Holy See authorised the creation of two independent provinces, with the Australian houses forming part of the Irish province. The decree of erection was communicated to the new provinces on 1 April 1898, naming Andrew Boylan as provincial of the new Irish province. On Easter Sunday, 10 April 1898, the list of those attached to the two provinces of Ireland and England was posted in all the houses. The Irish province counted fifty-one priests, fourteen brothers and twenty-nine students. Five Irish priests opted to remain in England and two Englishmen to stay on in Ireland. The erection of the new province was celebrated with a formal liturgical celebration in all the houses. In Clonard, the redoubtable Michael McNamara who had set the movement towards independence in motion by his crusade for Irish classes preached a sermon in Irish to celebrate the occasion.

---

[29] Ibid.

[30] John Bennett to Edward Douglas, 14 June 1896, DO–0544, RGAR. The departure of the American Redemptorist, Isaac Hecker, in 1857 to found the Society of St Paul, already referred to in chapter one in the context of Vladimir Petcherine's departure from the congregation, had left a bitter memory among Redemptorists.

CHAPTER SIX

Independent Irish Province: First Decade

Andrew Boylan was fifty-six years of age when he was appointed the first provincial of the independent Irish province of the Redemptorists. He was born in Crosserlough, County Cavan in 1842. After studies in Maynooth College, he was ordained priest for his home diocese of Kilmore in 1867. He spent the first years of his priestly life in the diocesan college in Cavan before being assigned to Maynooth College as assistant bursar in 1875. He was bursar from 1883 until he entered the Redemptorists in 1887, leaving Maynooth, as he would quip later, 'to follow Christ'. Walter McDonald, a member of the academic staff in Maynooth during Boylan's tenure, described him in his memoirs somewhat acidly as 'good humoured, honest, weak'.[1]

Thomas Bridgett's account of the 1894 provincial chapter that elected Boylan as a delegate to the general chapter after a mere six years in the congregation suggests that he enjoyed a reputation as a moderate, acceptable to both English and Irish, or, as the chronicler of the province recorded in his death-notice, 'from the beginning, he gained the confidence of his confreres as well as that of his superiors.' His time as bursar in Maynooth College had given him some standing in the Irish Church. This, together with his proven skill in handling financial matters, was doubtless a factor in recommending him as provincial. It is no surprise that when his native diocese of Kilmore became vacant in 1907, the bishops of the Armagh province added him to the *terna*, or list of three names forwarded to Rome for consideration for the appointment, although he had received only a single vote from the clergy of the diocese. The plain-speaking Redemptorist, Edward O'Laverty, who preached the panegyric at Boylan's month's mind in the cathedral of Ss Patrick and Felim, Cavan in April 1910, observed that while none of his friends would claim for him exceptional intellectual gifts, he made the best use of what he had and 'from first to last, he was straight, sincere, simple and unselfish.'[2]

---

[1] Walter McDonald, *Reminiscences of a Maynooth Professor*, edited with a memoir by Denis Gwynn (Cork: Mercier Press, 1967), 98.
[2] For a sketch of Boylan's episcopacy, see Anthony Mulvey, 'Most Rev. Dr Andrew Boylan CSsR, bishop of Kilmore (1907–1910)' in *Breifne: Journal of Cumann Seanchais Bhréifne*, vol. 8, no. 2 (1991), 145–54.

As has been shown, the first Redemptorists who came to Ireland in the early 1850s were in the main Belgian, Dutch and Austrian, with a handful of English upper-class Catholic converts, one Russian and one Irish-born priest, William Plunkett. There was a surge in vocations to the priesthood and religious life in the last four decades of the nineteenth century. Emmet Larkin has estimated that in 1860, Ireland had 3,000 priests and 1,500 religious women serving a population of 4.5 million. By 1900, there were 3,700 priests and 8,000 sisters for a population of 3.3 million.[3] By 1898, there were over 120 Irish Redemptorists. During the first ten years as an independent province, the figures continued to rise markedly, as shown in Tables 1 and 2.

Table 1. Number of Redemptorists in Irish Province,
including Australia, 1898 and 1909

	Priests	Brothers	Students	Choir Novices	Lay Novices
Redemptorist Province of Ireland and Australia, 1898	50	21	29	5	–
Redemptorist Province of Ireland and Australia, 1909	88	38	30	3	14

Table 2. Number of Redemptorists attached to Irish Communities,
1898 and 1909

	Priests	Brothers	Students	Choir Novices	Lay Novices
Redemptorists in Ireland, 1898	32	14	29	5	–
Redemptorists in Ireland, 1909	62	23	30	3	11

Source: Based on statistics in Provincial Chronicle, vol. 1,
RPAD for years 1898 and 1909

The growth of the new province was steady, but not dramatic. Three or four ordinations each year was the norm. The number of professed clerical students held at around five per annum, making for a student body of about thirty over the six years of study. Comparatively few students left after first profession. Members leaving after ordination to enter a diocese were exceptional; still more exceptional was the case of any one leaving priestly ministry completely after ordination. Between 1898 and 1909 there were fifty ordinations.

---

[3] Emmet Larkin, 'The Devotional Revolution in Ireland' in *The Historical Dimensions of Irish Catholicism* (Dublin: Four Courts Press, 1997), 57–90, here 84.

During this same period, twelve priests died. Deaths of young men were not uncommon. John Ryan died as a student in Belfast from tuberculosis at the age of twenty-five. Edwin Stephenson was forced to interrupt his studies due to ill-health. He was ordained in Limerick in 1904, just some months before his death. Edward Cahill, the first member of the newly-founded Philippine mission to die, was thirty-seven at the time of his death in 1909.

Membership of the new province was not exclusively Irish. Two Belgians, Jules Peeters and Henri Berghman, chose to remain in Ireland. A surprisingly high number of the first generation of the independent Irish Redemptorist province were former diocesan priests. Ten of the fifty listed as assigned to the new province in 1898 had been ordained for Irish or Australian dioceses prior to entering the Redemptorists. The diocese of Ferns was particularly well-represented. Most were former Maynooth men, though some of the Australians had been students at All Hallows College and one, Patrick Lynch, had completed his studies in Clonliffe College, Dublin. At the erection of the new province, John Magnier cautioned against making too many of the former diocesan priests superiors, 'lest the spirit of secular priests should dominate in the province'. In the event, several did hold positions of authority in the new province. Apart from the provincial, Andrew Boylan, they included the novice master, Michael Somers, and two rectors, Edward O'Laverty in Limerick and Patrick Griffith in Clonard. The superior of the Australian mission, Thomas O'Farrell, was also a former diocesan priest. Three more diocesan priests were professed in the period under review: Patrick Cussen in 1900, Patrick Crotty in 1903, and Bernard Hackett in 1905. A number of others joined the congregation after having spent several years in seminary training. Patrick Sampson was a student of All Hallows College, while Patrick Murray and Michael Geoghegan had almost completed their Maynooth courses. Noticeable too is a group of young men who had been contemporaries in the 'apostolic school' at Mungret, County Limerick. This was a college under the direction of the Jesuits founded to provide young men of slender means with the opportunity to begin studies for the priesthood on condition that they would eventually volunteer for service in the 'mission territories' of the English-speaking world. Between 1884 and 1897, six students from the college entered the Redemptorists.

The story of every vocation is unique, but some recurrent elements can be detected. The reason most commonly given for entering the congregation in the *curriculum vitae* written by every novice shortly before profession has to do with the search for personal holiness. In many cases, the attraction to the Redemptorists came as a result of reading the works of St Alphonsus, which were popular spiritual reading at the time. Alphonsus's *Visits to the Blessed Sacrament* was read avidly by the young James Joyce, as he relates in the

Portrait of the Artist as a Young Man. The *Glories of Mary* had become a long-time staple of Marian devotion and many of the smaller works such as the *Meditations for Every Day of the Week,* translated by Nicholas Callan, priest-scientist of Maynooth, and circulated in the cheap editions. Callan's translation of *The Selva or a collection of Matter for Sermons and Instructions for Ecclesiastical Retreats and for Private Spiritual Lectures* (1844) was the regular source used in Maynooth for grounding the students in the spirituality of priesthood.[4] For others, the attraction lay in the work and ideals of the Redemptorists, especially the prospect of helping 'the most abandoned souls'. Many of the diocesan priests who entered after several years on the Australian mission were attracted by the companionship community life offered. As one man put it in his novitiate *curriculum vitae,* many priests he had known had died without the last sacraments and he did not want to meet such a fate. Most candidates entered in their late teens but some were already mature men. Walter Lambert was fifty-eight when he joined, having spent many years as a priest in the diocese of Ferns. Boylan, the provincial, had himself entered at the age of forty-five. Three of the former diocesan priests – Andrew Boylan, Patrick Clune and Bernard Hackett – returned as bishops to their former dioceses.

More difficult to assess is the social origin of the early Redemptorists. It is likely that in the early years of the independent Irish province, it was more varied than was to be the norm in subsequent times. William Plunkett was the son of an earl and a former army officer. Thomas Power is described as 'the son of a wealthy merchant family'. Henry Halson was an Oxford-educated convert, who had served as an officer in the Crimean war before spending some years prospecting for gold in Australia to where he returned after ordination.[5] Edward Cahill had been apprenticed to a draper. Christopher Craig, Australian child of a mixed marriage, had been to university where he had taken his MA and gone into business before entering the Redemptorists at the age of thirty-seven in 1910. Thomas Campbell of Hollywood, County Down belonged to a family that had made a significant contribution to the Irish literary revival: his brother was the poet, Joseph Campbell, and a cousin was the writer, Helen Waddell. Thomas J. Walsh was the child of a broken marriage who was educated at home by his father and a governess. The largest number came from the Limerick, Clare and Tipperary regions, with a small number from other places, including three from County Down. Dublin was proportionally under-represented in the

---

[4] Corish, *Maynooth College,* 169.
[5] Samuel J. Boland, 'A Redemptorist from the Goldfields: Henry Halson CSsR, 1833–1900' in *SHCSSR,* vol. 53, no. 2 (2005), 275–90.

number of men applying for entrance. In most cases, generic descriptions such as 'farmer' in their *curriculum vitae* makes it difficult to assess the social standing of the family with any greater precision.

The bulk of candidates entered immediately after completing their secondary education. Increasingly after 1884, their education had taken place under Redemptorist auspices in the Limerick juvenate or preparatory college. The provincial, Andrew Boylan, once recommended a candidate for the novitiate on the grounds that 'he will be a good solid lump of a religious, never very brilliant, but he will be industrious and obedient, and he appears to be strong and healthy.' Unfortunately, as student and later as a priest, this man proved incapable of writing sermons and had little taste for the common life. His superiors' mistaken judgement that he was simply lazy led to many unhappy years. Popular reaction to him was different: at the time of his death, the people near the monastery regarded him as 'a terrible saint of a man' with a reputation as a kindly confessor. Some men were late vocations. When Christopher McDermott's family lost most of its savings through the collapse of a bank, he was forced to go to work as a 'pupil monitor' in the Christian Brothers' school in Limerick for some years before he was able to go back to study for two years at St Patrick's College, Thurles at the age of twenty-eight.

Independent house of studies: from Clonard to Esker
Boylan's mettle as provincial was to be tested in the continuing negotiations for a house in the west of Ireland. Patrick Griffith and Michael Somers had investigated an apparently endless succession of properties, including Dunamon Castle, Clonalis House, Mount Florence and Edmundstown, near Ballaghadereen – all four in County Roscommon – without success. Their perseverance eventually bore fruit. After a brief stay in Killukin House near Carrick-on-Shannon from1899 to 1901, a permanent community was established in Esker, County Galway in August 1901.

The foundation at Esker came at an opportune time. When the Irish and English provinces separated in 1898, they agreed that their students would continue to be educated together at Teignmouth in Devon. This arrangement lasted only two years as the English province found itself unable to carry the financial burden of Teignmouth. When they decided to send their students to the Austrian house of studies at Mautern, the Irish were left to make their own arrangements for the academic year of 1900–1901. Providentially, the newly-built monastery at Clonard in Belfast became available at this time. Built according to the rule's stipulation that there be sufficient rooms for retreatants, it proved large enough to provide temporary accommodation for the students. Boylan had not been in favour of building such a large house in

Belfast, but the plans had been approved before he took up office as provincial. He had written, probably half-jocosely, to John Magnier in Rome:

> May the Lord forgive the whole seven of you [the members of the general council] for approving such a house for Belfast: 54 bedrooms!!! We shall make a boarding school of it and send the students down to the Queen's College for lectures. Fifty-four rooms!! Oh my eye, what shall we do with them all?[6]

The students arrived in Belfast at the beginning of the summer holidays. Built in the middle of a working-class area of a large industrial city with only a cramped garden, half of which was occupied by a foul-smelling, disused millpond, it could be at best a temporary residence for a large group of young men. Esker in County Galway had a long tradition as a house of formation and study stretching back to the medieval Dominican priory of Athenry. The dilapidated buildings the Redemptorists found there needed to be rebuilt, so it was a comparatively easy matter to include accommodation for students in the plan. The students remained in Clonard until the alterations of Esker were complete in 1905. It was to remain the house of studies until 1940. A more detailed history of the houses of Clonard and Esker will be the subject of the next chapter.

Apostolic life

Independence as a province brought little change to the style of parish missions or to the internal life of the Irish communities. It did offer, however, an opportunity for reviewing existing practices. A provincial consultation brought together the rectors of the various communities with the provincial and his consultors. One of its results was the publication of the first official *Directory for Missions* of the Irish province, officially promulgated after Roman approval in 1903.

It stipulated that a 'closed season' was to be maintained, free from missions, from mid-December until mid-February of each year. During that time, the fathers were to remain in the monastery, apart from the few days of convent retreats traditional at the turn of the year, and to devote themselves to the exercises of the common life in keeping with a traditional maxim of 'Carthusian at home, apostle abroad'. It recommended that the younger priests be given help in preparing their stock of mission sermons. It stressed that in preaching on chastity, 'our missioners have well thought out what they wanted to say, written it out and committed it to memory' – possibly a sign that some preaching on this topic left something to be desired. It proposed establishing a fund to finance missions for poorer parishes and that

---

[6] Andrew Boylan to John Magnier, 19 Apr. 1898, 30130001015, RGAR.

benefactors be made aware of its existence and invited to contribute to it. The tendency of parish priests to scale down the duration of the missions was to be resisted, and rectors were enjoined to ensure that they accepted enough men and allowed enough time for the work to be done well. As far as practical, the normal mission was to run for three weeks, with three men.

Returns from the provincial chronicles, shown in Table 3, for missions conducted by all the houses over the twelve mission seasons from 1898 to 1909 reveal the growth in mission-giving during this period.

Table 3. Redemptorist Missions in Ireland, 1898–1909

Year	Missions	Year	Missions
1898	56	1904	88
1899	54	1905	73
1900	60	1906	75
1901	80	1907	73
1902	81	1908	74
1903	83	1909	73

Source: Annual returns, Provincial Chronicle, vol. 1. RPAD

The sudden surge in the number of missions in 1901 coincided, as had been predicted, with the foundation of a community in the west of Ireland.

The wisdom of the decision, despite the difficult birth, is confirmed by the number of missions given by the temporary community at Carrick-on-Shannon and later by the men at Esker. In the years from 1902, the number of missions given in the west of Ireland climbed steadily from just over 20 to more than 70 per year. In 1909, six full missions and 87 temperance missions were given by the community at Esker. Temperance missions were part of a short-lived and ineffectual campaign to promote temperance, sponsored by the bishops of the Tuam province. They consisted of three or four days' preaching in every parish throughout the diocese. Although they did the lion's share of temperance missions in the western dioceses, the Redemptorists were never fully convinced of its usefulness, as they believed the time available for preaching and confessions was too short.

The content of the mission sermons continued to be resolutely traditional proclamations of the 'great truths' of salvation. That is not to suggest that the missioners' interests in the people's welfare were exclusively spiritual. The temperance mission campaign, and the promotion of an 'anti-treating pledge' were attempts to address a major social evil, as was Boylan's advice to his men to include references to emigration in their preaching:

It appears part of our spiritual duty to convince people of this truth and to discourage emigration as far as lies in our power ... If we can do anything to keep the people in the country by encouraging home industries and by securing employment for young men in public companies, I would say that it is well within our sphere of duty to do so.[7]

He reminded those who might be reluctant to deal with social issues in their preaching, that 'if emigration goes unchecked, there will soon be no missions for us to give.'

It is more difficult to assess the quality of the work done in the monastery churches. The temporary church at Clonard in Belfast, erected within a few months of the Redemptorists' arrival in 1896, was soon rivalling the longer-established Mount St Alphonsus church in Limerick in the numbers attracted by its confraternities and in the round of daily services and confessions. Apart from special times like May, October, and Lent, which had their traditional devotions as well as the weekly confraternity meetings, there was an evening service at least three nights each week – Sunday 'evening devotions', devotions in honour of St Joseph on Wednesday and of Our Lady on Saturday.

In addition to a short instruction at the later Sunday Masses, a longer sermon was the principal feature of the Sunday evening service. The preaching does not always seem to have reached an acceptable standard, for the report at the end of Andrew Boylan's first canonical visitation in 1899 instructed the rectors to mark preachers for these sermons well in advance, since the people were complaining that they were being treated week after week to re-hashed mission sermons. They were also recommended to offset complaints of this type by drawing up 'useful and attractive' courses of sermons to be preached over a given period of time, for example, Sundays of Advent or Lent.

The figures for communions distributed in each of the churches, as reported annually in the provincial chronicles, show enthusiastic acceptance by the faithful of Pius X's *Decree on Frequent Communion* in 1905. Communions at Mount St Alphonsus, Limerick, for example, almost doubled in the year of the decree's publication.

Confraternity and city
By the time of the celebration of the golden jubilee of their arrival in Limerick in 1903, the Redemptorists occupied an important place in the public life of the city. This high profile was due mainly to the influence of the archconfraternity of the Holy Family. The number of men attending the weekly meetings was impressive by any standard. There were more than five

---

[7] Circular letter to superiors, 1903, Box LB-BO 1, RPAD.

thousand men on the books of the confraternity in 1903, with an average attendance at the weekly meetings of 3,992.[8] The members still belonged solidly to the working and lower middle classes: the *Bona Mors* sodality of the Jesuit church in the Crescent saw to the spiritual needs of the professional classes. While the ordinary weekly meetings in the church on Monday and Tuesday evenings were predictable in format, with major emphasis falling on an instructional sermon of about half an hour, the confraternity marked occasions of special celebration, with public processions through the decorated streets of the city. The first of these was held to mark the jubilee of Pius IX's consecration as bishop in 1877. As well as traditional banners, at the end of the procession came

> … the figure of Pope Pius carried, as in Rome, on his chair of state, clad in his robes and wearing his triple crown. Around were grouped flags and banners and close by walked the survivors of those who had gone in former years to fight for the temporal power in the ranks of the Papal Zouaves.[9]

The hymns sung at the meetings were rousing, with strong and simple tunes – the Catholic version of Victorian 'muscular Christianity'. 'Confraternity men to the fight' and 'We stand for God and for his glory' were favourites. The militaristic language of such hymns – and of their Protestant counterparts like 'Onward Christian soldiers' – may not appeal today, but it can be traced back to the New Testament injunction that Christians should arm themselves for the struggle against the powers of evil (Ephesians 6:10 ff).

The director of the Limerick archconfraternity was, after the bishop, arguably the most visible Catholic religious figure in the city. Individual parish priests may have been men of importance in their own right, but their influence was confined to their own parishes. Each week, the director addressed two large meetings of the confraternity. No confraternity director could survive long without a gift for direct and colourful language that appealed to his members. In days before the presence of mass-media of communications, sermons, especially when they touched on controversial themes, were discussed in the home or in the workplace the following day, ensuring that the words of the director reached a wider audience than his members alone. Directors were conscious too of the pastoral obligations they owed the men. Although the Redemptorist rule forbade social visiting, this did not apply to the spiritual visits of the director of the confraternity. He visited the men when they were sick or failed to show up for meetings on a

---

[8] Figures from the commemorative brochure, *Fifty Years at Mount St Alphonsus, Limerick. Golden Jubilee 1853–1903* (Limerick: CSsR, 1903), 58.
[9] Ibid., 54.

regular basis; he attended their funerals, instructed them week after week on the duties of Catholic men towards God, their wives, their families and employers. Some directors tried to do more. Thomas Bridgett, first director of the confraternity for instance, had founded a lending library in 1868 that continued in existence until 1882.

Occasionally, the interventions of the director of the confraternity in the life of the city over-reached the boundaries of acceptability. The muscular Christianity they preached and their high public profile led some directors to assume the role of champions of the faith. In 1901, Fr Daniel Tierney embarked on a public controversy with Dr J.J. Long, a Protestant medical missionary. In an unseemly confrontation between the two in the public street, Tierney shouted to Long to 'go off to England and strive to convert some of its heathen inhabitants'. Dr Long replied with a dignified letter of protest but Tierney's antipathy to the medical mission smouldered on. Later in the same year, the annual Limerick regatta on the Shannon clashed with the weekly meetings of the confraternity. Tierney denounced the regatta organisers from the pulpit the week before it was due to begin and called on the confraternity members to assemble the following Monday to mount a protest demonstration. The protest was timed to coincide with one of the gala events of the festival, so a trial of strength between the confraternity on the one side and the middle-class organisers of the regatta seemed inevitable. Tierney had asked one group of men to assemble in the church of Mount St Alphonsus: the other, led by two brass bands, filled the church yard. The regatta organisers, in an attempt at conciliation, had, in the meantime, written to the bishop of Limerick, Edward O'Dwyer, apologising for their mistake in timing the event. The bishop in turn directed Tierney to call off his protest. Tierney cancelled both his demonstration and the following night's confraternity meeting, allowing the men to attend the regatta. The confrontation left a bitter taste. At Christmas time the following year, the Limerick domestic chronicle recorded, 'a small book of verse, a parody of the *Jackdaw of Rheims*, was circulated in Limerick ridiculing and attacking Fr Tierney, director of the Holy Family confraternity. In it he was called *Fr Tyranny*.'[10] Tierney remained, nevertheless, a popular figure with the confraternity men. When he left Limerick early in 1902, he was presented with an address by the mayor of the city, James F. Barry, and the confraternity men took turns to draw the carriage carrying him to the station, accompanied by five bands.

---

[10] Limerick Domestic Chronicle, vol. 3, Dec. 1901.

Fr Creagh and the Jews

The most infamous incident associated with the confraternity came two years later. Tierney's successor, Fr John Creagh (1870–1945), preached a series of sermons to the confraternity denouncing the Jews of Limerick for extortion. Creagh effectively called for a boycott of Jewish businesses in the city that lasted for several months, resulted in several outbreaks of violence and forced a number of Jewish families to leave the city.[11]

Creagh's concern for the plight of the poor of the city has not always been given due credit. He has often been presented simply as a racist demagogue whipping up anti-Semitic hatred. When he took up the post of director of the confraternity in 1902, he was still a relatively junior priest and had spent most of the time since ordination in the seclusion of the house of studies in Teignmouth. He first came to public prominence in his new role in the course of a campaign against intemperance that he preached shortly after his arrival. Creagh branded the publicans of the city as Judases: 'Judas sold his master for thirty pieces of silver, and these publicans will sell souls, that Jesus Christ died to redeem, for the sake even of a pint of stout or a half-glass of whiskey.' He did not confine his campaign to the pulpit, for he appeared before a committee investigating the problem of public drunkenness in the city where he gave eloquent and detailed testimony from his experience as director of the confraternity of the effects of alcoholism on the lives of the poor.

That there was a social problem of money-lending at high interest rates among the poor of Limerick is not in doubt. Creagh's error, and it is an appalling one, was to turn a small emigrant community into a scapegoat and in doing so, to feed his audience with the worst dross of anti-Semitic legend. In his defence, however, it is right to observe that his sense of social justice was not confined to pulpit denunciations but led him to find ways of addressing the social scourge of money-lending. He opened a shop that sold goods at low profit margins and established a 'confraternity bank', a type of forerunner of the credit union movement, as ways of tackling the problem of money-lending. Social action of this kind was not normally associated with the role of directors of the confraternity.

Creagh launched his attack on the Jews at the first confraternity meetings of the new year on 11 January 1904 and followed it up with a second sermon a week later. He claimed to have first-hand knowledge of how Jewish peddlers were exploiting the poor of Limerick and tapped into his audience's latent fear of the foreigner. He described how the Jews had arrived in the city just a short time before as penniless emigrants:

---

[11] For a well-researched account of the events, see Dermot Keogh, *Jews in Twentieth-Century Ireland, Refugees, Anti-Semitism and the Holocaust* (Cork: Cork University Press, 1998), chapter two, 'The Limerick "pogrom", 1904', 27–53.

... but now they have enriched themselves and could boast of very considerable house property in the city. Their rags they have exchanged for silk. They have wormed themselves into every kind of business. They are in the furniture trade, the mineral water trade, and in fact in business of every description, and trade even under Irish names.[12]

Invoking the old notion of the curse on the Jews for their rejection of Christ, he then turned to the current persecution of the Church in France, where the 'Law of Associations' (1901) was being applied to limit the power and influence, and even to ensure the expulsion, of religious communities.[13] Creagh laid this development firmly on the influence of the Jews in the French anti-clerical government, claiming that 'there are no greater enemies of the Catholic Church than the Jews.'

The campaign against the Jews became a *cause célèbre* of national proportions. Public figures, like Michael Davitt and John Redmond, defended the Jewish community, while others, like Arthur Griffith, took Creagh's part. Griffith, editor of the *United Irishman* newspaper, raised the spectre of an influx of Jews into Ireland at the cost of the emigration of the native Irish:

When fifteen hundred of our strong men and good women sail on a liner from the Cove of Cork, we can count on receiving a couple of hundred Jews on the North Wall to fill their places. But has Ireland gained or lost by the exchange?[14]

Questions were asked in the House of Commons, and calls were made for Creagh's prosecution.[15] The Synod of the Church of Ireland became embroiled in the debate and Creagh's position was becoming an embarrassment for the bishop of Limerick who was unable to intervene since he had no jurisdiction over a member of a religious community. The affair petered out by the summer of 1904, but the Jewish community in the city had been dealt a blow from which it never recovered.

Creagh continued as director of the confraternity for a further two years but he directed his attacks more towards moral concerns such as drink or obscene literature and theatrical shows. He was named as a member of the pioneer team of Redemptorists who went to the Philippines in 1906. His stay

---

[12] Quotations from Creagh's sermons are from the press reports on the sermons in the *Limerick Journal,* 13 and 20 Jan. 1904, inserted into the Confraternity Chronicle.

[13] More than 400 religious orders and congregations, including the Redemptorists, were dissolved as a result of this law: see Jean Sévilla: *Quand les Catholiques Étaient hors la Loi* (Paris: Perrin, 2005).

[14] *United Irishman,* 24 Apr. 1904.

[15] Keogh, *Jews in Ireland,* 44.

there was brief and he was eventually posted to Australia. In 1916, he was named pro-vicar apostolic[16] of the Kimberlies in Northern Australia to replace the German Pallottine missionaries whose movements were restricted on account of their alien status during the First World War. His ecclesiastical rank gave him the authority of a bishop in all but name. The region was a difficult one and racked with poverty. It was fertile ground for an outspoken champion of the poor like Creagh. He attacked the pearl companies with a detailed exposure of how they exploited the pearl-divers – for the most part poor immigrants supporting families in Asia on the equivalent of slave wages. He embarrassed the government by attacking its grudging grant of one shilling a year to the Sisters of St John of God who ran the school and dispensary for the care of aborigine people. With the cooperation of the sisters, he arranged classes for the Asian crewmen, with the sisters teaching English and he himself offering courses in Christian doctrine.[17] Creagh remained in this difficult mission until 1923. Samuel Boland quotes an Irish St John of God sister who knew him in the Kimberlies as having 'a fiery temper but the heart of a mother'.[18] He spent the rest of his life attached to different Australian Redemptorist communities until his death in 1947.

Life in community

Redemptorist community life, in Ireland and elsewhere, continued to be shaped by the rule and constitutions of Alphonsus Liguori, as interpreted by the traditions of the founding fathers or by later decrees from rectors major or general chapters. The annual canonical visitation of each community by the provincial, or less frequently by the superior general, gave an opportunity to correct any laxity, and the visitors' observations, or 'recess', were written into a special 'recess book' for future reference.

Andrew Boylan's first recess as provincial made the usual observations about the observance of silence and the need to devote time to study and sermon-preparation. It reminded rectors not to dispense from reading at table too frequently, and to encourage some edifying conversation at the evening recreation. The 1904 visitation recess noted that porridge was not to be considered as a regular feature of the daily diet: the rule, reflecting southern Italian customs, made no provision for breakfast, and the usage introduced by the first continental Redemptorists was a cup of coffee and a roll.

John Magnier, as general consultor in Rome, continued to play the role of an *éminence grise* in the affairs of the province. Petty issues, such as

---

[16] Ecclesiastical administrator of a mission area that did not have a bishop.

[17] Boland, *Faith of our Fathers*, 128.

[18] Samuel J. Boland, 'Fr John Creagh in the Kimberlies' in *Old Limerick Journal*, 22 (1988), 151–3.

permission to smoke or whether the rector of Dundalk might require the novices to serve Mass against the wishes of the novice-master, were referred to his judgement. Some proponents of the language revival movement conducted their correspondence in Irish, which Boylan feared was a ploy to avoid the censorship of outgoing mail by the superior as the rule required. In an outburst of strong feeling, he blamed Magnier:

> You and our superiors in Rome are responsible for all this patriotism. The latitude given for Irish has caused all this trouble and some disunion among us. Some of the patriots misspent their time and called their neighbours offensive names because they were not enthusiastic about the Irish language.[19]

In response to a complaint 'that we are becoming increasingly secularised by attending at concerts, lectures and meetings held for outside temporal purposes', Boylan in 1902 forbade any Redemptorist to attend any gathering of the sort outside a church. Although he recognised that many of them might be in the promotion of worthy causes, he believed that religious life would be best promoted by avoiding them.

> I suppose meetings will be held in favour of home industries, in favour of fair play for Catholics and in favour of the Anti-Emigration League. It is with considerable reluctance that I say we must abstain from personal attendance at these meetings.[20]

For active men, such petty restrictions were irksome, and led to an unhealthy preoccupation with the inner life of a small closed community. Andrew Boylan's major achievement as provincial, however, is that he broadened the perspective of the province by accepting the first foreign mission. This will be considered in chapter nine.

---

[19] Andrew Boylan to John Magnier, 13 Jan. 1900, 13-D, RGAR.
[20] Andrew Boylan, letters to rectors, 19 July 1903, Box LB: BO 4, RPAD.

CHAPTER SEVEN

A Crown of Brothers

The complex Redemptorist world, with its travelling missionaries and strict monastic routine at home, would have been impossible to sustain without the presence of the brothers in the community. It was they who kept the monastery clean and in good repair, cooked the meals, ran the farm and, when the majority of the fathers were out on mission, ensured the continuance of the round of daily common prayer. They were the community's public relations officers who met callers at the front door and saw to it that the church was well ordered and fittingly decorated for the many celebrations that took place in it. They also nursed the sick and elderly members of the community and tended the guests who came to make retreats.[1]

The First Brothers
The first Redemptorist brothers in Limerick were as international a group as the priests. They included the Germans, Peter Franken, Joseph Sturm and Paul Faber; a Pole, Charles Moucha; the Belgian, Felician Dubuquoi, and Joachim Kelly. Walter Kelly was born of Irish parents in London in 1831. He trained as a colour printer or lithographer and entered Clapham as a postulant in 1853, receiving the name Joachim. He was professed in 1857 and would go on to become one of the founders of the Australian mission in 1882. He returned to England in 1894 suffering from ill-health and depression, having lost an eye while in Australia. He died in Clapham in 1898.

The first house at Bank Place was cramped and the high turnover of brothers in its early years may have been an attempt to distribute the small number of available brothers equally among the growing number of foundations in the two islands. Brothers Peter and Felician eventually became members of the new house at Courtbrack and maintained longer associations with Limerick. Peter was a quiet prayerful man, virtually unknown outside the community.[2] It was said of him that he had placed his tailor's sewing machine at an angle that allowed him to see the sanctuary lamp in the community

---

[1] For a summary of the history of the Redemptorist brothers see Santino Raponi, 'The Redemptorist Religious Brother', issued by the Commission for the Brothers, General Government CSsR, Rome, 1983.
[2] *Fifty Years at Mount St Alphonsus,* 75.

oratory as a constant reminder of the tabernacle. He prayed the rosary as he worked, counting the Hail Marys by associating each Hail Mary with a particular thought, so that he did not need to hold the beads in his hand. Born in Dottiginies in Belgium in 1816, Felician was professed at Tournay in 1841. In 1843, he accompanied Fr Louis de Buggenoms to the first foundation in England. He spent the next eleven years in England until he came to Limerick in 1855. Felician was the first of the province's great 'brother sacristans'. He began his work in the temporary church of Limerick, putting his skill in church decoration to good use especially in the elaborate Christmas crib that has remained a feature of Mount St Alphonsus to the present. He was responsible for training the altar boys: Felician's boys 'loved him and feared him. They felt how great was his joy when the rector gave them a feast: but they knew how exacting he was as to their conduct before, after and during the services in the church'.[3] Brother Felician died in 1897.

The Brothers of the New Irish Province
The Irish Province at its inception counted fourteen professed brothers and seven novice brothers, in addition to those who remained in England or were serving on the Australian mission. From 1898 until 1968, 184 men made profession as Redemptorist brothers. Of that number, forty-five were eventually dispensed from vows. The first upsurge in vocations to the brotherhood appears to have coincided with the canonisation of the Redemptorist brother, St Gerard Majella, in 1904, as twelve candidates received the habit over the next four years. The biggest influx of brothers' vocations came in the 1920s: thirty-five men entered between 1920 and 1929 (compared with 16, 30, 24 and 21 for the following four decades). In the years 1963 and 1964 there were sixteen novices in the brothers' novitiate in Dundalk, slightly outnumbering the choir-novices in Esker, where there were fourteen. The novitiate lasted two years for brothers: while choir novices spent only a year in the novitiate, their religious formation continued in the house of studies. There was a sharp decline in the number of brother candidates from the 1960s: very few professions are recorded in the 1970s and 1980s.[4]

Table 4. Brother Entrants by Decade, 1920s to 1960s

1920–1929	1930–1939	1940–1949	1950–1959	1960–1969
35	16	30	24	21

Source: Based on the Brothers' Profession Registrar, RPAD

---

[3] Ibid., 76.
[4] See Brothers' Profession Register: 'Album Fratrum Laicorum Prov. Hibernicae qui ab ejus erectione die xxviii Januarii 1898, Vota CSsR Emissere', Bro. 5, RPAD.

Before it was stabilised by the Code of Canon Law in 1918, the formation of brother members of clerical communities was relatively unstructured. The candidate was admitted to a community as a postulant. He continued to wear his lay clothes while receiving some initial instruction in the religious life. Older brothers taught him the skills he needed for his work – in the church, kitchen, dining room and farm or garden. This period lasted several months, or even years in some cases, until he received the habit and was admitted to the first novitiate of six months for more intensive spiritual training. He was then assigned to a community as a novice brother until he was recalled to the novitiate for the second novitiate in preparation for profession of vows. Until the Code introduced the distinction of temporary and final profession, the vows taken at the end of the second novitiate were for life.[5]

It is regrettable that comparatively little has survived in the archives about the early brothers. The *curricula vitae* of many of the earlier entrants have disappeared and it is necessary to depend on the brief necrologies or death notices that are usually perfunctory in personal details and offer a rather stock summary of the virtues of the deceased. It is possible, nevertheless, to sketch a collective portrait with a few broad strokes. The geographical area from which the brother candidates came was relatively wide, since many first encountered the Redemptorists in the course of parish missions. The majority were from a rural or small-town background: only four Dublin-born candidates figure in the seventy years covered by the brothers' profession book, while Limerick, Dundalk and Belfast are well-represented.

The first Irishman to be professed as a brother was James McVeigh. He was an Irish-speaker from County Tyrone, born in 1829, the year of Catholic Emancipation. He had been apprenticed to a shoemaker in Omagh, where he assisted at one of the earliest Redemptorist missions in 1852. During the renewal of the mission the following year, James approached Father van Antwerpen, the leader of the mission, to ask if he might be accepted as a brother candidate. His delicate health told against him and he was refused. James was insistent. He took off to Bishop Eton, the Redemptorist house in Liverpool, the following year to renew his request. Again, the answer was far from encouraging. He was directed to the Passionists, but his poor health forced him to leave after a short stay. He returned to Liverpool and took up his trade near the monastery. His persistence was repaid when he was eventually accepted. He was admitted to profession in 1860. As is often the case in monasteries, James, now Brother Stanislaus, never got the opportunity to practise his trade again. He served in the various Irish communities, dying

---

[5] As a result of this change in canon law, the novitiate had to be performed for at least one unbroken year. Eleven brothers were professed in 1918, some of whom had been in the habit for as long as seven years.

in Esker in 1909. Like Stanislaus, Michael Molloy was attracted to the religious life by hearing the preaching of the early missioners. Born in 1836, he was raised by an aunt and uncle in Ramsgrange, County Wexford and was expected to take over their flourishing business. Instead, he followed the stirrings of a religious vocation first experienced during the Ramsgrange mission of 1857. He was professed in 1863 and died in Dundalk in 1909.

While the lack of secondary education may have determined many young men to opt for the brotherhood rather than the priesthood, the majority of them came from small farming backgrounds, had been apprenticed to a trade or had some experience in running a business: in other words, they did not come from the very bottom of the social ladder. This study has revealed only one reference to a brother candidate who was unable to read and write: although he made little progress with his books, he proved to be a man of great energy in manual work. A few came from relatively affluent back- grounds. Andrew Tierney was born in Portumna in 1845. His family later settled in Thurles where his father set up in business as a shopkeeper and auctioneer. Andrew was being groomed to take over the family business and his talent as a public speaker drew him into the Fenian movement. Despite stiff opposition from his father, he entered the Dundalk community in 1882, receiving the religious name of Francis. He was followed some years later by two of his brothers, Daniel, who became a priest, and John, who tried his vocation as a brother, but returned home. In keeping with the formation arrangements for brothers in those days, Andrew was only admitted to vows eleven years after his entry. He spent the first years after the division of the provinces attached to the English houses but eventually returned to Ireland, dying in Limerick in 1919.

The most striking example of multiple vocations from the same family is that of the Gleesons. Five members of the family joined the Redemptorists over two generations. They were descended from a blacksmith and small farmer in Dualla, County Tipperary. One member of the family, Tom, joined the Irish regiment of the Papal Zouaves, founded in 1860 to support the Papal States in the struggle against the forces of Italian independence. He later emigrated to Australia where he was followed by other members of his family. John, born 1840, enlisted in the Royal Irish Constabulary at the age of twenty, but abandoned the policeman's life three years later in 1863 to join the Redemptorists as Brother Joseph. He received the habit in 1865 and was professed in 1874. He lived until 1916. Another brother, Daniel, professed in 1881, was a companion of Joachim Kelly in the foundation of the Australian mission, where he died in 1892. Timothy, born 1836, was the eldest of the six brothers: he married and inherited the family farm and smithy. On the death of his wife and facing trouble over land, Timothy went to join his brother Tom in Australia. He left behind two sons, Edmund, a student for the priesthood in St Patrick's College, Thurles, and a younger boy, who also showed signs of a priestly vocation but died in his teens. Timothy's two daughters entered the convent in Australia. With all his family provided for, his thoughts turned to the religious life. He was professed as a brother in 1901 at the age of sixty-four. His eldest son, Edmund, who had already entered the Redemptorists after a spell as a diocesan priest in Australia, had the unique distinction of being his father's rector and assisting him on his deathbed. The last son of the family, Thomas, had entered as Brother Kieran, a year before his father and made profession a year after him. Edmund went on to become provincial superior of Australia and bishop of Maitland, dying in 1956.

Stephen Moloney was born in Limerick in 1863. Despite his early promise as a scholar, his education was cut short by the death of his father and Stephen was forced to go to work as an apprentice tailor. He worked for two of the major outfitting firms in Limerick, Revington's and Cannock's. He was encouraged in his vocation by two of his sisters who had entered the Faithful Companions of Jesus in Laurel Hill. They were somewhat disappointed when, rather than joining the Jesuits to which they had been steering him, he opted for the Redemptorists. Despite stiff opposition from his mother, Stephen entered Mount St Alphonsus in 1886, taking the religious name of Brother Columba. He confessed that the greatest trial of his vocation was having to abandon his passion for rowing on the Shannon. It was ten more years before he was admitted to profession in 1896. He spent the forty years of his religious life attached to the different houses of the Irish province as the community tailor and died in 1941. Matthew O'Brien was born in Limerick in 1880, where he attended the Christian Brothers' school until he was sixteen. He began his working life as a clerk but soon made his way to Dublin and apprenticeship in the tobacco trade. The young man found the social world of *fin de siècle* Dublin, with its theatres and music halls, attractive, but fearing its dangers, he returned to Limerick to work with a local tobacconist.[6] At the prompting of his Redemptorist confessor, he married a local girl in 1908 but she died just five years later. Matthew was admitted to the Redemptorists in 1914. Taking the religious name of Matthias, he was professed in 1918 and died in 1932.

Patrick O'Sullivan, born in London in 1860, had been a fashionable West End tailor whose 'stylish appearance and well-trimmed moustache caused some amusement to those accustomed to the simple plain bearing of our lay-brothers' when he arrived in Limerick as a postulant.[7] Patrick's first trial

---

[6] Bro. Columba (Stephen Moloney), *Curriculum Vitae*, Personal File, RPAD.
[7] Bro. Patrick O'Sullivan, Necrology, Personal File, RPAD.

of Redemptorist life was unsuccessful and he was asked to leave. He made a second attempt shortly afterwards. He was professed during his final illness in 1896 and died the following year. Thomas Blackstock was also professed on his deathbed. He was born in Belfast in 1881. On the death of his father, he and his sister both decided to enter religious life, she going to the Daughters of Charity, he to the Redemptorists. Thomas received the habit in 1910 but took seriously ill shortly afterwards. From his not inconsiderable income, he purchased the Stations of the Cross for the new church in Clonard and left an additional £800 for the two side altars dedicated to Ss Alphonsus and Gerard.[8]

Two versions of the vocation story of John Cusack have survived in his necrology. The first is a rather plain account that he came to Esker to consult Fr Coyle about his vocation and decided to stay. The other, owing not a little to the story of St Gerard, is more colourful. Born in 1875 in Killinkere in County Cavan, John was set to inherit the family farm. Fearing opposition if he made his decision to enter religious life known, he left home in the middle of a bleak November night, and walked to the nearest railway junction, where he took the train for Athenry. From there he walked out to Esker but was unable to locate the monastery entrance. At the church door, he took out his pipe for a smoke. One of the neighbours came upon him puffing quietly. Learning of his proposal to enter, he told him that smoking a pipe would tell against him. John promptly handed over the pipe and went in search of the front door. Unused to doorbells, he knocked for some time, 'calling out in a neighbourly way, before the door to the fulfilment of his vocation was opened'.[9] He received the habit and religious name of Mel in 1911 and was the last to be professed under the old canonical form. He died in Esker in 1955.

Patrick Magee, born in 1902, left his home near Ballinamore, County Leitrim as a teenager to take up an apprenticeship in the bar trade in Belfast. As he notes in his *curriculum vitae*,

---

[8] There is little information about the Blackstock family in Redemptorist sources. According to the online version of the 1901 census, the family lived in Union Street, Belfast. Thomas was aged twenty in 1901. The archivists of the Daughters of Charity in Dublin and London have supplied the following details. Thomas's sister, Annie Teresa, was born in Belfast and baptised in St Mary's in 1876. Her father's profession is given as 'merchant' on her baptismal certificate. She entered the Daughters of Charity in 1909, receiving the religious name of Sr Veronica. She spent all her religious life in their houses in Scotland and England, and died at Mill Hill, London in 1959.

[9] Necrology: 'A Short Account of the Life and Death of Bro. Mel CSsR (John Evangelist Cusack), 1875–1955', Personal file, RPAD.

> Luckily enough for me, I had a brother in this black city before me who, I must confess, had often to admonish me and even at times hold a stiff rein or I might otherwise forget myself, and many a time, I kicked over the traces to get to see the famous stage-actors and comedians at the local theatres and picture-palaces.[10]

The young men were on the point of setting up their own business in the licensed trade, but the final asking price of the pub was beyond their means. This turned out to be a blessing, as the pub was destroyed during the Belfast pogroms of 1920 to 1922. Nothing daunted, Patrick now turned his attention to Irish dancing, at which he became quite proficient. He found spiritual encouragement in Clonard and entered as a postulant in 1922 at the age of twenty. Cuthbert, as he was henceforth known, remained an enthusiastic long-distance cyclist all his life, and it was ironic that he should die in 1971 as a result of a traffic accident near Limerick.

Brothers in Arms

Some of Cuthbert's contemporaries had taken part in nationalist politics. George Heydon (1885–1962) was an enthusiastic republican but eventually distanced himself from the movement as he had scruples about binding himself by an oath that did not have the approval of Church authorities. Michael Bradley (1898–1991) had fewer scruples. Like Cuthbert, he left home in Draperstown, County Derry in 1913 at the age of fifteen for an apprenticeship in the liquor trade in Belfast, with a promise from his father that he would set him up in business when he turned twenty-one. Michael joined the Irish Volunteers in 1916. The following year he was arrested and sentenced to nine months in prison.

> When the agreement entered into after the death of Thomas Ashe was broken, my three companions and myself started a hunger-strike. My companions who belonged to the southern area were removed to Dundalk. On being left alone in Belfast, I began to prepare for death. I did not expect to be released. That preparation was very bitter. I could not think of my past life: there was nothing in it for God. All I could offer was my death. The mission of 1913 [preached by Redemptorists in his home parish] and its consequences troubled me and I resolved that, if I came through the hunger strike, I would give the remainder of my life to helping the foreign missions. After this resolution, I no longer feared death. On 3 December, I was released and sent to the Mater Hospital [Belfast] where I remained for a month.[11]

---

[10] Bro. Cuthbert (Patrick McGee), *Curriculum Vitae*, Personal file, RPAD.
[11] Bro. Michael Bradley, *Curriculum Vitae*, Personal file, RPAD.

Michael's health had been severely undermined by his ordeal and he received the last rites twice in the following months. His first thought on his recovery was to apply to the recently-founded Maynooth Mission to China [later known as the Society of St Columban], but its founder, Fr John Blowick, told him they only accepted men for the priesthood, a path Michael had no desire to pursue. A chance meeting with a Redemptorist brother as he was praying one evening at Our Lady's altar in Clonard was decisive. As Michael prayed at the altar rails, the brother came behind him and whispered, 'Pray for a vocation.' The two fell into conversation and the brother brought him to see the rector. Michael entered on 23 August 1920. Despite the near-fatal outcome of his hunger strike, he lived until he was ninety-three. He spent many years as publications manager of the newly-founded *Redemptorist Record* and as assistant bursar at Clonard.

Patrick Brennan was born in Clontibret, County Monaghan in 1898. Reared in a staunchly Catholic and nationalist home, he joined the volunteer movement in 1918 and took part in several guerrilla actions. As a result of one raid, Patrick had to go on the run. On another occasion, his company was ordered to shoot an informer who had given evidence against a volunteer at a court-martial in Belfast.

> I did not like the idea of him being shot without giving him time to make his confession and I told this to the brigadier. He agreed, but it was turned down by the others. I then prayed to the Sacred Heart that his holy will would be done. I also said the rosary many times and when we entered his house, he was gone and was never seen in the country after.[12]

Patrick was present when his company took Castleblayney, County Monaghan. They held it for some hours and conducted an arms search. During an ambush on the Ulster Special Constabulary in South Armagh, two of his comrades were killed and another wounded. The Brennan family home was raided several times and Patrick had a few narrow escapes from arrest. In 1921, Patrick met the Redemptorists during the course of a mission in Derrynoose, County Armagh, as a result of which he decided to enter as a brother. Even the offer of the captaincy of his unit did not deter him. He resigned from the Republican Army on 9 October 1921 and entered the Redemptorists in Dundalk the following day, receiving the name of Brother Thaddeus. He died in 1983.

One man's spirit broke under the weight of the heavy-handedness of the regime. Brother Xavier – another Patrick Brennan – was assigned to the Philippines shortly after his final profession in 1924. By 1928, he was

---

12 Bro. Thaddeus (Patrick Brennan), *Curriculum Vitae*, Personal file, RPAD.

undergoing something of a crisis of vocation and applied for his dispensation to the superior general, Fr Patrick Murray. Murray replied kindly enough, advising him against making a hasty decision. Xavier alleged that

> ... there has been nothing only harshness and bitterness towards the lay-brothers since the death of poor Father Hartigan [the previous provincial] in the Irish Province and every bitterness possible put into action. And it is on the increase day by day, and the young Fathers are simply Tartars.[13]

A subsequent letter to the vice-provincial was more specific in its allegations: superiors were inaccessible, the younger members from their earliest days in the congregation were being trained in a kind of contempt for the brothers and how to keep them in their place. 'Is it a mortal sin to read the news-papers?', he asks. Xavier's isolation in the Philippines did not help matters and he took a very gloomy view of what lay in store for him if he returned to Ireland. In his superior's view, he was losing the run of himself and he would be happy to see the end of him, but the problem was how to dispose of the man while avoiding any scandal. If he returned to Ireland, it would cause talk; if forced to stay, there was a danger that he might run off and turn for help to some of the community's benefactors, bringing the entire affair to public notice. From the superior's point of view, the best outcome was quietly to arrange his passage to America where some members of his family had settled. A reading of this fragmentary correspondence suggests that Xavier had put his finger on a painful issue. It depicts a young man – he was still only thirty-one years of age – living in an alien culture, trapped in a depression with no way out and with little by way of support at hand. His request for a dispensation may have been a cry for help to the highest authority known to him. Murray seems to have replied with some show of kindness but Xavier's isolation needed something more humanly tangible and that was not forthcoming.

Reality of the Brothers' Life

While the rule claimed that all were equal as religious and members of the same religious family, in practice, 'a great gulf was fixed' between the two classes of Redemptorist. Fathers and brothers may have shared the same fasts and feasts, but they ate at separate tables in the refectory and recreated in different parts of the common room. Their place was fixed by an order of precedence that placed the most senior brother after the youngest cleric, no matter how long his service. The brothers had no voice in the election of delegates to chapters, whether provincial or general, could never hold any office in the community, even one that did not require the exercise of priestly

---

13 Undated letter, Bro. Xavier Brennan to Fr Patrick Murray, Personal file, RPAD.

orders such as bursar, or minister, as it was known among Redemptorists. They were distinguished by small but obvious details in the habit they wore: they did not wear a white collar on their habit like the clerics and wore a different form of winter cloak to their *zimarra* (a cloak with a shoulder cape). There were also many petty, if relatively minor, irritants. With his passionate interest in national affairs, Brother Thaddeus must surely have found particularly trying the regulation that forbade brothers to read the newspapers provided daily in the common room for the use of the priests. When his rector noticed that pages of it disappeared regularly, he suspected Thaddeus and reported him to the provincial.[14] Old Brother Peter's devotion to Our Lady led him to sign on as a member of Our Lady's confraternity in Clonard. His rector thought he should be doing spiritual reading and meditation in his room rather than attending the Sunday afternoon meetings. It could hardly have escaped the superior's notice that Peter was illiterate and unable to do spiritual reading, yet he publicly reprimanded him at the weekly chapter of faults and reported his 'headstrong' behaviour to the provincial.

Brother Xavier in the Philippines may have sounded a warning that all was not well in the lives of the brothers in Ireland. As will be seen in a later chapter, the 1920s and 1930s were difficult years that superiors attempted to control by a heavy-handed and literal interpretation of the rule. Some sense of how this impinged on the lives of the brothers might be gleaned by reading between the lines of a series of circular letters to them by Fr Hugo Kerr. Kerr was provincial from 1936 to 1947. No provincial before him had used such a direct means of communication as circular letters. In his first letter, Kerr sketched a picture of the ideal Redemptorist brother.

> As apostolic zeal abroad and study at home should be the chief characteristics of the Redemptorist priest, so humility, modesty and religious reserve, with diligent attention to domestic duties and love of cleanliness should be the characteristics of the Redemptorist brother. We require brothers who have good sense, and are efficient in their various charges. But over and above all, we require Brothers who are good religious, observant of the rule, humble, mortified, and devoted to prayer.[15]

Kerr put flesh on the ideal by appealing to the example of the recently-deceased Brother Columba, whose story was outlined above.[16] Columba, Kerr said, was above all, a man of prayer and when his sight began to deteriorate, 'the eyes of his soul were opened more and more to the things of God and the truths of eternity were seen more clearly by the light of faith.' He 'was deeply appreciative of all that was done for him and his beautiful spirit of

---

[14] Bro. Thaddeus, Personal file, RPAD.
[15] Letter to the Brothers, Jan. 1938, LB–K7, RPAD.
[16] Letter to the Brothers, 24 Feb. 1941, LB–K22, RPAD.

humility was troubled by the care and attention of which he was the object in his last illness'.

The publication of a new edition of the *Brothers' Manual of Prayers* was the occasion for yet another circular. Kerr stressed that the interior life was, if anything, more important for brothers than for priests:

> But though a Redemptorist Father who is not a spiritual man, may in a certain sense, be a successful preacher and save souls, a Redemptorist Brother who is not an interior man, since he only exercises the apostolate by means of prayer, cannot seriously hope to afford spiritual help to others. He will neither sanctify his own soul nor save the souls of others.[17]

Kerr suggests that the interior spirit was being undermined by the brothers in their dealings with one another and suggests that cliques or even bullying were not unknown: 'for some brothers, the early years in religious life have often been tragically unhappy by reason of want of kindness and consideration shown them.'

Kerr's final letter to the brothers was written shortly after one of them had been dispensed from vows, the fifth finally-professed brother to have left within the previous two years.[18] Such a high number of departures within a relatively short space of time should have signalled that all was not well. With the benefit of hindsight, one might suspect that the brothers were raising fundamental questions about the nature of their life, questions that would be faced more honestly twenty years later when the Second Vatican Council addressed the question of the authentic renewal of religious life. In the meantime, the only view of religious life ready to hand was a narrow one that assumed it was a hard way that made sense only when the entire package was accepted unquestioningly in the light of faith. To raise unsettling questions was to reveal a 'lack of a supernatural outlook'. Issues such as rights and equality that would appear perfectly natural after Vatican II seemed to Kerr suspiciously like socialism or a trade union mentality:

> Judged by a worldly standard, there are many points of regular observance that are 'hard' and many traditional practices of good Redemptorist Brothers are 'out of date.' If we let the spirit of the world into our religious life, we will be quick in the assertion of our rights, but slow in the performance of our duties. We shall be quick to claim what the rule allows, but slow to do what the rule enjoins. Insistence on our rights may suit a Trade Union Hall. But it is entirely out of place in a religious house.[19]

---

17 Letter to the Brothers, 1 Dec. 1945, LB–K50, RPAD.
18 Letter to the Brothers, 4 Aug. 1947, LB–K56, RPAD.
19 Ibid.

The contribution of the brothers to Redemptorist life in Ireland has been considerable, if often unacknowledged. They were often the permanent public face of the community. Always at home, meeting callers at the door, working unobtrusively in the church, training altar boys, they were the unsung heroes of the past century-and-a-half. Their role was a contemplative one that combined manual work with prayer and many men found it genuinely fulfilling and satisfying. Yet their role was often misunderstood and misinterpreted in a class basis that was out of place in Ireland. There is even a degree of confusion in the names applied to them in various editions of the Redemptorist rule. Santino Raponi states that the earliest term 'serving brothers' was changed to 'lay brother' in the 1921 edition of the rule, then to 'coadjutor brother' in 1947, until the simple term 'brother' becomes accepted in the post-Vatican II legislation.[20] There was an element of upstairs/downstairs in the petty distinctions that were created between ordained and non-ordained members of all religious orders. The emphasis on virtues such as humility, obedience, modesty and religious reserve assigned an exclusively passive role to the brothers. While their role as homemakers and providers was appreciated, they were given little that would allow them to develop the more active virtues or open to them the riches of the larger world of Catholic culture.

Some of these tensions, it might be said, go back to the earliest days of the congregation. Alphonsus, the founder, faced down some of his earliest brother companions when they tried to insist on equal rights with the priests in the details of the habit or the order of the day. Yet the story of the patron saint of the brothers, Gerard Majella, portrays him as someone who was actively involved in the life of the community around the monastery and often far beyond it. Outside of Ireland, some brothers found ways of using God-given talents, such as the artist Max Schmalzl (1850–1930) or the architect Gerard Knockaert (1845–1928), of the Bavarian and Belgian provinces respectively. Profound social change in Ireland in the latter part of the 1960s played a part in undermining the traditional understanding of the vocation of the brothers. Not least of these was the spread of free secondary education to all who wanted it. This in turn created new expectations. It was unlikely that the children of the 1960s would be content with the vocation of the brother as outlined by men like Hugo Kerr. The Second Vatican Council and the Redemptorist chapters that followed it would redefine the nature of life in religious community. Many of the brothers in the Irish province rose to that challenge but the overall decline in religious vocations over the past forty years has severely reduced their number: in 2009 there were only thirteen brothers and the youngest of them was sixty-two years of age.[21]

---

[20] Raponi, 'The Redemptorist Religious Brother', 3.
[21] *Conspectus Generalis* CSsR, 81, Rome: 2009.

CHAPTER EIGHT

New Houses: Clonard and Esker

With the foundation at Esker, County Galway in 1901, there was now a Redemptorist community in each of the four provinces of Ireland. Although Clonard and Esker have already been referred to, the circumstances that led to the foundation of each is given here in some detail.

Clonard Foundation

The expansion of Belfast as an industrial centre from the middle of the nineteenth century had led to a considerable growth in the Catholic population. Many of the new Catholic arrivals settled along the axis of the Falls Road leading westwards from the centre of the city.[1] Most Irish cities or larger towns outside of Ulster had one or more communities of friars – Dominicans, Augustinians and Franciscans – with long roots stretching back to medieval times. During the period of the Penal Laws, the friars managed to survive in the vicinity of their former houses, administering what pastoral service they could in unsettled times. In the aftermath of Catholic Emancipation in 1829, they re-established themselves in the towns and cities, where their churches provided Masses, confessions, sodalities and other forms of popular devotion alongside the parish churches, and helped to solve the problem of accommodating the large, urban Mass-going population. Relations between diocesan and regular clergy were sometimes tense: the events surrounding the Redemptorist foundation in Dundalk already recounted is a not-untypical example of how deeply feelings could run.

Belfast grew up as a town around the new castle founded by Sir Arthur Chichester in 1611. With growing industrialisation in the nineteenth century, it emerged as the second city in Ireland, outstripping Dublin in population briefly for a time in the early twentieth century. It received its urban charter in 1888. The first Catholic church to be built was St Mary's in 1784, catering for a congregation of less than 400. Five other churches were built in the course of the nineteenth century to cope with the increasing Catholic population. A. C. Hepburn has noted that 'nineteenth century Belfast was a city of migrants. In 1901, only an estimated 39 per cent of the population

---

[1] For a comprehensive account of the foundation of Clonard and its social setting, see Grant, *One Hundred Years with the Clonard Redemptorists.*

had been born in the city.'[2] The only other house of a clerical religious community in the city was that of the Passionists at Ardoyne, founded in 1868. As a condition for the foundation, the Passionists had been obliged to assume parochial responsibility for a large area of the northern part of the city, extending from the upper Shankill to the village of Ligoniel at the foot of Wolf Hill.

Dr Henry Henry was appointed bishop of Down and Connor in 1885. During his consecration retreat in the Redemptorist monastery at Dundalk, he intimated to the rector, Fr Edward O'Laverty, that he would welcome a foundation in Belfast. The bishop had a number of possible locations in mind, all in the western end of the city. O'Laverty was a former priest of the diocese of Down and Connor who had served in the city's oldest Catholic church, St Mary's, in Chapel Lane, prior to joining the Redemptorists. The prohibition on accepting parishes in the Redemptorist rule counted as an advantage in the bishop's calculations. It meant that their church would provide relief to the strained resources of the three existing parish churches along the Falls Road axis – St Mary's, St Peter's and St Paul's – without interfering with the vexed question of parish boundaries. Two of the bishop's proposed sites proved unrealistic. The first, at Cullingtree Road, was too small. The second, directly on the Falls Road, would have entailed moving the Bon Secours Sisters from the house they had been using as a convent and centre for their home nursing ministry since 1879. While the bishop was prepared to take such a step, the Redemptorists recognised that public sympathy would be with the sisters if they were 'evicted' to make way for an unknown community of men. They opted to make the best of the third site, Clonard House, the former home of the Kennedy family, members of the Belfast 'linen aristocracy'.

During October 1896, a general mission was preached in all the churches in Belfast by a team of fourteen Passionists and fourteen Redemptorists. Bishop Henry had agreed that the best time for the Redemptorists to commence their foundation would be at the end of the mission. Early on the morning of 1 November, two Redemptorists, Patrick Griffith and Walter Lambert, left St Patrick's presbytery in Donegal Street and walked across the city to Clonard to say the first Masses in the house. The house was empty, but they had sent ahead what was needed for the Mass. A picture of Our Lady of Perpetual Help hung over the kitchen table borrowed from a neighbouring house, which served as a makeshift altar. Griffith recorded the event later:

> We prepared the altar, placed our coats on the floor and commenced holy Mass … When I had vested and Mass commenced, we heard

2 A. C. Hepburn, *Catholic Belfast and Nationalist Ireland in the era of Joe Devlin, 1871–1934* (Oxford: Oxford University Press, 2008), 10–11.

footsteps hurrying over the gravel walk and by the time Mass was over and Fr Lambert had commenced his, the room in which we said Mass was almost full from panting and awe-struck people. The news had spread that priests were saying Mass in Kennedy's house. The remark of an old woman was eloquent. With hands raised towards heaven, she cried 'Glory be to God! Mass in Kennedy's house and in the old days, a Catholic crow daren't fly over it!'[3]

When his companion had concluded Mass, Griffith addressed a few words to the people, telling them that Our Lady of Perpetual Help had come to establish a new sanctuary among them. The neighbours took the new priests of Clonard to their hearts. Local women volunteered to scrub the house from top to bottom. Others contributed pieces of furniture to make the large empty house more like a home. Earnings in the linen mills, where most of the people worked, were at subsistence level, yet the mill-girls spontaneously set up the 'Pious Union of the Most Holy Redeemer', whose members promised to contribute 6d. or 3d. per week to support the community and to build the new church.

Clonard House had been set in an imposing parkland of fine trees, but already narrow streets of redbrick mill-workers' houses were encroaching on it and the rest of the estate would soon be staked out for the future Clonard Gardens, Kashmir Road and Bombay Street and their neighbours, until they in turn were cleared in a new development programme one hundred years later. With the arrival of two more priests in the community, four public Masses could be celebrated each Sunday in the temporary chapel, with congregations spilling over into the adjoining rooms. By Easter Sunday 1897 a temporary church with brick walls and a corrugated iron roof had been erected on the other side of Clonard Street on the site of the future monastery. It was known affectionately to the generation that had worshipped there as 'the wee tin chapel'. It could seat 800 people, but the head-count at one of the earliest Sunday Masses revealed a congregation of 1,100. Building work on the monastery according to the plans of the Belfast architect, John J. McDonnell, proceeded rapidly. Work began on 15 August 1898 and the community was able to move in by 2 May 1900. In keeping with the Redemptorist tradition of providing accommodation for retreatants, the monastery was larger than the needs of the community demanded. Some clerical wags in the city nicknamed it 'Griffith's folly' after its rector and founder.

---

[3] This and subsequent details about the early days of the Clonard foundation, unless otherwise accredited, are taken from the account of the foundation in Clonard Domestic Chronicle vol. 1, Domestic archives, Clonard.

As in Limerick, almost half a century earlier, the first retreat was held for the clergy of the diocese. Redemptorist financial circumstances had improved somewhat since the building of Limerick, but they were unable to defray the entire cost of the building alone and there were few wealthy Catholics in the Belfast area with money to invest in religious causes. The temporary church had cost £900 to build, apart from what had been spent on furnishings, and the monastery an additional £10,000. Bishop Henry was unwilling to allow the Redemptorists to undertake public fund-raising lest they compete with his own building projects, in particular the building of the new Mater Hospital on the Crumlin Road. It was January 1903 before he permitted Patrick Griffith to undertake a door-to-door collection to raise funds for the monastery and church, which brought in £1,500.

The services provided by the Clonard community won the loyalty of the people in the streets of little houses springing up around the monastery. Work in the linen mills began at 6.00 a.m., with a half-hour break for breakfast at 7.30 a.m. Many of the workers took advantage of this interval to hurry to Clonard for a quick Mass before returning to snatch breakfast as they worked. The same programme of confraternities for men and women as in Limerick was soon in place. Temporary transfer of the students to Clonard from Teignmouth in 1901 made it possible to conduct the liturgy with a great deal of splendour, with the students acting as servers and choir.

Construction of the permanent church did not proceed smoothly. Some of the local clergy prevailed on the bishop to scale down its proposed size by one bay. It was 1906 before permission to build was granted, and a further year before the contract was signed. The foundation stone was laid in October 1908 by the new bishop of Down and Connor, John Tohill. The builder's bankruptcy delayed it further and it was three years before the new church was completed for its solemn dedication on Rosary Sunday, 11 October 1911 by Bishop Tohill in the presence of the Irish-born superior general of the Redemptorists, Patrick Murray. Murray, a native of Donegal, had been prefect of students in Clonard, and later in Esker, from 1900 to 1907. He served as provincial from 1907 until he was elected superior general in 1909. The most striking feature of the interior of Clonard church was the enormous white marble and mosaic reredos of the high altar that is its focal point. Both it and the altar of the Sacred Heart were designed by a Belgian member of the community, Fr Henry Berghman, and executed by John Francis Davis of Cork.[4] The mosaics of the nativity and ascension were

---

4 Grant, *Clonard Redemptorists*, 64–6. Davis was a native of Kilkenny and had his studio in College Road, Cork. His works include the figures on the National Monument in the Grand Parade, Cork, and other monumental and ecclesiastical sculptures (details from the online *Dictionary of Irish Architects 1720–1940*, www.dia.ie/architects view/6027, accessed 29 November 2010).

designed by the German Redemptorist Brother, Maximilien Schmalzl. Berghman's design did not meet with the universal approval of his confreres, many holding that it was too massive for the space it occupied. Some of its upper parts were subsequently removed, and the simplified design which exists today was considered to be more harmonious. During renovations of the church in the late 1950s and again in the 1990s, proposals to remove the high altar on the grounds that it was out of keeping with the rest of the architecture of the church or the demands of modern liturgy were met with stiff resistance on the part of the people, as the archives of Clonard for the periods in question show.

The Foundation of Esker

The determined efforts to found a house in the west of Ireland have already been noted. While more numerous than in Ulster, clerical religious communities outside of the larger towns were still comparatively few in number. It was a poor region, and the slender economic base that might have supported religious communities alongside the diocesan clergy may have been one reason why the western bishops were reluctant to encourage religious communities to take up residence within their dioceses.[5] It is owing to the friendship between John Clancy, bishop of Elphin, and Andrew Boylan, the Redemptorist provincial, that the prospects of finding a house begin to materialise. Clancy had been professor of English at Maynooth while Boylan was bursar there. He was appointed to the diocese of Elphin in 1895 at the relatively young age of thirty-nine. Aware of Boylan's difficulties, Clancy suggested his mensal parish of Rosses Point, County Sligo as a location. In return for a foundation, the bishop expected the Redemptorists to assume responsibility for a home for sick and 'unemployed' priests (a euphemism for men with a drink problem). In 1877, Paul Cardinal Cullen had raised the possibility of establishing such a residence on the site of the Dominican convent at Esker with Laurence Gillooly, Bishop Clancy's predecessor in Elphin. Esker's remoteness appeared to recommend it, since Cullen believed that it was 'desirable that the fallen members of the clergy should be kept far away from cities, but they should be kept under severe and strict discipline. Esker appears suitable.'[6] Cullen believed that the Alexian Brothers would staff it, but when they proved unwilling, he entered upon negotiations with

---

[5] A request to make a foundation in Balla, made in 1894, was refused by Dr McEvilly of Tuam. See O'Laverty's request (18 Dec. 1894), and McEvilly's reply (1 Feb. 1895), Box D. 5.3, RPAD.

[6] Paul Cullen to Laurence Gillooly, 11 Jan. 1877, no. 270 in Peadar Mac Suibhne, *Paul Cullen and His Contemporaries*, vol. 5 (Naas: Leinster Leader, 1977). See also letters 278, 289 and 290 in this volume.

the Cistercian abbot of Mount Melleray. As the correspondence shows, the abbot drove a hard bargain and the proposal was abandoned.

The condition of running a hospice for priests was unacceptable to the Redemptorists, despite the bishop's argument that Alphonsus Liguori, when he was bishop, regularly sent his problem clergy to Redemptorist houses for a period of reflection and rehabilitation.[7] Finding a house in the west was proving so intractable that Boylan was prepared to grasp at any straw, even this unlikely one. He pondered the proposal with a combination of flexibility and the sound business sense of a former bursar, hoping that his Roman superiors would look benignly on his plight. He wrote to Patrick Griffith, one of the two men deputed to find a suitable house:

> What about Rosses Point? You know how anxious I am to have a house in the West, and although Sligo is not altogether in the West, I don't think that in our time we can get a better place ... The hospice is the great obstacle and you are placed between the bishop on one hand and Rome on the other. What is the very least the bishop will demand? What is the very most we can concede? Could we promise (a) daily Mass, (b) visit to the hospice by one of our Fathers at some time each day? (c) spiritual consolation and advice each day, (d) a boy (postulant or messenger) to make the beds, sweep, polish, coals, water etc. (e) the cooking and serving of meals – ordinary charge, say 35 shillings a week? Extra for wine, spirits, medical attention, special nursing etc. In no case could we allow the patients to have free access to our grounds. What about the sanitary arrangements and the water supply?[8]

John Magnier, the consultor general who oversaw Irish affairs in Rome, was unyielding on a precedent that ran so contrary to the rule, so the proposal died despite Bishop Clancy's pleading. A chance meeting on a train between Boylan and Bishop Clancy in the closing days of 1898 opened up another possibility. Both were on their way to the funeral of Bishop Thomas Nulty of Meath. Bishop Clancy told Boylan that the parish of Croghan, on the Elphin side of Carrick-on-Shannon, was vacant, and that he was prepared to allow the Redemptorists to set up a house there before he appointed the next parish priest.

Boylan travelled to Carrick-on-Shannon with Michael Somers a few days later. They found a suitable site for a future monastery on high ground about fifty yards from the bridge. In the meantime, they leased the vacant Killukin House a few miles outside the town as a temporary residence for a mission community. The nucleus of a community was in place by the end of January

---

[7] John Clancy to Michael Somers, 10 Feb. 1898, Box D.5, RPAD.
[8] Andrew Boylan to Michael Somers, June 1898, Box D, RPAD.

1899. Although the site for the future monastery was technically within the diocese of Elphin, it was only a few yards away from the Shannon that separated it from the neighbouring diocese of Ardagh and Clonmacnois. This made it altogether too close for the comfort of either the parish priest of Carrick-on-Shannon or the bishop of Ardagh, Joseph Hoare.

Bishop Hoare immediately lodged a vigorous protest with both Bishop Clancy and Boylan. More seriously, he submitted his complaint for decision by the Congregation of Propaganda in Rome. Boylan stubbornly proceeded to stake out the land for the new church and monastery. By June the following year, 1900, Rome ruled that the Redemptorists might build halfway between the parish churches of Drumlion and Carrick-on-Shannon, but no nearer. Although Bishop Clancy renewed his offer of Rosses Point without the condition of running the hospice, Boylan was anxious to extricate himself as quickly as possible from what had proved an embarrassing debacle.

Boylan had in any case already opened negotiations for the purchase of the former Dominican priory at Esker, near Athenry. The first time Esker was mentioned as a possible home for Redemptorists seems to have been in 1892. Fr Michael Geoghegan recalled that when Bishop John Healy of Clonfert was in Dundalk to preach at the opening of the church in that year, on hearing that the Redemptorists were anxious to have a foundation in the West, had remarked: 'There is Esker, take it.'[9] Healy had bought Esker from the Dominicans in 1889 with a view to using it as a diocesan college. The inaccessibility of Esker made it unsatisfactory for that purpose and the college was eventually transferred to Garbally Park, near Ballinasloe. Boylan purchased the house and lands from Healy in August 1900, paying £5,500 for the buildings and land, more than four times the original asking price, with an additional £2,250 to buy out the interest of the landlord, William Daly. He took possession in May 1901. The following day, he and Michael Somers said Mass in Esker church. This was the first time Boylan had seen the property. He was disheartened by the chaotic disarray and run-down state of the Esker buildings. It had suffered a disastrous fire in the last days of its Dominican occupation, and the diocese of Clonfert had done little by way of repair.

On 31 August 1901 the sanctuary lamp in the oratory at Killukin House was extinguished and the community made its way to its new home in Esker. The first community was composed of Frs Michael Somers, Edmund Langly, Richard Stack and Patrick Cussen along with Brs Bartholomew Lally, Thaddeus O'Connor and the novice brother, Casimir O'Gorman. They were joined some weeks later by Frs Patrick Sampson, Henry Berghman and John Creagh. The long search to find a home in the west of Ireland was finally at an end.

---

[9] Michael Geoghegan to Michael Somers, 6 Mar. 1895, Box D, RPAD.

'They shall spend their lives among books' (*Redemptorist Rule*). Fr Paddy O'Donnell, historian of the Province, in the library of Clonard Monastery. *Photograph courtesy of the late Liam McAreavey.*

Fr Louis de Buggenoms, first superior of the Redemptorist temporary residence at Bank Place, Limerick, 1853.

Fr Robert Aston Coffin, first provincial of the Anglo–Irish Province and later Bishop of Southwark.

Fr William Plunkett was the first Irish-born Redemptorist to be professed for the Anglo–Irish Province.

A group of early Redemptorist missioners includes two Irishmen (Frs Thomas Doyle and John Connolly); a Dutchman (Fr John Van der Aa); a German (Fr John Nicholas Schneider), and a Belgian (Fr Francis Theunis).

Fr Patrick Griffith was rector of Clonard Monastery, Belfast.

Fr Thomas Bridgett founded the Archconfraternity of the Holy Family in Limerick.

John Quin, a Limerick merchant who donated the bell tower and a peal of bells to the Redemptorist church in Limerick.

Cartoon of William Monsell MP, later Lord Emly. Monsell was a supporter of the first Redemptorists in Limerick.

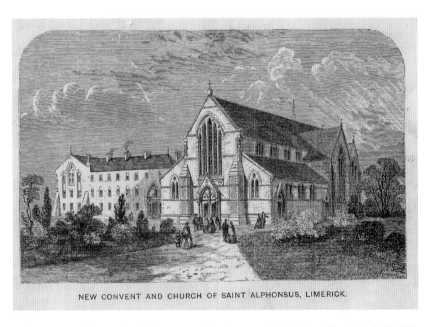

NEW CONVENT AND CHURCH OF SAINT ALPHONSUS, LIMERICK.

Earliest picture of Mount St Alphonsus, circulated as part of the fund-raising drive for building the church and monastery. The bell tower was added later.

Juvenists with their teacher. A preparatory college for secondary education of candidates was opened in Limerick in 1884.

Irish and English student community, House of Studies, Teignmouth, 1896.

At the student holiday house in Clifden, County Galway *c.*1958. (*Left to right*): Br Michael Brown receives a pitch and putt prize from Fr Michael Baily, while Br Patsy Cunning looks on.

Fr Alex Reid gives his first blessing to his mother.

Ordination liturgy in Cluain Mhuire, Galway, 1968.

Young Redemptorists and Redemptoris
after profession ceremony, Dublin, 201

Fr Stiofán Conneely with parishioners attending mission, Tully, County Galway, *c.*1930.

Fr Stiofán Conneely at mission on Inis Meáin, Aran Islands, *c.*1930.

Parishioners on way to mission in Carna, County Galway pass the mission stalls selling religious goods.

Fr John Gorey addresses the people at the close of a mission while the poitín stills burn. The burning of stills was a feature of some missions in the west of Ireland in the late 1920s and early 1930s.

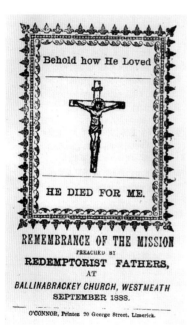

During missions, small leaflets containing the main points of the preaching and daily prayers were distributed. This one is from a mission at Ballinabrackey, County Westmeath, in 1888.

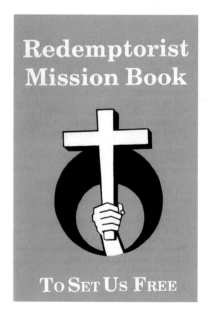

Cover of a mission prayer book from 1990 containing prayers and hymns.

Confraternity procession, Belfast, 1958. Three large processional cars were made in honour of joyful, sorrowful and glorious mysteries of the rosary.

Benediction in the monastery garden given by Cardinal Van Rossum to celebrate the diamond jubilee of the Limerick confraternity in 1928.

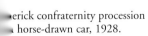

Limerick confraternity procession, horse-drawn car, 1928.

Gathering for a confraternity
procession in Limerick, 1928.

Men's confraternity, Clonard prepare
to depart in procession *c*.1924.

Past and present directors with secretaries of Limerick and Clonard confraternities
c.1947. The four Redemptorists in the photograph are (*left to right*): Frs Con
Mangan, James Reynolds, David Harris and James Cleary.

Fr John Doyle CSsR was a chaplain
in France in the First World War.

Fr Harry Potter CSsR in chaplain's
uniform during the First World War.

Four Irish Redemptorist chaplains who served in the Second World War.
(*Standing, left to right*): Frs Peter Mulrooney and Joseph Tronson.
(*Sitting, left to right*): Frs Daniel Cummings and Luke Hartigan.

The Devil at Dances?, a pamphlet that originally appeared as a series of articles in the *Redemptorist Record*.

The Perpetual Novena was established in Clonard by Fr Matthew Meighan CSsR, chaplain to the American forces in Belfast

The Perpetual Novena in Clonard attracted large crowds several times every Thursday.

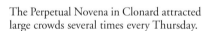

Postcard showing detail from Clement's Retreat House at A County Down, which opened in

Br Felician Dubuquoi, a Belgian, was a member of the first community assigned to Limerick in 1853. He spent more than forty years as sacristan in Mount St Alphonsus.

Photograph, dating from the nineteenth century, of a brother engaged in carpentry in Limerick.

Br Jerome (Hugh Murray) prepares chalice for Mass, while novice brothers Raymond (Eamonn Kavanagh) and Majella (Martin Carey) cut communion hosts.

Br Martin Mulholland at work in the reception office, St Joseph's Dundalk.

Br Gregory (Alphonsus Doran) at prayer in his room.

Fr John Torney (novice master) receives the vows of Br Kevin McDonnell. Brs Raymond (Eamonn Kavanagh) and Majella (Martin Carey) serve.

Early Redemptorists in the Philippines.
(*Standing, left to right*): Frs Thomas O'Connor, Matthew O'Callaghan, Br Hugh King, Frs Cyril Cahill, Edward Gallagher, Br Colman McHugh.
(*Seated, left to right*): Frs John Doyle, Edmund Gleeson, William Byrne.

Frs John Anthony and Stan Mellett at the close of a village mission in Madras State, early 1960s.

Fr Peadar Duffy with congregation at the close of a mission in a Filipino barrio, 1954.

Redemptorists at the Eucharistic Congress of 1932. Group at front of old Marianella includes Archbishop Nicholas Charnetskyi CSsR (centre front row), who celebrated the Congress's pontifical Byzantine liturgy. He died a martyr's death in 1959 and was beatified in 2001.

Redemptoristines in cloister garden of new monastery in Drumcondra, 2010.

Little has survived by way of a first-hand account of the Redemptorists' arrival in Esker since the domestic chronicle does not begin until 1903. A letter in the general archives in Rome from Michael Somers gives the impression that they were less than impressed by the conditions they found there. The house had lain empty for some time. It was rat-infested, many of the windows were broken, and it would need a thorough rebuilding operation before it would be habitable by a religious community.[10] The small and unpretentious church, built in 1845, was in a similar state of disrepair, with its walls bulging outwards and its roof threatening to collapse. Since the monastery was to become a house of studies, the sanctuary needed extending to accommodate more solemn liturgies such as ordinations. In the course of extending the sanctuary, a fine stained-glass window of Our Lady of Perpetual Succour, which had been installed by the Dominicans, was removed and put in storage in the cellar. It would only see the light of day again when it was placed on the stairwell of the new novitiate wing almost fifty years later, in 1949. The church also needed a new high altar which was ordered from Rome at a cost of £350; the two main side altars in marble were the work of the same Davis who did similar work in Clonard, at a cost £120 each. Four additional wooden altars were erected in the body of the church. Benefactors of the new foundation included the Misses Margaret and Mary Anne Kelly of Limerick, who added to their longstanding generosity to the Redemptorists by donating the altar of Our Lady of Perpetual Succour, while the Misses Prendergast of Dublin gave £800 for a burse 'for a deserving young student without means who has a true vocation to the priesthood in the Redemptorist Order'.

On 1 May 1903, the community moved into the college block – later the retreat house wing – to allow building to commence on the central block. The architect was John J. McDonnell of Belfast, and the contractors were McNaughten Brothers of Randalstown, County Antrim. The shell of the new house of studies was largely complete by Easter 1905 and the students were due to take up residence at the beginning of the new academic year in August. With such a recent outlay on two new buildings in Clonard and Belfast, little money was available for books for the library. An appeal was circulated to religious houses to donate any duplicate copies of books they might have in their libraries. The students were greeted on their arrival with a chain of bonfires lighted by the local people from Athenry station to the new monastery. Esker would remain a student house until the opening of Cluain Mhuire, Galway in 1940.

---

10 Michael Somers to John Magnier, 14 Sept. 1901, XIII–D, RGAR.

CHAPTER NINE

First Foreign Mission

Redemptorist interest in the foreign missions can be traced back to the founder, Alphonsus de Liguori.[1] While preparing for ordination, and for several years after, Alphonsus had lodged in the Chinese College in Naples, a recently-founded institute for the education of priests for that mission.[2] In his original draft of the rule, he had inserted a vow to go on the foreign missions if required but this was removed by the Roman redactors of the final version approved of 1749. In 1785, he asked for volunteers to undertake missionary work in what is present-day Iraq, where the Holy See was preparing for reunification with the Assyrian Church, but the mission did not materialise.[3]

The Redemptorist congregation was too preoccupied with the question of its survival throughout the nineteenth century to give much thought to foreign missions. There were, nevertheless, fitful attempts at foreign missionary work, especially in the Americas in the middle years of the nineteenth century. The Redemptorists went to the United States of America in 1832, chiefly to undertake the pastoral care of German-speaking emigrants. Fr John Baptist Swinkels, who had been provincial of the Dutch province at the time of the foundation of Limerick, spent the latter part of his life, from 1865 onwards, as vicar apostolic of Surinam (Dutch Guyana). A diocesan priest who joined the Redemptorists in Surinam was Peter Donders (1807–87) who had devoted his life to the care of the lepers. He was beatified in 1982 by Pope John Paul II. Nicholas Mauron, the superior general, regarded foreign missions as he regarded running parishes – namely, something of a necessary evil that distracted the members from the congregation's basic activity of preaching parish missions. Missions were a tool of renewal, not of 'first evangelisation' and it was in keeping with this sense of

---

[1] For an outline of the history of Redemptorist foreign missions, see Samuel J. Boland, 'The Redemptorists in the Foreign Mission Fields' in *SHCSSR*, vol. XXXII, no. 1 (1984), 127–51.

[2] Jones, *Saint of Bourbon Naples*, 66.

[3] Circular letter, 18 July 1758. English translation in *Letters of St Alphonsus Maria de Liguori, Doctor of the Church, bishop of Saint Agatha and founder of the Congregation of the Most Holy Redeemer*. Ed. Eugene Grimm. Centenary edn, vol. XVIII, 507–8. (New York: Benziger, 1891–1896).

the proper place of Redemptorists in the scheme of things that the Australian mission was undertaken. That is to say, it was not the work of 'first evangelisation' or the difficult planting of the seeds of the gospel but the renewal of the faith of those who had already been baptised.

The first sign that attitudes to missionary work were changing came with the general chapter of 1894. It issued a tentatively-worded statement that 'missions to the pagans are not opposed to the purpose of the Congregation but are in keeping with it.' According to the official *acta*, or minutes of the chapter, the passing of this declaration was greeted with applause by some delegates.[4] In the light of the story to be told here, one of those applauding may have been Andrew Boylan, delegate of the London province, of which Ireland was then a part. Almost ten years later, Boylan would find the opportunity to put the declaration into practice.

East or West?
In 1903, Boylan was called to Rome to discuss the possibility of the Irish province replacing the Belgian Redemptorists in Antigua in the West Indies. News of the plan leaked out in Ireland but it received little support from the provincial's advisors. They believed that they were already over-extended from their commitment to the Australian mission, and protested vigorously that another foreign mission would take the best of the active priests, and that the fledgling province would depend on young, inexperienced missioners who would be left pretty much to fend for themselves. Boylan was not enthusiastic about the West Indies in any case, for he was already contemplating a mission to the Philippine Islands.[5]

The Philippines had been in turmoil for much of the previous decade. The two years of nationalist revolt from 1896 to 1898 had been followed by a change in colonial administration when the islands were ceded to the United States at the end of the Spanish–American war in 1898. Some sections of the Philippine clergy had become militantly anti-Spanish and formed a breakaway national church under the leadership of Fr Gregorio Aglipay in 1902. With the coming of American rule, the Philippines experienced a new wave of Protestant missionary activity. It was considered imperative to find

---

[4] 'Acta Capituli 1894', no. 1352, in *Acta Integra Capitulorum Generalium CSsR* (Rome: 1899).
[5] For the history of the Redemptorist Philippine mission on which this chapter is substantially based, see Michael Baily CSsR, *Small Net in a Big Sea: The Redemptorists in the Philippines 1905–1929* (Cebu: University of San Carlos, 1978). Michael Baily was by training both a historian and a biblical scholar. He spent some years teaching in the Philippines where he began the research for this study based on archival sources in Ireland, the Philippines and Australia, as well as on interviews with survivors of the early generation of Redemptorists in the Philippines.

new ways of ensuring the vitality of the Catholic Church in the archipelago, an issue that was addressed by Pope Leo XIII in the Bull, *Quae Mari Sinaico* (1903) reorganising the Filipino hierarchy. The Maltese Benedictine, Archbishop Ambrose Agius, was appointed apostolic delegate in 1904 with the commission to oversee the work of reorganising the church in the islands. He made his consecration retreat with the Redemptorists in Rome, during which he confided to the superior general, Fr Matthias Raus, his hope that the Redemptorists might join congregations such as the Scheut and Mill Hill Missionaries in making good the deficit of clergy left by the departure of the Spanish friars.

Boylan's interest in the Philippines was sparked by his conversations with two former Maynooth colleagues, Archbishop Thomas Fennelly of Cashel and Bishop John Clancy of Elphin. Both of them had entertained Thomas Hendrick, who had been consecrated bishop of Cebu in August 1903 and shortly afterwards had visited Ireland in search of nuns to staff the schools of his diocese. These conversations sparked something in Boylan for he invited Archbishop Agius to visit Ireland before leaving for the Philippines. Boylan suggested that he was willing to take the opportunity of an impending visitation of the Australian houses to see the situation in the islands for himself and even to be among the first volunteers. While welcoming Boylan's goodwill, Agius attempted to moderate his enthusiasm:

> From your letter, I can gather that you are full of the spirit of God and the like of you is what the church out there needs, but much as I should love to have you personally, I fear the climate would be too trying at your age – but you should certainly visit the Philippines in your tour. You will be able *de visu* [from sight] to see the needs of the place, and it will touch your good apostolic heart to make speedy provision for us to restore all things in Christ.[6]

Boylan departed for Australia in November 1904, breaking his journey in Rome to attend golden jubilee celebrations for the declaration of the dogma of the Immaculate Conception. He spent most of the next year in Australia and New Zealand. In December 1905, with Fr Thomas O'Farrell, the Visitor to Australia, as his companion, he continued on to the Philippines, arriving in Manila on Christmas Eve. By January 1906, they had reached Cebu, anxious to make the final decision about the foundation.

Despite the urgency with which he had described the situation while in Ireland, Bishop Hendrick was not at home to welcome his guests. When he finally appeared, he was slow to get down to the practical details of the foundation. On 15 January 1906, Boylan forwarded Hendrick's formal

---

6 Ambrose Agius to Andrew Boylan, Cebu, Box 1, RPAD.

application for a foundation to Rome. On the back of a copy of the letter he had received from the apostolic delegate, Archbishop Agius, Boylan drafted his reasons for accepting the foundation. They included the dire pastoral situation in Cebu, where there were almost two million Catholics with only one priest per eleven thousand souls. He considered the climate to be good; the language presented little difficulty and in any case, knowledge of English was widespread. Although the present situation was a grave one, the people were good and an upturn in the Church's fortunes seemed likely.

As events were to prove, Boylan's optimism was ill-placed on virtually every count. The shortage of clergy in the Philippines would eventually pose serious problems for the Redemptorists and they would be faced, like it or not, with the question of accepting a parish. While Bishop Hendrick did not insist absolutely on their taking permanent charge of a parish, he intimated nevertheless that it would be necessary to assume 'temporary charge' of the district around their monastery, while still leaving some members of the community free to go on missions. Boylan's assessment of the climate and language difficulties proved to be excessively naive: both were to take their toll on the enthusiasm of the first group of Redemptorists from Ireland.

Boylan formally accepted the foundation in Cebu in March 1906. He wasted no time in calling the pioneering band from Ireland. They were the priests Patrick Leo, John Creagh, William O'Sullivan, Matthew O'Callaghan and Thomas Cassin, along with two brothers, Casimir O'Gorman and Eunan Graham. The seven left in May, laden with the equipment to the tune of £800 they believed they would need in setting up their new home.

Realities of Missionary Life
Andrew Boylan took formal possession of the *convento* of Nuestra Señora de la Regla at Opon on the island of Mactan, off the coast of Cebu. Auspiciously, for an Irishman with missionary dreams, this event took place on St Patrick's Day 1906. He held the fort with the Filipino priest, Fr Vicente Roa, until his confreres arrived on 30 June. The real difficulties were, however, only just beginning.

Bishop Hendrick proved again to be singularly unhelpful. He failed to communicate to Fr Roa that a new arrangement was at hand. When the Irish group arrived on 30 June, Roa was still in possession of the *convento* with his staff of twelve houseboys. The Irishmen crowded into the two remaining rooms but at least each of them had a bed. When Fr Roa's new appointment arrived the following week, a crowd of relatives and friends appeared to help him move. They stripped the *convento* from top to bottom. The beds, crockery and cutlery the missioners had been using all disappeared: only determined opposition by the Irish men prevented the water tank, the only source of drinking water, from following suit. For several days, dinner consisted of ham sandwiches washed down with water and a little wine. There were days when even bread was not available. A boycott lasting several months was effectively enforced against the new priests by the locals, angered by the departure of Roa. Food and other supplies had to be brought in by boat from Cebu across the bay.

Little by little, matters improved. Another Filipino priest helped them to begin the study of the language. By the end of the year, they were kept busy preaching, hearing confessions, conducting marriages and going on sick calls, but difficulties both personal and pastoral were already looming.

In his history of the Redemptorist mission in the Philippines, Michael Baily has described Boylan as 'the prince of the play' whose warm humanity helped his younger confreres to settle into the new mission.[7] Although sixty-five years old and suffering from diabetes, Boylan's energy and good humour lifted the spirits of his companions with impromptu parties, even when supplies of basic food stuffs were running low. Fr Patrick Leo, the prospective superior, who was due to take over when Boylan returned to Ireland, had spent much of his priestly life teaching philosophy and lacked Boylan's spontaneous humanity. He had a logical, orderly mind, but was inflexible and stiff. As details began to trickle out of how badly Boylan had mishandled the negotiations with Bishop Hendrick, Leo was appalled: 'I had a very high idea of Fr Provincial's business capacity until I came to Cebu', he wrote. 'I honestly think he had bungled the affair outrageously.'[8] John Creagh, the director of the Limerick confraternity at the time of the anti-Jewish disturbance in 1904, had recorded enthusiastically the sights and sounds of the journey to the Philippines.[9] He proved unable to withstand the pressure of life in Opon, however, and was sent to Australia within nine months of arrival. Events would prove that of the remainder of the group, Tom Cassin and Matthew O'Callaghan, would be the real architects of the Filipino mission.

Although Andrew Boylan wanted to remain in the Philippines 'to do something for Jesus before I die', Patrick Leo was determined to ship him home as soon as he decently could. Boylan departed for Ireland at the end of 1906, calling at Rome to report progress on the new foundation. Unexpected news awaited him there: he was to be appointed bishop of his native diocese of Kilmore. He arrived back in Limerick in January 1907. On 19 March of that year, the triennial nominations arrived, appointing Patrick Murray provincial of Ireland and one month later, Boylan's appointment to the

---

[7] Baily, *Small Net*, 12.
[8] Cited by Baily, *Small Net*, 15.
[9] John Creagh, 'Account of the Voyage on board the SS Lopez y Lopez from Limerick to Cebu, 1906', Cebu Box 1.1, RPAD.

diocese of Kilmore was announced. His time as bishop there was destined to be comparatively short. He collapsed during the liturgy of his episcopal consecration and the ceremony had to be suspended for a half an hour to allow him to recover. Despite the foreboding of those present, he survived for three more years, administering his diocese in a spirit of quiet devotion. He died on 25 March 1910. It is a tribute to Boylan's peaceable temperament that the celebrant of his funeral liturgy was Bishop Joseph Hoare of Ardagh and Clonmacnois, with whom he had such a bitter dispute over the proposed foundation at Carrick-on-Shannon.

After Boylan

More important than personal differences of opinion and temperament were the serious ideological and theological ideas that went hand in hand with creating a new missionary apostolate from the beginning. Missioners in the early twentieth century did not have the opportunity of knowing foreign cultures, even superficially, through the media of television or film. People entering new cultures commonly experience a period of disorientation described in modern times as 'culture shock'. If the concept was unknown in the early years of the twentieth century, the reality was only too familiar. There was little, in any case, that would have prepared the Redemptorists for what they met on landing in Opon. They belonged to a congregation and church that had practically no trans-cultural missionary experience. The Irish church may have boasted of its 'spiritual empire' overseas but it was confined for the most part to the English-speaking lands of North America and Australia where the majority of Catholics were Irish by descent, at most a generation or two removed from the old sod. Irish missions in Africa and Asia were still a comparative rarity. There was a small 'Maynooth Mission to India' from about 1838, and an Irish presence in the Cape of Good Hope from about 1837. These missions attracted some Irish communities of sisters. Small numbers of Irish members of missionary societies, like the Congregation of the Holy Ghost (the Spiritans) and the Society for African Missions, worked with their continental brethren in Africa, but it was only in the early twentieth century that the Irish Church emerged as a cohesive, self-confident institution capable of directing its energies beyond its own diaspora.[10]

Although Irishmen might have been expected to have some sympathy for the people's desire for independence, Filipino nationalism was tinged with a suspicion of church control in a way that Irish nationalism was not. The Redemptorists found themselves at odds with, and suspicious of, the local leaders of the Catholic Centre that controlled much of the church life on the

---

[10] See Edmund Hogan, *The Irish Missionary Movement: A Historical Survey 1830–1980* (Dublin: Gill and Macmillan, 1990).

island. The shortage of priests made it imperative to assume *de facto* pastoral authority around the house. Michael Baily has observed that, in the critical years of the early twentieth century, the church in the Philippines was making a fresh start. In such a situation, it might be an advantage for the missionary to be a learner. It was more problematic for this group of Redemptorists, some at least of whom had come to bring to a new land the traditions of their order. One of these traditions was a profound suspicion of the appropriateness of parish work for Redemptorists.

A wide gulf of sensibility separated Andrew Boylan and Patrick Leo. Boylan was in many respects a natural foreign missionary who lost his heart to the Philippines the moment he had heard of the spiritually-impoverished state of the country. He had been led to the islands by the belief that the mission apostolate could contribute much to the revitalisation of the Church. As a latecomer to the Redemptorists, he was less wedded to the idea that missions were the only acceptable form of Redemptorist apostolic life. If the glory of God and the salvation of souls were to be advanced by other means dictated by pastoral needs, then so be it. Patrick Leo saw things more in black and white terms: as far as Redemptorists were concerned, parish work, even in a country as deprived of priests as the Philippines, was the 'abomination of desolation'.

After Boylan's departure, Patrick Leo's inflexible temperament put him even further at odds with the people. He had little instinctive feel for the ways of the Filipinos, especially when they offended his notions of propriety or the proper observance of the rule. The exuberant air of the Filipino fiesta was a sore trial for him as the people assumed the new padres would continue to allow them to celebrate in their traditional fashion.

> What touches us Redemptorists most closely is that during the fiesta we are supposed to keep open house, to allow men and women in through all parts of the monastery and regale them lavishly and even let them sleep in the monastery, the women on the ground floor … we should require ten or twelve fathers for the parish alone to do the work as we think fit.[11]

On the first Easter, he suspended at short notice the dramatic Holy Week processions which were a feature of the Spanish heritage of popular piety in the islands. The people believed the foreign *paris* [priests] had little time for them. The distance was further compounded by the language problem. Like many expatriates in trying situations, they looked for human support to the handful of English-speaking Catholics, most of whom were American in the colonial service or business, with the occasional Irish or English family, but failed to notice what message this was sending to the local population. A local

---

[11] Baily, *Small Net*, 27.

newspaper account, while generally sympathetic to the Redemptorists, noted that the Fathers seemed to be keeping them at bay.

> The Oponites wondered that we were allowed to enter the parlour of the Fathers, for they say that since their coming, not so much as one man of the place has entered it. We understood the reason for the prohibition to enter, it was because they do not understand English, for the Fathers do not well understand the Visayan. English is their language.[12]

Patrick Leo's appeal for reinforcements brought him four more priests and a brother to replace Boylan and Creagh. The handful of missions undertaken proved to be so unsuccessful that some of the community drew the inevitable conclusion that missions, as they were known in Ireland and Australia, would never work in the Philippines. Leo returned to Ireland in 1909 to report on the Philippine experiment and to take part in a provincial chapter preparing for a general chapter in Rome the following year. His report was bleak. He recommended withdrawal as soon as it could be decently done and he claimed to have all his community behind him but one. When the general chapter elected Patrick Murray, a friend of Leo's, as superior general in April 1909, it looked as though the days of the mission in Opon were numbered.

The dissenter to Leo's proposal to withdraw from the Philippines was Tom Cassin, the youngest member of the community. Cassin had, symbolically and literally, put down roots in Opon within days of his arrival by planting a crop of vegetables in the garden. In 1908, he wrote an outspoken letter to Patrick Griffith, the Irish provincial, arguing that it was necessary to keep the parish for two reasons. First, income from the parish would be vital for financing future missions. Second, given the dearth of priests in the islands, giving it up so soon after arrival would be an occasion of scandal. Half-hearted measures, he argued, such as a holding period for a year or two, would serve no purpose as it gave them no incentive to get down to diligent study of the language. He regarded Patrick Leo as an excellent priest but considered that his personality flaws told against his ability to work in the Philippines. Cassin's plea also had the support of the apostolic delegate, Archbishop Agius, who threatened to go over the superior general's head if necessary to save the mission. Despite his coolness towards the Philippine mission, Murray backed down and told the Irish provincial to give it a further trial of five years. Leo was called to Rome to take up more congenial work in the general archives. Some of the others who were finding life in the Philippines too difficult returned to Ireland or went on to Australia.

---

12 Translation of a clipping that appeared in a local newspaper, *Camatuoran*, which had been taken in turn from *Kausswagan*, a paper edited in the parish of San Nicholas, Cebu. Opon Chronicles, 30 May 1906 (typescript copy), 72 in Cebu 1:1, RPAD.

Second Attempt

The new superior of Opon, Patrick Maguire Lynch, was, in Baily's words, 'flamboyant, extrovert and full of charm', but his contribution to moving the experiment in the Philippines is difficult to evaluate. Lynch had impressive contacts among English-speaking expatriates and he devoted himself almost exclusively to developing a one-man mission for English-language work. He ventured far beyond the islands, going as far as Hong Kong, Malaya and even China, where he preached a short mission in Canton. Under his leadership a second house was established at Malate, near Manila, in 1913. Malate was in a different language area from Opon, but Tagalog proved no easier for the Irish than the Cebuano of Opon. Many tried to avoid the challenge of language-learning by working in English. Such little progress had been made on the language front that, even in 1923, sermons in the Malate church were still being read from a translated text.

The handful of missions attempted during the first year were dismal failures. For most of the period between 1914 and 1928, there were seldom more than six or seven priests available for mission work. During the year 1915, ten full-scale missions were conducted. Men like Tom Cassin and Francis Gilmartin would spend three months at a stretch going from *barrio* [village] to *barrio* without a break. Baily considers that the little band made an impact on the area out of all proportion to their numbers.[13]

The foreign priests cast a spell on the population that was further enhanced by the pageantry of processions, the hymn-singing and the general air of fiesta that surrounded the *barrio* for the duration of the mission. In more remote areas often far from ordinary pastoral care, people came long distances to attend with a zeal that recalled the Irish missions of the previous century. Those living in the mountains came down in relays, bringing provisions for some days and dwelling with their friends in the *poblacion* [town]. As soon as they had been to confession and communion, they returned home to send the other members of their families.

As in Ireland, the use of religious objects and the reading of pious books were promoted during the missions. The expense of missions was defrayed initially by funding from Ireland, but as the houses became more self-sufficient, they were able to share more of the burden of supporting their mission teams. Local contributions tended to be haphazard, coming in the main from fees for marriages and other sacraments performed during the mission. Gifts of produce and food, however, were given generously and helped support the missioners during their stay.

The theology of salvation behind the preaching was little different from that which pertained in Ireland. A man dying next door to where the Fathers

---

13 Baily, *Small Net*, 65.

were staying on one mission had refused to make his confession, 'but a few bars on hell softened him', as the missioner later reported. As in Ireland, the goal of the mission was to attract as many people to confession as possible. Hearing confessions kept the missioners busy for seven or eight hours each day. Two additional features of the Filipino missions were the high number of marriages regularised and the struggle for turf with Protestant missionaries and the local Aglipayan church. In a successful appeal to the government to introduce a change in the law that would allow marriages blessed during the missions to be given civil recognition, Fr William Byrne noted that from 1914 until 1928, 'no fewer than 20,260 marriages of those living in concubinage have been solemnised at the mission exercises'.

It was noted earlier in this chapter that the arrival of the Redemptorists in the Philippines coincided with the breaking away of the Philippine Independent Church under Gregorio Aglipay and with the arrival of American evangelical missionaries. The Aglipayans initially attempted to combine the outward forms of Catholicism with an aggressive nationalism. Within a few years they were slowly drifting towards Protestantism as they ordained local pastors without any episcopal mandate. In some cases, Catholic priests had led their entire flock into the Aglipayan church. This was the terrain in which the missions were most successful, and the missioners' antagonism towards the proselytisers was fuelled by the ingrained Irish Catholic memory of evangelical crusades against Catholicism. The mission was sometimes the scene of open confrontation with the Aglipayans accompanied on occasion by threats of violence against the missioners. Baily estimates that the mission campaigns in the island of Negros won back some 4,000 Aglipayan converts to the Catholic Church.[14]

Going on missions entailed hardship. In most cases, the only way to get to the inaccessible mountain *barrios* was on horseback. John Mary Magnier, a nephew of the consultor general of the same name, lost his life when the horse he was riding stumbled on a rickety bridge and he was thrown to his death. On arrival at the mission, food and accommodation were rough and ill-suited to Irish stomachs. Dysentery caused by polluted drinking water was a common complaint.

Vice-Province

In the early decades, the Philippine mission suffered from comparative neglect on the part of Redemptorist superiors in far-off Ireland. No provincial or member of the general council visited the islands for twenty years, though sometimes passing close by on their way to Australia. The vice-provincial of Australia, Edmund Gleeson, later bishop of Maitland, kept a watching brief,

---

[14] Baily, *Small Net*, 93.

and conducted visitations regularly, sending back reports which are models of insight and good sense.

By 1924, the time had come to give the Philippines a measure of independence as a vice-province: it would be subject to Ireland in major matters but with more room for local initiative. Matthew O'Callaghan, or Padre Matteo as the people knew him, was appointed vice-provincial and took Malate for his official residence. O'Callaghan immediately set about revitalising the dormant Tagalog missions from that house. He was not destined to last long as vice-provincial. He died after three years on the job, in April 1927. Like Tom Cassin, he had attempted to hold firm to a missionary vocation. Two years after arriving, he had written to an Irish confrere about his depressing view of the situation:

> The whole Philippine question I regard now, from two years' experience, as a bungle. We bungled into it. We are, as the Lord knows, bungling through it, and we cannot but believe that we shall bungle out of it.[15]

O'Callaghan, nevertheless, stood firm. As a confrere wrote of him, 'few who have lived longer have done as much as he, and the fruit of his labour remains.' Succeeding Patrick Leo as superior of Opon, he won over the people who had been alienated by Leo's touchy manner. He restored the fiesta and processions that Leo had banned. He had also founded the first parish school in the diocese of Cebu at Opon, yet he never ceased to appreciate the importance of the parish mission apostolate for the Philippines. O'Callaghan was succeeded as vice-provincial by the Australian, Fr William Byrne, who had proved to be a true leader of men and had already put the house of Opon on a sound financial basis.

It was not until 1927 that the first Irish Redemptorist provincial, John Fitzgerald, visited the Philippines. It was more than twenty years since his predecessor, Andrew Boylan, had launched the mission. One of the purposes of Fitzgerald's visit was to oversee the complete withdrawal from parishes, in accordance with the wishes of Patrick Murray, the superior general. The two original communities of Opon and Malate were abandoned in 1928 and 1929. Opon was taken over by the Missionaries of the Sacred Heart and Malate by the relatively new Society of St Columban, or, as it was then more widely known in Ireland, the 'Maynooth Mission to China'. The running of parishes had been a bitter bone of contention from the beginning, but the time was now ripe for concentrating on parish missions. The previous ten years had proved that missions had the potential for making a very positive contribution to the Church in the Philippines. There were now three communities: in Cebu,

---

15 From a letter to Fr Thomas Walsh, quoted in Baily, *Small Net*, 28.

Baclaran and Iloilo, catering respectively for the three linguistic groups of Cebuano, Tagalog and Ilongo. Australia, which had become a province in its own right in 1927, was given responsibility for the northern islands from Baclaran, while the Irish took responsibility for the south from Cebu.

The odyssey that had begun with Andrew Boylan's visit to the Philippines in 1906 was at an end. There had been much pain in the previous twenty years. There had also been much learning, both for the pioneers and for the Irish province. In his historical survey of the modern Irish missionary movement, Edmund Hogan has argued that there were ample grounds in the nineteenth and early twentieth centuries for the low esteem in which Irish missionaries were held. Both Rome and the leaders of the international missionary societies considered the Irish as 'temperamentally unsuited' for foreign mission work.[16] Much of the early experience in Opon might be said to prove the truth of this judgement. Boylan had accepted the mission with a great heart, but with little appreciation of the practical difficulties that lay ahead. More critical still was the fact that he had ignored the opposition of some of the most influential members of his province, including his closest advisors. Boylan's big-hearted generosity relied on admonitions to practice 'holy hope' and a spirit of camaraderie to see him and his companions through the difficulties of the early days in Opon. It might be argued that he had taken on the Philippines with his eyes at least half-shut, with scant consideration for how the details would be worked out in practice, and much less, how they would affect his successors.

The word most often used to describe the early days in Opon is 'bungle'. Men as different in temperament as Patrick Leo and Matthew O'Callaghan suspected that, for all his goodness, Boylan had bungled the details of the foundation. Many of the problems of the early years were caused by that profoundly disorienting experience known today as culture shock. Boylan, despite his years, and Cassin, despite his reputation as intellectually weak, seem to have been curiously immune to its symptoms. Nor did the pioneers simply experience it on their own account. There is a sense in which it was their lot to undergo a vicarious culture shock on behalf of the Irish province. The after-tremors reaching back to Ireland questioned some of the congregation's most cherished values. The inability to even countenance the temporary acceptance of parishes or the insistence on the observance of the minutiae of the rule in circumstances of almost heroic apostolic endurance points to that. The endurance of many men was to be tested to the limit. There were also cases of extremely bad judgement when men were assigned to the Philippines who were temperamentally and physically unsuited for the rigours of the climate.

---

[16] Hogan, *Irish Missionary Movement*, 161.

Time has proved Boylan's instincts to be right and providential. More than a hundred years since its foundation, the Philippines has a flourishing independent Redemptorist province with its headquarters in Cebu and a vice-province in Manilla dependent on the Australian province. The word, *kairos*, is used in the Greek New Testament for a critical moment of judgement that is also a promise of grace and openness to new life. Boylan's letter accepting the Philippine mission, for all its errors of fact and judgement, was such a *kairos* moment for the province he led.

CHAPTER TEN

Wars and Revolutions

Patrick Murray, the Donegal-born provincial of the Irish Redemptorists, was elected superior general on 1 May 1909 at the age of forty-four. The election of the comparatively young and unknown provincial was the result of a deadlock when neither of the two leading candidates proved able to acquire the two-thirds majority required for election. It was a remarkable boost for the self-confidence of the still-young Irish province. Murray would remain in office for thirty-eight years, until ill-health forced his resignation in 1947. While he scrupulously avoided playing any visible role in Irish political or ecclesiastical affairs, Murray was regarded as one of the few high-placed Roman ecclesiastics sympathetic to Irish national aspirations in the period of the struggle for independence.[1] It is regrettable that no complete study of Murray has yet been produced, for it might reveal that he played a significant role in the story of Ireland and the Irish Church during this critical time.[2] He was also leader of an international religious congregation during two world wars and the rise of fascism which profoundly affected the life of many of its members. The two decades following Murray's departure to Rome were difficult years for the Irish province, marked by the shadows of the First World War and the struggle for Irish independence.

---

[1] Dermot Keogh regards Murray as less militantly nationalist than either Fr Peter Magennis, general of the Carmelites, or Mgr John Hagan, rector of the Irish College, who were the chief contacts of the Irish Republican delegation with the Vatican. He had little interest in playing a political role but 'when called upon to exercise his influence on behalf of the Irish Church he was not found wanting': see Dermot Keogh, *The Vatican, the Bishops and Irish Politics 1919–1939* (Cambridge: Cambridge University Press. 1986), 6.

[2] Robert Culhane's essay 'Most Rev. Father Patrick Murray (1865–1959), Superior General, CSsR, 1909–1947. Biographical outline over the years 1865–1909' in *SHCSSR*, vol. IX (1961), 21–79, is rich in detail about his early life, but concludes with his election as general. Murray's voluminous correspondence in RGAR still awaits thorough cataloguing. Seán T. Ó Ceallaigh, a member of the Republican delegation in Rome in 1920, paid tribute to Murray's kindness to them in his letter of sympathy to the provincial on the occasion of his death: see Seán T. Ó Ceallaigh to Michael Curran, 6 June 1959, Murray box, RPAD.

Education and the University

The 'university question' dominated church–state relations in Ireland for much of the nineteenth century.[3] The bishops' attempts to set up a Catholic university under the direction of John Henry Newman in 1854 in opposition to both Trinity College Dublin and the new Queen's Colleges in Belfast, Cork and Galway, had proved a failure. As a compromise solution, the Royal University of Ireland was established in 1879 as an examining and degree-granting, rather than a teaching, body. Students read the prescribed courses under the direction of a tutor and were awarded degrees on passing the examinations. This opened a door for several Catholic diocesan and religious-run colleges to establish university tiers. Despite its small numbers, the Redemptorist juvenate in Limerick attempted to follow the trend. For some years, two members of the staff, Frs Patrick Hartigan and Thomas F. Walsh, taught the first arts course in classics to the more promising final-year students, but the small number of both staff and students did not make it possible to continue the full degree course.

The Royal University was dissolved by the passage of a new Universities Act in 1908. It broke up the former Queen's University, creating a National University with constituent colleges in Dublin, Cork and Galway, with an independent Queen's University of Belfast. Clonard was the only Redemptorist house convenient to a university, and for a time, superiors toyed with the possibility of sending students to Queen's. The proposal was rejected, if for no other reason than that the daily journey to lectures entailed passing through the Orange area of Sandy Row on their way to college, a prospect likely to have filled parents of boys from the south of Ireland with dismay.

Fr Thomas F. Walsh, director of the juvenate, needed little convincing that the changed university structure offered interesting possibilities to his students.

> As soon as actual attendance at lectures became a *sine qua non* of university degrees, it became apparent that to keep pace with the times in education and to avoid being looked upon as a body of uneducated priests unfit for our work as Redemptorists, we should give our students, or at least a certain number of them, a university education.[4]

With Walsh's encouragement, Patrick Griffith was prepared to gamble his ambitions for a full foundation in Dublin in favour of the province's educational needs. He sought the permission of the archbishop of Dublin, William

---

[3] On the university question, see P. J. Dowling, *A History of Irish Education: a Study in Conflicting Loyalties* (Cork: Mercier Press, 1971), and Thomas J. Morrissey, *Towards a National University* (Dublin: Four Courts Press, 1983).
[4] Circular letter to the rectors, 23 Jan. 1913, RPAD.

Walsh, to establish a university residence, without a public church. Patrick Murray, the superior general, was less enthusiastic about university education. The archbishop granted permission for a residence on Griffith's terms. After a few weeks in hired lodgings in Harcourt Street, Thomas Walsh and six students took up residence in a house in Highfield Road on 3 October 1910, naming it Marianella, after the country home of the Liguori family and birthplace of Alphonsus. Walsh himself enrolled for an MA so that he could share more fully the students' experience of university life. Despite his opposition to university education, Patrick Murray learned of Walsh's daily trips to the National University on Earlsfort Terrace by bicycle with a degree of amused tolerance.

Thomas Walsh was not destined to stay long in Dublin. In 1912, he succeeded Griffith as provincial. Given his interest in education, it was inevitable that he would use his new role to improve the educational standards of the province. A *Schola Major* [advanced institute] had been established in Rome by the general chapter of 1894 but only began receiving students in 1909. It was intended as a centre for the postgraduate education of Redemptorists destined to teach theology, and especially moral theology, in their home province. One promising student had been suggested as the province's first candidate for the new institute, but on taking soundings, Walsh decided that his views on morals were on 'the narrow side', and that he should never be allowed to teach for that reason.[5] What was needed urgently, in Walsh's view, however, was a well-equipped teacher of philosophy. In a province where the study of philosophy had been perfunctory, Walsh's sketch of the ideal programme for a future teacher was far-sighted: it would begin with primary degrees in science (particularly biology) and philosophy before continuing to post-graduate studies in Rome. Such a programme was a visionary one but, Walsh remarked: 'if someone does not look ahead, how can those who come after have the material?'

Walsh's concern with the intellectual life of Redemptorists extended to his criticism of the style of preaching generally in vogue:

> Someone may think that by conspicuous natural gifts joined to an earnest and animated delivery he is making a notable impression; and this, no doubt is sometimes the case. It is equally true that one whose sermon consists of ideas and illustrations flung together any how is violating the rule, is neglecting his duty to souls and to the Congregation, is failing to make proper use of his talents and incurs the reproach addressed to the unfaithful servant.[6]

---

[5] Thomas J. Walsh to Patrick Murray, 21 Aug. 1912, XIII-D Provincialia, RGAR.
[6] Circular letter to the rectors, 23 Jan. 1913, RPAD.

Although he had considerable qualities of leadership and much sympathy for the younger generation, Walsh felt himself unsuited for the role of provincial and begged not to be re-appointed at the end of his three-year period in 1915.[7] The following year, he went to serve in Australia, where he was eventually appointed vice-provincial in 1924 and first provincial in 1927. His greatest contribution to the development of the Australian province was once again in the field of education, as he oversaw the development of its studendate after the return of the Australian students from Esker. Walsh returned to Ireland in poor health in 1930 and died in Marianella the following year.

Wars and Revolution

Patrick Hartigan, Walsh's successor as provincial, was born in Banogue, County Limerick in 1873. His nine years as provincial, from 1915 to 1924, were a time of more than ordinary complexity and difficulty which spanned the First World War, the war of independence and the civil war. At the end of his third term, he was appointed rector of Esker in April 1924, but died while on a mission the following June.

Within months of the declaration of war, numbers attending the confraternities in Limerick and Belfast were showing the first signs of decline as men rushed to enlist in the British army. By the end of 1914, for instance, about 500 Limerick confraternity men were serving with the forces. Writing a summary of the year for the confraternity chronicle, Con Mangan, the director, remarked that 'we cannot but feel very sad when we think of the hundreds of our grand young fellows who have, since the last retreat, fallen on the field of battle.'[8] Communities felt the effects of the war most sharply in the rationing of food. Requesting Murray to mitigate the Lenten abstinence because of the scarcity of fish, butter, or even margarine, Hartigan observed that the price of eggs had risen to four pence halfpenny each.[9] The Clonard community purchased a small mill to produce its own flour for the making of altar breads 'as the flour to be bought is very unsafe and is much adulterated with all kinds of stuff'.[10]

Patrick Hartigan's sympathies were with the Redmondite home rule movement, and he was anxious for his men to undertake pastoral care of the soldiers departing for the Front. Writing again to Murray, he comments:

> It is a great pity that something more is not done for the poor soldiers before they leave Ireland by way of retreats. I suggested this to the

---

[7] Patrick Hartigan to Patrick Murray, 10 Nov. 1916, XIII-D, Provincialia, RGAR.
[8] 'Chronicle of the Arch-confraternity of the Holy Family', vol. 2, Summary for year 1915, Limerick Confraternity Archives.
[9] Patrick Hartigan to Patrick Murray, Feb. 1915, XIII-D, Provincialia, RGAR.
10. Domestic Chronicle, vol. 1, 31 May 1918, Domestic Archives, Clonard.

Cardinal: he agreed and said that the priests who had been at the front told him that very little could be done on the field of battle if the soldiers were not prepared beforehand. Now when the missions are over, I am offering through Dr Hackett [a Redemptorist who had been appointed bishop of Waterford and Lismore the previous year] to give retreats to the soldiers preparing for the front during the winter. We gave a few such retreats already. I gave one myself and it was the most consoling work I have ever done.[11]

Providing regular pastoral care for soldiers in the front demanded a more radical commitment. At the outbreak of the war there were only seventeen Catholic priests serving as commissioned chaplains out of a total of 117 clergy of various denominations attached to the Royal Army Chaplains' Department. As more chaplains were needed urgently to serve the increasing numbers of Catholic troops, it was to the religious orders that both the military and religious establishment turned. By the war's end, there would be 651 Catholic chaplains out of a total of 3,475.[12]

The first Redemptorist to offer his services as a chaplain was Fr Harry Potter who volunteered in 1914, but was only sent to the Front the following year. He was awarded the military cross for bravery in assisting two wounded soldiers to escape capture. Potter was followed by ten more Redemptorists from the Irish province in the four years that the war lasted.[13] Patrick Kilbride joined as a chaplain in 1915, at the relatively advanced age of forty-seven and served to the end of the war. Thomas O'Connor saw action at Ypres and the Somme. Michael Geraghty was awarded the rank of 'honorary chaplain of the forces' with permission to wear the service dress uniform of that rank while attending ceremonials or entertainments of a military character.[14] Michael Hannigan and Michael Cagney joined the chaplains' service in 1915

---

[11] Patrick Hartigan to Patrick Murray, 22 Aug. 1916, XIII-D, Provincialia, RGAR.

[12] Figures from Tom Johnstone and James Hegarty, *The Cross on the Sword: Catholic Chaplains in the Forces* (London: Chapman, 1996), 174. On how the ecclesiastical politics of providing chaplains, and perhaps even a bishop, with oversight for the combined forces, divided the hierarchies of Ireland and Great Britain, see chapter fourteen, 'An *Episcopus Castrensis* for the British Army', 179–90.

[13] It might be useful to compare the number of Redemptorists who served as chaplains with those from the dioceses or religious orders as given in the *Irish Catholic Directory* for 1919 (i.e. those serving by the war's end in 1918). The following are representative figures: Dublin diocese provided 15 chaplains, Derry 3, the Carmelites 2, Holy Ghost Fathers 3, Franciscans 9, Capuchins 4, Passionists 14, Rosminians 4, Jesuits 25. Several orders and congregations do not list any member on war service.

[14] Letter from War Office, London, 6 Jan. 1919. Copy in Michael Geraghty's personal file, RPAD. Fr Geraghty left the Redemptorists in the early 1920s.

and went to the Thessalonika and Souva respectively. Cagney had a relatively short war as he suffered from shell-shock.

> [He] arrived home early from the war as he was not able for the din of battle ... He was in the hottest of the struggle for a few weeks and his nerves got greatly shaken. Since then, he has been taken back to base and now he is being sent home altogether. I have failed to get anyone to take his place. All to whom I have written are afraid of it.[15]

Others, too, had relatively short periods at the Front. Both John Doyle and Patrick Carroll joined in 1918, just in time for the final few months of the war.

Thomas Campbell, a native of Hollywood, County Down, was serving in the Australian vice-province when war broke out and volunteered as a chaplain with the Australian and New Zealand Army Corps (ANZACS), serving from 1914 to 1918. He was still in Australia at the outbreak of the Second World War and despite his advanced age (he was now sixty-eight) he volunteered again, serving until the war's end. William Howes also served as chaplain to the Anzacs.[16] Not included among the active chaplains is Patrick Clune (1864–1935), a native of County Clare, who had been ordained in 1886 for the diocese of Goulburn. He entered the Redemptorists in 1884. As bishop of Perth since 1911 (archbishop from 1913), he was *ex-officio* chaplain-general to the Australian forces. He will appear later in this narrative in another role for which his standing as a chaplain lent him particular authority.

Fr Bernard Kavanagh, a native of Limerick, who had remained in the London province after the separation in 1898, volunteered as a chaplain at the age of fifty. He served with the Egyptian expeditionary force and was present at the taking of Jerusalem on 9 December 1917. He was shot by a Turkish sniper while administering the last rites to a dying soldier on the Mount of Olives on 21 December 1917 and is buried in the Commonwealth cemetery on Mount Scopus, Jerusalem.[17]

The provincial's difficulty in getting men to go to the Front may have been due, at least in part, to a resurgence of nationalist sympathies in the wake of the Easter Rising. Some men had never made any secret of their strong nationalist sympathies. As director of the Limerick confraternity, Con Mangan was likely to be drawn into the public eye more than most of his confreres. A nationalist crowd, protesting at an anti-home rule meeting in

---

[15] Patrick Hartigan to Patrick Murray, 22 Aug. 1916, XIII-D. Provincialia, RGAR.
[16] Like Michael Geraghty, William Howes also left the Redemptorists shortly after the war.
[17] O. R. V-P [Oliver Rodie Vassal-Philips CSsR], 'Chaplains in the Great War: Fr Bernard Kavanagh CSsR' in *The Dublin Review*, 165 (1919), 52–62 draws richly on Kavanagh's diaries and correspondence.

Limerick in 1912, was baton-charged by the Royal Irish Constabulary (RIC). A full-scale riot ensued, and Mangan was asked by the bishop to use his influence to put an end to the trouble. On another occasion Mangan averted a near-riot at the end of an Irish Volunteers parade in Limerick on Whit Sunday 1915. The attendance of over 12,000 men included Republican leaders like Tom Clarke, the Pearse brothers, Bulmer Hobson, Éamon de Valera, Seán Heuston, Liam Mellows, Tomás Mac Curtain and Terence MacSwiney. They did not get a friendly reception from the Limerick people, many of whom had relatives at the Front. When they returned to the station to take their train back to Dublin, the crowd was in ugly mood. Once again, the director of the confraternity was called:

> The director mounted a side-car and made a speech of five minutes' duration, called the confraternity men to join hands and make a passage and keep back the crowd, while the Volunteers marched in. Anyhow, about a hundred men came forward and with them on one side and the police on the other, a narrow passage was made, and the Volunteers under a heavy shower of stones and bottles, passed in. The mayor and the district inspector feared another row at night, so they begged the priests to come to the station at about 10.15. We did and all was well … When the mail train had gone, we returned home, thanking God for our lives and that no blood was spilled.[18]

At one point in the scuffle, a rifle was wrested from one of the Volunteers. Mangan, grabbing a walking-stick from the confraternity secretary who accompanied him, struck the man grappling with the Volunteer, ordering him to hand back the rifle as the frightened Volunteer fled to the safety of the train. Several years later, in the course of house visitation during a mission in Dublin, Con Mangan met the man whose rifle he had saved. He was Peadar Kearney, the composer of *The Soldier's Song*.

From references to the Rising and its aftermath in the domestic chronicles, it is possible to discern the shift in sentiment among the Redemptorists. Most make only passing reference to the events of Easter 1916, but the execution of the leaders was as much a watershed for them as it was for the rest of the nation. By the following year, the students in Esker had become enthusiastic Republicans, celebrating the first anniversary of the Rising with a bonfire.[19] When the prefect of students read them Thomas Ashe's poem, 'Let me carry your cross for Ireland, Lord' a few days after his death on hunger strike in September 1917, the entire poem was copied into the student chronicle. Sensing the mood of the country the Irish bishops, at their

---

[18] Necrology of Fr Con Mangan, 23–4, Personal file, RPAD.
[19] Student Chronicle, 8 Apr. 1916, RPAD.

Maynooth meeting in April 1918, joined other bodies in formulating a pledge to resist the conscription that the British government was attempting to impose on Ireland which read in part: 'Denying the right of the British government to enforce compulsory service in this country, we pledge ourselves solemnly to one another to resist it by the most effective means at our disposal.' This pledge was to be taken at the door of the parish church the following Sunday, 21 April. The students were granted permission for 'an extraordinary walk' on the day which enabled them to go as a body to Killtullagh to take the pledge. Two days later, to show that this was no empty formula, they joined the national strike by refusing to do any manual work in the house or grounds. Instead, with the rector's permission, they gave themselves over to the amusements of a recreation day![20]

Redemptorist missioners in the months following the Easter Rising realised that they were preaching in a rapidly-changing Ireland. The report on the annual Lenten mission in Berkeley Road, Dublin in 1917, noted that:

> a very intense spirit of patriotism prevails in the district according to the testimony of the canon, and the presence of Fr Mangan who was known to be a relative of the gallant insurgent leader of last Easter Week [the O'Rahilly] was a considerable attraction.[21]

The unsettled state of the country made travel on apostolic work difficult and missioners needed to be sensitive to how volatile feelings could change from place to place depending on the political allegiances. In Wexford, where Redmondite feeling was strong, for instance, they had to take great precaution 'against misconstruction of speech by reason of acute and petty local rivalries between labour and capital and different sections of nationalists among whom public and private feelings and opinions were very strained'.[22] It was also noted how the war and its aftermath affected the morals of the younger generation. Most missioners steered clear of political issues in their preaching. The provincial, Patrick Hartigan, fired a couple of warning shots across the bows of some of his more hot-headed men when they took what he considered to be an excessively anti-conscription line.[23]

The monasteries occasionally received unwelcome attention from the police and military in search of men reputedly 'on the run' or for incriminating documents. The Clonard community, caught between the nationalist Falls and unionist Shankill, was in a particularly vulnerable position. On 22

---

[20] Student Chronicle, 21 and 24 Apr. 1916, RPAD.
[21] Notice on Berkeley Road mission, March 1917, in Marianella Mission Chronicle, vol. 1, 4–25, Marianella Domestic Archives.
[22] Notice on Wexford mission, May 1920, Marianella Mission Chronicle, vol. 1, 80–2.
[23] Patrick Hartigan to Patrick Murray, 8 July 1918, XIII-D, Provincialia, RGAR.

July 1920, Brother Michael Morgan was shot dead when the monastery was raked by gunfire. In recording this event, the chronicler mentioned that firing on the house was sometimes so insistent that the community had to take refuge in the cellar. The rector was forced to issue an official denial of reports that there had been shooting from the bell-tower in the direction of the Shankill area.[24]

Fr John Baptist Coyle had strong Republican leanings, and jotted events of significance in a small notebook, which has been preserved in the Esker archives. While giving a mission in Dolphin's Barn in Dublin during the Lent of 1916, he records that there was:

> Much excitement on account of recruiting meeting in D[olphin's] B[arn] opposite the church gate. Great enthusiasm for the Irish Volunteers. I saw Commandant Eamonn Kent at the head of 500 men. They sang 'A Nation Once Again'. Had a chat with Kent.[25]

On Easter Monday 1916, he noted the beginning of the Rising in red ink in his notebook, adding a fervent *Deo Gratias et Mariae* [Thanks be to God and Mary – a traditional Redemptorist prayer formula]. The first executions of the leaders of the Rising occurred while he was giving a mission in Garrison, County Fermanagh. He commented on the response of the congregation:

> Pearse, McDonagh, Clarke, shot by English in Kilmainham. All mad with indignation and curse the self-styled defender of small nations. All proud of the glorious blood shed for Ireland's redemption. Read post-card from Pearse and got prayers. Never heard prayers said more fervently. God be with you Pearse, McDonagh and Clarke.

Coyle records meetings with the families of the executed men and other members of Sinn Féin. Coyle maintained a fairly close friendship with the de Valera family. When Éamon de Valera visited Belfast in 1920, he dined in Clonard with Coyle and a confrere of similar outlook. Coyle recorded the date, with the observation that 'all delighted with him', ending with the biblical quotation: 'A true Israelite in whom there is no guile.'

The death of Terence MacSwiney in 1920 raised the vexed issue of the morality of hunger striking. Many moral theologians regarded it as suicide. When the rumour circulated that a Redemptorist moral theologian attached to the general house in Rome had condemned hunger strikes as a political tactic, Coyle wrote to the superior general, Patrick Murray, claiming that he was asking for clarification on behalf of an unnamed Irish bishop. Murray

---

[24] Grant, *One Hundred Years with Clonard Redemptorists*, 97.
[25] Unless otherwise stated, citations in this section are from the notebook of Fr John Baptist Coyle, Domestic Archives, Esker.

replied that he believed hunger striking to be still a disputed question, and that those who undertook it in good faith were not to be disturbed by their confessors.[26]

The provincial, Patrick Hartigan, was uneasy about any strong display of nationalist feeling. When pondering the forthcoming appointment of a superior to Clonard, he thought that one man's politics disqualified him from consideration: 'We got a reputation in the last triennium for patriots [...] This would be in my mind an argument against Fr McCann's appointment there.' He did however consider nominating Coyle as rector of Limerick on the chance that having to cope with the day-to-day realities of administering a community might bring some realism to his thinking.[27]

Redemptorist Emissary for Peace

One Irish Redemptorist was to play an important role in attempting to broker a peace settlement. He was Archbishop Patrick Clune of Perth whose name has appeared above as chaplain-general to the Anzacs.[28] Clune's personal commitment to the search for peace was ignited by the torture and death of his nephew, Conor Clune, by the Black and Tans on the night before Bloody Sunday, 21 November 1920. Clune's public profile opened doors for him into the British establishment. The following week at a luncheon-party he was attending in London, Clune gave an account of a Black and Tan raid in Lahinch, County Clare. One of his fellow-guests, Joe Devlin, Nationalist MP for Belfast, arranged for Clune to meet Lloyd George who asked him to act as a mediator with Sinn Féin. Clune returned to Dublin, travelling under the name of 'Dr Walsh' and made contact on 7 December with Michael Collins, minister for finance of the first Dáil and director of intelligence of the IRA. Danger dogged Clune's footsteps in Ireland. He was followed by detectives during his stay in Dublin. The home of one of his contacts, Bishop Michael Fogarty of Killaloe, was raided while he was visiting Clune in Dublin. Clune met Arthur Griffith, acting president of Dáil Éireann, who was a prisoner in Mountjoy: a set of proposals for a truce ensued from their meeting. Two of Griffith's conditions proved a sticking point for the government, namely that the IRA would not decommission arms and that Michael Collins and Richard Mulcahy, chief of staff of the IRA, would be granted immunity during the truce. Clune returned to London, but Lloyd George, confident of an IRA surrender, sent Clune back to Dublin with the message

---

26 Patrick Murray to John Baptist Coyle, 30 Oct. 1920, Murray box, RPAD.
27 Patrick Hartigan to Patrick Murray, 8 July 1918, XIII-D Provincialia, RGAR.
28 D. F. Bourke, 'Clune, Patrick Joseph (1864–1935)', *Australian Dictionary of Biography*, vol. 8, 32–3 (Melbourne: University Press, 1981). Clune's part in the peace negotiations is described in Tim Pat Coogan, *Michael Collins* (London: Hutchinson, 1990), 194–202.

that the Dáil would be permitted to meet openly to discuss peace terms, but that neither Griffith nor Mulcahy would be permitted to attend and arms would have to be decommissioned. Clune spent the month of December 1920 engaged in shuttle diplomacy between Dublin and London.

The British were attempting to weaken popular support for the republicans in Ireland by working diplomatically for a Vatican condemnation of Sinn Féin. Clune was due to make his official *ad limina* visit to the Holy See early in 1921. On his way through Paris, he was entertained to a formal luncheon by Seán T. Ó Ceallaigh, the Dáil's European representative. Clune spoke glowingly of the courage he had witnessed on the part of the Sinn Féin leaders:

> During the negotiations, when my taxi would stop before the house where I was to meet one of the leaders I was exposing to certain death, I never saw one of them tremble. When Mr Lloyd George, the prime minister, in my presence spoke of them as 'assassins,' I corrected him, saying, 'No, sir, not assassins, but the cream of their race.'[29]

According to Coogan, the phrase 'the cream of their race' was a propaganda stroke that went around the world. Patrick Clune invited the Redemptorist superior general, Patrick Murray, to act as interpreter during his audience with Pope Benedict XV. In the course of the conversation, the Pope intimated that a condemnation of the IRA was almost ready for publication. Clune responded that such a course of action would be a disaster for the Church, not only in Ireland but in every country where there were descendants of the Irish race. Murray was taken aback by Clune's directness in the papal presence and remarked that 'I had to excuse him for speaking so strongly as the matter was so grave.'[30] Clune's outburst nevertheless made its impression, for the decree of condemnation was never published. Daniel Mannix, archbishop of Melbourne, an even greater thorn in the side of the British government, found on the occasion of his own *ad limina* visit that Benedict was more sympathetic than he had dared hope for, which he put down to the influence of his interview with Clune.

Civil War

When the lull in hostilities that followed the Treaty gave way to civil war, the divisions in the country were likely to have been as strong among the Redemptorists as they were elsewhere. The closed atmosphere of community life and the consequences of an unguarded remark in the pulpit made superiors anxious to keep political talk and action at a minimum. John

---

[29] Ibid., 200.
[30] Ibid., 202.

Baptist Coyle continued to confide his impressions to his notebook. He notes the beginning of the civil war in June 1922:

> The second great battle for the Irish Republic begins. The Republican forces in the Four Courts under Rory O'Connor attacked the Free State troops. On the anti-republican side, one of the blackest chapters in Irish history. May those misguided men live to regret turning their English guns on their brother Irish men whose only crime is that they are fighting for a free Ireland. Cathal Brugha wounded and died on Friday July 7 – a soldier without fear and without stain.[31]

The execution of the first members of the Four Courts garrison is recorded on 17 November 1922:

> Four Irish boys executed in Dublin today! Court-martialled and condemned because they fought for Irish Independence. The judges say that they fought for the same twelve months ago. The fools! The fools!'[32]

The execution of Rory O'Connor, Liam Mellows, Joe McKelvey and Richard Barrett on 8 December 1922 bears the marginal note 'martyrs for Ireland and Mary Immaculate'. Coyle describes the election of August 1923:

> In spite of trickery, propaganda, arrests, imprisonment of 13,000 men and women, intimidation and attempted murder, the Irish Republic has won 44 seats. *Deo Gratias et Mariae de Perpetuo Succursu* [Thanks be to God and Mary of Perpetual Help]. The attack on President de Valera and his arrest in Ennis absolutely infamous. It was a miracle of God and Our Lady (and to the eternal glory of Republican self-control) that the streets did not flow with blood.[33]

The Irish Catholic bishops in a pastoral letter of 10 October 1922 formally condemned the Republican campaign 'as a system of murder and assassination of the National forces without any legitimate authority'.[34] Patrick Hartigan took steps to ensure that his men toed the line.[35] He laid down strict rules of conduct to be observed both on the missions and in the monastery, pointing out how an unguarded comment in sermons exposed the Redemptorists to the risk of being excluded from entire dioceses. He warned them that 'it would be folly, it would be worse, it would be criminal,

---

[31] Notebook of Fr John Baptist Coyle, Redemptorist Archives, Esker.
[32] Ibid.
[33] Ibid.
[34] 'Pastoral Letter of his Eminence Cardinal Logue, the Archbishops and Bishops of Ireland to the priests and people of Ireland' in *Irish Ecclesiastical Record*, vol. XX (1922), 542–6.
[35] Patrick Hartigan, provincial: Circular Letter to the Province, Feb. 1923, RPAD.

in a Father for the sake of his own private sentiments, so to act as to turn priests and bishops against us.' He forbade anyone to advocate in any way, the republican side in the civil war, or to maintain any contact, even by letter, with known republicans. Although he denied that these measures were aimed at anyone in particular, men with strong views like John Baptist Coyle were among his targets.

Hartigan's uncompromising stance may have been provoked by a threat from Cardinal Logue that, unless something was done, he would take action himself against certain members of the Dundalk community. The cardinal had written to Fr John Kelly, the rector of Dundalk, probably on receipt of some information regarding one or other member of his community: 'If you have reason to suspect any of your community, it would be better to get him changed to some of your houses in England where there would be no danger of his doing mischief.'[36] In informing the provincial of the cardinal's communication, Kelly hinted that he suspected some of his men of hearing the confessions of 'Irregulars' and, despite the provincial's prohibition, of carrying on correspondence with known republicans.

De Valera's call to 'the soldiers of the Republic, legion of the rear-guard' on 24 May 1923 to abandon the campaign of armed struggle brought the civil war to an end. Its legacy of bitterness would linger on for many years. It had been almost a decade since the beginning of the First World War, a decade that had created tensions from which men living in a religious community were no more immune than any other inhabitants of Ireland. As a later chapter will show, Hartigan was successful in preventing whatever political divisions there may have been between individual Redemptorists from spilling over into their mission apostolate. By the same token, concern for how a mission preacher's militant past might affect the success of his future preaching ministry led to a certain caution in accepting candidates in the years following the civil war. Although never officially stated, the Irish Redemptorists did not accept anyone who had actively borne arms in the 'troubles' as a candidate for priestly ordination. This proved no barrier, however, to accepting as brother candidates men like Michael Bradley and Patrick Brennan, who had been actively involved in the IRA (see chapter seven), since they would be spending most of their lives in the comparative seclusion of the monastery and would only be known by their religious name. When Liam (Bill) Pilkington, who had been general officer commanding the third western region of the IRA during the war of independence and the civil war, felt the stirrings of a vocation and made enquiries about joining the novitiate in Dundalk in 1924, he was directed towards the London province, where his military exploits were less likely to

---

36 Michael Logue to John Kelly, 23 Jan. 1923, Redemptorist Archives, Dundalk.

be remarked upon. He was accepted and ordained in Hawkstone in 1932. The Irish provincial, John Fitzgerald, objected, however, to his accepting a public presentation in Sligo on the occasion. Pilkington was well-regarded in his home province. He spent much of his priestly life as a foreign missionary in South Africa and the last twenty in several communities in Britain before his death in 1977.[37]

The effects of this decade on community living are more difficult to assess and will be treated in the following chapter. One index of a degree of unrest may be the number of men who, during this period, left the Redemptorists and in some cases, the exercise of priestly ministry. Six priests, all of them comparatively young men, left the congregation between the years 1916 and 1924. In at least one case, the departure was due to differences of political opinion. Some of the returning army chaplains also found readjustment to community life difficult. A few made their way into English and American dioceses. Of the remainder, there is sadly little trace.

---

[37] Michael MacEvilly, 'Pilkington, William (Liam, Billy)' in James McGuire and James Quinn (eds), *Dictionary of Irish Biography* (Cambridge: Cambridge University Press, 2009). Online edition accessed 2 Jan. 2011 at http://dib.cambridge.org/viewReadPage.do?articleId=a7342

CHAPTER ELEVEN

Taking Stock

In 1924, Patrick Hartigan handed over to his successor, John Fitzgerald (1883–1971), a province that had just celebrated the silver jubilee of its independence. It had many signs of vitality. The house of studies in Esker was full of students, and there was a thriving vice-province in Australia. The mission in the Philippines was approaching its twentieth birthday and, despite the reservations of the early years, it had become a vital part of the work of the Irish province. The unsettled state of the country during the years of the civil war had made missions difficult. Despite this, as the table below shows, the number of missions held throughout the country was growing steadily in the 1920s, apart from a dip in 1921 and 1922.

Table 5. Number of Redemptorist Missions held in Ireland, 1920–6

Year	1920	1921	1922	1923	1924	1925	1926
Missions	135	91	81	102	146	134	141

Source: Based on annual returns for apostolic works in
Provincial Chronicle, vol. 1, RPAD

It has been suggested, and with some reason, that the missions of the late 1920s and early 1930s were instrumental in helping to bridge the great fissures in Irish society that had opened up during the civil war period. The diverse political views on the Treaty expressed by members of the congregation appear to have become less pronounced.

Fitzgerald, professed in 1903 and ordained in 1908, belonged to the first generation of Irish Redemptorists who had received all their religious and theological formation within the Irish province. As a student in Belfast and later in Esker, he had been under Patrick Murray, director of students and now superior general. The narrowness of his formation may have contributed to Fitzgerald's literal and sometimes rather wooden interpretation of the rule that marked the twelve years of his time as provincial superior. It may be a sign of a return to comparative normality that the new provincial was not exercised by problems such as finding chaplains for the troops or calming down the political enthusiasm of his confreres. He was instead preoccupied with the problem of the *fáinne*. The *fáinne* is a badge in the form of a ring that testified the wearer's proficiency in Irish and willingness to speak it. It raised no great nationalist or ideological cares for Fitzgerald but he was concerned whether wearing it infringed the rule on religious poverty that forbade the use of articles of gold or silver for personal adornment.[1] He was relieved to learn that the Redemptorists wore the cheaper model of *fáinne*, made from brass, which avoided the problem with poverty, but was soon wondering if the same applied to the silver version.[2] He would later wonder whether gold-rimmed spectacles contravened the same regulations on poverty.[3]

The Canonical Visitation of 1926

It has been already observed that the reports – known as 'recesses' – of the canonical visitations conducted annually afford some insight into issues affecting the daily life of communities. Traditional themes dominated the agenda of visitations in the 1920s and 1930s. Redemptorist discipline was very strict about comparatively minor issues such as smoking and the use of spirits. One canonical visitor warned about the thin end of the wedge: if a little brandy were permitted in the after-dinner coffee on the occasion of a feast day, it might soon become brandy with a little coffee! Only the superior general could give permission to smoke on a regular basis and the general archives witness to the frequency with which requests to smoke flowed into Rome from Ireland.

More painful tensions ran deeper. The report of an extraordinary visitation undertaken by a member of the London province, Fr Cyril Ryder, in 1926 at the request of the superior general, Patrick Murray, is the nearest example of an independent audit of the Irish province and its administration in this period. Running to almost nineteen pages, it raises a number of serious issues. Ryder was reluctant to criticise Fitzgerald, whom he regarded as a young and inexperienced superior. He pulled fewer punches in his criticism of his principal consultor, Fr Eugene O'Donnell, laying at his door responsibility for most of the bad decisions of the administration. Although Murray listened to the Visitor's advice and removed O'Donnell at the earliest opportunity, he appointed him novice master, a post in which his influence was to continue in the formation of a generation of young Redemptorists.

Ryder paints a fairly sombre picture of the Irish province, describing it as over-stretched, disgruntled and in some respects, seriously unhealthy:

---

[1] John Fitzgerald to Patrick Murray, 9 Mar. 1926, XII-D, RGAR.
[2] John Fitzgerald to Patrick Murray, 12 Mar. 1927, XII-D, RGAR.
[3] John Fitzgerald to Patrick Murray, 24 Nov. 1927, XII-D, RGAR.

The province is suffering very seriously from its life-blood, so to speak, being drained from it by two vice-provinces, Australia and the Philippines, but especially the former. All the houses in the mother province are undermanned. The result is that they have to refuse more work than they accept, and there is always the temptation to accept more than they have real strength for, which alas, happens not infrequently, for fear of driving their best supporters to go elsewhere.[4]

Ryder thought that the health of individuals might be an index of the health of the province. He considered that the frequency of breakdowns in health and cases requiring serious surgery were so 'extraordinarily numerous' that it was clearly a sign of that difficulty.

There is little doubt that the difficult living conditions of war and civil unrest, together with the tight regime of the home life, contributed in some measure to the state of nervous tension in which several confreres passed their lives. Alphonsus Liguori's rigorous theology of vocation, with its steely insistence on the virtue of perseverance, reflected his struggles with the Mediterranean family model current in the Naples of his day that had prevented many young men from leaving home to follow a religious vocation. It was interpreted in Ireland with rigid and almost wooden literalism, leading to earnest efforts to hold on to candidates who were temperamentally unsuited to religious life. The effects of this ideology on a nervous and impressionable mind can be seen in a distressing case to which John Fitzgerald returns frequently in the course of his correspondence with the superior general, Patrick Murray. Within several months of his ordination in 1916, this unfortunate man had developed serious scruples about its validity. He had been sent for a time to a nursing home in England, but it was increasingly clear that he would never again be fit for the rigours of community life. He was still haunted by the cardinal sin of the Redemptorist tradition – loss of vocation: 'He thinks of nothing, speaks of nothing but mortal sin and damnation. I tried my best to console him, but in reply he quoted the teaching of our Holy Father [Alphonsus], especially that a dispensation from vows is the passport to hell.' Fitzgerald treated him with great kindness, and eventually he was able to take up a light convent chaplaincy. It was more worrying when such tensions affected the students. The visitation report noted that several students were unable to study due to nervous trouble: one had become so reclusive that he had even taken to cutting his own hair. He also detected signs of a spiritual malaise in the comparatively high number of departures referred to in the previous chapter, six within four years.

---

[4] 'Report on visitation of Irish Province', Cyril Ryder, 1926, XIII-D, RGAR. Quotations following are taken from this source.

The view that 'loss of vocation' was due to the lack of generosity on the part of the individual, however, precluded any search for an underlying malaise. The activism of the province worried Ryder. He believed that it led to 'the loss of feeling for the home [community] life', and created the impression that it was driven by a desire to make more money, for there was an impression abroad that 'confreres are valuable in proportion to their wage-earning capacity'. Each of the houses needed stronger mission teams, he suggested, especially Belfast.

Fitzgerald had attempted to restructure the order of the day by changing the rising time of the communities from 5 a.m. to 6 a.m. and then moving every religious exercise in the daily timetable one hour forward, without any attempt to rationalise either their number or their order. As a result, the community dinner took place at 2 p.m. followed by an hour of recreation until 3.30 p.m. With dusk falling by 4 p.m. in wintertime, even a brisk walk or a game for the students became virtually impossible. The most popular early morning Mass in several of the public churches at 6.30 p.m. had to be abandoned: within the first month, communion numbers had fallen by 5,000. Ryder suggested the compromise of changing the rising time to 5.30 p.m. It would remain the norm until the 1960s.

Ryder's report noted the harsh social conditions in the country in the aftermath of the foundation of the Free State. The economic outlook was bleak: 'trade is decreasing and unemployment is increasing.' The situation was particularly acute in Belfast. The people who came to Clonard had traditionally been generous. The Visitor recommended that the interest on Clonard's savings be used for local poor relief during the coming winter. In making this recommendation, he was challenging the provincial's right to control the funds of local communities, for Fitzgerald had disposed of practically the whole of Clonard's savings through a forced loan in favour of one of the Australian houses. Ryder conceded that levying a reasonable tax on a house might be acceptable, but 'wholesale confiscation is quite another thing, and in my humble opinion, quite unjust.'

The recent divisive politics of the civil war still hung like a cloud over the province. Strong political feeling may have gone underground, but Ryder noted the need for special vigilance in Belfast:

> I have heard that some took up the Republican side very strongly, and spoke about it most imprudently from the pulpit. Though this seems to have ceased for the present, there is danger of the fire breaking out again at the elections or any time of disturbance. There is special reason for care in the Belfast house. There, Mr Devlin, the member [for West Belfast who had broken with the nationalist abstentionist policy] has taken his seat in the Northern Parliament in order to use his influence for the good of the Church. One can see therefore how

imprudent it would be of a Father on mission to speak imprudently at table of Mr Devlin who may be a friend of the parish priest. The priests of Belfast apparently do not go in for politics as professedly as they do in the south, but simply for religion, trying to get the best terms for it, no matter from whom.

He recommended the strict enforcement of Patrick Hartigan's 1923 regulations on politics and that, even within the community, it should be forbidden to speak strongly in support of any side.

Formation for Priestly and Religious Life

Ryder concluded his visitation report by commenting on the formation system. A policy of sending candidates to university in Dublin after they had finished their secondary education in Limerick had been in place since 1910. The fewness of the numbers currently going to university gave cause for concern and Ryder suggested that, unless the numbers could be improved, the arrangement should be reconsidered and students sent directly to the novitiate and then to the house of studies. If there was need to train some for teaching, they could go to the university after ordination. The Redemptorists' experiment with university education came to an end in 1928: it had lasted just short of twenty years. During that time, twenty-six students had passed through the doors of Marianella, the Dublin student residence. Seventeen, or 68 per cent, were eventually professed, a high number by today's standards. Some in the province were happy to see university education go. They believed that exposure to university life weakened students' commitment to religious life. That was certainly the opinion of the superior general, Patrick Murray, from the beginning. It may have been in deference to his wishes that John Fitzgerald, the provincial, decided that all students should go directly to the novitiate at the end of the secondary school course, and then proceed directly to the studendate at Esker. It would be another twenty more years before university education became a practical proposition again, with the founding of a house of studies in Galway.

Esker continued to grow as a house of studies. Gary MacEoin (1909–2003), who arrived there as a student after his profession in 1928, describes how the appearance of the house differed from the earlier and rather harmonious designs of the previous century:

> The Irish priests … started off by buying a three-storey rectangular building without architectural character, and added to it – as the need to expand became acute – first one, then another wing, each with less beauty than its predecessor, fewer architectural pretensions and greater sacrifice of function and efficiency in order to cut costs.[5]

5 Gary MacEoin, *Nothing is Quite Enough* (London: Hodder and Stoughton, 1954), 77.

Five students were sent to do part of their studies at Attert in Belgium in 1921, with four more following in 1922. This decision may have been prompted as much by shortage of space in Esker and a sense of solidarity with the Belgian province rebuilding in the aftermath of the war than with any educational benefits to be gleaned from studying theology in a new country. Even after the departure of the Australian students in 1927, space was at a premium in Esker. The bulge in numbers towards the end of Fitzgerald's time as provincial led to serious problems of accommodation in both Esker and the Dundalk novitiate. Plans to purchase an estate at Collon in County Louth as a site for a new novitiate house came to nothing. The land was subsequently purchased by the Cistercians as the site for the new Mellifont Abbey. The solution to overcrowding was to await the arrival of Fitzgerald's successor.

Retrieving Confidence and Celebrating Two Hundred Years
If the Redemptorists were still feeling somewhat chastened by their internal difficulties at the end of the 1920s, and by the political ambiguities that the Irish men and women of their generation had inherited, the 1930s would become a time for rebuilding confidence. It is suggested that Irish Catholic culture became particularly narrow and inward-looking in what has become known as 'the age of de Valera', from approximately his victory in the 1932 elections to his election as president in 1959. The Redemptorists played some part in the process of forging a new identity through their missions which reinforced many of the Catholic attitudes to the individual and society at the period. The Eucharistic Congress in 1932 marked the emergence of a stronger and more self-confident Catholic identity after the exhaustion and divisions of the civil war period.

The Eucharistic Congress coincided with Fianna Fáil's first accession to power. It was preceded by two weeks of retreats for women and men in all the churches of the city of Dublin. Redemptorists preached in ten churches during this fortnight, with the help of reinforcements drafted in from England. A congregation that prided itself on its founder's devotion to the Blessed Sacrament was not to be outdone in its support for the event. Two Redemptorist bishops and numerous other members of the congregation attended. One of the bishops, Nicholas Charnetskyi, belonged to the Ukrainian Church. When the Soviets disbanded the Ukrainian Catholic Church, he was arrested and spent years in labour camps. He was beatified by Pope John Paul II during his visit to the Ukraine in 2001. The other bishop was Archbishop Cesarano of Conza in Italy.

The bicentenary of the Redemptorist Congregation also fell in November 1932. It provided the Irish province with an opportunity to present itself more positively in the public eye. Redemptorist impact on Irish Church life since their arrival in Limerick eighty years before had been considerable. Apart from the local celebrations in each of the communities, the public face of the Redemptorists was revealed to a wider public through the bicentenary book *Two Hundred Years with the Redemptorists*.[6] It was a handsome production, well printed on good paper, with ample illustrations and solidly-bound in the traditional red and blue colours of the congregation. The general editor of the enterprise was Fr Eugene O'Donnell, and he had gathered a team of Redemptorists who wrote well in the formal ecclesiastical style of the time.

The nine essays have something of an apologia for the congregation, a way of answering some of the most frequent charges brought against it by its critics. The tone of the book is caught by the quotation on the title page of a poem by T. H. Mahoney (I have been unable to identify Mahoney):

> In search of straying souls, they stride along
> The highways of the world. Their constant song
> His word. They fight man's envy, pride and lust
> To save the gem before the setting's dust.

Apart from a survey of Redemptorist history, the book included chapters on formation, home and foreign missions, the apostolate in the Irish language, 'Redemptorists in the field of literature', and 'Redemptorists in heaven', with a final appendix listing all the houses of the congregation worldwide.

Of particular interest, to friends and critics alike, were the three chapters purporting to lift the veil on the inner workings of Redemptorist formation, community life, and the spirit of the congregation. All three writers agreed in presenting the congregation as a community of prayerful, studious men living under a detailed, rather austere rule, which stressed the virtues of prayer, obedience and hard-work, but who took a certain pride in their reputation for standing at some distance from the larger world. Eugene O'Donnell, for example, highlighted the moderation of the Redemptorist rule, but emphasised how it was through the discipline of common life that Redemptorists were formed:

> With them it descends into many little details, but in truth, the smaller the details, the greater its power in training men. It thus becomes *a mighty engine in breaking down the self-will of the individual*, [italics added] and welding all into one solid body, where the will of one is the will of all, the good of one becomes the good of all, and the loss of one is felt by all. By it, the corners are worn off the individuals, and they fit into one another as easily as pebbles on the shore of the sea.[7]

---

[6] *Two Hundred Years with the Redemptorists* (Dublin: At the Sign of the Three Candles, 1933).
[7] Eugene O'Donnell, 'The Redemptorist in the Making', in *Two Hundred Years*, 20–35.

John Doyle painted a picture of the ideal Redemptorist community as a place where prayer and study 'alternate with pleasing and helpful variety in the daily round' and where the apostolate of the monastery church corresponds to Clement Hofbauer's ideal of a continuous mission.[8] For James Coogan, what the rule lacked in severe forms of bodily penance, it supplied abundantly in other ways:

> Many of the little concessions granted to human frailty in the more severe orders are denied to Redemptorists. He has no holidays, he cannot play games, 'even in jest'. When a man makes up his mind to become a Redemptorist, he must throw away his golf-sticks, put aside his pack of cards, and bid farewell even to his pipe.[9]

Eugene O'Donnell addressed directly the challenge that his confreres stood aloof from the concerns and interests of the rest of Ireland:

> Why do you, Redemptorists, keep so far away from political gatherings of any hue? Neither do we ever meet you at concerts or *ceilidh* or amid the enthusiastic crowds at Croke Park, or Lansdowne Road or even at such sedate nerve-soothing assemblies as the classical, literary or philosophical societies of our university colleges. Why this remarkable aloofness?[10]

For him, it sprang from the rule's insistence on recollection, the wisdom of which had been well tested by experience.

James Coogan admitted that a Redemptorist might be attached for several years to a large church, but in the time, he would have made '*few acquaintances, few if any personal friends* [italics added] – probably he has not been inside the door of a house in the neighbourhood of his monastery except when called to visit the sick'. No matter how mildly the friends of the congregation might protest at this severe aloofness, Coogan hoped they might agree with the friend of St John of the Cross who told him: 'when you come to visit us, you entertain us, when you stay in your monastery, you edify us.'[11] Like O'Donnell, he insists that 'the political arena is closed to the Redemptorist', and notes that missions have 'proved one of the best means of allaying political feeling in a parish and healing the wounds caused by party friction', and that all of this would be nullified if the missioners were to make even the slightest political reference in a sermon. What made such a demanding lifestyle bearable was the spirit of camaraderie within the community.

---

8 John J. Doyle, 'The Redemptorist at Home' in *Two Hundred Years*, 36–48.
9 James Coogan, 'The Redemptorist Spirit' in *Two Hundred Years*, 103–15, 108.
10 O'Donnell, 'Redemptorist in the Making', 29.
11 Coogan, 'Redemptorist Spirit' in *Two Hundred Years*, 106.

Anthony Kieran's outline of the Redemptorist contribution to literature begins naturally enough with Alphonsus de Liguori, and sketches the leading contributions of Redemptorists to the theological sciences, with particular attention to the work of moral theology.[12] With such a distinguished list at their finger-tips, could they any longer meet in silence the insult of being an ill-educated group of popular missioners?

Two Hundred Years was well received in both the Catholic and national press. It gave a public profile to the congregation, and – perhaps even more importantly for those who had planned its publication – it became the handbook of Redemptorist self-definition for a generation. Seen at this distance, and in the light of the tumultuous years which preceded it, it is possible to suggest that the collection of essays presented a 'revisionist view' of a way of life which had, in fact, been more open to, and more shaped by, the world that it sought to exclude.

---

[12] Anthony Kieran, 'The Redemptorist in the Field of Literature' in *Two Hundred Years*, 85–104.

CHAPTER TWELVE

Second Spring for Parish Missions?

In his study of Redemptorist missions in the nineteenth century, John Sharp concludes that by the end of the century, the missions had reached a point of exhaustion, and that the emphasis had shifted from winning souls to maintaining the strong Catholic communities that were the results of the missioners' success.[1] The continuing success of missions in Ireland in the middle decades of the twentieth century points either to the fact that their practitioners had uncovered new needs to which they attempted to respond, or that the missions continued to respond to deeper needs in the Irish Church and society in this period.

Speaking at the close of the 1926 general mission in Cork, Bishop Daniel Cohalan said:

> Some foolish people outside the Church and some prophets of evil within the Church have been proclaiming a decline in loyalty of Irish Catholics and prophesying an abandonment of the Church by Catholics or at least a luke-warmness in regard to the sacraments and observances of the Church. Let the great mission give the answer.[2]

Cohalan had been the only Irish bishop to formally excommunicate republicans within his diocese in 1920.[3] Relations between republicans and the Church had become more than ordinarily tense after 1922 and raised the question of the future relationship between the Church and the republican movement. Cohalan's closing address at the end of the Cork general mission suggests that its success gave the lie to those who claimed that the difficulties of the civil war years had left the Church's authority wounded.

This chapter will look at how Redemptorist missions during the period immediately after the civil war responded to some of the needs of the church between the end of the civil war and the beginnings of the Second World

---

[1] Sharp examines the weakness of the mission apostolate at length in chapter ten, 'Missions: their shortcomings', *Reapers of the Harvest*, 211–36.
[2] Reported in *Cork Examiner*, 15 Mar. 1926.
[3] Pádraig Corkery, 'Bishop Daniel Cohalan of Cork on republican resistance and hunger strikes: a theological note' in *Irish Theological Quarterly*, vol. 67, no. 2 (June, 2002), 113–24.

War. It will also suggest that the mission-preaching of the Redemptorists endorsed, and even to some degree gave religious authentication to, the same social vision of sober, respectable Ireland that was being created by those who had fought in the struggle for independence in the preceding decade.

The Missioner in the Field
The mission chronicles kept by each community are a valuable and largely unexploited resource for the social history of Irish Catholicism in the first half of the twentieth century.[4] Although the entries are in the main extremely brief and conform to a well-tried formula, they can sometimes provide a unique snapshot of individual parishes in a way that few other Redemptorist sources do. The missioners knew their reports would be scrutinised by the brethren at home, so it was in their interests to write up their successes and write down their failures. On the other hand, since the justness of their observations would be tested in time by the next group of preachers, it was scarcely in their interests to over-emphasise the results they had achieved. They were, besides, writing for members of the club: the parish clergy probably never suspected that their parishes would be the subject of mission reports preserved in the archives of a monastery, and this may have given them a certain freedom of comment.

The literary form of the report follows a set formula. It records first the available facts about the parish which could be gleaned either directly from the pastor or constructed from other sources in the course of preparing for the mission. It is a rough and ready statement of statistics: the number of people in the parish, their main occupations, their socio-economic status, existing patterns of religious practice and finally, the numbers attending the mission, especially for confession and communion. These figures are likely to be fairly accurate, for most of the missioners carried a counter in their habit pocket to keep a tally of the number of confessions. The additional details, the fruit of personal observation, are often informative.

Many missioners were sensitive to the needs of Irish speakers. The language revival had given most of the younger missioners a basic knowledge of the language which they were encouraged during their student days to work up to at least sufficient proficiency to hear confessions. Several were native speakers themselves and particularly at home in gaeltacht missions in Ireland.

---

4 The Mission Chronicles are variously styled 'Apostolic Labours', 'Labores Apostolorum' or 'Labores Apostolici'. The name by which they were best known in Redemptorist communities is given here. Those consulted are to be found in the domestic archive of each of the houses, for example, 'Limerick Mission Chronicles' is in the Limerick archive. Since mission chronicles were kept in chronological order, references here are to the dates on which the mission was held.

When the opportunity offered, they also conducted missions in the Gaelic-speaking areas of the Scottish highlands and islands.[5] Even where a parish was considered as being in an English-speaking area, it was noted where people wanted to make their confession in Irish. Parish clergy were sometimes reluctant to have the mission in Irish. In Clockbrack [Cloughbrack] near Clonbur, County Galway, for instance, it was noted in 1927:

> English is not understood by the people. The ministrations on that account fail to satisfy the needs of the parish. The excuse of the priests, 'They must be educated for England' is fictitious. The education is a fraud and the ministry is abused. The affair of English speaking on the part of the priests is shockingly scandalous.[6]

Given the way in which bad weather affected mission attendance, missioners were acutely sensitive to the weather. Prior to rural electrification and the widespread use of the motor car, the most favourable time of year for country missions was between high spring and late autumn. There were areas in the west of Ireland, however, where seasonal migration to England and Scotland by a large proportion of the male population made the winter or early spring a more suitable time. An observation on the 'suitability of the time of year' was imperative for planning the next mission, so the records sometimes provide interesting information on the climate of Ireland over this period. The missioners were required to note for future reference what were termed 'the principal abuses of the place' or any particular difficulties encountered. In practice both are often ignored. Where the reporter does allow himself freedom to comment, the alert reader may often pick up some threads of the ebb and flow of local social life or a missioner's judgement, not always flattering, accurate or even sympathetic, of how parishes were run.

The number of people attending the evening sermon was the most obvious gauge of the success of a mission, but experienced missioners con-sidered numbers coming for confession and communion and so reflecting the number who had 'received the grace of the mission' as a more accurate guide. In rural areas where distance from the church was often great, assistance at morning Mass and mission-instruction was considered a better measure of fervour. Changing patterns of rural employment were already beginning to interfere with this: a not infrequent complaint, for instance, was that people were unable to attend in the morning because of their work in the creameries.

---

[5] There were occasional mission campaigns in the diocese of Argyle and the Isles. One, from 17 Oct. to 8 Dec. 1926, included the parishes of Inverie, Morae, Arisaig and Mingarry, as well as their out-churches: see Esker Mission Chronicle, vol. 3.

[6] Clockbrack [Cloughbrack] Mission, 12–19 June 1927, Esker Mission Chronicle, vol. 3.

Sometimes, a devout creamery manager might be persuaded to allow the workers time off for Mass, and this was generally acknowledged in the reports.

Occasionally, unsolicited comments on housekeeping arrangements in presbyteries and boarding houses appear. The preacher of one convent retreat advised his successors: 'if the bed is damp where you put up, take off your boots and go to bed in your clothes.'[7] Since the effect of the mission depended on maintaining good relations with their clerical hosts, one report offers the advice that 'two things must be avoided at Fr. H.'s table, the Irish language and Mr de Valera.'[8]

The Missioners and Politics

As has been suggested in the previous chapter, one of the effects of the Redemptorist missions in the 1920s and the 1930s was the reconciling of political differences that continued to smoulder after the end of the civil war. This was not something the missioners deliberately set out to do, but the sense of the mission as a celebration of the whole parish community united for a time of faith, prayer and preaching that tried to reach to the heart of the 'great truths of salvation' may well have been a factor in restoring relationships, especially in small places.

The first indication of how deeply local political differences were beginning to complicate relationships in parishes appears in 1920 in the report of a mission in Passage East, County Waterford:

> There was a sharp split between the village people and the country folk over a dance which was held by the farmers at a time when Sinn Féin prisoners were supposed to be dying in English prisons. The dancers were dispersed and the dance house wrecked. The bishop suggested allowing ill feeling on both sides to die down without much attempt to settle it up. Many on both sides anxious to have it settled. The split in no way interfered with the attendance. There were a few Catholic gentry – greatly admired by the P.P. by the way – who turned up only for Mass on Sundays. They sent the servants on the week-night.[9]

During a mission in Killarney in Lent 1923, the missioners noted the problems arising from the civil war but also how both sides availed of the presence

---

[7] Retreat in Convent of Mercy, Cashel, County Tipperary, 28–31 Dec. 1926, Limerick Mission Chronicle, vol. 4.

[8] Parish mission, Killenaule, County Tipperary, Dec. 1926, Limerick Mission Chronicle, vol. 4. The two priests on this mission were stout partisans of one and the other!

[9] Mission, Passage East, County Waterford, 25 July–5 Aug. 1920, Limerick Mission Chronicle, vol. 4.

of the mission. Despite the bishops' condemnation of the republicans in the civil war and the difficulty many had in receiving the sacraments in their local church, the missioners made a point of treating all alike in the confessional. The divisive political scene was noted among 'the abuses of the place':

> The most glaring abuse were the results of the 'Irregular campaign' of warfare on the citizen population and the disregard of episcopal authority. Having suffered much from the rebels, the people turned for consolation to religion Despite many difficulties, arising from the conditions of weather, roads, commercial depression, military activities and political propaganda, the work was blessed by God. Both nationalists and republicans attended well, and all sections approached the sacraments, notwithstanding the temporary estrangement between the extremists and the clergy who had openly denounced the wickedness of the Irregular campaign.[10]

Another retreat in 1923, at Tahilla, the out-church of Sneem, County Kerry, was regarded as successful since everyone profited by it, including the men 'on the run' who came to confession and communion. In Emly, County Tipperary in 1924, the Irregulars just released from internment camps made the mission and 'peace seemed quite restored'. Places regarded as 'storm centres' during the civil war such as Foynes, County Limerick and Castletownroche, County Cork also had missions in 1924 with good results. Kilmichael, County Cork, scene of an ambush in which seventeen Auxiliaries were killed, was described as 'the scene of strife and blood-shed in the civil fighting as well as in the Black and Tan days'.[11]

Not all divisions between priest and people were political: 'apart from politics, there is still a great deal of discord and quarrelling. The P.P. is losing his sight and seems to be perpetually quarrelling with someone in the parish.'[12] A land dispute in the area near Mount Melleray Abbey in County Waterford features on more than one occasion in the Limerick mission chronicles. Retreats had been given there quite frequently, but even a successful mission of 1924, 'failed to eradicate completely the habit of taking lawsuits and keeping up enmities between families: a habit which has been strengthened by the political quarrels of 1923 and 1924'. In some places, the effects of the unrest struck deeper levels of bitterness. The report for the mission in Dunhill, County Waterford noted that:

---

[10] Mission in Killarney, County Kerry, 18 Feb.–19 Mar. 1923, Limerick Mission Chronicle, vol. 4.

[11] Mission in Kilmichael, County Cork, 27 June–18 July 1926, Limerick Mission Chronicle, vol. 4.

[12] Ibid.

There had been a class-war in this and surrounding parishes – a strike of labourers against farmers – fomented from without and led to many outrages. This had died away before the mission, which helped to heal the wounds.[13]

Political differences between pastor and people occasionally ran deep. In one parish, the people's lack of enthusiasm for the mission was put down as 'owing perhaps to differences between people and priests in politics – priest being a violent imperialist and unsociable' and it was observed how political feeling had weakened the lever of the clergy on the control of the people.[14]

The mission in Gowel, Carrick-on-Shannon, County Leitrim earned a lengthy account of almost two pages in the Dundalk mission chronicle. It is of particular interest since there was a sequel to the story more than ten years later on the occasion of the next mission held there.[15] The abuse singled out for comment in 1922 was socialism. The Soviet revolution had taken place less than five years before. There had been some abortive attempts in the country to marry the republican idealism with a socialist vision. The main leaders of the movement in Carrick-on-Shannon were a returned emigrant called James Gralton and his sister. Gralton, a native of Effernagh, near Carrick-on-Shannon, had emigrated to America about 1909 where he became involved in radical socialist politics, but returned home in 1922.[16] According to the missioner, he had won the people's respect by his kindness. When the local hall was burned down by the Black and Tans, Gralton built a new one at his own expense, or rather, the chronicler suggests, with the large amount of money rumoured to be at his disposal for socialist propaganda purposes. Along with the dances, Gralton organised educational activities in the hall, with the accent on discussion of social questions. His sister gave music lessons and was rumoured to advocate divorce. Although they had both initially attended Mass on their return from America, they criticised the Church and 'then openly denied the existence of God'. To the obvious horror of the missioner,

---

13 Mission in Dunhill, County Waterford, 14–28 June 1925, Limerick Mission Chronicle, vol. 4.

14 Ibid.

15 Mission in Carrick-on-Shannon, County Leitrim, 28 May–6 June 1922, Dundalk Mission Chronicle, vol. 2.

16 Tim Pat Coogan, *The IRA* (London: Pall Mall Press, 1970), 105. Coogan, however, appears not to know of the earlier part of Gralton's career, since the only incident he describes is that associated with the mission in 1933, which will be described later, and he implies that Gralton returned from the United States immediately prior to this event.

It is almost incredible, but it is an absolute fact – that whilst preaching these doctrines night after night, the hall was crowded to the doors, and even respectable women, and mothers of families (wearing shawls on their heads to hide their identities) went to hear him.[17]

The missioner sprang into the fray with the opening sermon based on the text 'Beware of false prophets'. According to the missioner, Gralton had to go on the run after the second night and he returned to the United States. From then on, the missioners regarded their work as a glorious success. With the Graltons' departure, the hall stood empty. Carrick-on-Shannon had been reclaimed for the Church and the supporters of private property.

Trouble erupted again during the next Redemptorist mission at Gowel, County Leitrim in 1932.[18] Gralton had returned and was reported to have gathered twenty-four adherents. According to the mission chronicle, most of them were related to him, with the exception of a returned American called O'Beirne, who professed 'not to believe in the divinity of Christ'. The strength of public opposition generated by the mission once more forced Gralton on the defensive. His hall was burned down on Christmas Eve 1932. Gralton was arrested and his deportation under the Aliens Act was ordered by the Minister for Justice in the first Fianna Fáil cabinet, James Geoghegan, in February 1933. Since Gralton went on the run, the order could not be executed until the following August.[19] The minister's order had excited much comment, with demands that he be given a legal trial and questions were raised about the use of the Aliens' Act to deport a native-born Irishman. The case was taken up with particular intensity by the Revolutionary Workers Group, as the Communist party then styled itself, and they launched a 'Keep Gralton here' campaign. Seeing how high popular feeling was running against Gralton, the Leitrim IRA refused to become involved in the affair. That did not deter Peadar O'Donnell, who had founded *Saor Éire* as a radical socialist republican group just two years previously. When he attempted to address a public meeting after Mass at Drumsna, County Leitrim, he was pelted with mud by the congregation who had been warned by the celebrant to ignore the speakers. According to the *Irish Times* report, with the help of the clergy, the local garda superintendent 'appealed to the people to stop and they desisted but began to booh and cheer, and shouts were raised of "Down with Soviet Russia"'.[20]

---

[17] Carrick-on-Shannon, mission, 28 May–6 June 1922.
[18] Mission in Gowel, County Leitrim, 12–19 Mar. 1932, Dundalk Mission Chronicle, vol. 2.
[19] 'James Gralton Deported: Captured after six months' chase', *Irish Times*, 14 Aug. 1933, 8.
[20] *Irish Times*, 11 Mar. 1933, 17.

Saor Éire was condemned in a joint pastoral by the bishops in October 1931 as 'frankly communistic and working for the overthrow of Christian civilization in Ireland'.[21] The missioners also regarded what remained of the IRA with growing concern as being 'tainted with communistic and revolutionary doctrines'. The missioners preaching in Tralee, County Kerry in 1935 found that it existed in some strength there and 'their activities had to be denounced and the people warned against them.'[22] The major coup of the Kilkenny mission the same year was recorded as follows:

> Best of all, a little band of communists who were causing a great deal of worry and trouble submitted. They nearly all came from the cathedral parish. Having publicly abjured their errors, they were admitted to the sacraments.[23]

Even in the quiet backwater of Kiltulla, County Galway, two miles from Esker, 'communism was beginning to creep into certain quarters, but it was stopped.'[24] In the nearby parish of Fahy, 'the missioners warned the people of the dangers of communism creeping in amongst them and with good effect.'[25] There is no indication how precisely 'it was stopped' or what local conditions in such quiet places gave rise to advanced radical socialist thinking.

Redemptorists and 'the Ballrooms of Romance'

As political differences became less of a burning issue, the missioners' attention was taken up increasingly by matters of sexual morality. The development of dancehalls in rural Ireland is a social phenomenon that has received frequent attention. While the Redemptorists were not unique in their opposition to dancehalls, they did reflect a growing concern with the changing patterns of entertainment among young people made possible by the arrival of the motor car.

From the later 1920s, the missioners conducted a running battle with the promoters of dancehalls, particularly in the Cork–Kerry area. Dancehalls are mentioned as a problem in the Limerick mission records of the late 1920s and early 1930s in places such as Ballyporeen, Abbeydorney, Kilflynn, Clashmore, Milltown, Kenmare, Templemore, Ballylanders, Knocknagoshel, Kilgarvan, Dingle, Aghinagh and Liscarroll, in addition to the places which

---

[21] Keogh, *Vatican, the Bishops and Irish Politics*, 180.

[22] Mission in Tralee, County Kerry, 10 Mar.–7 Apr. 1935, Limerick Mission Chronicle, vol. 5.

[23] Mission in Kilkenny, 10–24 Mar. 1935, Limerick Mission Chronicle, vol. 5.

[24] Mission in Kiltulla, County Galway, 23–30 July 1933, Esker Mission Chronicle, vol. 3.

[25] Mission in Fahy, County Galway, 30 July–6 Aug. 1933, Esker Mission Chronicle, vol. 3.

will be discussed at some length below. The Esker and Dundalk mission chronicles also refer to dancehalls in places such as the parish of Backs, County Mayo, which had four, and Navan, County Meath, Ballyconnell, County Cavan, and Tarmonbarry, County Roscommon.

When interest in one mission in 1930 was slow to develop, the missioners embarked on a campaign of house-visitation and concluded that the cause of the spiritual lassitude was the local dancehall. The chronicler recorded that in the preaching:

> A dance-hall in the village was denounced as an occasion of sin, and when the owner refused to close the hall – by express command of the bishop – he was denounced *nominatim* [by name] at the close of the mission. A stiff and obstinate people![26]

The impression is given, particularly from the final comment, that the people did not share the indignation of either missioners or bishop regarding the dangers of their dancehall. The number of dancehalls either had grown rapidly at this time or else the Church authorities had only just become aware of a reality that people had been taking for granted for a long time. Dingle, for example, was reported as having three dance-houses open during winter and spring, especially on a Sunday night, to a late hour. 'All-night dancing', often used as a term of abuse, meant, in fact, dances that continued until 2 a.m.

Some indication of what the missioners regarded as the depravity of the dancehalls can be gleaned from the following account from Ballyvourney and Coolea in the Cork Gaeltacht in 1932:

> There was a dancehall there to which hundreds of people come long distances by motors. The hall was a scandal. There are sixteen share-holders in the hall, some of whom created difficulties. Although the bishop had come and spoken against the evil of all-night dancing, after that the committee defied him by holding two all-night dances. Over fifty motors from Cork city, Kinsale, Bantry etc. invaded the little village and held dances for two days and two nights from Whit Sunday to the following Tuesday. Over 750 strangers and natives celebrate Pentecost in that way.[27]

Fourteen of the shareholders in the hall gave written promises of better behaviour to the administrator at the close of the mission. The solemn blessing traditionally given to the parish and all its inhabitants at the end of the mission was framed in terms that excluded two shareholders who remained

---

26 Mission in Kilgarvan, County Kerry, 8–22 June 1930, Limerick Mission Chronicle, vol. 5.
27 Mission in Ballyvourney, County Cork, 7 Sept.–12 Oct. 1932, Limerick Mission Chronicle, vol. 5.

obstinate and the prayers of the congregation were asked for their conversion, effectively branding them as public sinners.[28] It is understandable why dance-hall owners at another place shirked meeting the missioners, who, with a degree of smug self-satisfaction, recorded that the people closed it by not attending the duration of the mission, as they were pledged to do.[29] The missioners were not alone in their opposition to dances. According to the *Irish Times*,

> The clergy, the judges and the police are in agreement concerning the baleful affect of drink and low dancing upon rural morals. Further restrictions on the sale of drinks, a remorseless war on the poteen industry, the strict supervision of dance halls and the banning (by law if need be) of all night dances would abolish many inducements to sexual vice.[30]

Opposition to dancehalls dwindled with the passing of the controlling legislation of the Public Dance Halls Act, 1935.

Similar campaigns were waged against immodesty in women's dress and immoral literature. There are several references in the mission records to a campaign for 'Modesty of Deportment and Dress'.[31] It is reported, for instance, that one hundred and twenty women and girls signed up for the campaign in Clashmore, County Waterford in 1928 and another large crowd did so in Piltown, County Kilkenny. 'Immodest dress', by definition, included swimwear, and the new fashion of slacks for women. As they had become more accessible, seaside resorts were attracting the young. It is not difficult to see how, in the missioners' eyes, Ballybunion in County Kerry could earn a reputation for 'much public immorality and "marriages of necessity"'.[32] In a quiet backwater like Roundstone, County Galway, the missioners noted abuses such as:

---

[28] Ibid.

[29] Mission in Kilflynn, County Kerry, 16–23 Sept. 1934, Limerick Mission Chronicle, vol. 5.

[30] Cited by Gearóid Ó hAllmhuráin in 'Dancing on the Hobs of Hell: Rural Communities in Clare and the Dance Halls Act of 1935' in *New Hibernia Review*, vol. 9, no. 4 (Winter, 2005), 9–18, at 10.

[31] James S. Donnelly, 'The Peak of Marianism in Ireland, 1930–60' in Stewart J. Brown and David W. Miller (eds), *Piety and power in Ireland, 1760–1960: Essays in honour of Emmet Larkin* (Notre Dame, IN: University of Notre Dame Press, 2000), 252–84, refers to this as coming into being in the 1940s through the work of the Sisters of Mercy at Mary Immaculate Training College in Limerick. According to Sr Loretto O'Connor, the Modest Dress and Deportment Crusade was founded by a group of students of the college in 1927: see *Passing on the Torch: a history of Mary Immaculate College, 1898–1998* (Limerick: Mary Immaculate College, 1998), 40–1.

[32] Mission in Ballybunion, County Kerry, 3–17 Sept. 1931, Limerick Mission Chronicle, vol. 5.

Mixed bathing by strangers, all-night dancing in farmhouses, company keeping ... The parish priest formed a vigilance committee to stamp out mixed bathing. Visitors had introduced men's dress for women [slacks!] but the Legion of Mary is going to deal with this scandal.[33]

A Redemptorist in a small town warned future missioners not to take its peaceful appearance for granted and advised that:

The missioner to this place should make it his first duty to find out and to visit those who are publicly known to be living an immoral life. One or two such were in the Children of Mary.[34]

During a mission in Navan in 1928, a promise not to sell bad books and papers was exacted from the local newsagents and 'a secret vigilance committee was formed of seven men whose business it will be to see that the promise is faithfully kept and report to the priests any information they may obtain about bad literature coming into the parish.'[35]

The 'Poitín Missions'

The abuse of drink had been long regarded as a serious social evil in Ireland. The great temperance campaign of 1909 in the west of Ireland and the Redemptorists' part in it has been mentioned in an earlier chapter. Experience of mission-preaching in the 1920s and 1930s suggested that a major cause of alcoholism and other social ills in the rural west sprang from a thriving trade in poitín. The first references to poitín in Redemptorist mission records is in connection with abuses that came to light during a mission in Carraroe, County Galway in 1926[36] and in the Pullathomas–Aghoos district of north Mayo two years later.[37] The response to it was a series of missions preached by two Redemptorists, Frs Stiofán Conneely and John Gorey, mainly in the

---

[33] Mission in Roundstone, County Galway, 7–28 Aug. 1935, Esker Mission Chronicle, vol. 3. As early as 1920, the public abuse mentioned during a mission in Rosses Point, County Sligo, 1–15 Aug. 1920, was 'mixed bathing': see Dundalk Mission Chronicle, vol. 2.

[34] Mission in Kinvara, County Galway, 8–22 Apr. 1934, Esker Mission Chronicle, vol. 3.

[35] Mission in Navan, County Meath, 29 Apr.–30 May 1928, Dundalk Mission Chronicle, vol. 2.

[36] Mission in Carraroe, County Galway, 3–10 Oct. 1926. Fr John Gorey preached this mission along with Fr Michael McLoughlin. The profile of the parish describes it as inhabited by 'fishermen and small farmers. All knowing Irish, except half a dozen, few able to follow an English sermon well ... one abuse – making and drinking of potheen [sic]', Esker Mission Chronicle, vol. 3. The Esker Mission Chronicle is the major source for what follows. Entries for Gaeltacht missions are usually written in Irish: translations here are my own.

[37] Mission in Pullathomas–Aghoos, County Mayo, 3–17 June 1928, Esker Mission Chronicle, vol. 3: 'the poteen evil was universal.'

Connemara Gaeltacht and north Mayo between 1931 and 1935.[38] The opening salvos of the campaign were fired during the next mission in Carraroe in 1931. The report on the mission mentions clearly:

> Poitín was the abuse, and there was a lot of drunkenness as a result of it. We made the people bring down the poitín and on the last Sunday, we had a bonfire with about 14 gallons or so. The mission-cross was planted and there was a big procession the same day. We got about 1,000 names for the Sacred Heart Confraternity. The priest there is one in a million and they are a holy people who listened to everything. Apart from the poitín, everything is fine. In Tír an Fhiaidh, the out-church, 13 stills, 6 worms, 35 gallons and 6 bags of malt were handed in, and everyone took the pledge around the bonfire on the last Sunday of the mission. In Leitir Meallain, most of the people involved in poitín making again handed over 30 gallons, 14 stills and worms and 5 bags of malt.[39]

Flushed with their success, the two missioners moved on to Rosmuc.

> The blessing of God was on the work of this mission. The parish was destroyed (*mílte*) with poitín. The people handed up every drop they had and every worm. We had a bonfire in all the places. In Litir Mór, 50 gallons of poitín, 15 stills and worms, a ton of malt. In Camus, up to 70 gallons, 24 stills, 18 worms, 2 tons of malt. In Rosmuc, 5 stills, 5 worms, 4 bags of malt and 10 gallons of poitín. All the men took the pledge. The people showed strong faith. All the people came to the mission. Totally in Irish: not a word of English.[40]

In August of the same year, they were back in Connemara, this time in Carna where they found little enough poitín, except around Derryrush, with a little in Cashel. They also found a little in Rossaveel the following month, but there was no public burning of stills. The following year, they were in Moygownagh, County Mayo, in the diocese of Killala, where:

> the parish priest gave every assistance to make the mission a success. Young people making poteen. Ten stills were given in. The year before, two men died from the effects of poteen. Men, women and children

---

[38] Brendan McConvery, 'Hell-fire and Poitín: Redemptorist missions in the Irish Free State, 1922–36' in *History Ireland*, vol. 8, no. 2 (Autumn, 2000), 18–22.

[39] Mission in Carraroe, County Galway, 25 Jan.–22 Feb. 1931, Esker Mission Chronicle, vol. 3.

[40] Mission in Rosmuc, County Galway, 22 Feb.–22 Mar. 1931, Esker Mission Chronicle, vol. 3. As well as in the main parish church in Rosmuc, missions were also preached in the out-churches of Leitir Mór and Camus.

were drinking it. All night dancing another abuse. Poteen was brought in and sold at dances.[41]

A one-week mission in Kilfian, County Clare in 1932 brought in six poteen stills.[42] The following year, during a bi-lingual mission in Moycullen, County Galway, where every second sermon was in Irish, the missioners detected poitín-drinking in some places.[43] Two missions in the diocese of Killala had similar results: in Corballa, County Mayo, 'the holders of poteen surrendered or destroyed their stills.'[44] The mission in Ballycastle, County Mayo was described as 'most successful. Every poteen-maker gave up the trade. All took the anti-poteen pledge. One hundred and seventy became Pioneers, 4 stills given up'.[45]

Pullathomas, County Mayo, where the presence of poitín had first been detected in 1928, was revisited for a mission in the autumn of 1933. The list of abuses is extensive: apart from poitín-making, there was drinking at wakes, Mass-missing and neglect of the sacraments. It was reported that boys and girls aged twenty-two years had not been to Mass since their confirmation, and 'the people were destroyed with poitín'.[46] Twenty-three stills and seventy-seven barrels were handed up. The renewal of the Ballycastle mission the following year gave heartening results, for only two cases of poitín-making were discovered since the mission and all who had broken the pledge came to renew it.[47] The parish of Lacken, near Ballycastle in County Mayo, remained untouched by reform:

> People gone wild. Poteen, dancing, Mass-missing rife. Sheebeens abun-
> dant. People would not come out [for the mission]. Missioners spent
> Monday and Tuesday 'raiding' and afterwards there was no trouble …
> Eleven stills publicly burned. All the parish took the anti-poitín pledge.[48]

A mission in Oughterard, County Galway was preached by John Gorey and Tom Cassin in July–August of 1934. There were reported to be sheebeens,

---

[41] Mission in Moygowna, County Mayo, 7–21 Aug. 1932, Esker Mission Chronicle, vol. 3.

[42] Mission in Kilfian, County Clare, 21–28 Aug. 1932, Esker Mission Chronicle, vol. 3.

[43] Mission in Moycullen, County Galway, 23 Apr.–7 May 1933, Esker Mission Chronicle, vol. 3.

[44] Mission in Corballa, County Mayo, 11–18 June 1933, Esker Mission Chronicle, vol. 3.

[45] Mission in Ballycastle, County Mayo, 20–27 May 1934, Esker Mission Chronicle, vol. 3.

[46] Mission in Pullathomas, County Mayo, 24 Sept.–8 Oct. 1933, Esker Mission Chronicle, vol. 3.

[47] Mission in Ballycastle, County Mayo, 20–27 May 1934, Esker Mission Chronicle, vol. 3.

[48] Mission in Lacken, County Mayo, 27 May–10 June 1934, Esker Mission Chronicle, vol. 3.

especially in the village of Rusheens, but everyone took the pledge. Culnamuck, one of the out-churches of Oughterard, proved more of a challenge:

> A stubborn and ignorant people, debauched by poitín. They told barefaced lies and only with great difficulty did they surrender four stills. All except four took the anti-poteen pledge, but their earnestness is doubtful. The neighbouring parish of Killanin spoils them.[49]

Conneely and Gorey returned to Rosmuc in Lent of 1935. They began by calling in the poitín-making equipment which brought in five stills and three distilling 'worms', adding that 'there is no point of giving a mission here unless they hand in the stills.'[50] The three-day renewal in Lacken took place in June and the missioners may have congratulated themselves on the improvement in the parish:

> Last year people in a bad state with poitín. Renewal most consoling. People kept the pledges against poitín which abuse has been rooted out.[51]

The Redemptorist anti-poitín campaign lasted for a little over four years. It was pursued with the greatest vigour in gaeltacht parishes. It may be due to the fact that Conneely, who was a native Irish speaker from the Aran Islands, believed he had his finger more accurately on the pulse of the people of the Gaeltacht. It is difficult to assess its impact at this distance. The missioners' reports themselves would suggest, that despite the public burnings of stills, poitín-making was never totally eradicated, although there is some evidence that the making and sale of poitín was curtailed. The work of Conneely and Gorey was recognised by the commissioner of the Garda Síochána, who directed his deputy commissioner, Éamonn Coogan, to write a letter of appreciation for the missioners' efforts to the rector of Esker. Coogan commends them for doing 'more in a short time than the Gardaí could hope to accomplish even over a considerable period'.[52]

What methods did the missioners use? Apart from the dramatic burning of the stills and poitín-making equipment, the one tactic to emerge clearly from the reports is the administration of an anti-poitín pledge not to make,

---

[49] Mission in Oughterard, County Galway 15 July–5 Aug. 1934, Esker Mission Chronicle, vol. 3. Poitín-making was a 'reserved sin' in the diocese of Galway: it could only be absolved by a priest having special faculties from the bishop. The missioner's ire seems to be directed at the more benign approach adopted by a neighbouring pastor.

[50] Mission in Rosmuc, County Galway, 3 Feb.–3 Mar. 1935, Esker Mission Chronicle, vol. 3.

[51] Renewal of mission in Lacken, 27–30 June 1935, Esker Mission Chronicle, vol. 3.

[52] Éamonn Coogan to the Superior of Esker, 18 Aug. 1934, Esker Domestic Archives.

distribute or to use the illegal spirit. The pledge was administered with dramatic, if largely improvised, solemnity, including invoking spiritual threats on those who would dare break it. The text of none of the sermons preached by either Gorey or Conneely have survived. It is likely that references to the poitín trade would simply have been worked into their repertoire of major evening sermons. Reports have survived in the oral tradition of Connemara of the missioner throwing his stole into the congregation in a dramatic gesture of divine disapproval. There are occasional references to 'raiding' in the mission reports: presumably this refers to surprise visits by the missioners to places where they suspected that poitín or the equipment for its manufacture might be stored. A Redemptorist who in the course of a mission some sixty years later visited one of the parishes mentioned here has told the author how the 'poitín mission' of the 1930s still survived in the folk-memory. They included stories of the missioners entering the homes of suspected poitín-makers and turning the picture of the Sacred Heart towards the wall as a symbol of how the consecration of the family represented by the picture was being undone by the activity of poitín-making. It was inevitable that such tactics left much pain, humiliation and resentment in their wake.

The Faith of the People

Despite the strong tactics occasionally used in campaigns such as those against dancehalls or the poitín trade, the missioners treated the people for the most part with respect and even with stiff affection. They did not generally expect to find the average parish a sink of corruption. The reports record for the most part that there was 'no particular abuse' in the parish. The Redemptorists saw themselves as preaching by preference to ordinary people, with ordinary sins, and these were the people who responded best to them. If some members of the upper middle-classes attended, that was all to the good, but the missioners were not going to court their good will at the expense of the vastly more numerous popular audience. In Cobh, County Cork, it was noted in 1935 that 'as a body, the "aristocracy" of Ashbrook did not attend', but the elderly survivor of the O'Connell dynasty of Derrynane, Mme O'Connell, whom the writer of the mission chronicle regarded as heir to the real Irish aristocracy, attended morning and evening along with her household staff.[53] The missioners' commitment to fostering the declining Irish language has been noted already, and there were many instances asserting the importance of pastoral work in Irish in the already dwindling Gaeltachtaí. It was noted, for example, that in the apparently thriving Gaeltacht area of Ballyvourney, County Cork, the clergy 'for many years' had

---

[53] Mission in Cobh, County Cork, 28 Apr.–12 May 1935, Limerick Mission Chronicle, vol. 5.

spoken only English and although the administrator at the time of the mission in 1932 spoke Irish, he preached in English.[54]

The missioners frequently commented on the unobtrusive piety to be seen in the countryside and in the small towns. The people of one parish were 'nearly all total abstainers – there is no public house in the parish'.[55] A renewal of the mission in Corofin, County Clare prompted the observation that since the last mission, 'many young men are going to daily communion and some old women have begun to talk to their enemies.'[56] The retreat-giver to the Irish-speaking battalion at Renmore, County Galway in 1928 painted a glowing picture of the piety of some of the young officers of the fledgling Free State army. One captain kept the traditional 'black fast' for the whole of Lent, abstaining from butter, milk and eggs as well as from meat for the whole six weeks, while the commandant went daily to Mass and communion and made spiritual reading and meditation each day of Lent.[57] If less dramatic than during the earliest missions of the nineteenth century, the eagerness of the people to get to confession from the missioners was remarkable. Many stayed much of the day waiting in the queue at the confessional, often in damp clothes and with little to eat.

The final part of the Redemptorist mission, the 'exercises of the *vita devota*' or instruction in piety and prayer extending over the final few days, was the special contribution of Alphonsus Liguori to the traditional mission. It included the celebration of public devotions such as the way of the cross, the holy hour of adoration before the blessed sacrament and the consecration of the parish to Our Lady, as well as promotion of the rosary and visits to the blessed sacrament. Devotion to Mary often included the setting up of a picture of Our Lady of Perpetual Help in a prominent place in the church: it still remains the most common icon of Mary in Irish churches. The sense of warm devotion that these events created was in stark contrast to both the stern preaching of the 'eternal truths' in the early part of the mission, and to the normally frugal diet of Irish Catholicism, particularly in the rural parish churches. The same might be said for the promotion of congregational hymn-singing: although the mission hymn repertoire was not a large one, it did create an impression on the people.

---

[54] Mission in Ballyvourney, County Cork, 7 Sept.–2 Oct. 1932, Limerick Mission Chronicle, vol. 5.

[55] Mission in Drumraney, County Westmeath, 29 June–7 July 1924, Dundalk Mission Chronicle, vol. 3.

[56] Mission in Corofin, County Clare, 13–27 June 1926, Limerick Mission Chronicle, vol. 5.

[57] Retreat in Renmore Barracks, 25 Mar.–1 Apr. 1928, Limerick Mission Chronicle, vol. 5.

Customs that had been more common in the previous century survived in some places into the 1930s. Reservation of the blessed sacrament in the church was still not the universal norm, for one of the results of an increase in devotion to the eucharist promoted during the mission in Ballinhassig, County Cork in 1926 was to have the blessed sacrament reserved in all three churches of the parish.[58] None of the three churches of Kilmichael parish reserved the blessed sacrament: there had never been benediction in one of them before the mission and in another, it had been last given twelve years previously.[59]

Traces of Jansenism lingered in the devotional sensibility of some religious communities. A retreat-master records that in one convent 'a number of sisters have the custom of not going to communion several days during the retreat.'[60] Despite Pius X's decree on frequent communion in 1905, little had been done in some places to foster frequent reception of the eucharist. The only Sunday Mass available in many rural churches was at 11 a.m. or midday. The strict fasting regulations which required the communicant to fast – even from water – from midnight put regular communion beyond the reach of many, especially those who had to rise at an early hour to attend to the chores of house and farm. A report on religious practice in Lisgoold, County Cork in 1933 reads:

> Being accustomed only to receive the sacraments at the 'Stations', the people were slow to go to communion [during the mission]. Nor did they make much of the First Friday. By order of the PP, no confessions were heard on that morning, though the curate lives near the church. They must come the day before. The PP himself lives a mile away, and says Mass at home daily, except on Sundays and allows no bell to be rung during the weekdays, not even for the Angelus nor for the curate's Mass on weekdays, on the plea that no village exists in the place. It is ascribed by some to economic reasons that the Blessed Sacrament is not reserved and the bell is not rung in the church. The Blessed Sacrament has been removed on the pretext of dampness from the place.[61]

Full attendance at Sunday Mass was not the norm everywhere. A distance greater than three miles from the church and the absence of transport were

---

[58] Mission in Ballinhassig, County Cork, 16 May–19 June 1926, Limerick Mission Chronicle, vol.5.

[59] Mission in Kilmichael, County Cork, 27 June–18 July 1926, Limerick Mission Chronicle, vol. 5

[60] Retreat to religious, Convent of Mercy, Bessbrook, County Armagh, 13–20 July 1920, Dundalk Mission Chronicle, vol. 2.

[61] Mission in Lisgoold, County Cork, 3–17 Sept. 1933, Limerick Mission Chronicle, vol. 5.

regarded as excusing from the Sunday obligation, particularly in cold or wet weather. It was noted earlier that in places were poitín-drinking was wide-spread a corresponding drop in Mass attendance was observable. In Castlebar, County Mayo, 'many absented themselves from Mass and the sacraments. The number of these absentees was so remarkable that it might be considered a public abuse.'[62] The report does not pause to enquire why the practice rate was low.

The Redemptorists strenuously promoted confraternities on their missions or attempted to reform those already in existence as a way of continuing the practices of the 'devout life' that the mission sought to encourage. The experience of the Redemptorist confraternities in Limerick and Belfast had taught them that men needed the solidarity of other men and a shared sense of manly brotherhood if religion were to avoid the label of 'pious' or the suspicion that it was 'a women's thing'. In many places, confraternities existed only in name. Although the missioners exhorted the people to attend, they held out scant hope that the local clergy would run them with sufficient vigour or interest to ensure their survival. In the absence of regular sodalities, there was little enough spiritual nourishment for the average layperson, particularly in the rural parts. In running their confrater-nities, the Redemptorists had been able to draw on the assistance of their brethren in large religious communities. This made them sometimes unsympathetic to the burden that preparing material for the confraternity in addition to the normal work of the ministry entailed for the local clergy. In one place, the people were regarded as good but singularly unfortunate in the clergy they had been given, for 'in this ill-served parish, all they get is Mass and that is all.'[63] On the other hand, 'the mania for short sermons and quick devotions' meant that mission-preaching in Waterford was not easy as 'people here find it difficult to listen to a sermon over ten minutes.'[64]

Given the very public nature of the mission event in a rural community, attendance was usually large. The mission chronicle entries often note that everyone or nearly everyone attended at least part of the mission. Apart from those confined to home through old age or illness, failure to attend was often put down to mental illness or 'oddness'. When no signs of either were apparent, a common explanation was the effect of travel abroad. In Kenmare, County Kerry, for example, there were

---

[62] Mission in Castlebar, County Mayo, 4–25 Sept. 1927, Esker Mission Chronicle, vol. 3.
[63] Mission in Aglish, County Waterford, 10–24 June 1934, Limerick Mission Chronicle, vol. 5.
[64] Mission in Waterford cathedral, 22 Feb.–15 Mar. 1931, Limerick Mission Chronicle, vol. 5.

some negligees [sic] and absentees including drunkards and a few apostates who had travelled abroad and returned with their faith impaired. But nearly all the inebriates attended and some of the apostates promised to pray.[65]

Very occasionally, other reasons for non-attendance emerge. The dissenter is on occasion described as 'an educated man', the local doctor perhaps, who has intellectual difficulties with the faith. Very occasionally, the reason for non-attendance is that the person is in a second or 'irregular' marriage, that is, one contracted outside the strict norms of ecclesiastical law.

Attendance at missions was almost universal, and adherence to the church system that it implied was even more so. To a large degree, the agendas of church and state in post-civil war Ireland coalesced. In addition to measures to control the consumption of alcohol or control dance halls, acts for the censorship of films and publications were passed by the Dáil in 1923 and 1929 respectively. The local and national Catholic press could be relied upon to print glowing reports of missions and similar events, often citing extracts from sermons or clichés that the recent mission was 'the best in living memory'. While the Redemptorists did not lack criticism, much of it was behind hands. In the 1930s and 1940s, more searching criticism of an Ireland where, to quote James Joyce, 'God and Caesar were hand in glove' was the domain of creative writers. It may be appropriate to conclude this chapter with an extended look at how one novelist recorded his first-hand experience of attending a mission.

Tarry Flynn goes to the Mission

Patrick Kavanagh's *Tarry Flynn* is a semi-autobiographical and satirical novel set in County Monaghan in the 1930s.[66] Kavanagh, nevertheless, writes with the soul and the conscience of a believer, to whom the matters of the Spirit are as important as the energies of the life-force which he feels painfully has been stunted, both in himself and in the community in which he lives. The account of a parish mission in the second chapter is probably the longest account of a mission in Irish fiction. The parish priest, thinking his parish was 'in danger of boiling over into wild orgies of lust' following an attack on a young girl, summoned two Redemptorists 'who were such specialists in sex sins', from their monastery in Dundalk.[67] The excitement generated by news

---

[65] Mission in Kenmare, County Kerry, 4–25 Aug. 1929, Limerick Mission Chronicle, vol. 5.
[66] Patrick Kavanagh, *Tarry Flynn* (London: Pilot Press, 1948). The account of the mission is in chapter two, 37–61, *passim.* MacGibbon and Kee edition, 1968.
[67] The Dundalk Mission Chronicle provides evidence that missions were given regularly by the members of that community in Kavanagh's native parish of Inishkeen, County Monaghan.

of the mission grips everyone in the place. Tarry, for all his dreams of freedom, is little more than a dependent, overgrown boy. Despite their shows of bravado, he and his best friend, Eusebius, are still inexperienced sexually but bursting with curiosity. His mother warns him that he will have to attend every evening or face the risk of being talked about by the neighbours. The congregation gathered in the church for the opening sermon seemed to Tarry to be made up of grey-headed and bald old men with 'the look of old blackguards who are being flattered by bawdy suggestions' and elderly unmarried women. The young people who crowded into the gallery could not lessen the terrible impact of old age and sterility in the church. In the opening sermon, one of the missioners told a story about a boy whose sexual behaviour led to his girlfriend's suicide. At its conclusion, the preacher slammed the pulpit, crying out that the boy had damned the girl's soul. For all its passion, the sermon left Tarry indifferent as 'it lacked that touch of humour, that appearance of not being too earnest which is the real sign of sincerity.'

A meeting with one of the missioners, Fr Andrew, went badly. Tarry's second encounter with the priest in the confessional went even more disastrously wrong. Trying to think of something original to confess, he spluttered that he had read books. The words were scarcely out when he realised his mistake, for the priest pounced immediately and demanded to know the name of the writer. Tarry had read nothing more spiritually-damaging than old schoolbooks or an occasional newspaper. He grasped at the first name that came into his head and said 'Shaw, Father.' He had never read a line of Shaw but he had picked up the notion somewhere that Shaw was a radical writer. The missioner exhorted him to leave writers like Shaw aside and to read regularly the *Messenger of the Sacred Heart*, where he would find some of the finest literature known.

Kavanagh captures accurately the spirit of moral and social compulsion that forced even internal dissenters like Tarry to the mission, for if he stayed away, his absence would be noted and he would be put down as 'a queer fellow'. Not that Tarry had any intention of missing the carnival spirit of the mission. He had toyed with a possible token resistance by staying away on one evening. Part of the carnival atmosphere of the mission was created by the mission-stalls outside the church where colourful rosaries and other religious goods were on sale. The stalls were kept by 'fantastic dealing women with fluent tongues and a sense of freedom unknown in Dargan' who, unlike the missioners, had an easy manner with God – 'like poets or actresses'.

For all the excitement it brought, the mission's initial promise of life proved deceptive. As the crowds drifted homewards, Tarry sensed that 'once again the clay hand was clapped across the mouth of prophecy.'

Kavanagh's picture of the mission is accurate in its details. It is the writing of a man who has been present at more than one of them, who has felt the excitement and sense of occasion of the opening, who has seen the garish mission stalls and walked home with his companions discussing the merits of the preachers and comparing the confessors. He had associated them with life and hope, and above all with the symbols of burgeoning crops and the promise of sexual fulfilment, the assuaging of 'the great hunger' in the hearts of young men like Tarry and his companions, with little prospect of marriage. This was at once a social reality in the Ireland of Kavanagh's youth and a central metaphor in much of Kavanagh's poetry. More than most of the critics of the narrow morality of the sermons on 'the occasions', Kavanagh grasped how such preaching in fact generated a sense of desire and curiosity that might have served as an antidote to the life-denying financial ethics which kept young men unmarried until late in life.[68]

The portrait of the Redemptorists which emerges from Kavanagh's pages is not a flattering one. It contains an element of satire even to the point of caricature. The example of the boy and the girl was a staple one in sermons on the occasions of sin, and Kavanagh catches accurately the impression of triteness it created once the initial frisson of horror was past. He suspects, too, that the sermon was too highly wrought, too much of a product of pulpit artifice. Such a judgement may well be the poet's response to how many preachers with more good-will than imagination or talent filled the fifty minutes allotted to the evening sermon with hackneyed and borrowed material. He highlights, too, the missioners' inability to enter the world of young people with any degree of sympathy, deftly demonstrating the missioner's pompous ignorance of which he is supremely unaware. Despite its humour, Kavanagh's portrait is a searching one and there are probably few Redemptorists who would deny its perceptiveness.

---

[68] The chronicler of the mission in Murroe, County Limerick, 14–28 July 1936, regards 'late marriage and no marriage' among the 'abuses of the place': see Mission Chronicle, Limerick Domestic Archives, vol. 5.

CHAPTER THIRTEEN

The Making of a Missioner

The making of a missioner was the goal of the entire Redemptorist formation system, a process that lasted seven or eight years – longer, if the years of
secondary education passed at the juvenate or secondary college in Limerick
are included, or the time at university taking a degree in arts or science.
In addition to the standard academic training, emphasis was placed on
voice-production and elocution through public reading during meals in the
refectory or taking part in the plays or Gilbert and Sullivan operas which
were a major part of the student community's entertainment during the
Christmas holidays.

The spiritual foundation was laid in the novitiate, which prepared the
young man, usually entering in his late teens or early twenties, to make
profession of the vows by which he engaged himself to the imitation of Jesus
Christ the Most Holy Redeemer and to 'working for the salvation of the most
abandoned souls, especially of those who live in country districts'.[1] When the
Irish province became independent in 1898, a novitiate with six clerical and
four brother novices was established at Dundalk. It would remain there until
1949, when it was transferred to the accommodation in Esker vacated a
decade earlier by the transfer of the house of studies to Cluain Mhuire,
Galway. By the early 1970s, changes in the formation system brought the
novitiate back to Dundalk.

The regime was strict, with the emphasis on learning the basic spiritual
and community skills of Redemptorist life. Paramount among these was the
making of mental prayer or meditation which was practised three times a day
– morning and evening in common and in the afternoon in the privacy of
one's room. It also entailed learning how to cultivate the twelve 'monthly
virtues' that were regarded as the distinctively Redemptorist contribution to
the ascetical life. The 'monthly virtues' were faith (January), hope (February),
love of God (March), love of neighbour (April), poverty (May), chastity
(June), obedience (July), meekness and humility of heart (August), mortifi-
cation (September), recollection and silence (October), prayer (November)
and self-denial and love of the Cross (December). The earliest form of the

---

[1] Traditional formula of Profession, see *Ordo Suscipiendi Habitum et Professionem Emittendi in
Congregatione Ss Redemptoris* (Rome: CSsR, 1959), 157.

Redemptorist rule consisted of twelve chapters based on these virtues. They formed the basis of the meditations, spiritual talks to the community by the superior at the weekly chapter and the individual's twice daily examinations of conscience. They continued to hold a central place in Redemptorist spirituality until the post-Vatican II period. More attentive historical research showed that Alphonsus Liguori lived a freer kind of spirituality in which a regimented system such as the monthly virtues had little place. Their presence probably owed more to the influence of Bishop Thomas Falcoia, the first director of the new institute of Redemptorists and Redemptoristines, than it did to Alphonsus himself.[2] Still more important was the insertion of the candidates within the Redemptorist 'story' through the reading of its history and the lives of its saints. The test of whether a candidate had made a successful novitiate was how well, in the opinion of his novice master and others, he had absorbed the undefined, but identifiable, 'spirit of the Congregation'.

Up until the period immediately following the Second Vatican Council, the plan of philosophical and theological studies in the student houses at Clonard (1900–5), Esker (1905–38) or Galway (1939–68) followed in the main that laid down by Church law for the training of priests. If there was a particular Redemptorist edge to it, it was in the emphasis placed on moral theology, seen as the indispensable requisite for the confessor, especially one likely to be exposed to a range of unusual moral problems in the course of his work as a missioner. While the Latin manuals of philosophy and dogmatic theology were those used in seminaries throughout the Catholic world (for example, the two-volume *Elementa Philosophiae* of Joseph Gredt[3] or the four-volume *Manuale Theologiae Dogmaticae* of J.-M. Hervé),[4] the moral manuals were always the work of Redemptorist theologians, grounded in the moral theology of Alphonsus Liguori. The one most used in the Irish province was that of the Dutch Redemptorist, Joseph Aertnys (1828–1915), *Theologia Moralis Juxta Doctrinam S. Alphonsi Mariae di Ligorio*, subsequently revised through several editions by Cornelius Damen and finally by Jan Visser.[5]

The teaching method involved the explanation by the professor of the Latin manual in class, followed by private study. This entailed committing the principles learned from the exposition of the manual to memory in order to be able to repeat them back to the satisfaction of the professor at the beginning of the next class. It was not a taxing regime and talented students found

2 Raponi, *The Charism of the Redemptorists*, 466–9.
3 Joseph Gredt, *Elementa philosophiae Aristotelico-Thomisticae*, 2 vols, 7th edn (Friburg am Bresgau: Herder, 1937).
4 J. -M. Hervé. *Manuale theologiae dogmaticae*, 4 vols (Paris : Berche et Pagis, 1953).
5 Joseph Aertnys, C. A. Damen , J. Visser. *Theologia moralis secundum doctrinam S. Alfonsi de Ligorio, Doctoris Ecclesiae*, 3 vols (Turin: Marietti, 1956).

it boring. If they were lucky, they could do some independent reading or might have the good fortune to be assigned a 'thesis' in some area of study to be researched over several weeks, presented and publicly defended before the whole community. Training for preaching was begun and continued for the length of a student's stay in the formation house in the weekly 'mission academy'. Once a week, for about one hour, the students were brought together by the priest responsible for teaching them the basics of elocution and voice-production. They were put through their paces, delivering in turn a short fragment of a mission sermon from the stock available. Criticism concentrated on common faults such as failure to project the voice, woodenness of delivery, dropping the voice at the end of a sentence and so on. More formidable was the monthly general mission academy when, in the presence of the entire community, including veteran missioners, senior students close to ordination delivered a longer section, usually the first point of a mission sermon. The critique here was more searching. Comments of veteran missioners were welcome, especially when they were reassuring and predicting the neophyte preacher had the makings of 'a great missioner'.

Second Novitiate
The Redemptorist general chapter of 1764 had introduced a 'second novitiate' when formal study of theology in preparation for the priesthood was completed. It was intended to serve two purposes: to renew the spiritual enthusiasm of the young men after the years of study, and to provide them with a period of immediate preparation for the work of mission-giving. The 'second novices' spent six months living the full observance of the daily order prescribed by rule under the direction of the prefect of the second novitiate, who was chosen for his experience as a missioner and his ability to guide the spiritual development of the newly-ordained. He gave them talks on the spiritual life, directed their work of sermon preparation, and conducted practical workshops on preaching and the hearing of confessions. The obituary of Fr James McCann, prefect of the second novitiate in the mid-1930s, gives an indication of the ideal prefect of the second novitiate. McCann believed:

> The young fathers should be equipped with a complete set of mission sermons and instructions, and … in all their compositions, they should hold rigidly to the traditional methods of treating the subjects. He left nothing to chance … In sermons and still more in instructions, everything had to be clear-cut and to the point. 'Give it in tabloid form' was a common saying of his. With his practical mind, he went into every detail of a mission: how to recite the rosary, the manner of giving the notices, how to read the leaflet and announce the five *Paters* and *Aves*

[recited at the end of the evening session while the Church bell tolled for the conversion of sinners]. He was certainly thorough.[6]

The *horarium* of the second novitiate was a demanding one. Apart from two daily community meditations, the full divine office was recited in choir at the times prescribed by the rule. A half-hour was given to preparation for Mass and another for thanksgiving afterwards. Much of the afternoon was devoted to devotional exercises, including a half-hour of spiritual reading and another of meditation in one's own room, followed by the recitation of antici-pated matins and lauds of the divine office. Twice each month, the novices made a day's retreat in addition to the annual ten-day retreat. Each week the prefect gave a spiritual talk and met them once a month for *colloquium*, a session of spiritual direction.

The notebook of Fr James Cleary, director of the second novitiate in the 1930s, provides a rich source of information both about the daily routine and content of the lectures he held with the novices.[7] Cleary (1892–1968) became prefect of the second novitiate for the first time in 1936 and continued in the role for many years. He held an MA in classics from the National University of Ireland, was a prolific writer in theological journals and was regarded by his Redemptorist contemporaries as a man of considerable talent. His notebook allows much of the pastoral training given in the second novitiate to be reconstructed. It also bears the stamp of a rigorist moral theology. Cleary's instructions reflect the theological vision of the generation of Redemptorists who flourished between his ordination in 1923 and his death in 1968. Given his role in the formation of his younger contemporaries, Cleary was also one of the shapers of that tradition.

How to write a Sermon – Redemptorist Style
The work of sermon-writing began with a preliminary study of some principles of sacred oratory. The nearest the Irish province ever came to developing its own 'handbook of pulpit rhetoric' was a typescript of notes drawing on classical and eclectic sources complied by Fr Patrick Carroll (1889–1932), a native of Pallasgreen, County Limerick.

Public address systems were a rarity in churches in the 1920s and 1930s, especially in rural areas, so a preacher's greatest asset was a strong resonant voice, capable of filling a church without the aid of a microphone. During the initial weeks of the second novitiate, the voice training begun in the student house continued. The novices were also shown how to perform the simpler parts of the evening mission ceremony, from giving out the rosary

---

6 Necrology of Fr James McCann, Personal File, RPAD.
7 'Notes on Second Noviciate' by James A. Cleary CSsR, rewritten 1950–1, RPAD. Citations here are taken from this source.

with a brief meditation on each mystery, to reading the notices or teaching the forms for the 'daily acts' or prayers of faith, hope, charity and contrition.

The first step in sermon-writing entailed a close study of some works of master-preachers of the past, with an eye to their plan and construction. After that, the young priests were required to draw up a plan for their first sermon on one of the main themes of the mission, for example, death, judgement, the 'delay of conversion'. The ideal of this concentrated time of sermon-writing was to provide a young missioner with sufficient material in order to give a full one-week mission alone in a small parish. This required eight full sermons, each almost an hour in length, with six morning instructions on practical points, each about ten or fifteen minutes long. They did not eat much idle bread for the six months.

The initial advice on sermon-writing was severely practical. The young priests were recommended to rewrite and polish their text, before committing the final copy to notebooks. The notebooks, one for sermons and the other for instructions, should have differently-coloured covers and be small enough to carry around on missions (but not into the pulpit). They were advised to mark key-words in red ink, to keep a list of the contents of each book at the front, leaving two pages blank before each sermon to record where and when it was preached, and to leave some space on each page for the inclusion of additional material. They were recommended to find two good stories for each sermon, but were warned of the danger of relying on hackneyed ones. The stories did not have to be 'personal experiences'; they could be taken from the lives of the saints, from contemporary or recent history, or even from the newspapers. If one did choose to narrate a personal experience, it was imperative to avoid anything that might give the impression of violating the 'seal of confession' or being critical of any other parish. Cleary tried to teach his students to become aware of the power of language, warning them that 'the worst English is that which disguises poverty of thought by the use of big, hollow, lumbering words'. He quoted with approval an American advertising expert whose philosophy was 'Say it simply. Say it over and over, say it in one syllable words'. He pointed out how, at that level at least, the philosophy of the advertiser and the missioner was identical, citing St Leonard of Port Maurice (1676–1751), an Italian pioneer of parish missions, who claimed, long before the advent of advertising: 'To say a thing once on a mission is not to say it at all; it is like writing on water.'

A mission sermon was a solemn occasion, and the novice preacher was enjoined to develop a suitably grave demeanour and especially to avoid joking with the altar boys or the sacristan immediately prior to going into the pulpit. Gravity extended to the place of humour in the pulpit. Cleary held that:

Jokes should not be made *in* night sermons, especially on the Great Truths [Death, Judgement, Heaven, Hell], still less in the sermon on the Proximate Occasions [of sin]. Young people should not be encouraged by witticisms on this subject, to make light – as many alas, do – of the occasions of sin. A joke, in the notices before the sermon, is *useful.*

Preachers have always disagreed on the extent to which a sermon should be memorised. Cleary recommended that sermons be written in their entirety, read and re-read, almost as if they were to be preached verbatim. Nevertheless, when the moment for delivery came, the preacher should not feel enslaved to the text. The final arbiter of the success or failure of a sermon was the audience. Cleary reminded his students:

> Your listeners may be stupid: but their verdict is final. They want to hear about certain things, in words they know. All follow easily when you use words they use. If they do not follow you, they sleep.

The young preachers were given a rough guide on how to calculate the length of the sermon when it came to delivery. A good rule of thumb was to count the total number of words: solemn public speakers, such as preachers, deliver approximately one hundred words a minute, while broadcasters averaged 140 words. Everything on the mission had to yield in importance to the sermon. In Cleary's view, 'the sermon or instruction on the mission is even more important than the Mass', if only on the grounds that people could get other Masses but not other mission sermons.

The first essential for a good mission sermon was a clear plan. The plan of a mission sermon should be the essence of simplicity. The first topic Cleary set his students was on death, and he offered them a three-point plan as the framework around which to work. His three points were 1. Death is certain; 2. Death is uncertain; 3. We die as we live. The prefect oversaw the work in progress. As each point was developed and written, it was submitted for criticism and rewriting. When it passed muster, the student was permitted to pass on to another of the regular mission-sermon topics – for example, the opening of the mission, mortal sin, drunkenness, scandal, general judgement, proximate occasions of sin, prayer, hell, salvation, the mercy of God, confession, the *Amende* [in essence, a sermon on the Blessed Sacrament, but including topics such as Mass-missing, unworthy communion, irreverence towards the Blessed Sacrament], the Blessed Virgin Mary, an address to a confraternity and a sermon for the close of a mission.

A Sermon on Death
The liturgical and theological renewal of the 1960s and the advent of television as the primary model of mass communication spelled the end of the

mission sermon of forty-five or fifty minutes in length. Reading through the manuscripts of such sermons that have survived, it is striking how rapidly the system of beliefs and the assumptions on which they rested have disappeared beyond recovery. Taken on their own terms, many of these sermons are extra-ordinarily potent examples of mass-communication in which complex ideas are stripped down to their basic essentials and then expressed in carefully-crafted language, in which every word is chosen for its emotional impact. The aim of the sermon was not so much to impart new knowledge, but to recall a world of assumptions and emotions shared by preacher and congregation.

Cleary's own sermon on death is a notable example of the mission-sermon genre.[8] His manuscript records that it was first preached in Raphoe, in County Donegal in 1922 and had its last performance in Ashbourne, County Meath in 1953. Over those thirty years, it was preached well over one hundred times, to congregations as diverse as rural parishes and universities. It runs to approximately 4,350 words, and on the basis of the rule of thumb given above, it would have taken about forty-five minutes to deliver. If Cleary had followed the advice he gave to his students, he would have re-written and polished it repeatedly in the course of those years.

The aim of this close reading of a sermon text is not to critique its theo-logical assumptions, however foreign or even questionable they might appear to modern sensibility. It is rather to study its careful construction and its highly-wrought and skilful use of language. The advent of radio and televi-sion has contributed to a certain flattening and loss of formality in public discourse, every bit as foreign to the political orators of the 1920s or 1930s as it would have been to their ecclesiastical counterparts.

Particular attention in sermon construction has traditionally been given to the opening, or *exordium*, of the sermon. In his notes on the art of sermon-writing, Carroll described the objective of the *exordium* as gaining the attention of the hearers and concentrating it on the subject to be addressed. The essential qualities of a good *exordium*, as Carroll summarised it, were 'interest, vivacity, the striking'. A typical opening (*exordium*) of a Redemptorist mission sermon was made up of a text from scripture, a brief story illustrating the point, and concluding with a very short prayer to the Blessed Virgin to obtain for the hearers the grace or fruit of the sermon. A properly-constructed opening was virtually the complete sermon in miniature.

Cleary's *exordium* begins with a short biblical text: 'It is appointed unto man once to die' (Heb 9:27). It then recounted a story of how the dying Philip II of Spain sent for his son, and unwrapping the bandages covering his cancerous throat, announced 'my son, see how the glory of the world comes

---

8 Text cited throughout from James Cleary, 'Transcripts of my best M[ission] Sermons', 1954, RPAD.

to an end. Behold how kings and emperors die.' From this the preacher drew the moral that the world is steeped in sin because people do not think about death. The prayer to Mary which closes the *exordium* is a single sentence: 'May the glorious Mother of God obtain for us a constant remembrance of death, so that when death comes, we may be prepared to meet it.'

The body of the sermon proper opens with a concise but well-constructed paragraph:

> My brethren, we must die. One day, we must die. There is no escape. Death is a bitter word, but there is no escape. One day we must leave the world. We must bid good bye to our family, and friends and leave behind us all our worldly interests and ambitions. We must disappear into the grave: a long narrow wooden box will be our home – the house of our body until the day of judgement.

The sentences in this opening paragraph are very short, composed for the most part of monosyllabic words. Of the seventy-four words it contains, only ten have more than one syllable. There is also a considerable amount of repetition. The first sentence, 'we must die', is repeated immediately, separated only by the words 'one day'. It is likewise with the second sentence: 'there is no escape.' The five-fold repetition of the word 'must' ('must die … must die … must leave the world … must bid farewell … must disappear') creates a sense of the inevitability and relentless approach of death: it is a fate no human can avoid. The finality of death and the frailty of mortal life are conveyed by the word-picture of disappearing into the grave. The preacher avoids using the word 'coffin', substituting a more colourful but lugubrious expression 'long, narrow wooden box' with its series of long vowel sounds (of the six syllables, four contain long 'o' sounds, while the words <u>n</u>arro<u>w</u> and <u>w</u>oode<u>n</u> reverse in their opening and closing the consonant sounds 'n' and 'w'.

The second paragraph introduces the image of the death sentence by means of an anecdote describing a meeting with a condemned prisoner. Few circumstantial details of the meeting are given, for the effect the preacher is striving to convey is the condemned man's sense of horror as the time before his execution becomes shorter – the setting sun, the final visits of friends. If he is under sentence of death, then so just as surely are the listeners:

> But you and I, my brethren, we are no better off than he. We, too, are sentenced to death by a judge, who when our time has come, will listen to no appeal. The time is fixed, the place of our death is already determined, the manner of our passing into eternity is already decided. The sentence is pronounced. The judge is God and he has said: 'It is appointed unto man once to die.'

Again, a series of simple sentences identifies the place, manner, sentence, and the judge. The final sentence re-introduces the scripture text from the *exordium* ('it is appointed unto man once to die'), which is now expounded in detail. The exposition opens with a series of rhetorical questions: 'Where now are all the men and women of former times? ... All are gone.' The change which death brings is hammered home by means of a contrast. During life, great political leaders were escorted by processions and bands: now they sleep quietly in Glasnevin cemetery with 'only the night wind moaning through the branches of the mournful yew-tree'. The sound of this sentence is evocative, particularly its alliterative use of the nasal 'm' and 'n' consonant sounds (night, wind moaning, branches, mournful).

The incidental reference to political demonstrations and to Glasnevin prepares the way for an anecdote from the life of Daniel O'Connell. O'Connell is reported to have replied to a friend who congratulated him on his fame: 'Tell me, of what use will fame and reputation be to me when I am dead and gone?' The exposition of the text continues with three paragraphs constructed around a similar opening and closing sentence 'all must die ... it is appointed' – the young, the strong, the beautiful and lovely. On the third occasion, the scripture text is cited in its full form, 'it is appointed unto man once to die.'

At this point, the audience is invited to visualise the reality of their own death: soon, very soon, a name will be read from the altar and prayers will be offered; but you will not hear the name nor offer a prayer: 'because the name will be your name and prayers will be said for you, and you will be in the coffin and the funeral will be yours.' The natural world is cited to support this picture of the inevitability of death – the clouds, the flowers, the rivers, the dying day. The concluding paragraph of this section drives the point home by repetition: 'Other things may be doubtful, death is certain. Riches cannot bribe death. Beauty cannot charm it. Courage and strength cannot keep it off, or loosen its unrelenting grasp.'

An anecdote introduces a change of pace and prepares for the following section. A prison chaplain met a boy of seventeen who had not been to confession for a long time, but who thought he would have plenty of time later on. Next day, the chaplain found him in the hospital, and when he approached his bed, there was no answer; the boy was dead. This prepares for the moral reflection that follows. Each paragraph begins with an identical sentence structure: 'At the summons of death, the farmer (shopkeeper, young man, young woman) must obey.' It is the counterpart to the series noted earlier, except that now, the examples are closer to the state of the audience. It also gives the opportunity to introduce a number of common sins – Mass-missing, injustice, drunkenness, sinful company-keeping – and their relationship to death. The last in the series is developed at greatest length:

> At the summons of death, the young girl obeys. Her parents many times commanded her to avoid certain places of amusement, a certain dance hall, a certain bad companion, and she only laughed at them and sneered at their old-fashioned views. The confessor warned her to avoid a dangerous companion, to give up those lonely meetings. She had promised with her lips, but in her heart she never intended to obey. And suddenly in the dead hour of night, death lays his icy hands upon her brow and calls her to the cemetery. And now she leaves her sinful companion and hurries away from his passionate embraces, and away from the crowded dancehall, to sleep her long sleep in the lonely grave-yard. She had been proud of her beauty; she had been so fond of dress. And her dress, what shall it be in the tomb? The Sacred Scriptures tell us worms and vermin – 'worms and vermin shall be her covering.'

Several striking antitheses are implied in this paragraph: the disobedient girl who may have succeeded in fooling her parents and confessor cannot fool death. Death himself replaces the dangerous companion towards whom she is drawn. The crowded dancehall stands in contrast to the lonely grave, vanity in earthly dress to the clothing of worms and vermin in the grave. There is an almost archetypal quality in the implication that Death is the girl's real bridegroom. It suggests that the touch of the icy hand of death is the counterpart to the warm but 'immodest touch' of the lover. If death is the spouse, then the cemetery is the real trysting place. The equation of bride-groom and death is a common *topos* in poetry and mythology, for example, its use in the popular Irish song, 'She Moved through the Fair'.

Like many sermons of its time, Cleary's sermon on death reflects a negative and distrustful view of women, and especially of young women, to the point of caricature. The woman is presented as a liar and a vain one at that. The preacher is not beyond taking a liberty with the scriptural quotation: worms and vermin as a covering was applied originally to a male (the king of Babylon) by the prophet Isaiah (14:11), not to a woman, but given the poverty of Catholic scriptural science, it is unlikely that Cleary would have even bothered checking the reference.

As the sermon reaches its mid-point, the audience has been left in no doubt that death is approaching them. The death of the just is treated briefly. Another story taken from the life of St Margaret of Cortona who 'made the thought of death her constant companion' lightens the pace again, and it concludes with a biblical quotation: 'Remember your last end and thou shalt never sin' (Sirach 7:36). By this stage, more than half the sermon has been dedicated to the development of the first point ('death is certain'). The remaining two points are treated in a more summary fashion.

Cleary's transition to the second major point ('death is uncertain') is made in a brief paragraph which states the two truths side by side:

> Death, then, is certain. It is a solemn and impressive truth. But there is a truth more solemn, a truth more impressive. The time of death is uncertain. We know not the day or the hour.

The uncertainty of death is illustrated by three brief stories of sudden death, including one about a priest who came to attend a solemn requiem but died in the sacristy so that the Mass which he came to attend for someone else is celebrated for the repose of his own soul. To reinforce the truth of death's uncertainty, the preacher appeals to the evidence of scripture by a brief reference to the 'thief in the night' as well as to the parable of the rich fool. The concluding words of this parable: 'Thou fool, this night do I require thy soul of thee' serve as a conclusion to three paragraphs addressed in the style of an *ad hominem* argument (i.e. one that attacks the opponent rather than his argument) to three typical classes of sinners – the drunkard, the company-keeper, the unjust person who refuses to make restitution.

The final point ('we die as we live') is treated even more briefly. It is introduced by the sentence: 'Since the time of death is uncertain, follow the advice of Our Lord and always be ready, always be ready.' If the drunkard, the company-keeper, the unjust person had known they were to die so soon, would they have continued in their sinful ways? These three examples of unprepared death are balanced by three equally brief examples of the death of the just. The first two consist of a sentence each on the death of St Francis of Assisi and St Catherine of Siena. The third is delivered more in the nature of a personal anecdote:

> I remember a poor man – a faithful member of his confraternity and when he was dying he began to sing the hymn he had so often sung at his sodality *Tantum ergo, sacramentum, veneremur cernui.*

The sermon moves towards its conclusion with a final appeal to the audience:

> When your last moment comes, when you are lying on your last sick bed, when you can no longer speak, when your limbs are already cold with the icy chill of the grave, when your feeble hands are holding the blessed candle, then it will not console you to remember the money you made or the friends you had or the dances at which you were present, or the pleasures you enjoyed. But I will tell you what will console you then – it will console you to remember the masses you heard, even on weekdays, and the holy communions you received, and the rosaries you

said to God's Holy Mother, and the confraternities you attended, and the crosses you carried in patience. God grant too, that it may console you then to remember, that in spite of your faults, you made the mission, the greatest mission of your life, the turning point of your history, the time in which you began to serve God in real earnest.

The rhetorical construction of this paragraph is deceptively simple, but effective. It consists of four lists. The first, a list of signs of approaching death, linked together by a five-fold repetition of 'when', the effect of which is to stress their inevitability. The next two lists are held together by the word 'console' – things that will not bring consolation and those that will. The final list is shorter: it is a description of the mission, the turning point of personal decision.

The final paragraph of the sermon, the peroration, is in the form of a prayer. It is essentially an act of contrition and invocation of Mary, balancing the invocation at the beginning. It reaches its climax in the familiar words of the invocation to the Holy Family for a happy death ('Jesus, Mary and Joseph, I give you my heart and my soul'). It is probable that the whole congregation would have spontaneously joined in this final prayer.

The Art of Pastoral Care: Training for the Confessional

When a young Redemptorist arrived for his second novitiate, he already had the standard course of moral theology behind him. It consisted substantially of a thorough study of the textbook, by which he had committed to memory the basic principles of moral theology and had begun to learn how to apply them to cases he would be likely to meet in the confessional.[9] The student's grasp of the subject was tested formally in the *rigorosum*, or solemn final oral examination, presided over by the provincial and attended by all the rectors of the province.

It was the task of the prefect of the second novitiate to help his charges reduce this mass of theoretical detail to practice. They got some practice by hearing confessions in the monastery church. Much of the training for 'mission confessions' was done through lectures and practical discussion of cases, even at times role-playing the parts of confessor and penitent. Cleary was much admired as a theologian by his contemporaries. His notebooks were assiduously kept and constantly updated. The cross-references show a man who read widely and accurately. He was conscious that the special quality of the confessional relationship with the penitent threw young men back on their own resources and that they would often need to think quickly. Their

---

9 For a critique of the manual system and its weaknesses, see Raphael Gallagher, 'The Manual System of Moral Theology since the death of St Alphonsus' in *Irish Theological Quarterly*, vol. 51, no. 1. (March, 1985), 1–16.

only security could come from sound knowledge of the basic principles of moral theology and a lifelong study of reputable authors. The advice 'if you hear a doubt raised, look it up', was intended to encourage young priests to keep in touch with their moral theology by creating a personal programme of study based on questions they had encountered in the course of their ministry. Cleary's moral vision was narrow, however, but his standing among his contemporaries, and the confidence his superiors placed in him, guaranteed that his opinion would be taken seriously.

To young priests beginning work in the confessional, Cleary stressed the importance of basic issues such as the inviolability of the seal of confession. Although a novice confessor might find himself totally at sea when dealing with complex cases, if he needed advice from a wiser head, he had to be careful to let nothing slip that might betray the identity of the penitent. Under no circumstances was it permissible to deal with cases outside of the confessional on the basis of knowledge obtained there. This held, he warned them, 'especially in cases of seduction and pregnancy. *Such girls are often desperate liars* [emphasis added], and there is besides great danger *de sigillo* [regarding the confessional seal]'.

In Alphonsus's classic treatment of the confessor, his first role of spiritual father was to be shown first of all in the way in which everyone is welcomed.[10] Cleary stressed the obligation to receive penitents kindly, even advising the novice confessor to leave the box for a short time if he found himself lapsing into bad humour. The confessor's second role was that of judge. The confessor had a duty to ensure that the penitent had made a complete confession, holding back nothing that should be confessed due to shame or embarrassment. To perform this role, the confessor was obliged, if necessary, to question the penitent. Cleary offered a few guidelines to help the inexperienced confessor. He recommended the psychological value of an introductory question that suggested a worse state of affairs than was probably the case: 'I suppose you're away from confession for thirty years?', when the reality was likely to be a much shorter time, or to begin by mentioning serious sins the penitent was unlikely to have committed. The virtue he recommends most strongly in practice to novice confessors, however, is severity. Cleary returns so frequently to the confessor's duty to refuse absolution in certain cases that one might suspect that he regards the confessor's role of judge as paramount, almost to the exclusion of the other roles such as physician of the soul and spiritual guide. He believed that it might sometimes be the confessor's duty to defer

---

[10] 'The Confessor as Father' translated and annotated by Raphael Gallagher from *Prattica del Confessore*. 3, in *Alphonsus Liguori: Selected Writings*, Classics of Western Spirituality Series, ed. Frederick M. Jones (Mahwah, NJ: Paulist Press, 1999), 317–18, here 317.

absolution. Although he appeals to St Alphonsus in support of his position, it is based on a rigorist reading of Alphonsus's theology via the nineteenth-century manuals that systematised and commented on his thought. Cleary holds up the severe confessor as the model to be imitated, in contrast to more gentle confessors he characterises as 'easy', 'criminally indulgent', 'cruelly lenient', 'worldly' or striving after false popularity.

Confessors of a rigorist stamp were particularly concerned with the area of sexual morality. A directive ascribed to a seventeenth-century general of the Jesuits, Claudio Aquaviva, that there was 'no parvity of matter with regard to the sixth commandment' (i.e. that all sexual sins were objectively grave) had become axiomatic in moral theology.[11] What lessened the gravity of the sin in individual cases was the subjective state of the penitent (for example, lack of knowledge or defective consent). One of the standard mission sermons was on the need to avoid the 'occasions of sin': in the deceptively-clear logic of the catechism answer, an occasion of sin was 'any person, place or thing that entices us to sin'. The archetypal occasion of sin for the Redemptorist mission preacher was 'lonely company-keeping' between young people. The moral manuals of the nineteenth and early twentieth century had set down stringent conditions about company-keeping, which reflected eighteenth- and nineteenth-century bourgeois social conventions, where arranged marriages and chaperones for unmarried young ladies in polite society were the norm. Cleary's views on company-keeping were extremely negative. His working principle was that 'nearly all long company-keeping becomes sinful in the end' and he regarded anything over two years as long. His standards of what constituted privacy were equally strict. Company-keeping might be regarded as 'less lonely if in a room and the mother comes in from time to time to do her work: hardly lonely is a walk by day on a public road'. Anything more intimate, he held, was running the risk of serious sin.[12]

Redemptorist preaching and confessional practice on matters sexual from the 1920s into the 1960s did much to earn the missioners a reputation for holding an extremely narrow view of sexuality. In Austin Clarke's poem 'The Redemptorist', a poor urban woman with a drunken husband, caught in a cycle of annual pregnancies, who has been persuaded by her doctor to take the contraceptive pill, comes to make her confession. After a lengthy questioning, the confessor refuses her absolution, banging the confessional shutter in her face.

---

[11] Charles E. Curran, *Catholic Moral Theology in the United States: a History* (Washington: Georgetown University Press, 2008), 192.

[12] Slightly more genial in tone, but still representing the Redemptorist preoccupation with company-keeping, was the popular pamphlet by John J. Gorey CSsR, *May I keep company?* (Dublin: Juverna Press, 1944).

> Shutter
> Became her coffin lid. She twisted her hands
> And left the box.
> > The missioner
> Red-bearded saint had brought God's flame
> To frighten women on retreat.[13]

The slamming of the confessional shutter in the woman's face anticipates the slamming of her coffin lid at the end of the poem when she has died in her attempt to follow the confessor's advice. Clarke's treatment of the Redemptorist of his title is harsh, but the rest of the poem makes it clear that the Redemptorist is the vicarious representative of all the Catholic religious orders in Ireland. He has the red beard of the Capuchin, the 'black cross on his badge' of the Passionist, he preaches in the Franciscan pulpit of Adam and Eve's and the flame that he sends 'to frighten women in retreat' covers with its smoke even the urbane Jesuit in his castle at Rathfarnham.

By the time James Cleary had retired from active mission work in the 1960s, Redemptorist moral theology was beginning to take a fresh direction. Two factors contributed to this. The first was a more historically-accurate reading of the moral theology of Alphonsus Liguori, which had been one of the objectives of the foundation of the Alphonsian Academy in Rome in 1949 as a specialist institute for the study of moral theology. The second was the publication of the ground-breaking manual, *Das Gesetz Christi* by the German Redemptorist, Bernard Häring (1912–98) in 1954.[14] Häring had been a promising young doctoral student when military service in the German army snatched him from the comfortable world of academe. Exposure to war and suffering radically changed his vision and he has described the shock to his religious training, based on the doctrine of blind obedience when it came in collision with its secular counterpart as a medical orderly on the Russian Front.[15] The Irish province was fortunate in having one of its members on the staff of the Alphonsian Academy. Seán O' Riordan (1916–98) was appointed professor of moral theology there in 1960, the same year that the Academy was recognised as a specialised institute for the study of moral theology by the Lateran University in Rome. One of his areas of scholarly interest was the complex relationship between moral theology and the new vistas opened up by psychology and sociology. He continued to serve his home province by lecturing both the young men in formation, speaking frequently at seminars and acting as a conduit to the emerging renewed theology of the post-Conciliar period.

---

[13] Austin Clarke, *Old Fashioned Pilgrimage and Other Poems* (Dublin: Dolmen Press, 1967), 35.
[14] Bernard Häring, *The Law of Christ: Moral Theology for Priests and Laity* (translated by Edwin C. Kaiser CPpS), 3 vols (Cork: Mercier Press, 1963).
[15] Bernard Häring, *Free and Faithful: My Life in the Catholic Church* (Liguori, MO: Liguori Publications, 1998).

CHAPTER FOURTEEN

Twenty Years a-Flourishing

The two decades between the celebration of the bicentenary of the foundation of the Redemptorist Congregation in 1932 and the celebration of the centenary of the foundation of the first house in Limerick in 1953 were years of growth and diversification. Much of this growth took place in the shadow of the Second World War. Wartime conditions made communication with Rome and the men on the overseas missions virtually impossible. During these two decades, only three provincials served in the Irish province, the second of whom did not even complete his first term in office.

One man who put a decisive stamp on this period, Hugo Kerr (1895–1986), was provincial from 1936 until 1947. Kerr may have found the unprecedented freedom from Roman oversight that the provincial enjoyed under wartime conditions congenial. It spared him having to negotiate too closely with the increasingly inflexible superior general, Patrick Murray. Kerr was a member of a relatively small social group – an upper-middle class Belfast Catholic. His father, a wealthy solicitor, had made astute investments in land purchase and house-building along the rapidly-expanding Falls Road.[1] Hugo had been educated by the Jesuits in Clongowes Wood College, County Kildare. Among his closest friends was a doctor's son from Cavan called John McQuaid (1895–1973), the future archbishop of Dublin. An indication of the closeness of the friendship can be gauged from the fact that Kerr was one of the few friends to whom McQuaid confided the news of his father's remarriage. As he dreaded spending the summer holidays with his new stepmother, he spent it with the Kerrs in Belfast.[2]

Hugo Kerr was a man of strong personality and of more than common intelligence and ability. His Jesuit education left its mark on him, particularly in a respect for university education that was not shared by all his Redemptorist contemporaries. A certain hauteur of manner and accent was not calculated to endear him to all his confreres and some were more than

---

[1] Hugo Street on the Falls Road near St John's Catholic church was named after his son.
[2] The details of Kerr's early life given here are taken from a personal memoir, 'Before I go', written *c.*1977, professedly to help a future writer of his death notice. Hugo Kerr, Personal file, RPAD.

ready to complain that he lacked 'our simplicity of ways' or a taste for the common life. Gary MacEoin claims to have known him in the offhand way that schoolboys know their teachers, but that he got a deeper insight into his character when he was rector of Limerick and MacEoin was fighting his dismissal from the congregation:

> Then we had thought him worldly, offhand about rules. Now I uncovered less attractive characteristics. He fancied himself mightily as a power politician, and was typical power politician in his ability to persuade himself that the ends sought justified the means to hand.[3]

Given the tensions between Kerr and MacEoin, this may be an exceedingly negative view, but there can be no denying that Kerr's leadership of the Irish province during his years in office did at times involve the application of skills that might, depending on one's point of view, be called either firm and imaginative leadership or ruthlessness.

Some of the stories about the circumstances of Kerr's entrance into the congregation have acquired the patina of folklore. According to one version, the saintly Fr John Sullivan SJ 'advised him against entering the Redemptorists on the grounds that they were a bunch of uneducated men'.[4] Another version has it that the Redemptorists assured his father that he would be given an opportunity for a university education, but the promise was never kept. Whatever truth there may be in either of these tales, or to what degree they influenced his later thinking, Kerr made the education of Redemptorist students one of his priorities, and did not hesitate to invest in it some of the not inconsiderable family fortune that came his way.

Hugo Kerr was also the founder of the province's second mission in India. In many respects, his handling of this project showed insights into the nature of missionary work that were well ahead of their time. He realised that the British Raj in India had only a short time to run, and that Indian independence would pose new challenges for Christian missionaries in India. If the Redemptorist congregation were to flourish there, it would have to set down deep roots in Indian soil from the beginning, and a key to this was the fostering of Indian vocations. It is a tribute to his foresight that the Irish Redemptorists were able to hand over a flourishing independent province to Indian leadership within a quarter of a century of their arrival.

More of Kerr's circular letters to the members of the province have survived in the archives than have those of any other provincial before him.

---

[3] MacEoin, *Nothing is Quite Enough*, 207.
[4] In the memoir referred to above, Kerr mentions Fr Sullivan's encouragement of a possible Jesuit vocation, but makes no reference to any opposition to his joining the Redemptorists; see Kerr, 'Before I go'.

They cover a wide range of topics, including minutiae such as instructions to purchase small bells to signal the end of mission sermons,[5] the kind of games that might be played for recreation or exercise – football, tennis, croquet, bowls, clock-golf, ping-pong, but not chess, draughts, cards or any kind of board-game (25 June 1937), or permission for a cup of tea in the afternoon (21 February 1938). Kerr left little to chance, and was intent on tidying up loose ends or irregularities that had crept into the observance of the rule.

New Beginnings in Formation

A surge in vocations in the 1930s meant that the novitiate at Dundalk and the student house at Esker were both over-crowded. Redemptorist formation was usually done within the context of a working community composed of priests and brothers as well as the academic community of students and professors. This resulted in a very numerous community in the house of studies. In 1939, for example, the Esker community numbered eighty-three members, including forty-five students, as well as lectors, brothers and a sizeable mission team. Reference was made in an early chapter to the proposal to buy property at Collon, County Meath as a site for a new novitiate house. When Hugo Kerr became provincial in June 1936, finding a new home for the students had become a bigger priority. An important first step was the strengthening of the uncertain financial basis of the formation programme. Kerr established eight burses, each to the value of £1,000: every house, depending on its size, was required to find funding for one or two of them (16 August 1936). The following month, he opened negotiations with Bishop Thomas O'Doherty of Galway about the feasibility of transferring the seminary from Esker to a place closer to Galway city. Bishop O'Doherty readily granted informal permission, and the congregation's Roman authorities proved amenable.[6] Unfortunately for Kerr, the bishop died three months later, without having signed a formal agreement. In the meantime, a suitable property had been found, but it awaited the signature of the new bishop to proceed. Dr Michael Browne was conse-crated bishop of Galway in October 1937, and Kerr reopened negotiations with him. Brown was a more astute negotiator than his predecessor, and imposed several conditions on Kerr before agreeing to sign the agreement, which included a waiver by the Redemptorists of their canonical right to open a public church attached to the monastery. The agreement was signed on 8 February 1938. The interregnum in the diocese of Galway proved costly, as

---

5 Hugo Kerr, Circular Letter, 24 Jan. 1937, LB-K, RPAD. Unless otherwise stated, LB-K is the source of all documents of Kerr cited here and to avoid undue repetition of footnotes, quotations will simply be followed by date in the text.
6 'Statement on Congestion in the Irish Province and its proposed Remedy', XIII Hb, Kerr: 7, RGAR, Sept. 1936.

building costs were to rocket with the outbreak of the war the following year just as construction got underway. The house was completed and the students moved into Cluain Mhuire, Wellpark on the outskirts of Galway city after the summer vacation of 1940.

The principal reason Galway was attractive was the possibility it offered for students once again to take university degrees. University education of students, prior to their entry to the novitiate, at University College Dublin had been suspended since 1927. The superior general, Patrick Murray, had never been in favour of university education. Despite his grudging approval of Kerr's proposal when the Galway foundation was being planned, Murray dropped a bombshell two days before the opening of the new house by withdrawing permission for students to attend university. Not only did it undercut the main reason for going to Galway in the first place, it also left Kerr open to the accusation of duplicity in his negotiations with the bishop. He went through the formalities of the opening day with a heavy heart. In the face of threats of resignation from Kerr and one of his consultors, Fr John Doyle, Murray withdrew his opposition.[7] In October 1940, the first group of students set out for lectures at University College Galway.

A fresh problem arose in Galway some years after the house opened. Tuberculosis was a serious social and medical problem in Ireland in the 1940s. A national plan to combat the disease envisaged a rapid building programme of new sanatoria located strategically around the country. A report that the site earmarked for the Galway regional sanatorium close to a portion of Cluain Mhuire site became known in early 1945. It was with horror that Kerr learned of the decision to build a hospital within a stone's throw of his cherished project. The parents of the students, he argued, were likely to be concerned when they heard their sons were living so close to a sanatorium. Immediate representations were made to the highest level of state and a crusade of prayer was launched.[8] Mr de Valera replied to Kerr's letter of protest. He pointed out that no definitive decision had as yet been taken regarding the site for the proposed sanatorium, and that as soon as he heard of the Redemptorist concerns, he needed no urging 'with either whip or spur' to take a personal interest in the matter.[9] He reminded the provincial, however, that the minister responsible and his parliamentary private secretary had responsibilities that needed to be carried out without fear or favour and

---

[7] Hugo Kerr, 'Before I go'.
[8] In addition to Kerr's own letter of protest to an Taoiseach, Éamon de Valera (National Archives of Ireland, Department of the Taoiseach, 97/9/577), there is a draft of a personal letter sent to the Taoiseach by Fr John B. Coyle (undated) and his reply (Éamon de Valera to John B. Coyle, 1 Mar. 1945, H9, Cluain Mhuire Box, RPAD). Coyle was a personal friend of de Valera and his family.
[9] Éamon de Valera to Hugo Kerr, 9 Mar. 1945, H9.3, Cluain Mhuire Box, RPAD.

that every effort would be made to consider an alternative site, 'even though your objection is not considered reasonable'. In the event, a more suitable site was found at Merlin Park, a few miles further along the Dublin Road but the provincial's over-reaction to a matter of such public importance does him little credit.[10]

A New Mission
Shortly after concluding the arrangements with Bishop Brown for the foundation of Cluain Mhuire, Hugo Kerr left to undertake a canonical visitation in the Philippines. Prior to his departure, he had invited his consultors to consider undertaking a second mission in India. Kerr reasoned that the Irish houses now had more men than they had work for and made it clear to Patrick Murray that he intended to take advantage of his journey to the East to explore the possibility further.[11] On his return journey from the Philippines, Kerr stopped off at Ceylon (Sri Lanka), where the Italian Benedictine, Bishop Bernardo Regno of Kandy, welcomed the proposal to found a house in his diocese. Kerr also paid a flying visit to southern India. Bishop and provincial signed an agreement on 29 August 1938, and the December following, permission was granted by the Roman Congregation of Propaganda Fide.[12]

As war was looming, Kerr was keen to conclude the arrangements as quickly as possible. Realising that he would probably have to return to Ireland before settling the final details, he asked Fr John J. McDonnell, vice-provincial of the Philippines, to meet him in Kandy. Kerr left the business of finding a home for the community in McDonnell's hands and on his return to Ireland, set about preparing to take on the Indian mission. It was formally announced to the province in October 1938, and the chosen pioneers (Matthew Hickey, Gerald McDonnell, and Leo O'Halloran) were instructed to be at their posts by Christmas. Their brief was to begin mission work in English immediately, but also to begin the study of the local languages as soon as possible.

Kerr had failed to take into account the effect of his move on the Australian Redemptorist province. They had come to Singapore in 1935 and, having given several missions in India, considered it as falling within their sphere of influence. Although Kerr had broken his journey from the Philippines to Colombo in Ceylon (now Sri Lanka) at Singapore where he

---

[10] Handwritten copy of letter from J. C. Ward, parliamentary secretary of the Department of Local Government, to Hugo Kerr, 22 Mar. 1945. A note at the end of the letter records that the final meeting with Dr Ward, 'of which this letter is the outcome, took place on Thursday, 15 Mar. 1945,' H9.4. Cluain Mhuire Box, RPAD.

[11] Hugo Kerr to Patrick Murray, 16 Jan. 1938, XIII-Hb, RGAR.

[12] Congregation of Propaganda, Prot. 4760/38, India 1, RPAD.

had enjoyed their hospitality, he remained tight-lipped about his plans for India. If their suspicions were aroused when they learned that he proposed stopping over in Ceylon, they were confirmed by McDonnell's arrival a few weeks later on his way to Kandy to transact 'provincial business'. The realisation that Kerr had stolen a march on them unleashed a storm of protest, drawing a furious letter to Kerr from Fr William Byrne, the Australian provincial.

> I am exceedingly sorry to say that I and all who know the state of the case object most strongly to what we consider the shabby and unbrotherly and unjust way in which your Reverence has secured the Kandy foundation. We consider you have entered by stealth into what we had every right to regard as our proper field of labour … In several letters from confreres, your Reverence is likened to Hitler moving into Austria.[13]

While it is possible to sympathise with their sense of hurt and disappointment, it is an overstatement to accuse Kerr of high-handedly annexing Ceylon while Australian backs were turned. The matter was more complex, and some of the facts tilt the balance in Kerr's favour. In his memoir, he claims to have learned of the Australians' plans for expansion only after arriving in Bangalore. He also claimed that some of the Indian bishops to whom he spoke had made it clear that they regarded the Australian Fathers as unacceptable, but had no such reservations about the Irish.[14]

Some years later, in forwarding a request from the vicar general of New Delhi for a foundation in the Simla Hills to Kerr, Matthew Hickey made it clear that:

> The approach and application is made very definitely to the Irish province in view of deliberate policy concerning the new India … [which] arises no doubt from the All-White Australian policy which is made much of here.[15]

The White Australia policy, founded on the Immigration Restriction Act of 1901, sought to limit immigration to people of European origin. For a time, Kerr considered appeasing the Australians by dividing India and giving them the northern part. Still more drastic was his proposal to withdraw all the Irish from the Philippines to India and to leave the entire archipelago to the Australians. This proposal was never discussed with the Irish fathers working in the Philippines, but their response might be imagined. In any event, the Australians realised that their smaller numbers and extensive commitments in both Singapore and the Philippines made any further expansion unrealistic.

---

[13] William Byrne to Hugo Kerr, 5 Nov. 1938, RPAD.

[14] Hugo Kerr, 'Before I go'.

[15] Matthew Hickey to John Treacy, 7 Sept. 1949, India 1.10, RPAD.

The Indian mission flourished from the beginning. The difficult experience in the foundation of the Philippines more than thirty years earlier and the growth of the Irish missionary movement in the 1920s and 1930s had taught the Irish Redemptorists some valuable, if costly, lessons about missions abroad. The pioneers were fortunate, too, in that the local church was anxious to have them as parish missioners from the outset and they were able to get down to preaching missions in English within a short time of their arrival. By the following year, 1940, the arrival of two additional priests permitted a start to be made on the first foundation in the Indian subcontinent at Bangalore. For the first few years, they concentrated on English language missions, but Kerr had impressed on them the importance of knuckling down to the hard graft of learning one or other of the many Indian vernacular languages. As a result, the first mission in Tamil was preached in 1943. An extract from a letter from Matthew Hickey circulated by Kerr to the communities in Ireland gives some idea of the enthusiasm of the pioneers and the demands made on them. It evokes the atmosphere of the missions in Ireland almost a century earlier:

> Our missions here have been a phenomenal success. The attendance and fervour beats anything we have ever seen … The people follow us from one church to another. So there is how it is. The CSsR system can do untold good for these people whom one cannot help loving. But if only we had more help, and could do something for the poor Tamils who sit on the floor and look up at us. They are very wilful and ignorant. But religion means a great lot to their poor lives. If only our young men could see these poor Tamils, they would flock out to work for them. But physically, the work is as hard as one could undertake. Morally, it is depressing. All these people are wonderfully grateful. I believe they are very dear to God. One gets to love them … For the love of God, send us all the help you can. After Easter, there will be no rest.[16]

Letters such as this were intended as much for public circulation as they were for the provincial's information. Confidential letters between Hickey and his provincial gave a more sober view: it seemed unlikely that they would attract vocations quickly and there were continued difficulties about finding a permanent residence.

Despite the enthusiasm of many Indian bishops and priests for missions, Redemptorist mission preaching met with a cooler reception from the Jesuits, including Thomas Roberts, the English Jesuit archbishop of Bombay, who seems to have regarded his archdiocese as a Jesuit preserve.[17] According to

---

[16] Hugo Kerr to Rectors, Easter Sunday (probably 1943), India 2, RPAD.
[17] Joseph Morgan, *A Time to Remember* (Redemptorist Publications: Bangalore, 1992), 23–4.

Hickey, Roberts met the request for faculties for a forthcoming Redemptorist mission with the remark that Redemptorist mission preaching and confessional practice had often upset people in Ireland and that the Jesuits had to be called in to restore their peace of conscience. Hickey was not too downhearted and regarded the theatrical methods of at least one eccentric Jesuit missioner as his greatest ally:

> Fortunately for us, a Belgian Jesuit … has been giving missions, bringing men out into cemeteries at night, asking girls in church to touch a skull which he had carried in etc. He had to be sent away.[18]

Not that Hickey regarded all his own confreres as an unmixed blessing. The virtual hero worship of a pair of brothers for one another was trying the patience of a small community. Hickey realised that only a period of total concentration on the task in hand would permit the Redemptorists to set down a firm base in India:

> *We must get established* and our communities must be *mobile for the present.* For God's sake, stand by us and don't think this is a foolish sort of rivalry: it is not. [emphasis in the original].[19]

The outbreak of war closed the Suez Canal to merchant shipping. Fathers Michael Fox (1900–83) and Arthur Maloney (1903–76) left Ireland in 1941 in the hope of reaching India by going around the Cape of Good Hope. Twelve days out from Liverpool, their boat was torpedoed by a German rogue ship off the Cape Verde Islands. After drifting for three days in lifeboats, they were picked up by a cargo boat bound for South America. According to Maloney's sardonic description, it 'was of the type whose engines are held together by string and is driven more by bad language than by coal'.[20] Arriving eventually in the Argentine, they made their way by slow stages up through South America to San Francisco, where they crossed the Pacific, landing in Ceylon six months after their departure from Ireland.

The story of the Indian mission has been described in detail in Fr Joseph Morgan's *A Time to Remember.* Its outstanding and rapid success was due largely to the commitment of the men involved, particularly Fr Matthew Hickey (1896–1969). A native of Dublin, he had tried his vocation with the Cistercians in Mount Melleray Abbey, County Waterford, before coming to the Redemptorists. Professed in 1919, he spent a period of his theological studies at Attert in Belgium as that province was trying to reorganise its student house after the First World War, before his ordination in 1922. He

---

[18] Matthew Hickey to Hugo Kerr, 31 July 1939, India 2, RPAD.
[19] Matthew Hickey to Hugo Kerr, 22 Aug. 1939, India 2, RPAD.
[20] Arthur Maloney to Hugo Kerr from Monte Video, 16 Apr. 1941, quoted in provincial chronicle, vol. 3 (1938–44), 131, RPAD.

went to India at the age of forty-two and would preside over its growth for twenty years until he was replaced as vice-provincial by Fr William Hanly in 1959. Joseph Morgan singles out his deep loyalty to the Redemptorists, his sound judgement and his extraordinary charm of manner as the virtues which did most to advance the Redemptorist cause in India. His charm won him supporters and friends among the Indian bishops.[21] To this might be added his simple faith in the protection of St Joseph, especially in financial need. Hickey's first act in opening a house was to place in a prominent place the best statue of the saint he could find, confiding to the saint the needs of the new foundation. Under Hickey's leadership, Redemptorists criss-crossed the Indian sub-continent by train, preaching missions or giving retreats to clergy and especially to members of Irish religious communities.

Kerr had grasped that one of the problems in the Philippines had been the failure to foster local vocations from the outset and was determined that the same mistake would not be made in India. By the end of 1941, plans were in train for extending the tiny monastery in Bangalore to include a novitiate wing. The novitiate was formally opened in 1943. With the profession of the first two Indian novices in 1945, the time had arrived to establish a house of studies in Bangalore. Its short-term viability depended on having some students from Ireland to swell the numbers, and five Irish students set out for India the following year.

Hugo Kerr's contribution to the venture cannot be underestimated. He injected an awareness about the foreign missions into the members of the Irish province that anticipated the fresh thinking that would come to fuller expression in the era of Vatican II. The Philippine pioneers had not lacked enthusiasm or goodwill: what they did need was a vision that would explain why they had come all the way from Ireland and what they were to do when they got there. Hugo Kerr had a clearer vision than his predecessor, Andrew Boylan. He grasped that bringing the Redemptorist congregation into a new culture would entail helping it to find new ways of flourishing and he communicated this understanding to the pioneers. The situation may have been helped by a sense of urgency of the rapidly changing reality as India moved closer towards independence. No one could predict how long European missionaries might continue to be acceptable in India after the British withdrawal. It was imperative, therefore, to attract Indian Redemptorist vocations and to train them in India from the beginning if the congregation were to have any chance of survival.

Hugo Kerr's letter to the students in Galway preparing them for the selection of some of their number for India might be described as his missionary testament.[22] He sets out clearly in it his hopes for the Indian mission. He

---

[21] Morgan, *Time to Remember*, 12.
[22] Hugo Kerr to Students, 7 Oct. 1945, VR 13, RPAD.

begins by dispelling any notions they be tempted to entertain that volunteering for India might be a lark to brighten a few years now that the novelty had begun to wear off the new student house in Galway. He disabused them of any hope that the volunteers would be recalled to Ireland before ordination, or at least, within a few years of it. The call of the Indian mission, he insisted, was for life. Europeans found its dry heat more bearable than the damp heat of the Philippines, so the need to return home for health reasons every few years would not arise. If other Irish religious could stay in India for a lifetime, he asked, why should the Redemptorists want to be any different? Despite such difficulties, they should consider it a privilege to be chosen to help lay the foundations for a great new Redemptorist province. Using a traditional Redemptorist image that the congregation was called for the service of the 'most abandoned', Kerr identified the Dalits or people outside the caste system as the privileged objects of Redemptorist care.

Going on the Indian mission was not an occasion to teach anything to the people of India. Those going out would have to be open to being taught, to learning a new way of life. While drawing life from the Irish stock and the Redemptorist tradition, the congregation planted in India would 'develop on lines suitable for its own peculiar genius and culture'. The Irish were welcome in India because of the similarity of the two people's struggle for independence but they would have to accept the fact that they were exiles, and 'we must seek to identify ourselves in mind and heart with the people amongst whom God has called us to life and labour.' The Catholic tradition in India was a long and venerable one. Its roots went back to the earliest Christian times with the legend of St Thomas and to the glorious story of St Francis Xavier. The subcontinent of India bore the marks of centuries of colonialism:

> When we come face to face with them, we surely have reason to be ashamed of our colour in thinking how so many of the European nations in turn, Portuguese, Dutch and British, have so cruelly despoiled and exploited them. And when we think of the barbarism to which the white people of today have sunk in the prosecution of a fiendish war, we surely have no reason to consider ourselves a superior race, but rather we must feel a deep respect for the culture and civilization of a people remarkable for their gentle kindness towards all.[23]

He concluded by admonishing them to strive to develop the qualities they would need as young missionaries, and that the call could come at any time and not merely just for those finally professed, but even for those just recently out of the novitiate.

---

[23] Ibid.

A number of points are remarkable about this letter. The first is the way in which Kerr appealed directly to the idealism of his youthful audience. They had come into religious life with high ideals: he knew it was the time to put them to the test. He spared little in spelling out the demands of the missionary life. Second, he realised that mission was essentially a crossing-over into a new culture, that they could not afford to be looking backwards, hoping to transplant something of Ireland into the foreign field. Thirdly, there is an unusual respect for the distinctiveness of Indian culture and the recognition that the European Church had entered India under the banner of a colonialism that was exploitative and cruel and must now lay it aside. Finally, there was the recognition that the Church and the Redemptorist congregation had to strive to become Indian, and not think of themselves as simply another outpost of Western culture that co-opted Indian members. It anticipates some of the distinctive voices of a more contemporary theology of mission. With his strong sense of where mission was going, Kerr was to leave his mark not just on the Irish mission to India, but on the missionary sense of the Irish province in general.

The work of Kerr and Hickey in planting the Redemptorists on Indian soil would prove to be one of the international success stories of the congregation in the twentieth century. Within a little over thirty years of its foundation, it was an autonomous province under Indian leadership. Today, it is one of the largest provinces of the congregation. The province of Bangalore has fourteen houses and two regions of Colombo (Sri Lanka) and Mumbai that enjoy a measure of autonomy. There is also the vice-province of Alwaye composed of members of the ancient Syro-Malabar Rite, whose major archbishop, Cardinal Mar Varkey Vithayathil, was one of the first Indian Redemptorists to be professed, and second provincial of the independent province of Bangalore.

Parish Missions in Wartime

Attention to the work of parish missions on the home front was as much a priority for Kerr as it was for his predecessors, even if his period in office saw no dramatic innovation in style or content. He cautioned his preachers to review carefully the content of their sermons and to avoid making statements from the pulpit that were offensive to sound theology or good taste.

> A preacher who makes intemperate and extravagant statements in the pulpit generally shows that he has forgotten his manuscript, and is relying on the inspiration of the moment. It is often a dangerous and sometimes a fatal proceeding.[24]

---

[24] Hugo Kerr, Circular Letter, 31 Jan. 1939, LB-K, 10, RPAD.

Confessional practice also evoked some comment. Some missioners, he suggested, made severity in the confessional a substitute for theological knowledge, while others combined theological rigidity with a harsh manner in addressing penitents. 'Why scold?', he asked them, 'and why be sarcastic and ill-tempered, and why make no allowance for human nature and its weakness and the force of temptation?'[25]

The outbreak of the Second World War posed few problems to mission work in the Free State, apart from occasional delays in travelling due to fuel restrictions. The mission council of January 1945 reported a considerable increase both in the number of missioners and in the amount of work done. The number of active missioners had increased from forty-eight in 1927 to sixty-seven in 1945. The number of missions in the same period had soared from ninety-seven to 228, and parish retreats from 178 to 242. There was a corresponding increase in the number of retreats to clergy, religious and school-children. Kerr hinted that all was not entirely on the credit side and that work continued to be lost due to the manner in which some men had behaved. Disagreements with parish clergy continued to be a headache, as did the tendency of some retreat-givers who 'misled by false zeal, have made themselves a nuisance in religious houses by rigorous insistence on silence and interference with domestic arrangements'.[26]

Table 6. Missioners, Missions and Parish Retreats, 1926–45

Year	1926	1945
Missioners	48	67
Missions	97	228
Parish Retreats	178	142

Source: Figures based on provincial chronicle returns

The Apostolate of the Pen

Redemptorists had often pondered on how to keep 'the fruits of the mission' alive after they had departed from the parish. Their founder had encouraged the propagation of pious reading during the missions and had written many such works himself. There were frequent re-printings of the best-known of the works of Alphonsus, especially the *Visits to the Blessed Sacrament* which went through fifteen English editions in the nineteenth century alone.[27] John Baptist Coyle produced a selection of the spiritual writings of Alphonsus

---

25 Ibid.
26 Hugo Kerr, Circular Letter, 22 Jan. 1945, RPAD.
27 Statistics from Maurice de Meulemeester, *Bibliographie Générale des Ecrivains Rédemptoristes*, vol. 1 (Louvain: Imprimerie St Alphonse, 1933), 223.

arranged for daily meditation and spiritual reading in six volumes called *Meditations and Readings for Every Day of the Year*.[28] The Austrian Redemptorists had published *Unterrichts- und Andachtsbuch* ('Book of Instructions and Devotions') in 1826 for sale during missions. As well as popular prayers, it contained instructions on how to live the Christian life and, as the Redemptorists spread from Austria, it was translated into French, Dutch and English.[29] The first English version, *The Mission Book*, appeared in 1857 in the United Stares and several editions followed on both sides of the Atlantic. To the same genre belongs *Mission Keepsake: Devotions and Prayers taken chiefly from the writings of St Alphonsus*, compiled by Francis McNamara CSsR in Dublin in 1932, or the modest *Redemptorist Hymn Book and Prayers* of 1946. Probably the most successful examples of the prayer book cum manual were four short books produced by Fr Leo O'Halloran (1903–70). *Prayer Book for Men*, the first in the series, appeared in 1952 and reached its fortieth edition in 1959. *Prayer Book for Boys* saw nineteen editions by 1959. Only marginally less successful were the *Prayer Book for Girls* in 1956 and that for women in 1957.[30] Their small size – 8 cm x 11.5 cm – made them ideal for slipping into a handbag or inside pocket of a jacket. As well as the more common prayers, they contained instruction on aspects of the Catholic faith and the devotional life, adapted to the needs of the audience to which they were addressed. The longest section in each book is devoted to the preparation for confession, including a lengthy 'examination of conscience'. O'Halloran's prayer books paint a picture of the 'ideal Catholic' of the 1950s – prayerful, devout, sober, industrious, setting a premium on chastity and sexual restraint.[31]

---

[28] *Meditations and Reading for Every Day of the Year* (Dublin: Phoenix, 1922). It was reissued as *All my Days for God* (Dublin: Clonmore and Reynolds, 1947).

[29] Editions consulted include *The Mission Book. Instructions and Prayers to Preserve the Fruits of the Mission, drawn chiefly from the Writings of St Alphonsus Maria de Liguori*, new and revised edition (Dublin, 1891), and new and revised twelfth edition (Dublin, 1916); *Missionsbuchlein fur Junglinge und Jungfrauen. Ein Unterrichts- und Andachtsbuch als bestandige Hausmission* (15th Auflage, Munich 1909); *The New Mission Book of the Redemptorist Fathers*, ed. F. Girardey CSsR (St Louis, 1911; reprinted 1928); *Le souvenir de la mission ou le salut assuré aux âmes de bonnes volontés d'après St Alphonse à l'usage des personnes du monde qui veulent assuré leur salut*, ed. J-M Blancpied (Lyon and St-Etienne, Loire, 1913).

[30] They were all published by Fallon of Dublin, with a few British editions by Burns and Oates of London.

[31] See Brendan McConvery, 'The Redemptorists and the Shaping of Irish Popular Devotion, 1851–1965' in *Devotional Cultures of European Christianity, 1790–1960*, eds, Henning Laugerud and Salvador Ryan (Dublin: Four Courts Press, 2012), 48-59.

John Carr (1878–1962) made writing his main apostolate. He began his writing career while serving on the Australian mission. Much of his output consisted of popular lives of the saints, especially Redemptorist saints like Clement Hofbauer, Gerard Majella and Blessed Peter Donders, a Dutch Redemptorist who spent most of his priestly life ministering to lepers in Dutch Surinam in South Africa.[32] Carr kept up a steady output of short popular books and pamphlets until his death.

Several Redemptorist provinces issued religious magazines and the Irish province launched its *Redemptorist Record* in November 1936. It was the brainchild of Fr Thomas A. Murphy (1878–1950). It appeared every two months and the work of editing was done in Clonard by Murphy with the help of Brother Michael Bradley who looked after the accounts. One of the reasons for founding the *Record* was to present to a wider public, and to gain financial support for the Redemptorist foreign missions. TAM, as Murphy usually signed himself, wrote many of the articles himself or encouraged his brethren to write. He also secured contributions from a number of well-known Irish Catholic writers of the day such as Eoin MacNeill and Helena Concannon, the writer of saints' lives Alice Curtayne, and the popular novelist Annie M. P. Smithson.[33] Ten thousand copies of the first edition were printed, but the print-run for the second had to be increased to 15,000. Apart from his work on the *Record*, Murphy contributed to other Irish periodicals, including *Studies*, the *Irish Ecclesiastical Record*, *Irish Educational Review* as well as journals abroad, including *America* and the *Australian Catholic Record*. He was an early and staunch supporter of Frank Duff's Legion of Mary. Hugo Kerr encouraged the apostolate of the pen. One of the arguments he used to gain Patrick Murray's reluctant support for the decision to send students to University College, Galway, was that it could provide vital training for future writers. For much of the 1950s, the editor was Liam Gerard O'Carroll, under whose editorship the magazine was distinguished by several series of articles under the pen name of 'Bill Gerrard' on issues such as dancing, courtship, women's fashions and sex education which adopted a rigorous moral line and were eventually published as short pamphlets.[34]

---

[32] His published works include: *Truly a Lover, reflections on St Thérèse of Lisieux* (Dublin, 1925); *Christ is All* (Dublin: Clonmore and Reynolds, 1948); *Blessed Maria Goretti* (Dublin: Clonmore and Reynolds, 1948); *To Heaven through a Window: St Gerard Majella* (Dublin: Clonmore and Reynolds, 1949); *A Fisher of Men* (Dublin: Clonmore and Reynolds, 1952).

[33] Kevin H. Donlon, *And Ink be on their Hands* (Dublin: Veritas Publications, 1999), 108.

[34] *The Devil at Dances?* (1956), *Mary, Modes and Modesty* (1958), *Towards a White Courtship* (1958), all published by Redemptorist Record, Belfast and, under his own name, L.G. O'Carroll, *Educating to Purity* (Dublin: Redemptorist Record, 1961).

The *Redemptorist Record* changed its name to *Reality* in 1965, reflecting a change in perspective from being an in-house journal to being a journal of national comment. It has survived the circulation wars that saw the death of many religious periodicals in the latter decades of the twentieth century. As well as *Reality*, Redemptorist Communications publishes a youth magazine, *Face Up*, and other pastoral and liturgical resources, both in print and on the web.

Military Chaplains in the Second World War
Shortly after the outbreak of the Second World War, seven Irish Redemptorists, Frs Joseph Connolly, Daniel Cummings, Luke Hartigan, Harry McGowan, Peter Mulrooney, Joseph Murphy, James Scott and Joseph Tronson, volunteered for service as military chaplains. Kerr had a personal interest in this apostolate. His brother had been killed in action in France and, as a student, he had kept up a correspondence with Fr Patrick Carroll, an army chaplain.[35] Most of them saw action on the European Front, though Peter Mulrooney served in the Burma campaign with the Chindits. Kerr asked the young chaplains to keep in regular contact with him by letter and it is thus that a collection of letters from one chaplain, Fr Daniel Cummings, survive.

Dan Cummings (1907–77) was born in Belfast and belonged to a family with extensive Redemptorist connections. His uncle, the brother of Bishop Daniel Mageean of Down and Connor, was Fr Robert Mageean. Three of his cousins, Joseph Morgan, pioneer of the Indian mission, Robert Quinn and Richard McCall, who died as a student in Esker at the age of twenty-two, were contemporaries of his student days. After ordination, young Fr Cummings was sent to study in Rome and on his return, became professor of sacred scripture, first in Esker and later in Galway. His letters provide a vivid account of the day-to-day life of the chaplain in the days of the 'phoney war' to the anxious days of the Normandy landing and his arrival in Brussels with the first wave of allied liberators. Their vivid style merits more than passing mention.[36]

> I hope this won't alarm you – we have had the most trying time since we came to France. You have read of the spectacular advances – well, you can picture the long hours on the road, the want of sleep, the upsetting of the normal routine, and on top of it, all the cold nights.

---

[35] Two letters from Carroll are in Kerr's personal file, 13 Oct. 1918, 16 Dec. 1918, RPAD.
[36] Daniel Cummings, Letters to Kerr, Box NA, Chaplains, RPAD. See also Brendan McConvery, 'A Chaplain's War Time Letters' in *Reality* (Dec., 1994), 24–30.

I would not like to have to do it all again ... I saw a crowd of *Maquis* pushing an old man along – a *collaborateur*. He was supposed to have shot an American flier who was forced down. His face was scarlet, his eyes protruded wildly, he was covered with perspiration, an automatic was jammed into each ear – he was terror-stricken and I think with reason, for I feel sure they were marching him to his death ...

Father Cummings celebrated his first Christmas Mass in peace time under difficult conditions.

Wounded men swathed in bandages came down on trolleys and were placed before the altar. One young boy who had been wounded by a shell saw nothing, but kept saying his rosary. He said to me afterwards, 'You know, Father, it all becomes tremendous when your eyes are closed. If I still had my sight, I would be looking around me.' Another soldier whose head wound had injured the motor nerves controlling his speech lay still and quiet before the altar. Afterwards when I asked him did he like the Christmas Mass, he just blinked his eyes once to show me he was pleased.

Clonard: Novena and Ecumenism

As the war began to bite more deeply into the everyday life of Northern Ireland, there was a noticeable decline in the congregations attending Clonard. The 'black out' which made attendance at services after dark difficult and the increase of overtime and Sunday work required by the war effort had their effect on confraternity attendance. The constant wailing of sirens and air-raid warnings was taking its toll on the people's nerves, but as they came to terms with wartime conditions, the attendance began to improve again.[37]

Another army chaplain, this time an American Redemptorist stationed in Belfast who frequently visited Clonard, was destined to make a lasting contribution to the apostolic life of the Irish province. His name was Matthew Meighan. The American Redemptorists had adapted a form of devotion to Our Lady of Perpetual Help that had been first used by the Servites in the mid-1920s in honour of Our Lady of Sorrows.[38] It consisted of a short weekly service of prayers, hymns, brief sermon and benediction lasting a half-hour. During one of his visits to Clonard in 1943, Meighan described to the community the outstanding popular success of the new novena. As a result, he was invited to preach the annual novena in honour of

---

[37] Report on Clonard for 1942, provincial chronicle, RPAD.
[38] For an account of the origins of the novena in the United States see, Timothy Kelly and Joseph Kelly, 'Our Lady of Perpetual Help, gender roles, and the decline of devotional Catholicism' in *Journal of Social History*, vol. 32, no. 1 (1998), 5–26.

the Immaculate Conception beginning at the end of November. Attracted by the eloquence of the 'Yankee chaplain', the congregation overflowed from the church into the monastery corridors and crowded into the churchyard. The Clonard domestic chronicle records that

> the corridors were crowded to the refectory door with men [women at that time were not permitted into the lower part of the corridor due to the enclosure rule]. Sometimes at community supper, we were without a chair as all had to be used for the convenience of the men. The enthusiasm stirred up by the novena is the greatest ever seen in Clonard. The perpetual novena has come to stay.[39]

That last sentence would prove prophetic. Within a few weeks, perpetual novenas were established not just in the Irish Redemptorist churches of Limerick and Esker, but also in several parish churches in Down and Connor and throughout the rest of Ireland. The crowds flocking to Clonard were undiminished: in the bleak days of the war, the novena created an atmosphere of joyful faith and community solidarity. To help priests cope with the challenge of producing short sermons on Marian themes every week, 'novena sermonettes' were circulated as a few cheaply-printed sheets of sermon outlines for several months at a time. As a mark of their devotion, the people of Clonard responded generously: 'rings, brooches, cuff-links, watches and watch-chains, engagement and signet rings, earrings with all their precious stones were tastefully put into a beautiful gold monstrance to be used for the benediction at the novena devotions.'[40] Shortly afterwards, in June 1948, the images of Mary and the child on the icon were crowned with exact replicas of the crowns on the original in Rome and the material for their making was raised in the same way.[41] A year later, the ornamental gates around the shrine were put in place and blessed by Fr Leonard Buijs, the superior general.

Shortly after the end of the war, Clonard saw the birth of another new apostolate. It was the beginnings of the ecumenical outreach that was to become an enduring part of that community's mission. The dark days of the Belfast 'blitz' had broken down some of the hostility that traditionally had divided Catholic and Protestant in the city, and Catholic and Protestant neighbours from the surrounding streets had taken shelter in the church crypt during the worst of the bombing. One day, two young Protestants came to Clonard, anxious to learn more about the beliefs of Catholics. The rector,

---

[39] Clonard Domestic Chronicle, 8 Dec. 1943, Domestic archives, Clonard.
[40] Grant, *One Hundred Years with the Clonard Redemptorists*, 148.
[41] On the significance of crowning the image, see Anne Eriksen, 'Our Lady of Perpetual Help: invented tradition and devotional success' in *Journal of Folklore Research*, vol. 2, no. 3 (2005), 295–321, especially 315–16 for reference to Clonard.

Fr Gerard Reynolds, decided that the atmosphere in the city was right to offer a series of talks on Catholic beliefs to be known, perhaps unwisely, as the 'Mission to Non-Catholics'. The first mission, a series of six talks on each Sunday was set for the Lent of 1948. Two Redemptorists conducted each session. The format included bible-reading, hymn singing by the choir, a lecture on some aspect of Catholic belief, answers to questions sent in during the previous week and a concluding prayer.[42] It was an outstanding success. Even though it was attacked in some quarters as a Roman proselytising ploy, a claim given some credence by the inclusion of the word 'mission' in the title, the preachers were committed to a non-polemical presentation of the Catholic view point and were prepared to meet a group of their strongest critics from the National Union of Protestants in an atmosphere of tolerance and dialogue.[43]

One of the Redemptorists who devoted much of his energies to the development of the 'mission to non-Catholics' was Fr Daniel Cummings, the former army chaplain encountered earlier in this chapter. His wartime experience had convinced him that there was much ignorance about the basic facts of Catholicism even among well-disposed Christians of other denominations.[44] The 'mission to non-Catholics' continued in its original form until the mid-1960s. It was a child of its time, but it was also the beginning of the flourishing ecumenical apostolate that has been a feature of Clonard's ministry to the present. Speaking in 1950, Fr Gerard Reynolds, the rector, characterised the ideal of both the mission and what was to be Clonard's later ecumenical outreach:

> Our purpose is to build bridges of understanding in place of walls of misunderstanding. Differences there are. They were born at the

---

[42] The questions were published by the *Irish News*, the Belfast nationalist daily paper, in its Tuesday edition following each of the missions. The questions of the first decade were published as a set of three pamphlets entitled *Clonard Answers to Questions put by some Protestants during the Clonard Missions for all Denominations 1949–1959* (Dublin: Catholic Truth Society of Ireland, 1962). No. 1 discussed issues such as the Pope, indulgences, saints, marriage, drinking and gambling; no. 2 treated the Church, images, the bible, the Blessed Virgin Mary, Sunday, while no. 3 treated confession, tradition, the mass, sacraments and politics. The main contributors to the collections were Frs Seán O'Riordan and J. J. W. Murphy. O'Riordan was a young professor of theology; Murphy, a former chaplain to the British forces in Palestine, was no mean academic himself, having undertaken graduate study at the Pontifical Biblical Institute in Rome.

[43] Grant, *One Hundred Years with the Clonard Redemptorists*, 164–8.

[44] Dan Cummings wrote an account of the mission's progress in two articles for the *Irish Ecclesiastical Record* (*IER*): 'A Mission in Ireland for Non-Catholics' in *IER*, vol. xx (1948), 481–94, and 'Missions for Non-Catholics in Ireland', *IER*, vol. xxiii (1951), 3–24.

Reformation. But misunderstanding there need not be. We desire therefore in these talks to explain our Catholic faith that you may realise that we preach and teach only the Gospel of Jesus Christ.[45]

Enclosed Retreat Movement

Enclosed retreats for clergy had been regularly hosted in Redemptorist houses since the first for the priests of Limerick in the newly-opened monastery of Mount St Alphonsus in 1859. Organised residential retreats for lay people were rarer. In provinces like Holland and Belgium, the Redemptorists had for some time been organising retreats for lay people in purpose-built retreat houses. During the war years, an estimated 600 men had made one-day retreats in Clonard, a development warmly encouraged by Bishop Daniel Mageean of Down and Connor in his Lenten pastoral of 1945. The rector of Clonard, Thomas J. Regan (1893–1950) and his council sounded out the provincial about the possibility of acquiring a house exclusively for retreats somewhere in the Belfast area. Kerr readily gave permission and the hunt for a house began.

By a stroke of luck, the parish of Ardglass, County Down had recently acquired a dilapidated castle overlooking the harbour. The parish priest was willing to offer it to the Redemptorists. The first community took up residence in October 1946. Post-war conditions in the North were still grim. Getting building supplies or even a telephone would strain the ingenuity of superiors and builders alike for several years to come. The old castle was in a bad state of repair, and the winter of 1946–7 was one of the coldest in living memory. Nevertheless, preparations were complete in time for the first retreat in May 1947, to which the men of the parish of Ardglass and Dunsford were invited. As they were locals, they did not need to stay overnight. Despite the still makeshift arrangements of the house, the retreat was booked out. There was so little furniture in place that benches had to be borrowed from the local cinema after the last show on Saturday night. There was seating for only 130 in the second-hand Nissen hut that had been converted into a chapel. One hundred and fifty-three men had booked for the retreat, but 162 showed up. Somehow, 159 were squeezed into the dining room, while the rest took their meals outdoors in favourable weather.

After such a beginning, the problem was to ensure that the supply of retreatants continued. Dublin already had a number of retreat houses, mostly in the suburbs, catering for a sizeable Catholic market. Ardglass, by contrast,

---

[45] *Irish News*, 13 Nov. 1950. Fr Reynolds's nephew, also Gerard, was to play a prominent part in the development of Clonard's ecumenical work in the period of 'the troubles', see Ronald Wells, *Friendship Towards Peace: The Journey of Ken Newell and Gerry Reynolds* (Dublin: Columba Press, 2005).

was remote. It was twenty-five miles from Belfast, and in the immediate post-war years, private cars were still a luxury and petrol was severely rationed. The founders of Ardglass realised that Redemptorist efforts alone would not be able to fill the house on a regular basis. In January 1948, Fr John Gorey organised the first meeting of prospective retreat promoters: they included representatives from Catholic bodies as diverse as the Catholic Young Men's Society, Legion of Mary, Young Christian Workers, St Vincent de Paul, Knights of St Columbanus, youth clubs, and the Clonard choir. They were the nucleus of what would become the Down and Connor Lay Retreat Organisation.

A retreat house provided the opportunity for meeting the needs of groups, as diverse as university students, young people preparing for marriage (as long as they were men!), Irish speakers, workers and professional people. The retreat house staff was not slow in grasping the usefulness of new technology to promoting their work. A 'magic lantern' was acquired for slide shows. John Gorey commissioned a film on the work of the retreat house called *A Weekend with God.* Catholic-owned cinemas throughout Northern Ireland were happy to run the film as a 'short feature' and to allow Gorey to address the audience for a few minutes during the interval on the value of a retreat.

The retreat house attracted many who might not normally attend a Redemptorist mission such as the twenty-three 'Borstal boys' brought down for a day's retreat by a group of Belfast businessmen who defrayed the cost. Fifty-five Catholic members of the RUC made their first retreat in October 1948. In their letter of thanks they wrote:

> The Catholic police here have little chance of attending retreats in their local churches, as it's almost certain duty will intervene before it is complete, consequently a special one for themselves is all the more appreciated.[46]

Scarcely a minute of the timetable was left free from arrival at 7.15 p.m. on Saturday evening to departure at a sufficiently early hour on Monday to enable the men to get back home on time for work. On the first evening, they got two lectures, a rosary, and supper – all before night prayers at 9.30 p.m. They rose at 7.30 a.m. on the Sunday, had five lectures in the course of the day, as well as Mass, rosary, visit and way of the cross in common. The time that remained was for personal devotion and preparation for confession. The conferences or lectures were probably of the 'single transferable sermon'

---

[46] Brendan McConvery, 'Remembering Ardglass' in Michael Kelleher and Gerard Moloney (eds) *St Clement's 1947–2006* (Redemptorist Communications: Dublin, 2006), 15. Catholic members of the RUC continued to attend retreats as a group in the Belfast retreat house until the disturbed political conditions of the early 1970s made it impossible.

variety, administered with only minimal adjustment to groups as diverse as farmers, bar-workers and university students. A lecture plan from 1952 is typical of the style of retreat that remained in vogue until the late 1960s: an opening talk, talks on 'an eternal truth', supernatural outlook on life, some aspect of sin; duties of the state in life; Eucharistic life and Blessed Virgin Mary. The members of the retreat house team were totally involved in every aspect of the work. No lay help was employed, so apart from the hours of preaching and confessions, the priests and brothers of the community prepared the meals, served in the dining room and helped with a myriad other household chores.

Within the first five years, the number of weekend, mid-week and one-day retreats more than doubled and the numbers attending tripled. In 1950, 2,007 men attended at weekends, 273 at two- or three-day, mid-week retreats, and 282 one-day retreats.

Table 7. Enclosed Retreats in St Clement's, Ardglass, 1947–51

Year	Retreats	Attendance
1947	27	969
1948	44	1,660
1949	49	2,215
1950	52	2,562
1951	55	3,294

Source: Ardglass Domestic Chronicle, RPAD

By the time of the retreat organisation's annual general meeting of 1951, it was clear that space was a problem. The same groups were returning annually in larger numbers and filling every available bed, so it seemed pointless even to consider looking for new groups. The question of finding bigger premises became inevitable, especially if it could bring the retreat house closer to Belfast. House hunting came to an end in 1950 when an estate of thirty-seven acres with a large house became available on the slopes of the Cave Hill on the north side of Belfast. It is a sign of the times that negotiations to allow Catholics to purchase a prime site on the Antrim Road still had to be carried out discreetly. It was purchased through a third party in September 1950. Fr Michael Curran, the provincial, announced the following July that Bishop Mageean had granted permission for a new retreat house, as well as for a public church on the front of the Antrim Road. St Gerard's church was opened in 1956 and the retreat house followed in 1960. With it the Redemptorist presence at Ardglass came to an end.

The success of the Ardglass venture persuaded the Redemptorists that it was worth investing more men and money in the retreat house apostolate. The possibility of building a retreat house on the Marianella site in Dublin was considered. Hugo Kerr's successor as provincial, Jack Treacy, opened negotiations with Archbishop John Charles McQuaid to develop the Marianella site to provide accommodation for theological students and a retreat house.[47] McQuaid was favourably disposed to the idea, but suggested relocating the entire enterprise to a site in Raheny. The Redemptorists were less enthusiastic. They proposed instead buying 'Oaklands', a property that shared a boundary wall with Marianella (later the site of St Luke's Hospital). When the diocesan authorities refused permission for this, the project was abandoned.

So strong was Redemptorist support for enclosed retreats that little soul searching was required when it was proposed to build a retreat house in Limerick as a memorial to the centenary of the coming of the Redemptorists to the city in 1853. Permission was granted by Bishop Henry Murphy and the Retreat House of Our Lady of Perpetual Help held its first retreat in 1954.

Life in the Communities
The internal life of Redemptorist communities continued to be lived according to a rule formulated for eighteenth-century Naples, overlaid with traditions brought from Austria via Belgium and Holland and interpreted for more northerly climes by the generation of English convert superiors of the Oxford Movement. General chapters might introduce changes in minor points of regular observance: given the political conditions of the nineteenth century, they met erratically. The reform of the code of canon law in the early twentieth century ensured that chapters became a more regular feature of life in religious orders. It took the two Irish delegates, Hugo Kerr and John Fitzgerald, eight days to reach Rome for the chapter of 1936, as they undertook a little religious tourism on the side, travelling by boat and train via Bordeaux, Lourdes, Marseilles and Genoa. Although a revision of the constitutions was on the chapter's agenda, Murray made it clear in his opening address that no changes would be countenanced beyond what was strictly demanded by the changing times in which they found themselves. The 1936 chapter introduced a few changes that went towards making home life a little more bearable. Games might be played occasionally as part of community recreation, but strictly for exercise. Superiors of the Irish province interpreted this concession as applying only to priests or students: it did not apply to brothers since it was believed that the regular round of manual work of the brothers gave them all the exercise they needed. The full order of the day,

---

[47] Correspondence, John Charles McQuaid and John Treacy, Mar.–June 1948, RPAD.

from the rising bell at 5.30 a.m. to the last signal at 10.30 p.m., remained substantially unchanged from the days of Alphonsus Liguori. The 1936 chapter's concession of a cup of tea at 6.00 p.m. broke the long period between dinner at 1.30 p.m. and supper at 8.30 p.m. Redemptorist fasts were not particularly burdensome by the standards of some other religious orders, but abstinence from meat during the entire season of Advent, the Novena of the Holy Spirit from Ascension to Whit Sunday, and on each Saturday of the year remained in place until the mid-1960s, as did the minor fast on vigils of the main feasts of Mary and some other saints.

There were no regular holidays, except for the students who enjoyed a month's summer break in a rented house by the sea in Roundstone and later in Clifden, but even here the main outline of the day was followed. The only break from the daily round of life in community was through apostolic work outside the house or an occasional community day excursion during the summer time. Feast days, either for the major liturgical seasons of the year or to celebrate some internal event in the community's life such as the jubilees of profession or ordination were celebrated with a more abundant meal and a time of evening entertainment to which members of the community contributed their party-piece. In 1948, the superior general gave the Irish provincial permission on an experimental basis to grant a few days' *levamen*, or rest, to those confreres who believed they needed it, but on condition that this was not seen as a general vacation for everyone. The *levamen* could only be taken in a designated house, such as Ardglass or Galway near the sea, and the regular timetable of the community was substantially observed with some concessions. Smoking was a bone of contention, surrounded by regulations. A superior might give permission for a 'community smoke' on major feast days. On missions,

> if the Fathers are dining with the priests and the latter are smoking after dinner, the Fathers may have a cigarette, and sometimes even a second one, or if the priest offers one, sometimes even a cigar.[48]

Individuals sometimes attempted to evade the routine of community life by the stratagem of arranging a trip to Dublin to consult a medical specialist. If they were lucky, a few days in hospital might ensue, for what superiors suspected were comparatively trifling ailments. Hugo Kerr as provincial tried to exercise some control by issuing formal regulations: specialists were to be consulted only by way of exception and local superiors were to ensure that doctors did not prescribe prolonged periods of convalescence for, Kerr claimed, 'it is an undeniable fact confirmed by experience, that prolonged

---

[48] Regulations of provincial chapter and clarified by the provincial, 16 June 1948, RPAD.

convalescence is harmful to the religious spirit.' Visiting sick confreres in hospital provided some with a pretext for avoiding some of the more tedious religious exercises of the afternoon. Kerr warned superiors that they should not 'permit relays of fathers and brothers to visit hospitals the same afternoon. The law of charity towards the sick does not demand that we turn the hospital into a kind of clubhouse, causing serious disturbance of order and inconvenience to the nurses and sisters'.[49]

Six Lean Years

Much of this period reviewed here was lived under the shadow of war. It bit particularly deeply in the Belfast house, but elsewhere in the province, there were minor restrictions. If shortages and rationing led to an increasingly austere diet, it was little in comparison to what Redemptorist communities were suffering elsewhere.

The situation in the Philippines was particularly grim. For most of the war, the fathers and brothers were out of contact by post, apart from very occasional letters delivered through the Red Cross. Detailed news of how some of their confreres had fared only reached the Irish communities at the end of the war. Some had been forced to flee to the hills for safety at the onset of the Japanese invasion. Others had spent periods in Japanese detention camps. One, Fr Patrick Drumm, was murdered by guerrillas. He had initially worked with the guerrillas in the mountains but on discovering the extent to which they were terrorising the local community by a systematic policy of summary executions, he withdrew and offered his services to the local Filipino pastor instead. When he reprimanded two guerrillas publicly for their openly immoral conduct, they shot him dead on the spot.[50]

Houses like Esker with sizeable farms attached were better placed to withstand the challenge of the Emergency. The farm was put to its best use, and some additional land was leased to grow wheat to provide bread for the community. The flour was milled locally and the bread was baked in Cluain Mhuire, Galway, where a baking oven had been installed and one of the brothers passed on to his companions the bread-making skills he had learned in a crash course in baking with the Cistercians in Roscrea.

Conditions in the house of studies were particularly bad. There were more mouths to feed, and healthy young men have unfailingly good appetites. Matters reached such a state that Fr Anthony McHugh, the *socius*, or priest directly responsible for the daily needs of the students, felt bound in conscience to lay before the provincial some serious instances of

---

[49] Hugo Kerr to rectors, Dec. 1942, LB – K, 28, RPAD.
[50] There is a lengthy account in the provincial chronicle, vol. 3, RPAD, under the year 1947, of the Philippine communities during the war period.

maladministration affecting the students. His detailed account runs to sixteen specific charges, from stinting the students' butter ration in order to supply more to the senior professed, to depriving them almost altogether of fruit and vegetables, while selling much of the farm produce in town. McHugh alleged that the students were bearing the burden of rationing:

> Supper has been a travesty. Even before Lent, a potato cake, a little larger than a biscuit with a spoonful of jam, was all that was given. Extra was had for superiors (I write and confess this with shame!) but for the students – 'well, they eat too much.'[51]

McHugh believed the officials of the house were overstepping their authority in compelling the students to work on free afternoons. The minister [bursar], he alleged, had turned the Easter vacation into a kind of a work camp. There were undoubted tensions at work under the surface. Small privileges, such as the right to sleep an hour later in the morning if saying a late Mass, were guarded jealously by those who possessed them. Certain offices, like the direction of confraternities, brought with them a rich array of 'privileges' and were attractive prizes.

Most of the members lived productive and happy lives. The abundance of mission work meant that the priests who were available for missions and retreats were never subject to the full restraint of the common life for too long. The ending of wartime restrictions on travel meant that the foreign missions of the Philippines and India were once again open to Irish Redemptorists. Despite that, some found Irish Redemptorist life narrowly constricting. Some opted to go to other provinces. A few others opted for diocesan priesthood, especially in the United States. One or two dropped out from ministry leaving little trace, and attitudes of the time demanded that a veil of discretion be drawn around them. Superiors or friends might work discreetly to 'get them settled up', but little information about their current status was ever divulged.

Changing the Guard

On 26 April 1947, the first chapter after the war assembled in Rome. The eighty-two-year-old Patrick Murray was weakened by a stroke and exhausted by his efforts on behalf of the congregation during the war years. He presented his resignation to the chapter and it elected as his successor 'Fr Leonard Buijs (1896–1953) of the Dutch province. The nominations for the Irish province arrived the following September 1948, naming Fr John (Jack) Treacy (1889–1949) as provincial. Although he had been provincial for almost twelve years, Kerr was still only in his early fifties, having taken office

---

51 Anthony McHugh to Hugo Kerr, 3 Mar. 1943, VF 11, RPAD.

at the age of forty-one. Treacy was almost sixty years of age, in poor health and cautious by nature. It was not easy for a man of Kerr's energy and temperament to return to the ranks, and he clashed repeatedly with the new provincial for most of his short term of office.

Treacy began his first three-year period as provincial with extensive building plans. The Galway house of studies had not been completed due to a shortage of money and he made its completion his first priority. He also proposed expanding the secondary college in Limerick and building a new retreat house in Dublin. Finding that the door in Dublin was more open than he had suspected, he also obtained permission from Archbishop McQuaid to purchase land for building a house of theological studies at a future date. Treacy was critical of many aspects of his predecessor's reign. Finances were in a difficult situation: about £800,000 had been spent on the recent building programme at home and abroad, and the running of the student house in Galway was costing £40,000 a year. He faulted several of Kerr's decisions about Galway, alleging that he had ignored advice and gone ahead on his own plan 'with an impulsiveness that often betrays itself in him'.[52]

Treacy's suggestion that the easiest way to deal with overcrowding in Galway was to send the theologians back to Esker drew Kerr directly into the fray. He wrote to the general supporting the plan for a second house of studies in Dublin, suggesting also that the provincial residence be moved there, and that it should be done quickly in view of spiralling land prices. The suggestion of returning the students to Esker, he claimed, came from some men in the province who were 'very conservative (foolishly so) and reactionary who would prefer to see the students PERMANENTLY [capitals original] in Esker'.[53]

Kerr's long shadow made Treacy uneasy but he was not destined to bring any of his plans to fruition. He died unexpectedly on the following 15 November 1949 in the Philippines, where he was conducting a canonical visitation. Although Kerr's name was proposed as a possible successor to Treacy, the members of the provincial council made it abundantly clear to the superior general they were not endorsing him and that his support, even among former admirers, had declined.[54]

In the event, Michael Curran was appointed provincial at the age of sixty-three. His eleven-year term of office would prove almost as long as Hugo Kerr's twelve, but the similarity between the two men ends there. Curran's age and rather easy-going manner set the hallmark of his leadership style. If there was little dramatic happening throughout the 1950s, it would be a time for consolidating the gains made in the previous years.

---

[52] John Treacy to John Keogh, consultor general, 17 Dec. 1948, XIII Hib., RGAR.
[53] Hugo Kerr to Leonard Buijs, 12 Dec. 1948, XIII Hib. Provincialia, RGAR.
[54] Michael Curran to Leonard Buijs, 23 Dec. 1949, XIII Hib. Provincialia, RGAR.

In 1953, the Redemptorists marked the first centenary of their arrival in Ireland with elaborate celebrations in Limerick attended by leaders of church and state. The same year 1953 saw also the unexpected death of Leonard Buijs, the superior general, whose brief period of leadership had brought a new openness into Redemptorist life. He was succeeded the following year by Fr William Gaudreau (1897–1968) of the Baltimore province in the United States. The chapter that elected him also called for a thorough renewal of the rules and constitutions. By the time this was completed at the beginning of the 1960s, the Church was embarking on an unprecedented period of change that had been set in motion by the Second Vatican Council. That event and its impact on the Irish province will be treated in the next chapter.

At the beginning of this chapter, it was observed that the twenty years between 1932 and 1953 were a time of unprecedented growth and self-confidence for the Irish Redemptorists. One measurement of that might simply be in terms of membership and communities. By 1953, there were nine houses in Ireland, five in the Philippines, four in India. Its membership numbered 165 priests and 60 brothers, 73 students, 21 choir- and 5 lay-novices. Despite the outlay on new buildings, the financial situation appeared solid. The cocoon of Irish neutrality had protected the Irish province from much of the turmoil and questioning that the war had brought to the congregation elsewhere in Europe. This questioning was, in its turn, sowing the seeds of a renewed theology that was to flower in Vatican II. Very little of that questioning troubled the calm surface of Redemptorist life in Ireland. It might be suspected, however, that some Redemptorists entertained suspicions that all was not quite as placid as it seemed.

CHAPTER FIFTEEN

From Tranquillity to Change

The 1950s are often depicted as a colourless period in Irish history. It was a
time of high emigration, with little dynamism in the country. The govern-
ments of the Republic and of the North were firmly in the hands of the men
who had opposed each other over Home Rule and independence more than
forty years before. They were now a greying generation with little by way of
new ideas or energy. The same might be said of both the Irish and worldwide Church. There was little encouragement for imaginative initiatives. The
French Church in the post-war period, for instance, had tried to respond
with imagination to a growing awareness that France was once more a
mission country.[1] The worker priest movement sought to bring the leaven of
the Gospel into the world of factory work and trade-union activism. It was
suppressed by Vatican order in 1953. Some of the creative voices of the
French 'nouvelle théologie,' like the Dominicans, Marie-Dominique Chenu
and Yves Congar, had been effectively silenced some years earlier by the
encyclical, *Humani Generis*, of Pius XII.[2] The tide of what had seemed like
the beginnings of a post-war renewal of theology was being turned back by
increasing official caution.

The American superior general of the Redemptorists, William Gaudreau,
elected in 1953, presided over a congregation whose membership of more
than 9,000 put it among the ten largest religious orders of men in the world.
Gaudreau was a kindly man, but his style of government harked back to the
securities of the past. He had succeeded the Dutchman, Leonard Bujis, who
had lived through the Second World War in Europe and had seemed set to
bring the congregation forward but had died after barely five years in office.
The Irish provincial, Michael Curran, was in the Gaudreau mould. His term
of office was solid but unadventurous. He presided over what appeared to be
an energetic and growing province. Events had proved his predecessor's
forecast of a dramatic increase in student numbers to be justified. For most

---

[1] Henri Godin and Yves Daniel, *La France: Pays de Mission?* (Paris: Éditions du Cerf, 1943).
[2] *Humani Generis: Encyclical of Pope Pius XII concerning some false opinions threatening to undermine the foundations of Catholic Doctrine*, 12 Aug. 1950 (English translation, London:
Catholic Truth Society, 1952).

of the 1950s, there were ninety or more students in formation, with correspondingly high numbers in the novitiate. With two vice-provinces in the Philippines and India absorbing as much personnel as the mother province could send them, Curran could boast that he opened a new house almost every year, either at home or abroad.

A retreat house was begun in Limerick in 1954. By 1961, a new extension had been added at a cost of £135,000. The new church of St Gerard on the Antrim Road in Belfast was dedicated in 1956. Four years later, Ardglass retreat house transferred to a new building on the same site, with private rooms for over a hundred retreatants and a separate house for the members of the St Gerard's community. Parish mission work continued with little change in either content or style of delivery. The majority of missions were two weeks long, though some occasionally lasted a month. The triennial returns submitted to Rome, giving the statistics for work done in the year in question, may be taken as a guide to the number of missions preached annually:

Table 8. Number of Redemptorist Missions in Ireland, 1950–62

Year	1950	1953	1956	1958	1962
Missions	152	212	199	168	225

Source: Annual Returns, Provincial Chronicle, RPAD

The monastery churches were in an equally busy state. The confraternities of Limerick and Clonard reached their peak in these years. In the year of its diamond jubilee in 1956, Clonard had 7,172 members, with weekly meetings for three divisions of men, in addition to sessions for boys and young men. Each Thursday in Clonard was an additional day of intense activity, with six sessions of the perpetual novena in honour of Our Lady of Perpetual Help between 3.00 p.m. and 9.00 p.m., with confessions heard before and after each, in addition to the regular round of morning Masses. The churches of Esker and Limerick also had their perpetual novena devotions. In Dundalk, the major public devotion was a perpetual novena in honour of St Gerard Majella, the patron of mothers. Eamon Duffy, professor of the history of Christianity at Cambridge, who grew up near the Redemptorist church in Dundalk, recalls how, as a child, he was 'always baffled by the astonishing number of heavily pregnant women in the congregation'.[3]

The death of Patrick Murray at the age of ninety-four in 1959 marked the end of an era that stretched back to before the First World War. Since his

---

[3] Eamon Duffy, *Faith of Our Fathers: Reflections on Catholic Tradition* (London: Continuum, 2006), 11.

resignation as superior general in 1947, he had lived in retirement in Limerick, becoming increasingly incapacitated with the passage of the years.

Second House in Belfast: St Gerard's

In 1951 a Victorian villa, Ben Eaden, came on the market in Belfast on the death of its owner, Major William Adeley.[4] Originally part of the Belfast Castle estate, it was situated on a superb site of thirty-three acres of woodland, on the side of Cave Hill, overlooking Belfast Lough. To Fr Gerard McDonnell, rector of Clonard, it seemed like an answer to prayer, for the previous year, he had asked the congregation at the Clonard novena to pray 'for father rector's special intention' without specifying what it was. In fact, it was to find a suitable site in the Belfast area, preferably overlooking Belfast Lough, on which to build a new retreat house to replace the unsuitable one in Ardglass which had limited accommodation for the numbers it was attracting.[5]

Given the political situation of Belfast, declarations of interest in such a desirable property by a religious community needed to be circumspect. With the help of a Belfast solicitor, McDonnell took some initial soundings and then gained the approval of the provincial, Michael Curran, and of Daniel Mageean, bishop of Down and Connor, for his project. Bishop Mageean was particularly open to the idea, as he had long wished to see a Catholic church on a prominent site on the Antrim Road. The property was purchased for £14,000. The Adeley family left for England on 29 September 1951 and the Redemptorists moved in the same day.[6]

Gerard McDonnell celebrated the first Mass in the new house on 1 October. Shortly afterwards, he launched an ambitious campaign to raise funds for the construction of a new retreat house, church and monastery. Within the first six months, £30,000 was raised from fund-raising projects such as a carnival and a 'buy a brick' campaign, run from a premises near Clonard: the price of a brick was one guinea, in return for a certificate. In the meantime, the largest ground floor room of the former mansion served as a temporary chapel with a regular routine of daily Mass and devotions, while the rest became home to a small community. The new foundation was canonically erected in September 1953 under the patronage of St Gerard, with Fr James Reynolds as its first superior. The site, on a steep hillside, was not ideal

---

[4] The previous owner of the estate and builder of the house, was Valentine Whitla, a linen merchant who died on 12 Aug. 1865, leaving it to his daughter, Alicia (summary of will in the Public Records Office of Northern Ireland (http://www.proni.gov.uk/accessed 22 Dec. 2010).

[5] Éamon Phoenix, 'St Clement's 1947–2005' in Kelleher and Moloney (eds), *St Clement's 1947–2006*, 32.

6. O'Donnell, 'Story of St Gerard's', ibid., 27–9.

for building. In order to secure a foundation, concrete piles had to be sunk, some as deep as forty feet. The new church of St Gerard was finally completed and dedicated on 9 December, 1956. The architect was J. J. Brennan of Belfast. It was a single-nave, brick-built structure, without aisles in an adaptation of the Irish Romanesque style. Its most striking features were the long window at the west end and a mosaic of St Gerard Majella over the high altar. The refurbishment of the church in 2000 in accordance with contemporary liturgical requirements led to the mosaic being concealed from view.

It would be some years more before the building of the new retreat house could begin: it was not completed until 1960, as has been described in the previous chapter. The monastery for the community further down the hill, was completed in 1962 and the community of Fr James Reynolds, rector, Frs Matthew Hickey, John Torney, Denis Canny and Aodh Bennett and Brs Xavier McDonald and Joachim Murphy, took up residence in June.

The original idea behind the building of St Gerard's church was to establish a religious-run 'devotional church' with a regular programme of Masses, devotions and confessions like Clonard but in a part of the city where there were few public signs of a Catholic presence. By the 1960s, the Catholic population in the surrounding area was growing and in 1969, the Redemptorists agreed to take parochial responsibility for a new area carved out of the neighbouring Catholic parishes.[7] It was the first time the Irish Redemptorists had taken responsibility for running a parish. The first parish priest was Fr Thomas McKinley, with Fr Patrick McGowan as curate.

Third Foreign Mission
The situation in Latin America, where there was profound poverty, a serious lack of priests and a growing presence of North American Protestant missionaries, was causing concern at the Vatican. In preparation for the celebration of the fifteen hundredth anniversary of St Patrick's arrival in Ireland, Pope John XXIII wrote to the Irish bishops in 1961 confiding to them his distress and anxiety at the 'exceptionally grave and difficult circumstances of the priestly ministry in Latin America' and requesting their aid in meeting them.[8]

A similar request had come to the Irish Redemptorists just a year before. Confirming Michael Curran in his third term as provincial in September 1959, William Gaudreau wrote:

---

[7] 'Agreement between the Bishop of Down and Connor and the Father Provincial of the Irish Province of the Congregation of the Most Holy Redeemer regarding the Parish of St Gerard in Belfast, 14 July 1969.' The signatories were Bishop William Philbin and Fr John Whyte CSsR, Box L, RPAD.

[8] Apostolic Letter to Irish bishops, 14 Dec. 1960. English translation in *The Furrow*, vol. 13, no. 2 (Feb., 1961), 126–9.

After much pressure from the Holy See and from the bishops of South America, I am knocking on your door to ask the Irish province to take over a mission area there, specifically in the state of Goias, Brazil, in the diocese of Porto Nacional.[9]

There was already a strong Redemptorist presence in Brazil. The Dutch province had established a mission there in 1894, followed by the Germans in the same year. It was, however, a vast country, and could absorb as many priests as were available. Although it was twice the size of Ireland, the diocese of Porto Nacional in the central region of Brazil had only seven or eight priests at its disposal. Gaudreau agreed to Curran's request that Fr Arthur Maloney, his consultor, should make a fact-finding visit to Brazil. Maloney was a veteran foreign missionary who had spent time in the Philippines where he proved remarkably gifted at learning local languages, even producing an elementary grammar of the Cebuano language for the use of his confreres. He was then sent to the nascent Indian mission, enduring the trials of a ship-wreck to arrive at his destination. The poverty he saw on the ground and the scant resources of the local church shocked Maloney. With little hesitation, he urged Curran to accept the offer.

The pioneers left for Brazil in April 1960. They were Frs James Collins, as superior, John Myers, James McGrath, and Michael Kirwan. Apart from Collins, who had spent some years in the Philippines, the rest were young men who had recently completed their studies. Their first mission station was Pedro Afonso in the state of Tocantins. The Irish Redemptorists came to Brazil in much the same spirit of guileless enthusiasm as they had gone to the Philippines more than fifty years before and to India thirty years later. They were keen to transplant a tradition of parish missions as a way of serving a deprived local Church. They were prepared to work hard and be generous in adapting to a country they must have found bewildering in terms of language, culture, climate and sheer physical size. The experience of the still-young Indian mission had probably taught them a little more realism. Their predecessors who had gone to the Philippines almost fifty years before were unwilling to accept responsibility for running parishes. The Brazilian pioneers accepted that parish responsibility in a Church so deprived of priests was the inevitable, but they regarded it as the short-term price they would have to pay before getting down to their 'real work' of the parish missions they believed would prove an ideal way of reaching out to scattered communities of believers whose contact with the Church was very limited.

In an article for the *Redemptorist Record*, Michael Kirwan recorded some of the first impressions the country made on him and his companions. What was only too clear was 'the immensity of the task that awaits us'. The grave

9 William Gaudreau to Michael Curran, 4 Sept. 1959, Fortaleza 1, RPAD.

shortage of priests – one for every five thousand widely scattered people – created three serious problems. The first was the growing influence of fundamentalist Protestant missionaries, often from North America, among Catholic communities deprived of priests. The second was the growing influence of Marxism, especially following the success of Fidel Castro's Cuban revolution in 1959. The third was the persistence of cults such as Candomblé, which combined elements of Catholicism, such as the invocation of the saints, with the vestiges of the African folk-religion of their slave ancestors. If they were bewildered by some of these, what was clear was that 'there is far too much poverty in Brazil' and side by side with the plush apartments of the rich, 'there are shanty towns that are a disgrace to a Christian community.'[10]

A second house was established in the city of Fortaleza, the largest city of north-east Brazil, in 1962. The intention was to build a college that would serve as a juvenate for the secondary education of local boys likely to have a vocation to the Redemptorists. The vast territory within their remit proved capable of absorbing as many men as could be spared from Ireland. Fortunately, at the beginning of the 1960s, ordinations were plentiful so that by the end of its first seven years in 1967, the vice-province numbered five houses and twenty-six members, as well as a residence for James Collins now known by his Brazilian bishop's title as Don Jaime, who had been appointed administrator of the prelacy of Miracema do Norte in 1967 and raised to the episcopacy the following year.

The first canonical visitation was held in 1962 by Fr Tom McKinley on behalf of the provincial. The early visitation reports convey a sense of the work the pioneers were doing.[11] The community of Pedro Afonso had charge of a territory of more than 17,000 square miles – little more than half the size of Ireland, but with only 48,000 inhabitants. Distances between the municipalities or small towns and the centre were vast to Irishmen: Lizaida was 300 miles from Pedro Afonso and Itacaja was 120. Roads, where they existed at all, were often rudimentary, making travel uncomfortable and difficult. The chief means of transport was a jeep, wrote James McGrath, but getting it across swollen rivers was a problem. An improvised ferry consisting of planks slung between two of the largest canoes in town was the usual method, but if there were no canoes, then 'we have to get the local inhabitants (if there are any) to help us cut down trees and improvise a bridge.' Travel into the interior was only possible on horseback: 'with the help of a guide, we move around for nine or ten days at a time … no sign of life anywhere. An amazing silence: no sound apart from the soft plodding of the horses' hooves.'[12]

---

10 Michael Kirwan, 'Report from Brazil' in *Redemptorist Record* (Sept.– Oct. 1961), 360–1.
11 Visitation Reports, 1962, Brazil 1, RPAD.
12 James McGrath, 'This is Brazil' in *Redemptorist Record* (Nov.– Dec. 1961), 566–7.

Apart from looking after the Sunday liturgy in three main churches and their work in the school, the priests made apostolic tours, or *desobrigas*, into the interior. The families who hosted the *pousas*, or stations, were alerted of the impending arrival of the missionary several weeks or even months in advance, usually by word of mouth passed on through visitors to Pedro. On the evening of his arrival, the priest said the rosary, preached and heard confessions. The following morning, he celebrated Mass and administered whatever sacraments the community needed. Then it was on to the next station where the same routine was repeated. It was impractical to spend more than one night in each place, as the burden of providing food and lodging for all who came, as well as for the priest, was a heavy one for the host families.

The canonical visitors from the mother province reported that their confreres lived by the Redemptorist rule in very much the same way as they had done in Ireland, with due allowance for the difference of climate. The months from November to March were, as far as was practical, to be regarded as the 'repose season' demanded by the rule, during which apostolic activity would be reduced in the parish and *sertao* (backlands) and the community be bound to a more monastic lifestyle in which the 'afternoon acts' (spiritual reading and meditation each for a half-hour) took pride of place. Allowing for differences of climate, the order of the day and other regulations drawn up in the course of the 1962 visitation were not very different from what pertained in Ireland. The day began at 5.00 a.m. with meditation for a half-an-hour later, followed by celebration of Masses; at midday, there was community prayer, followed by dinner, recreation and a short siesta. When the 'afternoon acts' were to be performed, they took place between 2.30 and 3.30 p.m. The third period of meditation took place at 6.00 p.m. followed by supper, recreation and night prayers, with the last signal at 10.00 p.m. It was forbidden to arrange parish activities during the times of community prayer. The men were expected to wear the habit regularly, to have reading at table normally, and, despite the heat, but in keeping with Irish notions of priestly respectability, to wear socks at all community prayers, and especially when saying Mass and in public.

As he struggled to come to grips with the new reality, James Collins the vice-provincial, tried to think ahead.[13] He believed that it was imperative to plan for the future so that the mission could become an independent Brazilian province as quickly as possible. His assessment that 'perhaps it might be three or four years before we may be in a position to establish mission bands' proved to be wildly optimistic. Collins was, in any case, critical of the Brazilian

---

13 'Proposed outline of future developments of vice-province', Brazil-1, RPAD. Although this document is unsigned, its author was probably James Collins the vice-provincial.

missions he had attended, considering them more of 'a big tent performance' than a genuine effort at spiritual and sacramental revival. Too much time was given, he thought, to processions and long devotions, with too little time available for confession or else the people were too tired after all the other celebrations to go. He considered that the style of *barrio* or village missions he knew from the Philippines, with emphasis on house visitation, would be more effective. As regards the work in the interior:

> Our aim should be to build throughout the *sertao* chapels which when the father is not in the place, can be turned into schools where the teacher will teach Christian doctrine, prepare the kiddies for First Communion … beside the chapel, a *barracao* should be built – merely a roof where the folk can swing their hammocks during the time of the Padre's visit; thus as the visits of the Padre become more frequent, there will be no burden on the *fazendeiro* [farmer] beside whose house the chapel is since he does not have to provide hospitality for the people.[14]

Fortaleza was the first Irish Redemptorist mission to avail of the contribution of lay people to a foreign mission. The Legion of Mary had been sending lay folk on its extension-work in Africa and elsewhere since the 1930s. By 1960, the concept had broadened to include lay people who had a qualification in some technical field and who would devote their professional services for some years to the foreign missions as *Viatores Christi* ('Travellers for Christ'). Two County Galway brothers, Jim and Marcus Thornton, came to work with the Redemptorists in Brazil in 1963; one was an agricultural instructor and the other a carpenter. They were joined by Gerry Cassidy who added the skills of a motor mechanic and opted to join the Redemptorists on his return to Ireland.

Tensions over financial matters plagued the relationship between the Brazilian missionaries and the Dublin bursar's office. Poverty in the north east of Brazil was of an intensity unimaginable even in Ireland which was still a relatively poor country by international standards. At first, the Redemptorists thought that if they had sufficient financial resources, they could organise a programme of community development. The income of the entire mission-team from local sources was estimated at about £300 a year and in its first two years, the Brazil mission had cost the Irish province more than £13,000. The home province was in fairly straitened circumstances. It had a total debt of £269,000 in 1962 and formation and education was a constant drain on resources. In 1965, the Irish provincial administration complained to the general government in Rome that Brazil had cost over £140,000 to date and that

---

14 Ibid.

From this seemingly endless supply of funds from Ireland, there developed an unreal approach to self-subsistence in the vice-province of Fortaleza. Income from normal sources of revenue was ploughed back into parish development, even social projects – a very laudable thing in normal circumstances – but in this instance such a policy could create a complete and utter dependence on outside help for subsistence … We feel it would not be fair to the home province or to the other vice-provinces … if we allow the present attitude in the vice-province of Fortaleza to continue.[15]

In the event, matters did not work out the way Collins had anticipated. The Second Vatican Council brought in its wake a new emphasis on the local Church, and on the need for religious to identify with its needs and to share in its pastoral strategies. Ongoing discussion about 'the purpose of the congregation' initiated by the general chapter of 1967–9 eventually caught fire throughout the congregation and put paid to the urgency of establishing parish mission teams. If the whole congregation was missionary and was to approach all its works in a missionary spirit, was there really such a need for Redemptorists to define themselves primarily as givers of parish missions in the way their predecessors had?

Both James Collins and his successor as vice-provincial, Joseph Hanrahan, would go on to become bishops of dioceses in the interior of Brazil. Collins was named to the prelacy of Miracema Do Norte in the state of Goias (raised to the status of a diocese in 1981). He retired to Ireland in 1996, and died in Limerick in 2002. Hanrahan was appointed bishop of Santíssima Conceição do Araguaia in the state of Para in 1979, where he remained until his death in 1993. The territories for which they had responsibility were vast, and their clergy were few. Their new responsibilities led to a greater sense of partnership with the local Brazilian Church.

The Second Vatican Council released a new energy in the South American Churches. The opening paragraph of the encyclical, *Gaudium et Spes*, stressed that the Church shared in 'the joys and hopes, the grief and anguish of people of our time'. Becoming more aware of those hopes and griefs would open up the question of the meaning of existence in a world torn by poverty and striving for justice, and lead to a rediscovery of a 'Third World' alongside the power blocs of the capitalist West and Marxist East. For the South American Church under the leadership of a number of charismatic bishops, such as Dom Helder Camara, who wrote the appeal of the Brazilian bishops to the Redemptorist general that resulted in the coming of the Redemptorists to Brazil,[16] the

---

[15] John Whyte to William Gaudreau, 17 Nov. 1965, copy in Fortaleza 1, RPAD.
[16] Helder Camara to William Gaudreau 10 Apr. 1959, copy in Brazil 1, RPAD.

consequences of that discovery would mean a radical commitment to becoming a 'servant Church', the Church of the poor. The response of the Latin American Church was given its first authoritative expression in a set of documents on justice, peace and the family issued by the Conference of Latin American Bishops (CELAM) at the end of their meeting in Medellín, Columbia, in September 1968. Medellín was a foundational moment in the development of what came to be known as the theology of liberation.

It took the first Irish Redemptorists some time to realise that commitment to preaching the Gospel was commitment to its message of justice. That is not to say that they were complacent about the poverty and deprivation they faced to an extent unimaginable in Ireland or that they lacked compassion for its victims. From the beginning, most of the communities had a social dimension to the work they were doing in their parishes. Within a few years of the Council, prophetic voices of the Brazilian churches were becoming clearer and more insistent. The Irish Redemptorists in Fortaleza began to listen and to identify with the truth of what they were saying.

The focus of their thinking began to move from how to undertake small acts of development in favour of local communities towards deeper questions about structural injustice and how the Church might more effectively perform its role as the midwife of a new society which would ensure liberation rooted in God's preferential option for the poor.

A new and rich theology was being born in South America. Its birthplace was among the poor rather than in the classrooms of the European universities. This 'theology of liberation' was both biblical and political. It would affect much of what the Irish Redemptorists in Fortaleza did during the following two decades. On their return on leave to the mother province, they would bring back many of its insights which would influence their Irish confreres who were also becoming conscious that they, too, were facing the same challenges, if in a much less dramatic way.

A Council and a Chapter

Michael Curran died in office as provincial in 1961. Fr Arthur Maloney, his vicar, was nominated provincial in his own right the following year, 1962. The precarious state of the province's finances came as a shock to Maloney. The upkeep of three foreign missions and a full seminary were proving to be an unending burden on the province's finances. The debt was further increased by investment in a series of new buildings during the previous decade.

In the course of a canonical visitation in 1962, the superior general, Fr Gaudreau, suggested to Maloney that he should reopen negotiations with the archdiocese about building a retreat house in Dublin. Maloney made a formal petition to Archbishop McQuaid for a retreat house on the Marianella site and proposed to begin building in 1963. Negotiations with the archdiocese were not easy and Maloney eventually withdrew the application but asked permission instead to move the provincial's office from Limerick to the new extension (Liguori House) that he had recently built at Marianella for the editorial team of the *Redemptorist Record*.[17]

As a steady stream of decrees and constitutions emanated from the work of the Second Vatican Council in Rome, it was became clear that the Council had tapped into a deep hunger for a thorough-going renewal in the hearts of many of the leading scholars, bishops and ordinary faithful of the Church. The Redemptorist general chapter scheduled for 1963 had set itself a programme of some fine-tuning and updating the rule of 1749 as though it could continue without substantial change. The chapter elected an Irishman, Fr Frederick Jones (1921–97) to the general council. The impact of the still-unfinished Council, however, made it apparent that the 'authentic renewal of religious life' it had called for in its decree on the adaptation and renewal of religious life, *Perfectae Caritatis*, of 1965, demanded a more thorough-going approach. A new chapter was called to begin work in 1967: it would only complete its labours in 1969. One of the first acts of its president, Fr William Gaudreau, who had been elected superior general for life in 1954, was to offer his resignation and the chapter elected as his successor the Brazilian, Fr Tarcisio Amaral (1919–84) for six years, the first superior general with a fixed term of office.

The chapters of 1963 and 1967–9 revealed both deep divisions and new thinking in the congregation worldwide. Chapter delegates, who thought they had been elected to vote on ways which would enable their brethren to say their prayers and undertake the work of the apostolate better, found that they were being challenged to look closely and critically at the whole vision of religious and Christian life which undergirded the presuppositions of their vocation. Much of the debate centred on the meaning of the very first constitution – *De Fine Congregationis* – on the end [purpose] of the congregation. Like most religious, Redemptorists saw themselves as having two ends or purposes. The first was to sanctify themselves through the imitation of the virtues of Jesus the Redeemer and the second was to preach the Word of God to the poor, 'especially to those who lived in country districts', as the opening article of the 1749 rule put it. European Redemptorist scholars like Francis-Xavier Durrwell and Paul Hitz, who were invited to assist in laying out the theological groundwork for the new rule, would argue that this represented a fundamentally skewed view of religious life. It was based on an

---

impoverished view of the mystery of redemption and of the Church, and it was at a distance from the founding vision of Alphonsus Liguori. They proposed that the new rule should express a more biblical and theological vision of Redemptorist life, beginning from a reflection on God's plan of salvation and the place of Redemptorists and their tradition in the mystery of the whole Church. For some, this was so radical a step that it seemed the death-knell announcing, in quite a different sense, 'the end of the congregation', as they had known it. The first session of the chapter ended indecisively. Over the next few years, the work of renewal gathered momentum as the vision of the Second Vatican Council began to make its impact on the Church at large and in individual communities scattered from Brazil to Esker.

The work of the chapter was not confined to formal sessions in Rome. The chapter members continued their work at international meetings between sessions. They also realised the crucial importance of drawing the entire membership into the discussion and communities were required to engage in a process of discussion that was intended to feed into the chapter sessions in Rome. For many, it was a confusing time, as old certainties seemed to be breaking down. Drafts of possible rules circulated, including one drawn up by the Irishman, Michael Baily, then teaching in the Philippines. They all looked decidedly different from the pontifical rule of Benedict XIV promulgated in 1749. The chapter completed its business in 1969, handing over to the communities a 'provisional constitution'.[18] The Holy See had wisely permitted religious communities to work with provisional texts for several years in order to discover from lived experience what they really wanted the final text to include. For Redemptorists, this meant in effect a period of four years until the next general chapter was due in 1973.

Time of Change, 1964–73
The first major decision taken by John Whyte on his appointment as provincial in 1964 was to bring to resolution the long-standing question of the Redemptorist presence in Dublin. The last provincial to be directly appointed by the superior general, Whyte had spent the early years of his priesthood as a member of the Indian vice-province. On his return to Ireland, he had served as rector of the Limerick retreat house and later of Esker.

The lodging for a group of university students at Marianella on Orwell Road had eventually become a mission residence, but without a public church. Since 1962, it had become the base for the publications office and later the provincial's residence. Plans to develop it as a student house and

---

[18] For details of the chapter's work, see the *Acta Integra Capituli Generalis XVII Congregationis Ssi Redemptoris Romae Celebrati 1967–1969* (Rome: Redemptorist General Council, 1970).

retreat house in the late 1940s had come to nothing. The option of moving to a different site had been tentatively explored on several occasions, but financial considerations and lack of diocesan encouragement had never made any of them viable. Within weeks of taking office, Whyte invited the Limerick architect, John Thompson, to draw up a feasibility study for a new seminary building on the Marianella property. He specified that it should include adequate living space for a mission community as well as for a student population of about fifty students, with a corresponding number of teachers, in addition to provision for ancillary services such as library, classrooms and chapel. Whyte's proposal met stiff opposition, partly on financial grounds and partly from the fear of some that bringing the students to Dublin would further undermine aspects of religious formation already endangered by changes initiated by the Vatican Council. The provincial in the meantime had got the support of the superior general and the archbishop of Dublin for his proposal.

For the first two years after its opening in September 1968, Marianella functioned as an independent house of studies, with all theology courses being taught in the house by a small team of Redemptorist teachers. The renewal of theology following Vatican II had effectively spelled the end of small independent houses of study. Some religious orders had joined together to form the Milltown Institute in Dublin in 1968. The long-term aim of Milltown at the time was to offer a joint philosophy/theology course, taught over six years. For several reasons – not least the desire to keep the older and younger students separate and to retain the links with University College Galway – the Redemptorists declined to join the Milltown consortium. They sought instead a partnership with the Spiritan (Holy Ghost) congregation at Kimmage Manor. The joint venture began with the first semester of the academic year of 1970/71. Twenty years later (1991), this partnership formed the basis for the Kimmage Mission Institute, which transferred to the Milltown Institute in 2003.

Marianella had been built with a student body of about fifty students in view. By the time the first students arrived there, numbers had already begun to decline. In addition to the rooms intended for the students and their teachers, it had a number of large classrooms, a well-equipped library and a small television studio now lying idle. It was decided to make it available as a pastoral centre to provide updating courses in theology and allied areas for clergy and religious. The central element in the annual programme, a three-month course of priestly renewal offered twice yearly in the spring and autumn, began in 1974. It attracted clergy from the United States, Australia and many developing countries. Apart from members of religious communities who regularly sent members, it was not well supported by the Irish Church.

In time, the three-month courses were opened to women as well as to men. The annual summer programme included a one-month introductory course in pastoral counselling which introduced many pastoral workers to basic skills in counselling work. It also offered retreats and shorter courses in scripture, theology and spirituality as well as evening courses for lay people. By the 2000s, the facilities of Marianella were in need of radical updating for which the money was not available. It ceased to operate as a pastoral centre in February 2008.

When John Whyte's term of office ended in 1969, he was succeeded by James McGrath (1931–89), a pioneer of the Brazilian mission. McGrath was the first directly-elected provincial of the Irish province since the revised constitutions had returned that right to the provinces. His relative youth and missionary experience equipped him for the task of leading a religious community struggling to come to terms with internal change and with the necessity of redefining its place in a society in rapid transition. His absence from the province for most of the previous ten years gave him a degree of freedom, for it meant he could plead ignorance about potentially divisive issues and offer his own assessment as one that was not dependent on any preconceptions.

The first major issue that faced him was how to confront the question of the province's burden of debt that had hung over his predecessors. The cost of formation, the support of three foreign missions and the building of the new Marianella had added considerably to the overdraft, while income, dependent on church receipts, Mass-offerings and stipends for apostolic work, showed little increase. In 1970, with the guidance of an American professional fund-raising consultant, Mario Martinez, McGrath set about harnessing the goodwill of his brethren and their lay friends to clear as much of the debt as possible with an intensive campaign lasting six months. The financial campaign succeeded in reducing the debt considerably. McGrath's Brazilian experience had also sharpened his pastoral sensitivity and he was eager to encourage experimentation and new thinking.

McGrath assumed office at a challenging time for religious life. No Council in the history of the Church had received such detailed and critical reporting of its debates and the Church was beginning to learn to live, however uncomfortably, under the critical scrutiny of the media. Signs of unrest had been felt in the student house of Galway, even before the theological students departed for Dublin. In one year, 1967, fifteen students left, prompting the question of whether the existing structures of religious life could answer the needs of a new generation. Psychology and the social sciences were gaining acceptance as primary tools for interpreting human experience and the answers they provided were radically different from those supplied by the age-old theological and spiritual tradition. In his 1967 encyclical on priestly celibacy, Pope Paul VI noted that 'it is said that in the world of our time the observance of celibacy has come to be difficult or even impossible.'[19] The encyclical was a response to a debate that emerged following the Council. As well as facing a natural decline in numbers by death or a falling vocations rate, Irish Redemptorists, like every other community and diocese, had to reckon with the unexpected departure of men who were several years ordained and who seemed assured of a long life of active priestly ministry. The papal encyclical, *Humanae Vitae*, issued in 1968, had sought to bring closure to a debate on birth control that had been removed from the Council's remit. While the encyclical's teaching was clear, it opened up a wider debate that was not confined to the issue of artificial contraception, but touched on serious underlying issues such as the rights of conscience, the teaching authority of the Church and the role of local churches and theologians in arriving at the formulation of Church teaching.[20] The late 1960s also witnessed a growing debate on marriage as the ecclesiastical courts in some places took a wider view in interpreting aspects of the Church's law on the nullity of marriage.

McGrath encouraged a number of the province's theologians to assist the members to assimilate the new thinking. Fr Seán O'Riordan (1916–98) had been appointed to the Alfonsian Academy in Rome, a specialist institute in moral theology, in 1960 after many years of teaching in Galway. He was a gifted theologian, with a journalist's skill in making complex ideas accessible. Residence in Rome during the Council had brought him into contact with many of the architects of its documents and he had contributed a series of articles on the Council to the *Furrow*, of which he had been one of the founding editors. O'Riordan was generous in making his expertise available to his confreres, especially in the area of moral and pastoral theology. Others, like Gerald Crotty and Frederick Jones, had taken a particular interest in the Council's renewal of religious life and spirituality. Along with O'Riordan, they steered their brethren through the sometimes choppy seas of the newest debates. Their work was not confined to their brethren. O'Riordan was a popular lecturer at home and abroad. The retreat houses organised updating seminars for laity, religious and clergy. Jones's years in the general government from 1964 to 1969 had given him a valuable insight into the issues religious communities addressed as they embarked on the rewriting of their constitutions. He was invited by several

---

[19] *Sacerdotalis Caelibatus, Encyclical Letter of Pope Paul VI on the celibacy of priests,* 24 June 1967 (London: Catholic Truth Society, 1967), para. 1.
[20] For a sense of the direction of the debate, see Charles E. Curran. *Transition and Tradition in Moral Theology* (Notre Dame, IN: University of Notre Dame Press, 1979); Janet Smith, *Humanae Vitae: A Generation later* (Washington: Catholic University of America Press, 1991).

Irish bishops to help the sisters of their dioceses,   especially the Sisters of Mercy, to rewrite their constitutions and to prepare for the reorganisation of their communities at diocesan and provincial level.

Renewing Parish Missions

The three years during which the Second Vatican Council was in session (1962–5) were a steep learning curve that touched every part of Catholic life. It was inevitable that the Redemptorists would set about applying the Council's programme of *aggiornamento* to the work of parish missions. In early September 1964, a commission of six missioners and theologians met for the first time to prepare an agenda for discussion on mission work to be held in each community. The following month, the provincial, John Whyte, announced the formation of a mission council that would be representative of the various communities.[21] At its first meeting in February 1965, a number of diocesan priests were invited to share their experience of missions in urban, rural and growing industrial towns. The mission council's first decisions were modest enough. The evening mission service was limited to one hour, provision might be made for the use of a short scripture reading, the missioners were reminded of the need to include reference to the Resurrection when preaching the way of the cross to reflect the 'theology of the paschal mystery'. The traditional topics were to remain the focus of mission preaching but 'they should be treated in such a way as to adapt them to present developments in the life of the Church, so that the preaching of God's word will be really practical and up to date while remaining true to its "prophetic" character.'[22]

It soon became clear that more radical surgery was required. The more optimistic view of salvation and 'theology of the last things' implicit in the decrees of the council spelled effectively the end of the individualistic 'save your soul' theology of former days. The emphasis on liturgy, the participation of all the faithful in the life of the Church and of community as the place in which conversion and personal renewal takes place meant that the ancient communitarian dimension of faith had to be rediscovered. The evolution to a new type of mission was gradual. John J. Ó Riordáin, who was a participant on many of them, remembers that 'what would became known as the new mission began when Fr Liam O'Connell, a returned missionary from India, set up a meeting in a private house in Clonmel' during the course of a mission in that parish in May 1970.[23] In Dungarvan, in October of the same

---

21 John Whyte: Circular letter to the province, 2 Oct. 1964, NA 5, RPAD.
22 'Decisions of the Mission Council' (Feb. 1965) and 'Further decisions of the Mission Council' (Sept. 1965), NA 5, RPAD.
23 John J. Ó Ríordáin, *Before the Night Grows Late* (Dublin: Columba Press, 2009).

year, the group meetings were extended to include sessions with the urban district council, chamber of commerce, trade unions and credit unions. In the mission in Carrick-on-Suir in March 1971, the meetings were extended still further to include the teachers, and a 'summit meeting' with representatives of all the groups was held at the end of the mission.[24] Other mission-giving congregations were also struggling with the challenge of updating the mission format. At a congress of missioners held in Blackrock, County Dublin, the Redemptorists and Passionists presented blueprints of what they were doing to update missions.

It was imperative to win the approval of the bishops for what was a very different form of mission. As chair of the pastoral commission of the Conference of Major Religious Superiors (CMRS), James McGrath sent Archbishop Joseph Cunnane of Tuam a document entitled 'A Future for Parish Missions in Ireland', to be presented to the episcopal conference. At Dr Cunnane's request, he added a personal reflection on his own experience of giving new-style missions. McGrath suggested that no mission should be attempted in an urban area without a basic approach such as that outlined in the document.[25] He stressed the importance of 'close and collegial collaboration' between the parish team and missioners, both in preparation and during the mission itself. He underlined the importance of the first two weeks of visitation of the homes by day and meetings of neighbours and other community groups in the evening: group meetings gave the missioners an opportunity to see the reality of the local community and gave the people a chance to speak publicly about their faith, sometimes for the first time in their lives. They also allowed lay leaders to emerge from the groups. McGrath also outlined the themes of the sermons that would be preached during a typical mission. The opening sermon was on the human person and their 'call to grandeur and the depth of human misery' (a reflection of the theology of *Gaudium et Spes*, the Council's document on the Church in the modern world, paragraph 11). The second major theme was Christ, the way, the truth and the life. The following evenings treated sin and conversion, the family as the nucleus of the Christian community, work and leisure, a Eucharistic night with a concelebrated Mass which laid the emphasis on Christ as the centre of the community, and Mary, the mother of Christians. The mission ended with the renewal of baptismal vows and a final sermon on the community of faith, worship, charity and mission. The theological difference between this kind of preaching and that of the traditional mission is striking.

Although most of the bishops were in favour, the new mission plan encountered difficulties in some places. Seven parishes had invited the

---

[24] Report of the Secretariate for Apostolate (undated, *c.*1972), NA 5, RPAD.
[25] James McGrath to Joseph Cunnane, 31 May 1971, NA 5, RPAD.

Redemptorists to deliver the new-style mission during the Cork general mission in the Lent of 1972. They were prepared to send in a large team of between sixty and seventy priests for at least part of the time since the proposed programme of house meetings was intensive. Bishop Cornelius Lucey (1902–82) imposed some restrictions on the mission and used his Lenten pastoral to explain that getting enough suitable missioners had made this necessary. A newspaper report of Lucey's pastoral placed the Redemptorists in an embarrassing dilemma.[26] In the course of his report, the journalist stated that the new mission was 'intended to serve as a means of establishing anew the relevance of the Gospel to all aspects of man's life, with particular stress on the need to move from an individualistic to a communal understanding of faith', an approach, he implied, that was in conflict with the bishop's theology. In the course of his article, he quoted two Redemptorists, James McGrath himself and Stan Mellett, the rector of Limerick, who was reported as saying that the new type of mission would always get priority. Anxious to extricate the Redemptorists from any appearance of having briefed against him, McGrath wrote to inform Lucey that the journalist had only asked their permission to quote from two articles they had written without giving them any idea of the content of his article.[27]

New-style missions were particularly successful in large and medium-sized towns. A mission in Sligo during March–April 1973, with James McGrath as leader, had fifteen Redemptorist priests with four students for part of the youth week. In addition to house and other group meetings, there was a programme of factory visitation, including on one occasion what was regarded as a very successful celebration of Mass in the factory itself.[28] The Esker mission chronicle records new-style missions in towns such as Athenry in 1971, Athlone in 1975 and in 1981, Ballina in 1975 and Castlebar in 1979, as well as in rural parishes where the house-meetings sometimes followed the pattern of the traditional 'station', with a discussion after Mass or occasionally after the reading of the gospel. Many priests welcomed the new mission enthusiastically: Kilfenora in County Clare had two new-style missions within the space of three years (1972 and 1974). Priests were sometimes reluctant to have the new mission, or changed their mind after having initially agreed.[29] A few refused to countenance even modest changes: in one parish, the closing eucharist 'had to be trimmed to the liking of the parish priest who does not

[26] T. P. O'Mahony, 'Bishop says "no" to new missions. Redemptorists Restricted', *Sunday Press*, 26 Mar. 1972.
[27] James McGrath to Cornelius Lucey, 31 May 1972, NA 5, RPAD.
[28] Sligo Mission, 10 Mar. to 15 Apr. 1973, Esker Mission Chronicles.
[29] Cong, County Galway Mission, 17–24 Feb. 1974, Roscrea. County Tipperary Mission, Mar. 1975, Esker Mission Chronicles.

believe in "French things" like readings or prayers of the faithful by the laity and offertory processions etc.'[30] Even when a full-scale new mission was impractical, the traditional mission was absorbing some of its techniques, especially in the matter of subjects for preaching.

The new mission enjoyed a life cycle of about ten to twelve years. It was never formally abandoned but by the mid-1980s, it was becoming rarer to find a mission that included the intensive programme of visitation and home meetings that were deemed its distinctive feature. There are several reasons why it faded. Its creators had hoped it would revolutionise the Irish parish community. Despite their best efforts, it did not do so in any dramatic way. The returns for the effort invested, especially in disadvantaged urban areas, were often meagre. A large Dublin working class parish was divided into three sectors for its mission in 1972. Intense efforts had been made to visit every house, yet out of 230 houses visited, only 120 people came to a general 'street meeting' with Mass, of whom 110 were women. The preaching week for men drew a maximum congregation of 350 out of a total of 2,500 men in the area. While observing that 'we are far from complacent: we are equally far from despair', the chronicler noted, with some measure of foreboding, that as 'Dublin goes, so goes the rest of the country.'[31] Another reason for its decline is that it required an intense investment of personnel. The rule of thumb for calculating the size of a mission team was one priest per thousand people. This brought in turn the question of payment. In the early years of the mission, the suggested stipend was £20 per man per week. Some parishes gave more generously, such as Ballina, County Mayo, where the team of six priests received £900 for three weeks.[32] For others, finding accommodation, feeding and paying such a large team was prohibitive. The missioners paid in other ways for the intense work of the mission. Some found living out of a suitcase for a month in a boarding house or as guest of a family with little personal space difficult. The work of door-to-door visitation in all weathers for five days each week, unsure of what reception awaited them, and then spending the evening conducting two or even three house meetings was draining for many. The days in which a missioner could simply deliver a prepared text were gone: one of the reasons for house meeting strategy was to give the preacher the opportunity to see what life was like on the spot and to respond to it in his sermon. It was characteristic of the new mission that many of the sermons were hammered out by discussion during the week or two of the preached mission itself. Nor did it help that the missioners were

---

[30] Mullagh, County Galway Mission, 1–8 June, 1975, Esker Mission Chronicles.
[31] Ballyfermot, Dublin Mission, Mar. 1972, Dublin Mission Chronicle, Marianella Domestic Archives.
[32] Ballina, County Mayo Mission, 11 Sept.– 2 Oct. 1975, Esker Mission Chronicle.

channels of communication between parishioners and priests, especially when the message they were receiving at the house meetings was critical of the local Church.

An alternative to the intensive mission appeared in the late 1970s. Long a feature of the annual calendar of Redemptorist churches, the solemn novena in preparation for the feast of Our Lady of Perpetual Help was held each June. As director of the novena in Limerick, Fr Vincent Kavanagh had trans-formed it into an annual 'festival of faith', with up to twelve sessions daily and a correspondingly brisk confessional ministry. So successful were his efforts that he was invited to lead novenas elsewhere. The first was at Holy Cross Abbey, County Tipperary in 1977. It was followed by similar novenas in Tuam, Carlow, Longford, Galway, Tralee as well as in smaller towns and villages.[33] His confreres were not slow to imitate his example and the novena proved a popular alternative to the mission. Like the parish mission, the novena stressed the importance of what Redemptorists call 'the extraordinary proclamation of the Word'. It is 'extraordinary' in contrast to the 'ordinary' homiletic preaching of the Sunday liturgy. The topics for preaching were chosen with the intention of striking to the roots of Christian life. It was also extraordinary in terms of length – the average liturgical homily seldom goes beyond seven to ten minutes: mission or novena preaching is longer. Like the mission, the novena gave people the opportunity to make a well-prepared and unhurried confession. The main difference between the two was that the focus of mission was firmly set on the parish: this was less the case for the novena when the whole surrounding area was welcomed and made aware of the novena by means of an advance advertising campaign. Both set out to present their message in warm personal tones that reached to the heart.

The new-style mission had several significant strengths. It introduced people to the reading of the scriptures. Just as an earlier generation of missioners had encouraged the sale of prayer books, rosary beads and holy pictures, the new missioners sold the popular paperback, *Good News Bible*, and encouraged people to use it in their daily personal or family prayer, showing them how to use it by basing the first part of the mission service on prayer and bible reading instead of the rosary. It was possibly the first time that many Irish Catholics had a bible for personal use as distinct from a large family bible that was more of an ornament than something to be read regularly. There was also their contribution to the congregational singing required by the new liturgy. As an earlier generation of missioners had introduced congregations to traditional Catholic hymns like *God of Mercy and Compassion* or *Holy God, we praise thy name* (translated from the German by an American Redemptorist for the first edition of the *Redemptorist Mission Book* in 1853), the new missioners

---

33 Anne Dempsey, 'The man behind the Novena' in *Reality* (June, 2009), 16–20.

produced a folded card containing about twenty modern hymns that could continue to be used in the parishes after they had departed.

The new mission also forced Redemptorists to ask themselves what was the core of the message they preached. Traditional mission preaching was based on 'the great truths' of salvation – sin, death, judgement, heaven and hell. It had little of the 'good news' of the gospel about it. The renewal of theology had insisted that the heart of the Christian message was the *kerygma*, the proclamation of the good news of God's salvation in Christ. The question that faced the missioner was how to identify the essence of the *kerygma* and how to clothe it in modern language. The Council had attempted to do this in *Gaudium et Spes*. Its main themes, such as the mystery of human existence, the dignity of the person, the human community, the value of human activity, the Church's role in the world, the dialogue between faith and culture, justice, marriage and family – proved a major source of inspiration. While the actual form of preaching remained for the most part the traditional one of the speaker in the pulpit, there were experiments with what was known as the 'dual pulpit' or two preachers conducting a dialogue on some aspect of the faith such as how to make a mature confession, or the use of visuals such as a slide lecture on the Holy Shroud. The solemn celebration of the eucharist, the high point of the mission, was usually preceded by a short drama of the last supper in which members of the congregation played the part of the apostles while a missioner gave a commentary from the pulpit. Communal celebrations of the liturgy of reconciliation along the lines recommended by the Revised Rite of the Sacrament of Reconciliation (1973) stressed the communitarian aspect of sin and repentance.

'The Troubles'

Just before midday on 15 August 1969, a sniper on the roof of an old linen mill near Clonard Monastery began shooting at people in the street below. In an effort to dislodge the sniper, some of the people set fire to the mill. It was so close to the monastery that it was decided to move elderly members of the community for safety to homes of friends of the community. By mid-afternoon, a full-scale riot was in progress in the streets nearby. Within a short time, the houses in two streets at the rear of the church, Bombay Street and Kashmir Road, were blazing. Since no fire engine could venture into the area, it seemed as though the flames would eventually reach the monastery itself. As a precaution, the Blessed Sacrament was removed from both the church and community chapel. By six o'clock in the evening, British troops finally arrived to restore order. The monastery became a centre for immediate relief operations. 'With the help of the Sisters of Charity [who lived in the first residence of the Redemptorists across the street from the church] we set up tables in the corridor where people could have a meal', noted the chronicler. What few pieces of furniture people had been able to retrieve from their burning homes were stored in the monastery and garden. 'The Troubles,' that had been ushered in by the first civil rights demonstrations the previous year, and would drag on for another thirty years, had begun.[34]

The thirty years between the burning of Bombay Street and the signing of the Belfast Agreement on Good Friday 1998, deeply affected not just the Redemptorist communities of Belfast, but the whole Irish Redemptorist province. Only one other clerical religious order, the Passionists, had a house in Belfast at that time. Nearly all Redemptorist priests and brothers had served in Clonard even for a short period: many were natives of the city and indeed of the immediate area around the monastery. They followed events in Belfast with interest. One of the earliest offers of help came on the day following the attack on Bombay Street from the Limerick confraternity.[35] Limerick retreat house offered to take some people who had been made homeless, while others were accommodated in St Clement's retreat house on the Antrim Road. Fifty-two people made the journey to Limerick.[36] Unrest in the city grew in intensity over the following years. It came to a head in 1972 with the introduction of internment without trial, the Northern Ireland government's attempt to control the growth of the Irish Republican Army. As bomb outrages increased, the monastery was often subjected to searches for weapons and explosives. While Clonard's position on the boundary between the nationalist Falls and the unionist Shankill areas made it vulnerable, the two houses on the north side of the city were even more so. Some of the parishioners of St Gerard's who lived in the Whitewell Road area felt particularly vulnerable to attack. The large wooded parkland surrounding the church and monastery and St Clement's retreat house further up the hill made security at night difficult. St Gerard's church was subject to acts of vandalism on numerous occasions. On one occasion, 25 May 1982, a bomb did serious damage to the main entrance of the church and the large stained glass window.

The political situation in Belfast faced the Redemptorists with a number of stark choices. It was impossible to live and minister in such a situation of unrest and injustice without trying to come to grips with some of the challenges it posed. Many people came to the monastery in search of comfort at the loss of a family member through violence or internment. Others came with questions of conscience that challenged the Church. Some who had once been loyal and practising Catholics ceased practising, either because they

---

[34] Clonard Domestic Chronicles, 15 Aug. 1969. For a complete account of Clonard during this period, see Grant, 'Clonard and the Troubles 1969–1994' in *One Hundred Years with the Clonard Redemptorists*, 205–24.

[35] Ibid., 208.

[36] Clonard Domestic Chronicles, 22 Aug. 1969.

believed the Church's position on the issue of justice was complacent on the one hand or because they believed the Church had been too indulgent towards the republican paramilitaries on the other. During the bleakest and worst of times, the annual Clonard novena offered for nine days a respite from violence and a breath of peace. Fionnuala O'Connor has called it 'a phenomenon that draws on a sense of shared trauma and strengthens a sense of community with each repetition'.[37] Many young men and women of the Catholic community, who in normal circumstances would never have seen the inside of a prison, spent lengthy terms of imprisonment in the course of 'the troubles'. Some were among the first rounded up on internment day, 9 August 1971, and held without trial for up to four years until internment ended in 1975. Others were sentenced for their involvement in republican paramilitary activities. Retreats were organised for republican prisoners in the Maze (Long Kesh). The internees were originally receptive but retreat-giving became particularly difficult during the days of the 'blanket', later the 'dirty', protest of 1976–81, which was a struggle for non-criminal status. Prisoners called from their cells for confession arrived to meet the priest girded only in a towel: 'once the confession is over, they shrink down into the corner of their respective mattresses to escape the icy blast that comes through the windows. Some of them ask for news, a cigarette, a message to be brought to someone outside, a pencil. Here the priest is embarrassed for the rules forbid such things.'[38]

While they enjoyed the confidence of the people in nationalist Belfast, the Redemptorists realised that fidelity to the gospel demanded that they explore other means of peace and reconciliation. Chief among these was a new direction given to the community's ecumenical work which had begun with the Clonard Mission for Non-Catholics in the years following the Second World War. It would bear special fruit in the formation of the Clonard–Fitzroy Fellowship which began life in 1981 as a Presbyterian–Roman Catholic bible study programme and has become an important means of promoting dialogue between all Christian Churches. Clonard formed links with other ecumenical groups, including the Cornerstone Community. Fr Alex Reid who had spent his early years in Clonard developing the ecumenical work, was a constant visitor at the Maze prison, where he celebrated Mass most Sundays. His contacts with republicans and their families convinced him that the ongoing conflict was exacting too high a price from ordinary people and that the time had come to take the gun out of Irish politics. The patient work in building bridges of dialogue between John Hume and Gerry Adams initially, and then between them, the Irish government and loyalists would only become publicly known after the Good Friday Agreement was signed. That Good Friday marked the end of a long and painful Lent.

---

[37] Fionnuala O'Connor, 'Unifying effect of a novena', *Irish Times*, 16 June 2006.
[38] Clonard Domestic Chronicles, 21 Dec. 1978.

EPILOGUE

One Hundred and Sixty – Not Out

It is not easy to bring this narrative to a conclusion. The Redemptorists have been in Ireland for more than 160 years and the story continues to unfold. The writer is too close to the people and events of recent times to record them objectively and has chosen to invoke the safety of the archival 'thirty-year rule' for this period. Those thirty years, however, have seen profound changes both in how Redemptorist life is lived in community and in the forms of work undertaken, so a brief, if incomplete, sketch is necessary. During this period, the Redemptorists were under the leadership of six provincial superiors: John O'Donnell (1978–84), Stephen Mahoney (1984 –7), Raphael Gallagher (1987–93), Brendan Callanan (1993–9), Con Casey (1999–2008) and Michael Kelleher (2008–).

In every Redemptorist community in Ireland, there will be found men who have lived a considerable portion of their lives from their mid-twenties onwards in another culture, whether in the Philippines, Brazil or India. That fact alone makes for a certain richness in community life as well as for a readiness to think of how things might be done differently. Two of the three foreign missions – India and the Philippines – have become independent provinces and are self-supporting in personnel and finance. The foreign missionary impulse of the province is more modest today. It is centred, but not exclusively so, on its one remaining vice-province of Fortaleza, Brazil. The Irish province has been willing and able to lend support to other provinces in difficulties. In 1968, it agreed to provide personnel to help the Belgian Redemptorists in the West Indies who were finding themselves overstretched by commitments in the Congo and Lebanon. The first four priests took up their assignment the following year. For some, it was a short-term commitment, but Frs John Whyte and Michael Brosnan remained on for more than twenty years. The New Zealand Redemptorists, who are part of the Australian province, were anxious to revitalise the preaching of parish missions in their territory and asked for help from Ireland. Frs Frank Mullaghy and Patrick Clancy spent the years 1982 to 1984 working with them. In 1987, the small American province of Oakland accepted a mission in Nigeria but asked the Irish to help with personnel. Oakland later amalgamated with the larger American Chicago province to become the new province of Denver in 1996 which then assumed responsibility for Nigeria. The Nigerian mission has thrived and now numbers over forty professed priests and brothers and eighty students in formation. The last Irish Redemptorist to serve there, Fr Alphonsus Doran, returned to Ireland in 2008.

The Irish province has also links with other Redemptorist provinces in the European continent. Fr Tony Brannigan, after almost thirty years in Brazil, volunteered in 1986 to work with a mixed group of Ukrainian and Polish Redemptorists in a new mission area in Siberia. Financial assistance has been given to the Eastern European provinces in the Ukraine, Slovakia and Czech Republic as they emerged from the long night of soviet control. Some of their students have done part of their theological study in Ireland or have come for shorter spells in the summer to learn English. Fr Patrick Shields went to Copenhagen in 1979 as a temporary chaplain to the Filipino community: he stayed for thirty years, only returning in 2009. When Ireland entered the European Community in 1973, the Irish province was invited to provide a priest to join the team ministry of the European parish in Luxembourg coordinated by their confreres of the Strasbourg province. To date, three Irish Redemptorists have served in the parish, Frs Anthony Mulvey, Pat O'Connor and Éamonn Breslin, the present incumbent.

The Redemptorist churches of Limerick, Dundalk, Belfast, Esker and Dublin continue to provide religious services for the people of the surrounding areas. In Clonard and Limerick, especially, the regular church-going population has fallen sharply as a result of changing demographic patterns in the surrounding areas, as well as the gradual decline in regular religious practice. The confraternities of Limerick and Clonard hang on tenaciously, but they are a shadow of their former selves. The great annual event in most Redemptorist churches is now the solemn novena each June in honour of Our Lady of Perpetual Help, or in the case of Dundalk, of St Gerard in October. Even in these days when low rates of religious practice are considered to be the norm, the novena packs these large churches ten or twelve times daily, with a corresponding demand for confession and individual spiritual guidance. The Esker community also leads an annual novena each February in Galway Cathedral.

Parish ministry, once considered inimical to Redemptorist religious life, has been accepted in St Gerard's Belfast (1969), St Joseph's Dundalk (1976) and in the Dublin parish of Cherry Orchard (2003). Several priests serve in an individual capacity in Dublin city parishes. Others have taken on parish ministry in the diocese of Clonfert and in Down and Connor while remaining members of the Esker and Clonard communities respectively. There are also ministries that engage the energies of individual members on a more or less full-time basis, such as the Family Prayer Movement, led by Fr Peter Byrne from Limerick, the teaching of theology or hospital chaplaincy. Although it only involves one priest full-time as editor and another part-time as designer and graphic artist, Redemptorist Communications is one of the province's major undertakings. Apart from the monthly publication of *Reality* and the youth magazine, *Face Up*, it is also responsible for the production of resources for the ministries of the province such as the hymn and prayer books for the annual novena, as well as resources for liturgy and bible study. A new but growing area of communications is the Internet.

By the mid-1970s, the province had five retreat houses/residential pastoral centres in Belfast, Limerick, Esker, Galway and Dublin. Economics and declining numbers made it impossible to sustain all of them with an equal level of commitment. Limerick was the first to close in 1987. It was followed a few years later by Galway, when it was decided to close the house and to reunite the students in a single community in Dublin. St Clement's retreat house in Belfast closed in 2007. The Marianella Pastoral Centre which had put the emphasis on theological renewal for clergy, religious and laity, ceased operations in 2008. Esker alone continues as a residential centre for retreats and spiritual development. A small community in Cork since 1988 has developed an outreach to young people, including small group residential retreats. It is now based at Scala, Castlemahon House, Blackrock, County Cork. With a similar objective in mind, Esker converted some buildings in its disused farmyard into a 'youth village' with accommodation for school groups during term time and for other groups of young people, including those from abroad, during the summer holidays. Work for young people is regarded as a major priority of the province. In addition to youth ministry teams in Clonard, Esker and Scala, there is the SERVE project, which offers young Irish people the opportunity of spending some time each summer in a developing country.

St Clement's college in Limerick was opened as a juvenate or minor seminary in 1884. As free post-primary schools sprang up throughout the country from the mid-1960s, its future as a small boarding school of about one hundred boys looked more and more precarious. Today, it is a day school with more than 400 students housed in newly-built premises since 2008. Although the teaching staff is made up exclusively of laymen and women, it continues to glory in its strong Redemptorist associations, particularly through chaplaincy work.

During more than thirty years of 'the Troubles' the Clonard community pioneered a brave apostolate of dialogue, combined with social and ecumenical outreach, and has played a not undistinguished part in the painful search for a new and imaginative solution to the Northern dilemma. Fr Alex Reid, through his patient dialogue with all parties, deserves to be considered as one of the principal architects of the Northern Ireland peace process. A picture flashed around the world of Alex Reid kneeling beside the bodies of two dead British army corporals, shot by Republicans on 19 March 1989.

The 'explicit and extraordinary proclamation of the Word' remains a central preoccupation of the Irish province. Parish missions are less in evidence than they were a generation ago and the proportion of Redemptorists who are full-time missioners relative to the total number of active priests has also declined. Nevertheless, mission teams of Redemptorists and lay people continue to work from Limerick, Esker, Dundalk and Belfast. The intensive 'new mission' of the early 1970s that saturated parishes with a large team of Redemptorists did not survive, if only because it had become prohibitively expensive and such large teams of Redemptorists are no longer available. In many instances, the new-style 'solemn novena' serves the purpose of bringing the people of a parish together in an atmosphere of celebration to hear the Word of God and to celebrate the sacraments for a week or more. The annual Galway novena that packs the cathedral several times daily each February, and causes major traffic disruption in the city, is a case in point.

Deaths, departures from the ministry and the relentless decline in religious vocations over the past three decades have meant that the median age of Irish Redemptorists has continued to rise steeply. There are 135 Redemptorists in Ireland; 106 of these are over the age of sixty (figures from *Conspectus Generalis CSsR*, 2009). There has been a steady trickle of new entrants which provides grounds for hope that Redemptorists will still be around for many years to come, even if they will be much fewer in numbers. In part, the lack of professed Redemptorists has been met by inviting lay people to share in the work of ministry. Currently, nearly all the communities have one or more lay person contributing to their regular ministries on a professional, fixed-term contract basis. There are also countless unpaid helpers who give regular service in the more established works of the province. Shrinking numbers also demand thinking again about resources, especially buildings that were constructed to meet the needs of an earlier age. Successive chapters and provincial councils set up working parties to look at the Redemptorists' use of their resources and the future of their ministry. The outcome of these were the reports, 'Review of the Redemptorist Apostolate in Northern Ireland' (1989), 'Facing the Future' (1996) and 'Holding Fast to our Hope' (2002). All the churches have undergone periodic refurbishment to make them worthy places of worship. The national and international financial crisis which began in the autumn of 2008 raised questions about the future of some other planned projects, including the renewal of some buildings.

To think of religious life exclusively in terms of works done or investment in projects would be to miss its mystery. The renewal of the spirit and enthusiasm of individuals is as important as the renewal and development of an apostolic work. The new expression of religious life emanating from the Second Vatican Council forced the generation of the 1960s to re-evaluate the tradition they inherited. The 'return to the sources' that was set in train by the Council entailed a re-earthing of the individual and the community in the riches of liturgy, bible and theology, as well as the new dimensions of personal development introduced by a more generous appreciation of the role of human dynamics in the quest for God.

The celebrations of the two hundred and fiftieth anniversary of the foundation of the congregation in 1982, the three hundredth anniversary of the birth of the two major founding figures of the Redemptorist tradition, Alphonsus Liguori and Maria Celeste Crostarosa, in 1996, have encouraged the search for a more accurate and realistic telling of the story of the origins. Both Alphonsus and Maria Celeste have emerged from that history as more creative, but also as more vulnerable and wounded figures than an earlier generation might have allowed. There is a fresh appreciation of Alphonsus's venturesomeness as a moral thinker and his originality as a teacher of the spiritual life for everyone and of Maria Celeste's mystical insight of the importance of 'living memory' (*viva memoria*). The Irish province made its not insignificant contribution to that process of rediscovery of Alphonsus through the work of confreres who served as teachers and researchers in the Alphonsian Academy, Rome, like Seán O'Riordan, Raphael Gallagher, Seán Cannon, Martin McKeever or of Frederick Jones, historian and biographer of Alphonsus. The recovery of a virtually forgotten woman, Maria Celeste, in the story of Redemptorist origins led to a renewed and deeper friendship with the Sisters of the Order of the Most Holy Redeemer. Their contemplative community life continues in Drumcondra, where in the year 2000 they took up residence in a new monastery built on part of the old site and better adapted to the needs of a smaller and older contemplative community. After many lean years, they have begun to experience a surge of new vocations in recent times with the profession of six Irish and Slovak sisters.

The return to origins and sources was imaginatively symbolised for the Irish Redemptorists by their pilgrimage to the Alphonsian 'holy places' in two large groups during the jubilee year 2000, then to places in Poland and Austria associated with Clement Hofbauer, the second founder, in 2004 and finally to the Holy Land in 2008. The process of renewing community life does not stand still. If communities are smaller, and sometimes give the impression of being more shapeless than they were in the past, that may reflect much better the story of how grace is at work in the human condition than the former ideal of 'regular observance' did in the past.

Tradition has been described as the line of twenty or thirty old men and women that separates the Church today from Jesus Christ. The people in the line pass on the story from one to another. In terms of the Redemptorist presence in Ireland that line is shorter still. Novices who entered in the early 1960s knew the last generation of men who had received their theological education in Teignmouth in Devon at the end of the nineteenth century, who had lived under Andrew Boylan, the first provincial of the Irish province in 1898 and were among the pioneers of the Philippine mission in 1906. They, in turn, had known men who knew Thomas Bridgett, William Plunkett, Vladimir Petcherine and Robert Coffin, the pioneers of the Irish foundation. The line that separates today's young Irish Redemptorist or Redemptoristine from their origins is a relatively short one – four, five or at most six old men and women stand between him or her and those beginnings.

Bibliography

Acta Integra Capitulorum Generalium CSsR. Rome: CSsR, 1899.

Acta Integra Capituli Generalis XVII Congregationis Ssi Redemptoris Romae Celebrati. 1967–1969. Rome: CSsR., 1970.

[Alphonsus de Liguori,] *The Complete Ascetical Works of Saint Alphonsus de Liguori.* Centenary edition. Edited by Eugene Grimm CSsR. New York: Benziger, 1891–96, 24 vols.

[Alphonsus de Liguori,] *Alphonsus de Liguori: Selected Writings,* Classics of Western Spirituality Series. Edited with an introduction by Frederick Jones. New York/Mahwah: Paulist Press, 1999.

Baily, Michael, *Small Net in a Big Sea: The Redemptorists in the Philippines, 1905–1929.* Cebu: University of San Carlos, 1978.

Baily, Michael, 'The Parish Mission Apostolate of the Redemptorists in Ireland, 1851–1898' in Raphael Gallagher and Brendan McConvery, eds, *History and Conscience: Studies in Honour of Father Seán O'Riordan CSsR.* Dublin: Gill and Macmillan, 1989, 274–96.

Béco, Jean, *Vladimir Petcherin (1807–1885): Mémoires et Correspondance.* Rome: Redemptorist Historical Institute, 2006.

Becqué, Maurice, *Le Cardinal Deschamps,* 2 vols. Louvain: Biblioteca Alphonsiana, 1956.

Boland, Samuel J., 'R.A. Coffin and the English Oratory' in *SHCSSR,* vol. 28, no. 1 (1980), 147–74.

Boland, Samuel J., 'R.A. Coffin's Departure from the Oratorians' in *SHCSSR,* vol. 27, no. 2 (1980), 431–56.

Boland, Samuel J., 'The Conversion of Edward Douglas CSsR' in *SHCSSR,* vol. XXIX, no. 2 (1981), 291–322.

Boland, Samuel J., *Faith of Our Fathers: The Redemptorists in Australia 1882–1982.* Armadale, Vic: H. H. Stephenson, 1982.

Boland, Samuel J., 'The Redemptorists in the Foreign Mission Fields,' in *SHCSSR*, vol. XXXII, no. 1 (1984), 127–51.

Boland, Samuel J., *Dictionary of Redemptorists*. Rome: Redemptorist Historical Institute, 1987.

Boland, Samuel J., 'A Redemptorist from the Goldfields: Henry Halson, CSsR (1833–1900)' in *SHCSSR*, vol. LIII, no. 2 (2005), 275–90.

Boland, Samuel J., 'Fr John Creagh in the Kimberlies' in *Old Limerick Journal*, vol. 22 (1988), 151–3.

Bourke, D. F., 'Clune, Patrick Joseph (1864–1935)' in *Australian Dictionary of Biography*. Melbourne: University Press, 1981, vol. 8, 32–3.

Bowen, Desmond, *The Protestant Crusade in Ireland, 1800–70: a Study of Protestant–Catholic Relations between the Act of Union and Disestablishment*. Dublin: Gill and Macmillan, 1978.

Bowen, Desmond, *Souperism: Myth or Reality?* Cork: Mercier Press, 1970.

Buckley, Daniel, *The Miraculous Picture of Our Lady of Perpetual Succour*. Cork: Mercier Press, 1949.

Capone, Domenico and Sabatino Majorano, *I Redentoristi e le Redentoriste: Le Radici*. Materdomini: Valsele, 1985.

Carty, Mary Rose, *History of Killeen Castle*. Dunsany: Carty/Lynch, 1991.

Centenary Souvenir: St. Joseph's Dundalk, 1876–1976. Dundalk, CSsR, 1976.

Chiovaro, Francesco, *The History of the Congregation of the Most Holy Redeemer, vol. 1: The Origins (1732–1793)*. Ed. J. Robert Finelli. Liguori, MO: Liguori Publications, 1986.

Clarke, Austin, *Old Fashioned Pilgrimage and other Poems*. Dublin: Dolmen Press, 1967.

Clonard Question Box, Belfast: Clonard Monastery, 1951.

Codex iuris canonici Pii X Pontificis Maximi iussu digestus, Benedicti Papae XV auctoritate promulgatus. Romae: Typis Polyglottis Vaticanis, 1917.

Codex iuris canonici/auctoritate Ioannis Pauli PP. II promulgatus. Città del Vaticano: Libreria Editrice Vaticana, 1989.

Conspectus Generalis Congregationis Ss Redemptoris. Rome: CSsR, 2009.

Coogan, Tim Pat, *The IRA*. London: Paul Mall Press, 1970.

Coogan, Tim Pat, *Michael Collins: a biography*. London: Hutchinson, 1990.

Corish, Patrick, *Maynooth College, 1795–1995*. Dublin: Gill and Macmillan, 1995.

Corkery, Pádraig, 'Bishop Daniel Cohalan of Cork on Republican resistance and hunger strikes: a theological note' in *Irish Theological Quarterly*, vol. 67, no. 2 (June, 2002), 113–24.

Coyle, John B., *An Appeal to Ireland*. Dublin: O'Brien Printers, 1910.

Coyle, John B., *Our Lady of Perpetual Succour and Ireland*. Dublin: M. H. Gill, 1913.

Coyle, John B., *Meditations and Readings for Every Day of the Year. Selected from the writings of St Alphonsus Liguori*. Dublin: Phoenix, 1922.

Coyle, John B., *All my Days for God*. Dublin: Clonmore and Reynolds, 1947.

Culhane, Robert, 'Most Rev. Father Patrick Murray (1865–1959), Superior General, CSSR, 1909–1947: Biographical outline over the years 1865–1909' in *SHCSSR*, vol. IX, no. 1 (1961), 21–79.

Cummings, Daniel, 'A Mission in Ireland for Non-Catholics' in *Irish Ecclesiastical Record*, vol. XX (1948), 481–94.

Cummings, Daniel, 'Missions for Non-Catholics in Ireland' in *Irish Ecclesiastical Record*, vol. XXIII (1951), 3–24.

Cummings, Daniel, *Facts about the Catholic Church*. Dublin: Catholic Truth Society of Ireland, 1968.

Curran Charles E., *Catholic Moral Theology in the United States: A History*. Washington: Georgetown University Press, 2008.

Curran Charles E., *Transition and Tradition in Moral Theology*. Notre Dame: University of Notre Dame Press, 1979.

Decreta Synodi Plenariae Episcoporum Hiberniae apud Thurles habita Anno MDCCCL. Dublin: James Duffy, 1851.

Dempsey, Anne, 'The Man Behind the Novena' in *Reality* (June 2009), 16–20.

Donlon, Kevin H., *And Ink be on their Hands.* Dublin: Veritas Publications, 1999.

Donnelly, James S., Jr., 'The Peak of Marianism in Ireland, 1930–60' in *Piety and Power in Ireland, 1760–1960: Essays in Honour of Emmet Larkin*, ed. Stewart Brown and David Miller. Indiana: Notre Dame University Press and Institute of Irish Studies, Queen's University, Belfast, 2000, 252–84.

Dowling, P. J., *A History of Irish Education: A Study in conflicting Loyalties.* Cork: Mercier Press, 1971.

Duffy, Eamon, *Faith of Our Fathers: Reflections on Catholic Tradition.* London: Continuum, 2006.

Eriksen, Anne, 'Our Lady of Perpetual Help: Invented Tradition and Devotional Success' in *Journal of Folklore Research*, vol. 42, no. 3 (Sept.–Dec., 2005), 295–321.

Farina, John, ed., *Hecker Studies: Essays on the Thought of Isaac Hecker.* New York: Paulist Press, 1983.

Fifty Years at Mount St Alphonsus. Limerick, 1903. Limerick: Redemptorists, 1903.

Fleischmann, Kornelius, *Klemens Maria Hofbauer: Seine Leben und seine Zeit.* Graz: Verlag Styria, 1988.

Gallagher, Raphael, 'The Manual System of Moral Theology since the death of Alphonsus' in *Irish Theological Quarterly*, vol. 51 no. 1 (Mar., 1985), 1–16.

Gallagher, Raphael 'Moral Theology' in *Alphonsus Liguori: Selected Writings.* Classics of Western Spirituality Series, ed. F. M. Jones. Mahwah, NJ: Paulist Press, 1999, 315–29.

Gallagher, Raphael and Brendan McConvery, eds., *History and Conscience: Studies in Honour of Father Seán O'Riordan CSsR.* Dublin: Gill and Macmillan, 1989.

'Gerrard, Bill' [Liam G. O'Carroll CSsR], *The Devil at Dances?* Belfast: Redemptorist Record, 1956.

'Gerrard, Bill', *Mary, Modes and Modesty.* Belfast: Redemptorist Record, 1958.

'Gerrard, Bill', *Towards a White Courtship.* Belfast: Redemptorist Record, 1958.

'Gerrard, Bill', *Educating to Purity*. Dublin: Redemptorist Record, 1961.

Gerouille, Henri, *Father Joseph Passerat: A Great Pioneer Redemptorist*, English translation by John Carr. London: Sands and Company, 1928.

Godin, Henri and Yves Daniel, *La France: Pays de Mission?* Paris: Les Éditions du Cerf, 1943.

Gorey, John J., *May I keep company?* Dublin: Juverna Press, 1944.

Grant, James, *One Hundred Years with the Clonard Redemptorists*. Dublin: Columba Press, 2005.

Hanmer, Anthony John, *Mrs Sophia Ainsworth* (for private circulation). London: Privately published 1889.

Häring, Bernard, *The Law of Christ: Moral Theology for Priests and Laity*, 3 vols. Cork: Mercier Press, 1963.

Heinze Clement, *Die Redemptoristinnen*. Bonn: Hofbauer Verlag, 1931.

Heinzmann, Josef, *Preaching the Gospel Anew: Saint Clement Maria Hofbauer*. Liguori, MO: Liguori Publications, 1998.

Hepburn, A.C., *Belfast and Nationalist Ireland in the era of Joe Devlin, 1871–1934*. Oxford: Oxford University Press, 2008.

Hogan, Edmund, *The Irish Missionary Movement: A Historical Survey 1830–1980*. Dublin: Gill and Macmillan, 1990.

Hosp, Edward, 'First Redemptorist Missions in Ireland according to Fr Joseph Prost's Diaries' in *SHCSSR*, vol. VIII, no. 2 (1960), 454–85.

Hosp, Edward, 'Leben des Paters Josef Prost, 1804–1885, nach seinen eigenen Aufzeichnungen' in *SHCSSR*, vol. XI, no. 2 (1963), 375–432.

Johnstone, Tom and James Hegarty, *The Cross on the Sword: Catholic Chaplains in the Forces*. London: Chapman. 1996.

Jones, Frederick M., *Alphonsus Liguori: The Saint of Bourbon Naples*. Dublin: Gill and Macmillan, 1992.

Jones, Frederick M., ed. *Alphonsus Liguori: Selected Writings*. Classics of Western Spirituality Series. Mahwah, NJ: Paulist Press, 1999.

Kavanagh, Patrick, *Tarry Flynn*. London: MacGibbon and Kee, 1968.

Kelleher Michael and Gerard Moloney, eds, *St Clement's, 1947–2006.* Dublin: Redemptorist Communications, 2006.

Kelly, Timothy and Joseph Kelly, 'Our Lady of Perpetual Help, gender roles, and the decline of devotional Catholicism' in *Journal of Social History*, vol. 32, no. 1 (1998), 5–26.

Keogh, Dermot, *The Vatican, the Bishops and Irish Politics 1919–1939.* Cambridge: Cambridge University Press, 1986.

Keogh, Dermot, *Jews in Twentieth-Century Ireland.* Cork: Cork University Press, 1998.

Kirwan, Michael, 'Report from Brazil' in *Redemptorist Record* (Sept.–Oct., 1961), 360–1.

Larkin, Emmet, 'The Devotional Revolution in Ireland' in *The Historical Dimensions of Irish Catholicism.* Dublin: Four Courts Press, 1997, 57–89.

Livius, Thomas, *Father Furniss and his work for Children.* London: Art and Book Company, 1898.

Majorano, Sabatino, *L'Imitazione per la Memoria del Salvatore. Il Messaggio Spirituale di Suor Maria Celeste Crostarosa 1696–1755.* Bibliotheca Historica CSsR VII. Rome: EDACALF, 1978.

Meulemeester, Maurice de, *Bibliographie Générale des Écrivains Rédemptoristes*, 3 vols. Louvain: Imprimerie St Alphonse, 1933.

Meulemeester, Maurice de, *Histoire Sommaire de la Congrégation du Très Saint Rédempteur.* Louvain: Imprimerie St Alphonse, 1950.

Moffitt, Miriam, *Soupers and Jumpers: The Protestant Missions in Connemara, 1848–1937.* Dublin: Nonsuch Publishing, 2008.

Moffitt, Mariam, *The Society for Irish Church Missions to the Roman Catholics, 1849–1950.* Manchester: Manchester University Press, 2010.

Morgan, Joseph, *A Time to Remember.* Bangalore: Redemptorist Publications, 1992.

Morrissey, Thomas J., *Towards a National University: William Delany, SJ (1835–1924): an era of Initiative in Irish Education.* Dublin: Wolfhound Press, 1983.

Mulvey, Anthony, 'Most Rev. Dr Andrew Boylan, CSsR, Bishop of Kilmore (1907–1910)' in *Breifne: Journal of Cumann Seanchais Bhréifne*, vol. 8, no. 2 (1991), 145–54.

Murphy, James, 'The Role of Vincentian Parish Missions in the "Irish Counter-Reformation" of the Mid-Nineteenth Century' in *Irish Historical Studies*, vol. 24, no. 94 (Nov., 1984), 152–71.

Macauley, Ambrose, *Patrick Dorrian, Bishop of Down and Connor 1865–85.* Dublin: Irish Academic Press, 1987.

Macauley, Ambrose, *Patrick McAlister, Bishop of Down and Connor, 1886–95.* Dublin: Four Courts Press, 2006.

MacEoin, Gary, *Nothing is Quite Enough.* London: Hodder and Stoughton, 1954.

McConvery, Brendan, 'A Chaplain's War Time Letters' in *Reality* (Dec., 1994), 24–30.

McConvery, Brendan, 'Some Aspects of Redemptorist Missions in the New Irish State (1920–1937)' in *SHCSSR*, vol. XLVII, no. 1 (1999), 105–25.

McConvery, Brendan, 'Confraternity spirituality: the case of the Limerick men's Holy Family Confraternity' in *Spirituality*, vol. 5, no. 26 (Sept.–Oct., 1999), 291–4.

McConvery, Brendan, 'Male spirituality in Nineteenth Century Ireland: the case of the Limerick Holy Family Confraternity' in *Spirituality*, vol. 5, no. 27 (Nov.–Dec., 1999), 360–3.

McConvery, Brendan, 'Hell-fire and Poitín: Redemptorist Missions in the Irish Free State 1922–36' in *History Ireland*, vol. 8, no. 3 (2000), 18–22.

McConvery, Brendan, 'Remembering Ardglass' in Michael Kelleher and Gerard Moloney, eds, *St Clement's 1947–2006.* Redemptorist Communications, Dublin: 2006, 14–17.

McConvery, Brendan, 'The Redemptorists and the shaping of Irish popular devotion' in Henning Laugerud and Salvador Ryan (eds), *Devotional Cultures of European Christianity, 1790–1960.* Dublin: Four Court Press, 2012, 48–59.

McGrath, James, 'This is Brazil' in *Redemptorist Record* (Nov.–Dec., 1961), 566–7.

McLaughlin, Patrick, *Nicholas Callan, Priest-Scientist 1799–1864*. Dublin: Clonmore and Reynolds, 1965.

Mac Suibhne Peadar, *Paul Cullen and his Contemporaries*, vol. 5. Naas: Leinster Leader, 1977.

MacWhite, Eóin, 'Vladimir Pecherin, 1807–1885: The First Chaplain of the Mater Hospital, Dublin, and the First Russian Political Emigré' in *Studies: An Irish Quarterly Review*, vol. 60, no. 239/240 (Autumn–Winter, 1971), 295–310.

MacWhite, Eóin, 'Towards a biography of Fr Vladimir Petcherine (A Progress Report and Bibliography)' in *Proceedings of the Royal Irish Academy. Section C: Archaeology, Celtic Studies, History, Linguistics, Literature*, vol. 80c (1980), 109–58.

O'Carroll, Ciarán, *Paul Cardinal Cullen: Portrait of a Practical Nationalist*. Dublin: Veritas Publications, 2009.

O'Carroll, Liam G. (see 'Gerrard, Bill').

O'Donnell, Patrick, 'History of St Joseph's, Dundalk' in *Search*. no. 4 (Dec., 1978), 12–18.

O'Donnell, Patrick, 'The Story of St Gerard's' in Michael Kelleher and Gerard Moloney, eds, *St Clement's 1947–2006*. Dublin: Redemptorist Communications, 2006, 27–9.

Ó hAllmhuráin, Gearóid, 'Dancing on the Hobs of Hell: Rural Communities in Clare and the Dance Halls Act of 1935' in *New Hibernia Review/Iris Éireannach Nua*, vol. 9, no. 4 (Winter, 2005), 9–18.

Ordo Suscipiendi Habitum et Professionem Emittendi in Congregatione Ss. Redemptoris, Rome: CSsR, 1959.

Ó Ríordáin, John J., *Before the Night Grows Late*. Dublin: Columba Press, 2009.

O'Riordan, Seán and Joseph W. Murphy, *Catholic Answers to Questions put by some Protestants during the Clonard Missions for all Denominations 1949–1959*. Booklets 1–3. Dublin: Catholic Truth Society of Ireland, 1962.

Seán O'Riordan: A Theologian of Development: Selected Essays, edited by Seán Cannon and Raphael Gallagher. Quaestiones Morales 10. Rome: Editiones Academiae Alphonsianae, and Dublin: Columba Press, 1998.

Paiva, Gilberto, *A Vice-Província Redentorista de Fortaleza. Jubileu Áurea 1960–2010*. Aparecida: Editora Santuário, 2011.

Phoenix, Éamon, 'St Clement's 1947–2005' in Michael Kelleher and Gerard Moloney, eds, *St Clement's, 1947–2006*. Dublin: Redemptorist Communications, 2006, 30–54.

Potter, Matthew, *The Life and Times of William Monsell, First Baron Emly of Tervoe (1812–1894): A Catholic Unionist*. Limerick: Treaty Press, 1994.

[Prost, Joseph] *A Redemptorist Missionary in Ireland: 1851–1854. Memoir by Joseph Prost CSsR*, translated and edited by Emmet Larkin and Hermann Freudenberger. Irish Narratives Series, ed. David Fitzpatrick. Cork: Cork University Press, 1998.

Prunty Jacinta, *Margaret Aylward, 1810–1889: Lady of Charity, Woman of Faith*. Dublin: Four Courts Press, 1999.

Raponi, Santino, *The Charism of the Redemptorists in the Church: A Commentary on the Constitutions*. Rome: Centre for Redemptorist Spirituality, 2003.

Raponi, Santino, *The Redemptorist Religious Brother*. Rome: Commission for the Brothers, General Government CSsR, 1983.

Russell, Matthew, 'In Memoriam: R. P. Edmundi J. O'Reilly, S.J.' in *The Irish Monthly*, vol. 6 (1878), 695–700.

Ryder, Cyril, *Life of Thomas Edward Bridgett*, London: Burns and Oates, 1906.

Sampers, Andreas, 'Wladimir Sergejewitsch Pecherine (1807–1885). Sein Austritt aus der Kongregation der Allerheiligsten Erlösere (Redemptoristen), 1861' in *SHCSSR*, vol. XXI, no. 1 (1973), 165–97.

Sampers, Andreas, 'Institutum Oblatorum in Congregatione Ss. Redemptoris, Rectore Maiore N. Mauron 1855–1893' in *SHCSSR*, vol. XXVI, no. 1 (1978), 75–114.

Sampers, Andreas, 'L'ingresso di Eugenia Dijon e Antonia von Welserheimb nel monastero delle Redemptoristine di S. Agata dei Goti, 18 Novembre 1830' in *SHCSSR*, vol. XX, no. 1 (1972), 15–23.

Sharp, John, *Reapers of the Harvest: the Redemptorists in Great Britain and Ireland 1843–1898*. Dublin: Veritas Publications, 1989.

Smith, Janet, *Humanae Vitae: A Generation Later*. Washington: Catholic University of America Press, 1991.

Stebbing, George, *Father Edward Douglas*, London: n.p., 1917.

Tierney, Mark, *Blessed Columba Marmion: a short Biography*. Dublin: Columba Press, 2000.

Two Hundred Years with the Redemptorists, 1732–1932. Dublin: Sign of the Three Candles, 1933.

Vassal-Philips, Oliver R., 'Chaplains in the Great War: Fr Bernard Kavanagh CSsR', in *The Dublin Review*, vol. 165, (July, August, September, 1919), 52–62.

Vernoou, Joop, 'Cardinal Willem van Rossum, CSsR: "The great Cardinal of the small Netherlands" (1854–1932)' in *SHCSSR*, vol. 55, no. 2 (2007), 347–400.

Walter, Aloysius, *Villa Caserta 1855–1905. Ad aureum domus generalitae jubilarum*. Rome: CSsR, 1905.

Weiss, Otto, *Begegnungen mit Klemens Maria Hofbauer, 1751–1820*. Regensburg: Verlag Friedrich Pustet, 2009.

Wells, Ronald, *Friendship Towards Peace: The Journey of Ken Newell and Gerry Reynolds*. Dublin: Columba Press, 2005.

Whelan, Irene, 'The stigma of souperism' in Cathal Póirtéir, ed., *The Great Irish Famine*. Cork: Mercier Press, 1995, 135–54.

Wuest, Joseph, *Annales Congregationis SS. Redemptoris provinciae Americanae*. Ilchester: Typis Congregationis Sanctissimi Redemptoris, 1899.

Index